THE ONE YEAR®
UNCOMMON LIFE

DAILY CHALLENGE

THE ONE YEAR®

UNCOMMON LIFE

DAILY CHALLENGE

TONY DUNGY

AND NATHAN WHITAKER

TYNDALE
MOMENTUM™

The nonfiction imprint of
Tyndale House Publishers, Inc.

Visit Tyndale online at www.tyndale.com.

Visit Tyndale Momentum online at www.tyndalemomentum.com.

Visit the author's website at www.coachdungy.com.

TYNDALE, *Tyndale Momentum*, Tyndale quill logo, *The One Year*, and *One Year* are registered trademarks of Tyndale House Publishers, Inc. The Tyndale Momentum logo and The One Year logo are trademarks of Tyndale House Publishers, Inc. Tyndale Momentum is the nonfiction imprint of Tyndale House Publishers, Inc., Carol Stream, Illinois.

The One Year Uncommon Life Daily Challenge

Designed by Ron Kaufmann

Edited by Bonne L. Steffen

Published in association with the literary agency of Legacy, LLC, Winter Park, Florida 32789.

For information about special discounts for bulk purchases, please contact Tyndale House Publishers at csresponse@tyndale.com, or call 1-800-323-9400.

ISBN 978-1-4143-4828-5

Printed in the United States of America

23   22   21   20   19   18   17
19   18   17   16   15   14   13

How to Use This Book

We hope you will enjoy reading *The One Year Uncommon Life Daily Challenge* devotional as much as we enjoyed writing it.

For the last fourteen years, Tony has been in a Bible study with a number of other coaches. Reading *The One Year Bible* each year, they have not only engaged in a study of God's Word, but have engaged in the building of a community. As coaches from their original group in Tampa Bay have changed teams or left the National Football League altogether during that time span, Tony has found that the *One Year* format keeps them connected as a community.

On any given day, they all know what the others are reading. Essentially, everyone is on the same page. This knowledge sparks e-mails or voice mails or direct conversations—"What did you think about those verses from Ezekiel? I needed to hear that today. It really spoke to me because . . ."

With this *One Year Uncommon Life Daily Challenge*, our hope is that the format will create the same sense of community for you, which is why we have indicated dates for the readings, but have not tied them to any particular year. Wherever you are in life, jump right in with today's reading. And check out www.uncommonchallenge.com and www.coachdungy.com for more resources.

The book focuses on seven themes, with each theme repeating every seven days. Therefore, every week you will read one devotion from each of the themes:

> Core
> Family
> Friends
> Potential
> Mission
> Influence
> Faith

January 1 starts with Core. Every seventh day that follows (January 8, 15, 22, 29, and so on) will be an insight on Core. Each devotion stands on its own, so that no matter what date you begin, whether it's January 1 or August 27, you can jump right in. No matter what year you begin, you will always be in community with others who are reading the devotional.

Each devotion includes Scripture and an Uncommon Key—an application or action to implement based on what you've just read. This isn't just a "read-it-and-you're-done" type of devotional. The goal is to not only engage your mind, but to also challenge your heart. That, too, is worth sharing with the community that you may form with others.

If you miss a day, keep going. Don't try to catch up, and don't feel guilty. Yesterday is gone—spend time with God *today*. Our prayer is that every day you will be blessed by what you read and challenged to do more for God's Kingdom.

Tony Dungy
Nathan Whitaker

January 1

A Personal Training Plan

I discipline my body like an athlete, training it to do what it should. Otherwise, I fear that after preaching to others I myself might be disqualified. 1 CORINTHIANS 9:27

Self-control. Discipline. Getting in shape. A new commitment to stick to the plan.

How many times have you written down these goals or thought about them just before January 1? In a CNN report last year on New Year's resolutions, it wasn't surprising to learn that losing weight is the most common goal people set. In fact, I would guess that year after year that rarely changes—it will always be up there. It's what fitness centers across the country gear up for: an influx of new customers and increased revenue in January more than any other time of the year.

And then we come to our senses—around February.

When I was a player, we'd see that occasionally when training camp rolled around. Professional football wasn't a year-round enterprise then, and guys had jobs in the off-season. Some would show up totally out of shape when camp began.

As followers of Christ, we should maintain self-control and discipline, especially when it comes to taking care of our bodies. Getting in shape and making a commitment to stay that way honors God. He has given us our bodies through the miracle of creation. Taking care of them, watching what we put into them, and being careful about how we use them each day are responsibilities we shouldn't take lightly.

But that mind-set is not only important for our physical bodies. That desire and discipline also applies to the training we do and the commitment we make to ourselves and to God. We commit to learn more about Him and about how we can be better disciples. It's not a passive endeavor. It takes resolve and repetition, consistently working at it for maximum results. And results will happen as we grow closer to Him. Real success in achieving goals—whether they were set on January 1 or not—comes when we know we can't do it by ourselves and look to the Lord for strength.

Where do you need improvement? More physical training for your body, taking care of the temple He gave you? Or getting to know Him better, spending time in His Word and with Him in prayer?

I'd recommend both on a regular basis. And ask God to be your trainer, to be there when you need to be pushed a little harder. He will give you the strength to help make your resolutions realities.

UNCOMMON KEY > *Moving from desire to actually doing better is only achieved with self-discipline, and self-discipline only works effectively when you trust in Him to help. Amp up your self-discipline in the areas you need it most.*

January 2

The Importance of a Look Squad

> Then I saw a new heaven and a new earth, for the old heaven and the old earth had
> disappeared. And the sea was also gone. And I saw the holy city, the new Jerusalem,
> coming down from God out of heaven like a bride beautifully dressed for her husband.
> REVELATION 21:1-2

In practice each week, our team would run our plays against a "look squad." That's what
we call our backup players who simulate the other team's techniques as closely as possible.
The simulation helps the first team's players visualize how our plays will work against the
other team's. When we run a play and see it executed successfully in practice, we have the
confidence to run it successfully during the game.

Visualization increases chances of success—not just in football but in any area of life.
If we can't see ourselves succeeding as workers, leaders, parents, or spouses, for example,
we won't have any confidence in those roles and be able to perform them well. But if we
can see ourselves fulfilling our responsibilities effectively, achieving our goals, and relating
to others healthily, we are much more likely to have the vision and the confidence to do
those things. We tend to be able to accomplish what we can see.

God gives us a lot of pictures in the Bible—visions of who we are becoming and what
His Kingdom is like. Today's passage from Revelation is encouraging because it shows us
our future with Him forever, as members of His family. If we can see our tomorrow and
know how good it is, we can live in confidence today. We have courage to face anything
when we know this is what awaits us on the other side of it.

Think of life as practice and the visions and instructions of Scripture as a "look squad."
Those words aren't the full picture, because words can only tell us so much. The reality
of the actual "game" will look a little different. But like the look squad during a week of
practice, Scripture's descriptions of the future give us and our families an idea of where
we're headed and what it will be like when we get there. We can know that God is standing there waiting for us with outstretched arms. And if we can "see" that future, we will
have a much better idea of how to prepare for it, much more confidence as we move forward, and much more courage to handle anything today.

UNCOMMON KEY > *When you read God's Word on a regular basis, you'll discover
what your future holds. Claim His promises and pay attention to His instructions. Seeing God
in your tomorrow is the key to having confidence and courage today.*

January 3

The Best Role Model Who Ever Lived

> I don't mean to say that I have already achieved these things or that I have already reached perfection. But I press on to possess that perfection for which Christ Jesus first possessed me. PHILIPPIANS 3:12

We have a perfect role model.

Christ is our example on how to treat other people.

Christ is our example on the influence we can and should have on those around us.

Christ is the classic and eternal example of the role model we are called to be.

No other role model even comes close to Him. A tour through Scripture reveals a Christ who was always finding people where they were and taking them where they needed to be. He was always seeking people who thought they were nobodies and making them into somebodies.

In the verse above, Paul makes it clear that the goal we pursue—here on earth and in the hereafter—is Jesus Himself. He is the example we are to follow, the person we were meant to be like. We won't reach perfection until we see Him face-to-face, but we are called always to be moving in that direction. In His strength, we press on toward that goal one day at a time. He can make us who we need to be if we focus on Him and allow Him to work through us. The same Christ who went around making somebodies out of nobodies is still at work in our lives.

God has a purpose in shaping us to be like Jesus. We become His influence—His hands and heart—for everyone around us. Wherever we find ourselves, we can influence people for His glory. That begins at home in our families, but it extends to every other area: our friends, coworkers, neighbors, fellow church members, fellow students, teammates—everyone we come in contact with. God doesn't just glorify Himself by sending Jesus into this world. If we will let Him, He glorifies Himself by sending Jesus into this world *through us.*

UNCOMMON KEY > *Today and every day, remember that you are a personal representative of Jesus Christ. Always strive for the perfection of Christ—for yourself and for those around you.*

January 4

Reaching Incremental Goals

> Jabez cried out to the God of Israel, "Oh, that you would bless me and enlarge my territory! Let your hand be with me, and keep me from harm so that I will be free from pain." And God granted his request. 1 CHRONICLES 4:10, NIV

Few of us want to remain where we are without any improvement or increase. God has wired us to want to grow. But what kind of growth are we looking for? We have to be careful to focus on what's really important and within our control, rather than external results we can't really control.

My goals are usually qualitative, not quantitative. When I coached, my aim each season was not to win a certain number of games, but to have a team that played as well as it could and that was an asset to its community. I measured the team by whether it played up to its potential. And from year to year, I measured it by whether it improved.

That's also how I measure myself. When I was a young assistant, I wanted to learn enough to one day be considered for a coordinator position. Then as a coordinator, I wanted to learn and improve so I could become a head coach. Sometimes our goals are a steady step-by-step progression, and sometimes they require risk. Whenever we ask God to enlarge our territories, we need faith to move to the next level. That always comes with the possibility of failure, although we can trust Him to be with us either to help us get there or to catch us when we fall. Over time, those steps of faith pay off. We grow and improve and reach higher goals.

Remember to focus on goals that are within your control. As a coach, I worked on learning more and improving my coaching abilities in order to be qualified for positions with greater responsibility. I couldn't control whether I would be hired for those positions. When you do your part to prepare, you can trust God for the results. In His timing, He's the one who enlarges your territory. Your job is to make yourself ready for it.

UNCOMMON KEY > *A little improvement each day makes a big difference over time. Ask God to enlarge your territory, but prepare yourself along the way to handle it well.*

January 5

First Things First

> Seek the Kingdom of God above all else, and live righteously, and he will give you everything you need. MATTHEW 6:33

When people ask me to sign something, lately I've begun using this verse. Its truth is such a helpful way for me to structure the focus of my days.

How do you begin to set the right priorities for your life against the pull of the things the world says are important? It's not easy, but it's absolutely essential if you want to make sure you don't miss the things that matter most.

With today's verse, the natural tendency is to read the first part quickly in order to get to that last phrase: "and he will give you everything you need." I know; I've been there. And if we're honest about it, we would probably admit that we're usually inclined to live each day primarily focusing on "everything [we] need." It's the stuff that slams us smack in the face when we wake up each morning and becomes more and more pressing throughout the day. The pressing needs around us—even if they are good things—can take the focus away from what matters most: our relationship with God and the people He has placed in our lives.

But read the verse again: "Seek the Kingdom of God above all else" (another Bible translation says, "Seek first His Kingdom"). How can you do that? With all the challenges, obstacles, and urgent matters of each day, is it even possible?

Let me suggest that you keep doing what you are doing right now—taking a few moments to be quiet and spend time with God. When you do, you will be pleasantly surprised at how He will lessen your worries about tomorrow and release you from the breathless pace of the world's "urgent" priorities for today in order to make room for His priorities.

Dedicating time to the priorities that God has entrusted to you may not seem significant right now, but to someone who needs you, it could make all the difference in his or her life—and in yours.

UNCOMMON KEY > *Determine to seek God's priorities for your life. It begins by spending time with Him. Try to do it every day—for yourself and for those who matter most to you.*

January 6

Uniquely You

> "I know the plans I have for you," says the LORD. "They are plans for good and not for disaster, to give you a future and a hope." JEREMIAH 29:11

Have you thought about all the events that led up to this moment in your life—why you're here, how you've been shaped, what caused you to read this book or seek God's plans for your life? Have you wondered how much of it is accidental or random and how much is designed?

I believe God knew exactly where you would be right now and exactly what you would be like. He knew about your passions and gifts and the platform you have. In fact, I believe He was very purposeful in designing your life. He made you to be uniquely significant and to have an eternal impact on the world around you.

Let that sink in. How would you live differently if you really believed that God had intentionally designed you to impact others? What steps of faith would you take if you knew He had already planned them? What would you attempt if you were fully convinced He was backing you? Would you set out to accomplish big things in your community? Would you go into the local schools with a sense of mission? What impossible problems would suddenly seem possible to deal with? The fact is that when you believe you were designed for a purpose, you will live with purpose.

I realize we all have some areas we can improve, and just because we believe God designed us doesn't mean we know what for. But God is gracious. He knows we'll fall short, and He knows that finding His will for our lives will be a process. We'll make mistakes along the way. Grace isn't an excuse to give less than our best, but it is reassuring to know that God doesn't pressure us to be perfect. When we fall, we can get up, dust ourselves off, and keep moving toward the goal. Whatever our past, God has future plans for us. And those plans are good.

Don't be afraid to try big things that fit with God's purposes. No problem is too big for Him to solve, whether it's in the lives of people around us, on a national or global scale, or anything in between. That means no problem is too big for us to attempt to solve in His strength. We were designed for such purposes.

UNCOMMON KEY > *God was very intentional about your design, your opportunities, and your purpose. Thank Him and look for ways to use what He has given you in the best way possible.*

January 7

A Gift You Don't Want to Return

> God blesses those who are poor and realize their need for him, for the Kingdom of Heaven is theirs. MATTHEW 5:3

We would always ask the players to come in on Monday, then give them Tuesday off. As strange as it may sound, many times a player suffered an injury in the game and didn't know it until he did a little activity the next day. He'd think that he was okay, but he really wasn't. The day-after workout revealed the need for treatment.

The Bible says God blesses those who realize their need for Him. That seems like an easy way to be blessed, but a lot of people can't bring themselves to realize they need anyone, even God. Still, that doesn't keep Him from pursuing them. He wants all of us to spend eternity in heaven with Him.

Step one is to realize we need Him. Jesus made that clear. Not a single one of us is perfect, and because we have fallen short of God's standard for our lives—in other words, we have sinned—we are separated from Him. He is holy and perfect, and our sin puts a gap between us and Him. Without being holy, we can't be in a right relationship with Him or even come close to experiencing His presence—unless He makes a way.

God has provided that way in the person of His Son, Jesus Christ. God loved us so much that He sent His only Son to die for us and take the punishment for our sinful nature so that we could have a direct relationship with Christ and God. All we have to do is desire to be in a relationship with God, understand that we can't do it ourselves, and believe that God sent His Son for us.

That's a gift from God. It cost Him a lot, but to us it's absolutely free. Have you ever accepted that free gift?

When we truly believe in the free gift of Jesus in our hearts; acknowledge that we need that gift; accept Him as the Savior who died in our place for the consequences of our sin; and embrace Him as our Lord, making Him the number one priority in our lives, then we are absolutely assured of spending eternity with Him in heaven (John 3:16-17). Nothing we can do has greater power to change our lives than making this one decision.

UNCOMMON KEY > *God's gift is anything but common, and it's by far the most important key for living an uncommon life. The implications are huge. What is your relationship with Jesus Christ?*

January 8

Living Wisely

> | In the same way, encourage the young men to live wisely.   TITUS 2:6

What does it mean to "live wisely"? Other Bible versions translate the Greek phrase as "be self-controlled." It seems that we have lost that concept today, especially for our young people—the idea of embracing and knowing what it means to be self-controlled. As far as I am concerned, that's really one of the keys to life, to discipline ourselves to do what we need to do so that at a later time we can do what we want to do.

That belief was one of the reasons my coauthor Nathan and I wrote the book *Uncommon* to reach young men. Of course, we also wanted to reach others with what we felt were keys to living an uncommon life, since God's truths are timeless and not gender specific. However, as a coach, I have seen so many young men over the years who were searching for direction. Many of them came from homes with no fathers and no strong male role models to show them God's design for their lives. It was our desire to reach out to them with a blueprint for living a life of significance.

Self-control. It's just one of those keys that young men—actually, all of us—need to learn in order to live the lives they were intended to live and to become the men God created them to be. Whether you are a man or a woman, maintaining a core of self-control will set you on a path toward developing other basic qualities that are keys to living an uncommon and significant life, keys that focus on character, honesty, and integrity; the priorities of family and friends; embracing your full potential and mission; and living a life of faith and influence. All designed with the intention of helping you to grow in the wisdom of God's plan for your life and to live out His purpose fully.

How is your self-control? Strong in some areas, weak in others? Strive to strengthen the weak areas and remain disciplined in the strong areas.

UNCOMMON KEY > *Reading this devotional every day is a matter of discipline and self-control—keep it up! You are finding a key to heightening your impact for God's Kingdom.*

January 9

Nothing Means Nothing

> I am convinced that nothing can ever separate us from God's love. Neither death nor life, neither angels nor demons, neither our fears for today nor our worries about tomorrow—not even the powers of hell can separate us from God's love. . . . Indeed, nothing in all creation will ever be able to separate us from the love of God that is revealed in Christ Jesus our Lord. ROMANS 8:38-39

These verses from the apostle Paul are one of the greatest passages of hope, assurance, and comfort you will find anywhere in Scripture. For me, this passage has also been one of the ever-present reminders and renewal for the courage I have needed through the years and will continue to need to face the challenges and get past the obstacles of each day.

I'd venture a guess that you find reassurance in these verses too. Times get tough, things look bleak, the clouds roll in, and the sunshine rolls out. And yet there is nothing that can separate us from the love of Christ.

One of the things that caused me some reservations when deciding whether to write *Quiet Strength* was that I wasn't sure anything that I had done was worthy of mention. What parts of my life would interest readers? But then when Nathan and I began the process of writing the book, I realized that it wasn't just the joys that might be interesting for them to read about, but also some of the disappointments and heartaches and how I tried to walk on. What I went through might be a blessing and a comfort for others who have experienced similar trials.

In fact, we opened the book detailing a terrifically low point in my life—being fired by the Tampa Bay Buccaneers. It was a simple decision to start there—we knew that every reader could relate to a time when personal dreams have been dashed.

The one thing I knew to be true, but was reminded of through this process, was that I was never separated from God and God's love revealed through what His Son Jesus Christ did for me—and for you—on the cross. As Nathan and I recalled moment after moment of the events of my life and my family's, I could see even more clearly that God had been with me every moment and beside me every step of the journey, along with my wife and family.

What about you? Do you feel separated from God today because of your fears for today or your worries about tomorrow? The apostle Paul says, "Don't be! The God who loves us will take of those things." Whether you're aware of it or not.

UNCOMMON KEY > *Write down what you think could separate God's love from you or your family members. Now draw a cross covering everything you listed. It is an eternal promise of hope for today and forever—nothing will ever separate any of us from the love of God revealed in His Son Jesus Christ.*

January 10

A Genuine Interest

> After David had finished talking with Saul, he met Jonathan, the king's son. There was an immediate bond between them, for Jonathan loved David.   1 SAMUEL 18:1

Our son Jamie really exemplified a statement my parents always made: choose your friends for the sake of friendship. That seems obvious, but a lot of people choose friends because they are popular, good-looking, rich, or part of the "right" crowd. But Jamie was never concerned with someone's status. He was drawn to people who looked like they needed a friend. Sometimes it seemed like the less status someone had, the more likely Jamie was to hang out with them. He chose his friends for no other reason than that he enjoyed being around them.

Friendship is meant to have mutual benefits for both people, but we often evaluate others by how they might benefit us. We may criticize society for valuing star athletes more than nurses and teachers, but we often reflect the same distorted values in our personal relationships. We determine people's worth based on what they can do for us, how well-connected they are, or what their job is. We think more often about the benefits we might receive than the benefits we might be able to give. Rarely do people develop friendships based on the opportunities they give to pour into someone else's life.

Friendship runs two ways. Dale Carnegie said you can make more friends in two weeks by genuinely showing interest in them than you can make in two years by trying to get them interested in you. And he was right. If you choose your friends simply for the sake of friendship—two-way, mutual benefit—you'll not only have more of them, but the ones you have will mean more to you.

UNCOMMON KEY > *Choose your friends based on the fact that you enjoy being around them. Instead of thinking how they might benefit you, think about how you might benefit them.*

January 11

A Couple of Minutes a Day

> **Before daybreak the next morning, Jesus got up and went out to an isolated place to pray. Later Simon and the others went out to find him. When they found him, they said, "Everyone is looking for you."** MARK 1:35-37

Do you have moments in your life when you feel like everyone is demanding a piece of you, looking for you everywhere, armed with all their urgent requests and deadlines? So you try to find a place where they don't know to look. Or maybe you just turn off your phone for a few minutes of peace and quiet.

The Gospels mention some similar moments for Jesus (albeit I'm pretty sure without the phone). Times when He realized it was time for Him to get away to be by Himself. Times when He no doubt spent time talking with His Father about what He was going through. Times to put His feet up—a good thing for a lot of reasons—and think.

Maybe sometimes He went off to take a nap. With the amount of walking He was doing, He had to have bouts of fatigue. Perhaps while He rested, He thought about the next day's plan, what He hoped to accomplish, and asked for guidance from His Father on how to best go about it.

I certainly try to follow Christ's example. But this idea of stopping what we're doing and getting alone with the Father? For most of us it's not part of our DNA. It is certainly not embraced by society. They would most likely label us as recluses or as displaying anti-social behavior. Instead of pulling away, taking some time, getting some rest—society says charge on, full speed ahead.

Why not begin to find some time in your day to be alone and quiet? Find some moments of your day—perhaps in the morning before the day gets legs—to spend time alone with the God who created you and all you see around you. Why not find some time each day to put your feet up and think?

God wants for there to be times when you simply escape with Him, alone, and recharge. Like you are doing right now, reading this. He wants to be with you and help you to slow down for a few moments and seek Him. It will give the two of you the chance you need to hang out together.

UNCOMMON KEY > *Spend time each day with God. Start with a couple of minutes of no phone calls, no interruptions—just you and God. Then gradually increase your time together.*

January 12

Facing Reality

> Anyone who listens to the word but does not do what it says is like someone who looks at his face in a mirror and, after looking at himself, goes away and immediately forgets what he looks like. JAMES 1:23-24, NIV

Perceptions don't win ball games. No team can rely on its reputation as "a finesse team" or "a dome team" or "an offensive team." After all, it may not even be accurate—perception is not the same as reality.

I used to talk to my team often about the difference between perception and reality. The public perceives players as different from the ordinary people their families and friends know. But to win and be effective, our players needed to dig beyond perceptions and look at reality—not at their reputations, media personas, or past performances, but who they were on the field. And sometimes that process of uncovering reality could take a little work.

To develop a good game plan in life, we need to know who we really are—not how others perceive us, not the image of who we want to be or who society says we should be, but our true selves. That applies not only to us as individuals but to the "teams" we play on: with families, coworkers, church members, neighbors, and other groups we're involved in. We need to know our strengths and weaknesses and how they fit into the big picture.

How can we all do that? We must occasionally stop and take stock of who we are and what our goals are. And we need an objective standard to do that, not just our personal opinions. When we measure ourselves, our thoughts, our actions, and our goals by our own standards, we may end up missing the mark. Our perceptions aren't always accurate. But if we measure these things by God's Word, we are basing our lives on reality, not perceptions. That is the kind of game plan that works.

It's a process, and it isn't always easy. But if we want to "win"—to live effective lives that contribute to society and further God's purposes—we'll take the time to look in the mirror of truth, see who we really are, and base our lives in reality.

UNCOMMON KEY > *Perception doesn't accomplish goals; substance does. Know who you really are and where you are going, and then pursue your goals.*

January 13

Committed

| Commit your actions to the LORD, and your plans will succeed. PROVERBS 16:3

My parents raised my siblings and me on this verse. The words are so familiar that it's almost like a friend giving me encouragement and clear direction in every season of my life. My parents helped me understand at a very early age that God would walk alongside me and bless me as long as I remained in His will. That is, if my siblings and I were doing the right things and following the pursuits that God put on our hearts.

Note, however, that the verse doesn't give any indication of timing. We don't know if God's plans are for tomorrow or four years from now. For some people, the journey is long, like William Wilberforce, who worked for over forty years to abolish the slave trade in Great Britain. And it may be hard to recognize any discernible success. God calls us to be available and faithful to His ways and His Word. The result is up to Him; the impact and influence in the world and for His purposes happens in His timing, by His hand—and ultimately for our good and His glory. He has the big picture clearly in mind for each of us. If we commit to Him, our plans will succeed, as success is defined by Him.

Will it always be considered success in the world's eyes? Not always. Things will occur which may or may not be recognized by society as successful, but the standard we tried to be guided by was whether the success resulted from committing our actions, lives, day-by-day efforts, and decisions to the Lord.

It probably got me in a little trouble at times—especially as a head coach—when I would suggest that while our goal was to win football games, make it to the playoffs, and even win the Super Bowl, there were other things I wanted our team to focus on that were more important to me. The reason? Because that is what I believed God called us to. To build traits like integrity and character, to help others in need, to seek God's guidance and wisdom in every decision we made. To commit every action, everything we did, to the Lord.

What standard of success are you following? Are you seeking to make a difference and have a positive influence in the world around you? Are you committed to a plan or to Him?

UNCOMMON KEY > *Change your plan into His plan today. Do things for the right reason—to glorify God and be in His will. And your plans will succeed—at the time and in the way that God chooses.*

January 14

Working with the Amount of Faith You Have

> If you had faith even as small as a mustard seed, you could say to this mulberry tree, "May you be uprooted and thrown into the sea," and it would obey you! LUKE 17:6

The Lord asks us to have faith. Faith in His promises. Faith in His Son Jesus Christ. Faith in the hope of the resurrection of Christ. Faith in everything He has set forth in His Word.

He asks us to believe without doubting, to ask without stopping, to seek until we find, to knock because the door will be opened, and to pray without ceasing, believing that what we ask for, seek for, knock for, and pray for He will do something about. But God also realizes that sometimes it's tough to believe. Sometimes we feel like Thomas, asking for physical proof of Jesus' resurrection. Sometimes we want to get our finite brains around an infinite God and understand things without having to do it on faith alone.

And usually those times are when we need to have faith even more. Often it's in those times that the world keeps preying on us and nothing feels right. I've been there. There are days when I appreciate Thomas's assertiveness: "Show me, Lord. I need to touch Your hands." There are days when I, too, want to see the nail holes and hear His voice of quiet assurance. There are those days when I just seem to need a little more visible proof to go with the usual dose of faith.

Losing a playoff game. Being fired. Losing a child.

Some are important, some are not so important, but any of them can disquiet us or shake us to the core. Those are the days when I need to remember even more to just hang on, to clutch the faith He calls me to. The disciples had their moments of doubt, and Jesus was standing there, right in front of them. So I don't feel quite so guilty when I have my moments of doubt. The disciples were struggling on a regular basis, and Jesus told them that it doesn't always take much—it just takes some faith. Even faith as small as a mustard seed.

That's all we need—you and me—and He'll take it home.

UNCOMMON KEY > *Christ doesn't call us to understand it all, to see all of God's plan for His Kingdom and our role in it. Instead, He wants us to have just enough faith in Him to continue to follow Him day by day on the path He has set before us. Step out in faith today.*

January 15

"Just between You and Me . . ."

Every January there is a mad scramble for jobs in the NFL. Someone recently described it to me as "musical chairs for grown-ups." For every head coach who gets fired from a particular team, there are anywhere from sixteen to twenty-five other coaches and staff members from that same team who are fired too. In a given year, if seven or eight teams change head coaches, about 150 people are suddenly looking for work—trying to get up to speed as new coaches in new organizations, sliding into vacancies on other staffs, or heading into the college coaching ranks. A mad scramble.

People around the league end up spending hours on the phone swapping information: "I hear the guy in San Diego really doesn't want to be there anymore; his mother is in Cleveland and is ill, so he's trying to hook on with the Browns." Unfortunately, sometimes the initial private conversation that was told in confidence—"Just between you and me . . . my mother is ill, so I'm wondering if I shouldn't consider trying to move . . ."—becomes very public. And like the childhood game of telephone, the "facts" get muddled.

The next thing you know, it's all over the league: so-and-so wants out of San Diego. And when it comes back around to the front office of the Chargers, they might not be too happy.

Think twice before you say idle words, even if you think they are justified. Someday, we'll all be asked to account for what we say.

UNCOMMON KEY > *If you have been asked to keep a confidence, honor that request. Think carefully before sharing information with someone else. Make sure "just between you and me" stays that way. Deflect gossip about a person with uplifting and edifying words about them, and never say anything you wouldn't want that person to hear.*

January 16

Never Stop Skiing

> When I was a child, I spoke and thought and reasoned as a child. But when I grew up, I put away childish things. Now we see things imperfectly, like puzzling reflections in a mirror, but then we will see everything with perfect clarity. All that I know now is partial and incomplete, but then I will know everything completely, just as God now knows me completely. 1 CORINTHIANS 13:11-12

When he was nine, Nathan went skiing with his parents in Colorado. All along the ski slopes, signs were posted with the warning:

BEWARE OF SNOW CATS.

Each sign was approximately five feet high and eight feet wide—you couldn't miss these large warning signs strategically placed beside the ski trails heading down the mountain. After three days of skiing, Nathan pointed to one of the signs as he and his dad were riding the ski lift to the top of the mountain. "Daddy, have you seen one yet?"

"Seen what, Nathan?"

"A snow cat." Upon further discussion, Nathan's dad realized that the "snow cats" his son was keeping a sharp eye out for were of the mountain lion, snow leopard, or comparable dangerous-animal variety. Smiling, Scott explained to his son that what the signs were referring to were the snowplow-like machines that drove up and down the slopes packing down the snow, machines referred to as "snow cats."

"Oh." Nathan breathed a deep sigh of relief.

You may have experienced a similar situation of misinterpretation with your children from time to time. But here's what I want you to take from Nathan's story: despite believing that at any given moment a mountain lion or snow leopard could leap out of the trees while he was skiing down the slopes, Nathan never stopped skiing. Instead, he pointed his ski tips straighter to be ready to outrun the danger.

Things take on a different perspective through the eyes and heart of a child.

But as the apostle Paul says, it's not always going to be that way. Things that are a little muddied will be made crystal clear. God will dispel your fears, and you will be able to see things exactly as they are. Can you imagine the courage and hope you will sense when you stand before Him face-to-face?

Why not feel it now? No matter what you face, keep on skiing!

UNCOMMON KEY > *One day you will stand before the Hope of the world and see things more clearly. But you don't have to wait to ask for His clarity on matters you are dealing with now. He is accessible to you and wants you to live like you believe it!*

January 17

To Forgive or Not to Forgive?

If you forgive those who sin against you, your heavenly Father will forgive you. But if you refuse to forgive others, your Father will not forgive your sins. MATTHEW 6:14-15

These verses have always been a little disconcerting to me. I think I understand the plain message of the words, but does Christ really understand what He is asking me to do? I wonder if He knows about some of the things I still vividly remember that others have done to me through the years. And is He asking me to forgive them or I'm out of luck to receive His forgiveness for my wrongdoings?

I imagine proposing a simpler solution—why doesn't God just forgive everyone (including me) as I believe He did through His Son on the cross, and we'll be done with it? Don't ask me to forgive them as well. And don't put that contingency clause for my own forgiveness on the tail end of it.

And then I begin to look inside a little deeper, and I can't help but wonder sometimes if I don't have trouble forgiving others because I don't want to forgive myself for all the stuff I've done. What about you? I mean, it seems as though sometimes the baggage we carry isn't really something we want to carry around, but we do it anyway. Either we enjoy the misery and want the self-imposed pity parties we're throwing to continue, or more likely, we simply can't forgive ourselves for all the times we have fallen short of God's standard.

So we turn around and don't forgive others. And our hearts begin to harden not only toward others, but toward ourselves. But God's plan of forgiveness provides total freedom for us from guilt over what we have done and from the bitterness toward others for what they have done to us. The ability to forgive is a reflection of a repentant, spiritually reborn heart. That repentance begins one-on-one with God.

UNCOMMON KEY > *How willing are you to forgive yourself and others? Confess your lack of forgiveness to God and begin to change your attitude. And start making a list of people who have wronged you whom you need to offer grace to.*

January 18

Thoughts That Materialize

| **What I always feared has happened to me. What I dreaded has come true.** JOB 3:25

You have the ability to paint a picture of what your life is going to look like. You may not get all the details exactly right, but you certainly have a part in shaping your future. Your perspective today has a lot to do with what happens tomorrow. What you believe and what you expect have a tendency to come about.

This is why it's so important to be careful how you speak to yourself, think of yourself, conduct yourself, and develop yourself. The landscape of your future is in large part determined by what you think it will be and by how you see yourself in it. This is "the power of self-realization," which study after study seems to validate. That doesn't mean you can manipulate your future, but there's a strong connection between your perceptions and your outcomes. Those who have positive expectations experience positive results more often than those who have negative expectations. So it's vital to make sure your perceptions are positive.

If you have the option of painting a picture of your life, why not make it a good one? Envision your future, your accomplishments and achievements, and your God-given significance. Base it on what you know to be true, of course, not on your own sense of pride or unhealthy ways to satisfy your needs. But within the values and dreams God has given you, paint a picture of where you want to go, what you want to be like, and what you want to accomplish. Expect good and pursue it rather than simply going through life without a plan and seeing whatever happens.

I'm not suggesting life will always be easy if you have the right thoughts, or that blessings will be showered upon you if you simply start thinking positively. But negative thinking sets you back. I've seen it happen again and again with athletes and teams living out their self-fulfilling prophecies. The way I see it, if these "prophecies" tend to be self-fulfilling, they might as well be positive ones.

With God's help—His power, encouragement, and energy flowing through our lives along with the gifts, abilities, and talents He has given us—we can shape the future. Because He created us, we have the potential of living lives of significance, possibility, and impact.

UNCOMMON KEY > *For better or worse, what you envision often begins to take shape. Be intentional and choose to envision a life of significance, possibility, and impact.*

January 19

True Civil Disobedience

> Submit to governing authorities. For all authority comes from God, and those in positions of authority have been placed there by God. So anyone who rebels against authority is rebelling against what God has instituted, and they will be punished. . . . Would you like to live without fear of the authorities? Do what is right, and they will honor you. ROMANS 13:1-3

Not too long ago, the FBI investigated a "denial of service" attack against corporate websites. Apparently some hackers, who know far more about computers than I do, launched an "attack" through which they caused these corporate websites to crash. They did it quickly and anonymously.

In an article, some of the cyberspace criminals, who had either been apprehended or were speaking anonymously while still in hiding, used terms like "justice" and "civil disobedience" to explain their actions. But to my way of thinking, their actions lacked courage.

And without even understanding the full nature of their claims, for that reason alone—the lack of courage to face those they disagreed with as they acted in "civil disobedience"—their reasons didn't hold much water with me.

Contrast their approach—acting without courage behind the comfort of a keyboard—with that of Patricia Stephens Due, who in 1960, while a student at Florida A&M, was arrested for sitting in a whites-only section in a Tallahassee restaurant. She knew the penalties for her actions and faced them head-on to right a wrong. I'm grateful for her courage and the courage of other African Americans who, like her, stood up when necessary—just as people have done across the African continent throughout 2011, often armed with nothing more than their presence and their iPhones. Those protestors, like Ms. Due, truly did make a difference for justice. (As an aside, I played with J. T. Thomas with the Steelers. He was the first African American football scholarship player at FSU. He certainly would not have been there without people like Patricia Due.)

Christians should be careful in this age of easy anonymity. Too many people fall prey to posting harsh, inflammatory rhetoric on the Internet. If we disagree, we should speak out, civilly and openly. If something is wrong, we should take a stand with other brothers and sisters, or alone if necessary, and be prepared to face the consequences. That is civil disobedience—if we must disobey authorities, we should do so with courage.

Model yourself after Patricia Stephens Due and others in her era . . . not a bunch of hackers.

UNCOMMON KEY > *Submit to the governing authorities, but speak out with candor and grace when necessary when God calls you to do it. Starting today.*

January 20

What Others See in You

| And you should imitate me, just as I imitate Christ.   1 CORINTHIANS 11:1

It would be nice to reach the point someday where someone would say, "Tony, I've just accepted Jesus. What should I do now to grow?" And for me to respond, "Imitate me, just as I imitate Christ." I doubt I'll ever be confident enough to actually say that, but that is the kind of lifestyle we all should be moving toward, a lifestyle that Paul lived. He could legitimately say, "Follow me. Do what I do because I'm following Jesus."

Whether we realize it or not, we are being watched and our behavior is being followed. People are looking to us as examples of what the Christian life is all about, so we should be maturing and making ourselves better to help them grow. More than likely, new believers will incorporate into their lives what they see in ours, so let's work to make ours ones that look like Christ.

You see that with the veterans on football teams and pitching staffs. A coach with veteran players can take a step back because those seasoned players will model the behavior he wants in the younger players. During his last years as an active player, Andy Pettitte served as a positive influence with the younger New York Yankee pitchers. He had seen so many situations, survived the New York media for so long, and had dealt with pressure time and again that he was able to model, directly and indirectly, big-league skills and Christlike habits for others on the staff.

You should strive to do the same, whether in the church body as a whole, in a smaller accountability group or Bible study, or in your everyday life, knowing that people are looking for an example of how to be like Jesus.

UNCOMMON KEY > *What is something you can model today so that others can see Christ through you? Start with an attribute of Jesus to work on, such as joy or patience.*

January 21

Playing the Position God Gives Us

| **We live by believing and not by seeing.** 2 CORINTHIANS 5:7

Faith is a big component in a football team's game plan. Our team ran a "Cover 2" defense, an assignment-oriented plan that requires faith and trust to work. Players can't just run to the ball in a Cover 2, even though that's what their natural instincts tell them to do. They have to protect their areas, guard the gaps, and trust the system, whether it looks like they are going to be involved in the play or not. If each player can depend on the others to carry out their assignments, the defense works effectively. If they don't have faith in their teammates, they abandon the plan and open up holes for the offense to exploit.

Running an offense requires faith too. A quarterback has to throw the ball to a spot before the receiver has gotten there or even begun to cut in that direction. He has to trust that the receiver will run his route correctly, and the receiver has to stick with the route that was planned, trusting that the ball will arrive in the right place at the right time. If either player depends entirely on what he sees and not on the plan as it was designed, the pass will result in an incompletion or an interception. They have to believe in the route.

That's how life works too. We have to trust that the assignment God has given us is the right one, whether it looks like we're in the middle of the action right now or not. We need to know that the people and circumstances around us are running a pattern that will work out for good. Or that the route we're running is designed well and that the ball will get to us in the right spot at the right time. As we carry out our assignments faithfully, the results will come. We need to forsake our natural instincts and play our position, no matter how things look, and trust that the plan will work. That's what it means to live by faith, not by sight.

UNCOMMON KEY > *Play your God-given position as well as you can, realizing that your assignment fits into a bigger picture. Do your best, forget the rest, and trust that God really is in control.*

January 22

It Really Is the Best Policy

> Just say a simple, "Yes, I will," or "No, I won't." Anything beyond this is from the evil one.
> MATTHEW 5:37

I know a man who used to work in the front office of several teams in the National Football League, rising as high as vice president for one. He was the business equivalent of the "five-tool player" in baseball: he was extremely bright; well educated; comfortable dealing with players, business leaders, coaches, and fans; and was a great ambassador for the team and the league. He quickly grasped the issues facing the league, navigated his team through competitive challenges, and built a strong product for his team's owner, both on and off the field.

There were many observers around the league who anticipated that he might eventually end up as the next commissioner of the NFL.

He's now out of the league completely. What happened?

Sadly, he had a hang-up with honesty. He simply couldn't tell the truth. It got to the point where, on occasion, he even joked about it. Ultimately, however, that character flaw proved to be his undoing, outweighing any assets he brought with him. When people can't rely on your word, when they can't trust you, it undermines everything else you are trying to do.

Even sadder is that he was an enjoyable person to be around, as evidenced by his many friends. But at the end of the day, most of those friends proved superficial because they couldn't trust him either.

Honesty is a component of a person's character that is remembered far longer than an individual's words, talents, or accomplishments. All those things can carry a person to a point, but ultimately, without honing that deep core of honesty, they will all be for naught.

Be someone who tells the truth. Let your "yes be yes." Nothing more and nothing less.

UNCOMMON KEY > *Being less than honest with others will permanently mark your character if you don't change. Any attempt to stretch the truth, be all things to all people, or be "creative" in your truth-telling is a habit you need to change as quickly as possible.*

January 23

Peace Be with You

> You will experience God's peace, which exceeds anything we can understand. His peace will guard your hearts and minds as you live in Christ Jesus. **PHILIPPIANS 4:7**

Our feelings of self-worth are shaped by the opinions and attitudes of others. Some of us were surrounded by people who affirmed our worth again and again as we were growing up. Others of us weren't. But all of us have been affected at some point along the way by the thoughtless words and hurtful actions of others. Those words and actions color how we see ourselves. And no matter how much we have heard about God's love for us, we sometimes struggle to believe that we can actually experience that kind of love.

I know that's harder for some people, especially for those whose parents didn't give them a lot of support or show them the warmth of God's love. That makes it even harder to overcome those feelings of worthlessness we all have at times. But those feelings can still be overcome. That struggle to know God's love doesn't have to be our story. His can be the only outside opinion that we truly rely on to shape our sense of worth.

Whether you realize it or not, God has created you with unique gifts and abilities, called you to a fulfilling purpose, and plans to use you for extraordinary accomplishments. Maybe you don't even know what those gifts and abilities are yet or have only just begun to tap into them. Perhaps you haven't discovered the real purpose of your journey yet. Maybe there seems to be too many obstacles to get over—someone wounded you or did something that put you at a disadvantage in life, or you're in a situation that seems to have no way out or room for growth. Or maybe you think you've made too many mistakes. But God isn't limited by these things, and neither are you. The God who created you is still there and loves you with an unending love.

Regardless of how people have treated you or tried to define your worth, God stands ready to walk with you for the rest of your life. He will help you draw a line between your past and your future, and He will help you forgive and move into all the fullness and freedom of a brand-new day.

UNCOMMON KEY > *If you are unsettled about something in your life—past or present—ask God to bring you peace about it. Be assured that God has never left you, and He never will—no matter what.*

January 24

Prescribed by God to Make a Difference

> When Jesus heard this, he told them, "Healthy people don't need a doctor—sick people do. I have come to call not those who think they are righteous, but those who know they are sinners." MARK 2:17

How often do we minister only to those who are like us or have their acts together? I would suggest we do it a lot of the time—it's only natural since it's a more comfortable setting. We have an idea how to approach someone who is at least somewhat like us. But those are not the only lives where God call us to make a difference.

As a longtime fisherman, I appreciate the numerous fishing metaphors that Jesus used to make many of His points. I heard it said that Jesus asks us to bring the fish into the boat, not to worry about having to have them cleaned up first and *then* hauled aboard.

When I was coaching, there were a couple of times each year when that became more apparent to me and caused me to struggle with how to handle a particular situation and minister to a particular player. I would have to decide, despite the athlete's ability to play the game, whether that person's shortcomings in character or other things that needed to be cleaned up in his life were too great or too much of a distraction for our team to keep them.

At the end of every season, our coaching staff conducted overall evaluations. I had to determine whether I felt I could still help certain players with what was going on in their lives or not. And then as the season began and we went through the rigors of training camp, there were both veterans and newcomers whose immediate futures and livelihoods were in my hands, which for me was no small burden and responsibility.

Every now and then I'd have a coach or player who may not have had a perfect past, and people would ask me if I really wanted them on the staff or the roster, or even if I wanted to be associated with them at all. How else will we show the world that we're different and impact those who may need it? Jesus wants us actively ministering to people who need to be ministered to, who need to know the Source of that difference in our lives. Who need Jesus' healing words and grace.

UNCOMMON KEY > *Is the way you are living your life making a difference in someone else's? Someone you wouldn't readily gravitate to? There may be bigger things that Christ calls you to than what seems obvious.*

January 25

Refurbishing the Temple

> Don't you realize that your body is the temple of the Holy Spirit, who lives in you and was given to you by God? You do not belong to yourself, for God bought you with a high price. So you must honor God with your body. 1 CORINTHIANS 6:19-20

For me, whenever it's time for another birthday, it seems as though every year has passed by faster than the year before. Let's be honest with ourselves: life is short, and we need to be serious about taking care of ourselves.

Don't get me wrong; I'm as guilty as the next person. I've got a weakness for ice cream and other desserts. But I always try to keep my intake moderate, fitting it with everything I put into my body—water, juices, well-balanced meals, and no tobacco or alcohol. And now that I'm no longer coaching, I don't have easy access within the office to treadmills and StairMasters. I need the workouts more, but I have to make a more conscious effort to do them.

I'm not going to live forever. How long will this body that God created be around? Seventy years? Ninety? One hundred and ten? Only He knows.

Yet so often we don't pay much attention to what we're doing to ourselves, despite knowing the long-term consequences. God wants more from us!

Some of you probably have body issues. You aren't in shape and you don't like the way you look. Or you're frustrated that you haven't successfully kicked a habit that you've been wanting to kick. The truth is, your body is still a temple, whether it's run-down or not.

But where you are now doesn't determine where you can be if you decide to change. Make tomorrow healthier than today. And keep going. One day at a time. Transformation doesn't happen overnight, and yet incremental changes in diet and exercise can make dramatic differences when done consistently over a period of time. Health and satisfaction result. And hope.

Ultimately, God wants you to do His work here on earth. The more you honor Him with your body, the greater the likelihood that you'll have longer to do just that.

UNCOMMON KEY > *Your body is a temple, created by God. If you haven't been concerned about what you put into it or have been slacking off in keeping active, make a change. From this point forward, honor Him by taking care of yourself physically.*

January 26

When Expectations Derail Your Dreams

Don't copy the behavior and customs of this world, but let God transform you into a new person by changing the way you think. Then you will learn to know God's will for you, which is good and pleasing and perfect. ROMANS 12:2

Michael Westbrook was a gifted wide receiver for the Washington Redskins and Cincinnati Bengals during an eight-year NFL career. He had been an All-American at the University of Colorado and was known for catching one of the most dramatic touchdowns in Colorado history to beat Michigan. He had succeeded at every level. And at the relatively young age of thirty, he retired and became active in mixed martial arts. Why? Because apparently he never even liked football.

That's what he said in an article I read not long after he retired. He felt like he needed to play because it was expected of him. I was not only surprised that he didn't like the game, I was also saddened that he had spent so much of his life doing something he didn't enjoy. Like many other people, he had set his direction solely because of the expectations of others.

We see this all the time, don't we? Kids in my youngest children's classes are all planning to grow up to be doctors or artists, gymnasts or football players, presidents or police officers. Sometimes these are the children's plans, but often they're really their parents' plans. But as they get older, kids confess to no longer having those dreams, if they were theirs at all. They had learned to conform to the expectations of those around them. Many of us go through life trying to play a role expected of us by parents, spouses, or the culture itself.

God put certain things in your heart, passions and dreams that others don't have. It's true that some childhood dreams may prove to be unrealistic, but there's something in them that reflects God's fingerprints in your life. Those fingerprints are unique to you, and they shouldn't remain hidden. They shouldn't have to conform to other people's expectations or be quenched because someone has another plan for your life. If your dreams develop in the process of seeking God's will and fit within His overall purposes, follow them. He would not have given them to you if they were not important.

UNCOMMON KEY > *God made you the unique person you are. Discover your passions. Dare to dream, to reach, and to soar. The world needs what you have to offer.*

January 27

Embracing the Truth

> Jesus said to the people who believed in him, "You are truly my disciples if you remain faithful to my teachings. And you will know the truth, and the truth will set you free."
>
> JOHN 8:31-32

I've taught my children that telling the truth is the best way to deal with the consequences of something and that trying to cover up a lie or misstatement is often worse than the initial transgression. It's where our integrity and influence take a hit. We've seen that played out time and again in our culture—in sports, politics, business, and even some religious settings.

We've seen over and over that the cover-up often seems to have greater consequences than the initial action. In most of the situations, the public seems more than willing to forgive the initial action if the person comes clean and admits their knowledge or participation in whatever is under investigation. But that attempt to cover up the truth seems always to be what causes the curtain to fall on their careers and, eventually, their freedom and influence and impact for God's Kingdom.

In the verse today, Jesus had the bigger picture in mind, however. He's talking about the ultimate, eternal truth—the truth that He is the Savior and that by accepting Him as Savior, we will be set free from our bondage to sin and no longer separated from Him. So many people view the Christian walk as a series of dos and don'ts, a list of behaviors to be kept. Rather, Christ came for freedom so we would no longer be slaves to the law, but rather would be redeemed through His death—through grace.

It seems like such an easy thing. God takes something that seems incomprehensible to our finite minds—our redemption—and makes it accessible to us through Jesus' death on the cross. That in itself should make us take a serious look at the Truth embodied in Jesus Christ.

What truth do you know and understand?

UNCOMMON KEY > *It's simple: the Truth (Jesus Christ) will set you free! Why don't you claim Him for your life? And watch how He will use His truth in you to influence the world around you.*

January 28

Persevering to the End

> I have fought the good fight, I have finished the race, and I have remained faithful. And now the prize awaits me—the crown of righteousness, which the Lord, the righteous Judge, will give me on the day of his return. And the prize is not just for me but for all who eagerly look forward to his appearing.   2 TIMOTHY 4:7-8

How often have you seen a team jump out to a big lead and then change what they were doing? The game isn't over, and suddenly they move to a different offense or defense, thinking that the game is already won.

Here's the classic, which I have personally never understood or used, but for years team after team would do it. A football team would be well ahead—three to four touchdowns—and their defense was shutting the other team down. But for some reason they would go into a "prevent defense," with defensive backs playing deeper than usual to prevent the big play. Before you knew it, the team who was behind had scored two or three touchdowns against this defense, and all of a sudden, they have made what seemed like a lopsided loss into a competitive game. You'd think they would continue to play the same tough defense that had been successful—persevering until the game was won. But they don't. And they lose. There's always something left to be done, right until the very end.

Today's verses from the apostle Paul to Timothy—and now to us—encourage us to stay strong until the end of the fight. The fight isn't over yet, but what a day it will be when we stand face-to-face with God and say that we persevered to the end! And then we'll hear, "Well done, good and faithful servant!"

Note, too, that the prize isn't for accomplishments; it's for "remaining faithful." We can't earn it or achieve it, no matter how many wins we have or all the earthly rewards that come with them. The prize is the crown of righteousness that He will give us when He returns for finishing the race and remaining faithful to the end.

Are you someone who is "eagerly look[ing] forward to his appearing"?

UNCOMMON KEY > *The race of faithfulness is different for each person. Your job is to run it until the end, keeping the prize in your sights.*

January 29

Pulling Together

> If you think you are standing strong, be careful not to fall. The temptations in your life are no different from what others experience. And God is faithful. He will not allow the temptation to be more than you can stand. When you are tempted, he will show you a way out so that you can endure. 1 CORINTHIANS 10:12-13

We all have issues. We all have things that pull at us, tempt us, and distract us—constantly.

And if we are honest about it, we would have to admit that we usually allow ourselves to be pulled, tempted, and distracted by everything imaginable—often the wrong things—because we believe we're able to handle it all. No problem. More than likely we insist, once again, on going it alone.

But God doesn't ask us to walk alone. God specifically created us to be in relationship, relationship with Him and relationship with others. God is always bringing other people into our lives to walk with us, to help us do what He's called us to do even better.

During my years of coaching, I saw relationship in action. I called it a team—a group of individuals with a stated mission and purpose and a commitment to accomplish that mission successfully. Team members would interact in the locker room, in the classroom, and on the practice field, preparing for game day. They depended on each other to help us achieve our goal of winning football games. But I also saw that along the way, things would pull at the team to distract it, luring the attention of some individuals away from the game plan. It was never anything particularly surprising: injuries, concerns over individual playing time, contract renegotiations, and off-the-field distractions that came with the territory.

Successful, high-performance teams are aware of individual team members and the distractions and temptations they might be facing. Individuals don't have to walk alone on those teams—others come alongside them and keep them focused and encouraged.

Great teammates make for great teams.

UNCOMMON KEY > *You are not expected to be invincible. Life happens to all of us. No matter what you're facing, you don't have to go it alone. God created you to have a relationship with Him and with the people He puts in your life. Reach out and they'll be there for you.*

January 30

A Different Scoreboard

> This Book of the Law shall not depart from your mouth, but you shall meditate in it day and night, that you may observe to do according to all that is written in it. For then you will make your way prosperous, and then you will have good success.   JOSHUA 1:8, NKJV

Chuck Noll believed success wasn't always reflected on the scoreboard. I think he would rather have seen his team play well and lose than play poorly and win. Obviously, the nature of competitive sports defines success in terms of wins and losses, but that doesn't always measure matters of the heart. And in God's Kingdom, real success is a heart issue.

Leading a team to a Super Bowl win is considered the pinnacle of an NFL coach's profession, and I'm fortunate enough to have done that. But that was never an all-encompassing quest for me. I knew it would not make my life complete if we won or leave me feeling unfulfilled if it never happened. I wanted to win, of course—I'm as competitive as the next guy. But significance isn't found in things like winning a Super Bowl—or whatever is considered to be the pinnacle of your career or ambitions. No, significance is found in focusing on the priorities you know are important: doing as good a job as you can do, spending quality time with people you love, and investing yourself in ministry opportunities and influencing others for good. In other words, real success is about doing what God has called you to do as well as you can.

When we figure that out, it sets us free from a lot of pressure. We don't have to become a head coach, a CEO, a PhD, a billionaire, or a celebrity in order to be successful. There's nothing wrong with being any of those things, but our significance doesn't depend on them. In fact, we need to find our significance long before we ever step into one of those roles. We need to set our minds on discovering what God has put us here to do and then doing it as well and as faithfully as we can. When our hearts and our actions are true to our callings, God considers us successful. And in the end, His is the only scoreboard that counts.

UNCOMMON KEY > *God measures success by how faithfully we follow Him, not by outward accomplishments. Write down what you think your score with Him is this morning. Try and get it higher by the end of the day in ways that matter, starting with your family.*

January 31

MVP: Many Valuable People

> Just as our bodies have many parts and each part has a special function, so it is with Christ's body. We are many parts of one body, and we all belong to each other. ROMANS 12:4-5

Since the first Super Bowl was held in 1967, forty-six Most Valuable Player awards have been handed out, one for each of the forty-five Super Bowls (and one with two).

In the first four Super Bowls, the quarterback from the winning team was selected as the Most Valuable Player. Green Bay quarterback Bart Starr was selected in both 1967 and 1968 as the MVP, and in 1969 Joe Namath was selected following the New York Jets' historic win over the Baltimore Colts. In 1970 Len Dawson of the Kansas City Chiefs was selected after leading his team to victory over the Minnesota Vikings in Super Bowl IV. Every year since, the award has been handed out to a member of the winning team, except in 1971, when Dallas Cowboys' linebacker Chuck Howley won the award in the game against the winner, the Baltimore Colts.

During the course of the forty-five-year span of Super Bowl Sunday games, the breakdown by position of the Most Valuable Player selected is kick returner—1; running backs—7; wide receivers—6; defensive players—8; quarterbacks—24.

In the forty-five-year history of the Super Bowl, not one offensive lineman has won the award. Yet try to play the game without them. Try to win a Super Bowl without a stellar offensive line. And as to quarterbacks—how many Super Bowl MVP awards do you think they would have won if they had been consistently hurried, hit, or sacked during a game, watching the game from the vantage point of their backsides?

I know of one in particular—Peyton Manning, the MVP quarterback in Super Bowl XLI—who couldn't have won it without his offensive line. Or his running backs, receivers, and tight ends. Or his defense. Peyton's a great player, but he needed the rest of the supporting cast.

Many parts—one team, one body. All together.

UNCOMMON KEY > *You can try to make a difference in the world by going it alone. But there is strength and power in numbers. God designed one body with many parts, all working together and interdependent upon each other. Make sure you're part of one.*

February 1

The Four-Way Growth Plan

> | Jesus grew in wisdom and in stature and in favor with God and all the people. LUKE 2:52

It becomes too easy to say at times, and a bit glib and insincere-sounding: football is about more than the game; it's about life. Well, a friend of mine means it, his teams live it, and their individual lives after football prove it to be true.

At Liberty University in Lynchburg, Virginia, head football coach Danny Rocco took over a program that was 1 and 10, and in five years has taken the Liberty Flames' football fortunes to a consistent level of championship caliber. Since taking over in December 2005, he has led the team to four Big South Conference Championships in 2007 (the first in school history), 2008, 2009, and 2010; been selected as Conference Coach of the Year three times; and been nominated for the Eddie Robinson and Liberty Mutual National Coach of the Year awards on three different occasions.

He has done it with a relentlessly attacking offense that mixes a power running game and play action and a deep passing game that stretches the field, and a defense designed to play fast, smart, and aggressive. But more than that, Coach Rocco has done it by recruiting and developing character and by relying on the admonition and direction of God's Word, particularly the teaching in Luke 2:52.

Danny believes that part of his responsibility to the university, to his players and staff, and to the community the players serve now and the one they will serve when they graduate is to grow his players and staff in a number of different ways: intellectually ("Jesus grew in wisdom"), physically ("stature"), spiritually ("in favor with God"), and relationally ("and all people"). Coach Rocco calls it "whole-person development" and believes that the person who embodied it—Jesus Christ—is an unmatched role model for him and his teams to emulate.

And the bonus for them is winning a lot of football games!

UNCOMMON KEY > *Do you need a growth spurt? Everyone needs improvement with something. Write down Luke 2:52 and evaluate what area you need to work on. Explore ways to make it happen and then do it!*

February 2

Patting Yourself on the Back Can Be Hazardous

Let someone else praise you, not your own mouth—a stranger, not your own lips.
PROVERBS 27:2

My high school football coach, Dave Driscoll, drove home today's verse in another way: "Talent is God-given—be thankful. Praise is man-given—be humble. Conceit is self-given—be careful."

In his book *Through My Eyes*, Tim Tebow recounts that his parents made a rule when he was very young: he and his brothers couldn't tell about their own feats—usually sports related—unless they were asked about them. Apparently, there was quite a bit of bragging going on among Tim and his two brothers and subsequently to others, and their parents wanted it to stop. So at about age five, Tim, and his brothers, Robby (age eleven) and Peter (age eight) were forbidden to go on—unchecked—about what they had done well.

Friends at church learned about the Tebow rule, so whenever they wanted to know the latest news, they would walk up to Tim on Sunday and ask, "Timmy, have you had any games this week?" Once that question was asked, the boys were permitted to freely recap the weekend's highlights.

The lesson is a good one for all of us. When we've done something well or been recognized for our achievements, we can't help it—we want others to know about our accomplishments, including what others may have said. For whatever reason, nobody close to us seems to be impressed, or if they are, they're keeping it to themselves. Yes, we can be quick to praise or boast about ourselves and justify it in many ways, but in the process we lose focus on others and our call to service.

When I saw Tim during college press conferences—after years of practicing the lesson of Proverbs 27:2—he was slow to speak about himself. Years of good training paid off—he wouldn't even recap his exploits when asked.

As hard as it is at times to bite your tongue in those situations, let others do the talking and be the ones to praise you. When your focus in life turns inward—focusing on yourself—you begin to lose God's purpose for your life: to love Him and others.

UNCOMMON KEY > *Rather than patting yourself on the back in front of others, think of something to praise another person for. Who knows? They may return the gesture.*

February 3

Against All Odds

> Jesus replied with a story: "A Jewish man was traveling from Jerusalem down to Jericho.... Then a despised Samaritan came along." LUKE 10:30, 33

I remember it to this day. I had been wronged and was complaining about the unfairness of what had occurred. My dad agreed with me, but his response to me was by way of a story.

"When I was in the service," he said, "they didn't want to teach us how to fly planes, so we taught ourselves to fly."

We being blacks. African Americans. The Samaritans, perhaps, of that time. I didn't ask any questions about what he meant by "we taught ourselves to fly."

Tuskegee, Alabama, is near Montgomery. The town was named for a nearby Native American tribe called the Taskigis. It is still best known for Tuskegee University, whose first president was Booker T. Washington.

During World War II, the United States Army Air Corps needed a training location for a start-up program to train black pilots until 1946, when blacks were fully integrated into military training. In 1940, Tuskegee was selected as the training site. Roughly one thousand pilots—the Tuskegee Airmen—were trained there and first saw combat in 1943, finishing their service without any of their planes shot down in bombing runs in Europe. In 2007, the Tuskegee Airmen were awarded the Congressional Gold Medal for their service.

My dad was a part of this elite group of pilots, but I never knew it until his memorial service in 2004, where one of the eulogists shared the story about my dad and all the other black pilots trained to fly at that training facility. I wondered why he had never told me that story. There may have been a number of reasons, not least of which was my failure to follow up and ask about what he had meant by his comment.

It would have gotten lost in the lesson, anyway, which was that we should not let external issues hinder us and our objectives, goals, and performance, especially when those issues are based on race or any other factor.

Things will go wrong. We will be wronged. With Christ in our lives, He will help us get beyond it.

He will come up with a new and customized plan just for you.

UNCOMMON KEY > *Are there any barriers between you and others that need to come down? Read the entire story of the Good Samaritan in Luke 10:29-37. Who is the most like you in the story? Make any changes to be more like the Samaritan.*

February 4

Faithful, Not Successful

> "My thoughts are nothing like your thoughts," says the LORD. "And my ways are far beyond anything you could imagine. For just as the heavens are higher than the earth, so my ways are higher than your ways and my thoughts higher than your thoughts." ISAIAH 55:8-9

After the journey of writing my first book, *Quiet Strength*, God impressed upon me and Nathan that His measurement of success has little to do with sales numbers. We were blessed to have great numbers, but that's not what made the book a success in God's eyes. God's scorecard is different from ours. He judges not by money, statistics, or fame, but by the state of our hearts and our desire to serve Him.

God calls us to be faithful, not "successful." He calls us to follow the dreams He has put in our hearts. The outcome of those dreams may look successful in worldly terms, or they may not. They may look futile. We may not see any external results at all, or at least not for a few years. We may not see any lives that our dreams have changed—or notice how our own hearts have changed in the process. Our commitment and persistence, even if others admire us for those attitudes, may not seem to be paying off. But if we are faithful, God notices. And He calls that success.

Real success often happens behind the scenes, and only God can measure it accurately. The only thing that's really important is that His purposes are accomplished. He wants hearts to change—including ours—and lives to be impacted, even when those results aren't visible to anyone. His work is done deep inside. Our job is to be faithful; His job is to accomplish results.

Trust God to bear fruit in your life however He chooses to. Don't sell yourself or your dreams short. Be persistent in accomplishing whatever He has placed in your heart. Your diligence, persistence, and commitment to His purposes are the keys that define success.

UNCOMMON KEY > *God's purposes begin with His call to be faithful. Are you willing to answer that call today? Move forward with Him, and He will call you successful—no matter what the external results look like.*

February 5

Your Words

> Don't use foul or abusive language. . . . Get rid of all bitterness, rage, anger, harsh words, and slander, as well as all types of evil behavior.   EPHESIANS 4:29, 31

I've always heard that foul language is not only tolerated in football locker rooms and on the field, it's expected. People say, "It's just that kind of place." I don't get that. If I've got enough self-control to not use foul or abusive language other places, I clearly could do the same on the field. And I chose to do so.

The way I see it, abusive language toward officials will get your team penalized or get you ejected from the game. The same language, if used in a television interview, would draw a fine, suspension, or firing. So even those players and coaches who use that type of language learn to control it.

I've noticed that award shows on television aren't live anymore, but rather run off a five-second delay. That is absolutely no surprise to me; I wonder why it wasn't changed sooner. Radio talk shows have had five- to seven-second delays in place for years for callers. It's probably a wise strategy, given the things we've heard coming out of some people's mouths.

If you use unwholesome language on a regular basis and brush it off as "I'm just kidding around," people will lose their trust in you and it could hurt feelings and damage relationships forever. Even if you said something that might be considered complimentary, your words might be suspect as people think, *I wonder if he means it.* They won't know whether they can trust you enough to bring something serious for your counsel or input.

Similarly, let no bitterness or harsh words come out of your mouth. What do you do when someone hurts you by saying mean things? If it is directed personally toward me, I can handle it easier than if someone hurts or tries to hurt someone I love. In that case, my first instinct is for the gloves to come off. My better instincts cause me to wrap my loved one within my protective embrace—actually or figuratively—and try not to make the situation worse by lowering myself to the same level of bitterness, harshness, anger, or slander being thrown at them.

None of this is easy to do. In fact, we have to ask Christ to control our thoughts, words, responses, and behavior. When we do, we bring honor and glory to Him—for all of the world to see.

UNCOMMON KEY > *Don't shrug off foul and abusive language, in yourself or others. If you need to clean yours up, begin right now.*

February 6

What True Love Looks Like

> Love never gives up, never loses faith, is always hopeful, and endures through every circumstance. 1 CORINTHIANS 13:7

There is no clearer showcase of your character than your relationships—the way you treat others and expect them to treat you. And the way you handle relationships, particularly your close ones, will impact every other area of your life in one way or another.

I think a lot of people are confused about relationships, especially marriage. Some people seek to dominate the relationship, while others are almost completely passive. And it's hard to blame this generation for those extremes because we haven't had the best role models. Many moms and dads either weren't around or didn't demonstrate how to truly love someone else. Society hasn't taken up the slack, putting out movies and TV shows that focus more on erotic passion than on emotional and spiritual love.

And those who look to the church to clear up the confusion are often disappointed, finding either misinterpretations of Scripture that overemphasize "head of household" control or misinterpretations of Christ that depict Him as passive and weak and expecting us to be that way too. Good examples of true, sacrificial love that builds others up are hard to find.

According to 1 Corinthians 13, love means doing everything for someone else's benefit. That doesn't mean passively giving in to the other person's every wish or desire, and it obviously doesn't mean dominating a relationship. It means making every decision with the other person's well-being in mind. Whether in marriage, in other family relationships, or among friends, the principle is the same. Love seeks to strengthen and benefit others.

Be active in the lives of others—your spouse, your family members, and your friends. Talk to them and, more important, listen to them. Invest your time and your attention. Be interested in them, be supportive, and be involved. Real love changes lives—including yours.

UNCOMMON KEY > *Don't just show love to others. Show Christ's kind of love—sacrificial, others-centered, and enduring—by investing your life in other people's well-being.*

February 7

What Are You Willing to Do?

> This is my commandment: Love each other in the same way I have loved you. There is no greater love than to lay down one's life for one's friends. JOHN 15:12-13

I always considered the members of my teams as family. But Tom Walter, the baseball coach at Wake Forest, has taken that "family" relationship to an entirely new level.

He donated a kidney to one of his players.

Coach Walter didn't hesitate to volunteer to help Kevin Jordan, a freshman outfielder attending the school on a baseball scholarship. Kevin's athletic skills had not gone unnoticed: the New York Yankees had picked him in the nineteenth round of the amateur draft. But even that news didn't change the fact that Kevin was very ill. His first semester, Kevin was so sick from a rare kidney disorder that he was on a dialysis machine in his dorm room eight hours a day, attending classes and team practices when he wasn't. He wondered if he would ever be able to play ball again.

But there they were, together at Emory University Hospital in Atlanta, recuperating from the surgery and both thinking about future baseball seasons.

"It's something you can't imagine," said Kevin's father, Keith. "Somebody mentioned divine intervention when you look at how we got to Wake Forest. It's just one of those things you can't express in words."

Actually, it *is* something we can imagine—because Jesus Christ did it for us.

You may not be in a situation like Coach Walter and Kevin, but you may be called to do something else. It's not the "what" that is important; it's the "what will you do" that is important. As a follower of Christ, you are called to love the way Christ loved—to lay down your all for others the way He laid down everything for you.

What will you do for others on His behalf?

UNCOMMON KEY > *"Love each other in the same way I have loved you." As you strive to be like Christ, be ready to lovingly sacrifice something for others. It may be the most important thing He calls you to do.*

February 8

Turning Troubles into Opportunities

> When troubles come your way, consider it an opportunity for great joy. For you know that when your faith is tested, your endurance has a chance to grow. So let it grow, for when your endurance is fully developed, you will be perfect and complete, needing nothing.
> JAMES 1:2-4

Troubles as opportunities? Once again, God is turning the "wisdom" of the world on its head. The apostle James says that trials should be embraced rather than lamented.

Don't get me wrong. There were plenty of times when I wasn't particularly keen about a loss we had suffered—especially those playoff losses—or a key injury that we sustained. But I also understood that God was using all that for good by helping me and the team to grow.

Maybe you're someone who has followed your heart into something and it didn't turn out as you expected. Tough luck or wrong choice, huh? Maybe not. Consider that you may be planted exactly where God intended for you to be in order to grow your faith in Him, even though the rain and wind are blowing so hard it may have clouded the broader, bigger, better vision He had set before you earlier.

So instead of turning around and retreating, why not pick yourself up and throw yourself back into the fray, trusting that He is with you and will use all of it to strengthen and grow you? God never wastes what you are going through for Him. He will use it to grow you more into the person He wants you to be.

Look at it this way. As that great philosopher Yogi Berra said, "The game ain't over 'til it's over." A lot can happen in nine innings of a baseball game, four quarters of football, two periods of basketball, or every day of a lifetime. It's not about things or troubles, but it is about following your heart, a heart aligned with God, over, under, around, and through any mountain, sea, valley, or storm.

It's not about what you can get out of where you are, but what you can put into and do by enduring right where He has planted you.

UNCOMMON KEY > *When troubles hit, dig in deeper and grow—right where you are!*

February 9

Reaching Out in Innovative, Simple Ways

> There was a believer in Joppa named Tabitha (which in Greek is Dorcas). She was always doing kind things for others and helping the poor. ACTS 9:36

When speaking at an Impact for Living conference recently, I met a couple of guys who are finding unique ways to impact the poor. Steve Haas from World Vision establishes partnerships with other organizations or businesses to create ways in which they can take on a direct role to help others around the globe. John Kingston is a businessman in Boston, and he was becoming concerned that his children were detached from the issues of want and suffering around the world. So John started SixSeeds, an organization committed to helping families find ways to serve others.

In an e-mail to Nathan, Steve shared some of the challenges that they face at World Vision:

> *What was astonishing to me . . . was the amount of Scripture that underlined the fact that true justice was leveling the playing field.* How *we do it is everything, and simply having the mandate that we are to disadvantage ourselves for the advantage of others isn't license for us to run out and do this poorly—or haphazardly (although in some cases that is better than doing nothing at all . . . just ask the Haitians three days into the quake who had nothing to eat). We have to . . . find constructive ways to assist and strengthen rather than avoiding or, often as badly, taking or robbing the interest in self-reliance and ingenuity from the recipient of our charity. . . . The distribution of these items can be done in a way that restores self-respect, encourages self-reliance, and builds community and personal/corporate resourcefulness.* (emphasis added)

In that same vein, John has created various avenues that his family and others can take to help in hands-on ways and templates that allow families to tailor the approach to ones that work in their own areas.

In so doing, both have taken the emphasis off of the giver (Look what *we're* doing!) and placed it where the Bible does—on our duty to help those who need it, and to do so in a way that leaves the person's dignity intact and his or her future brighter.

And that's something we all can get behind.

What idea is God bringing to your mind?

UNCOMMON KEY > *What is a simple, tangible way that you can help the poor? Sometimes the best first step is a simple one. Check out www.worldvision.org or www.sixseeds.org for ideas if you need them.*

February 10

Choosing to Be a Positive Influence

> You say, "I am allowed to do anything"—but not everything is good for you. You say, "I am allowed to do anything"—but not everything is beneficial. Don't be concerned for your own good but for the good of others. 1 CORINTHIANS 10:23-24

I don't have a particular problem with alcohol. I get that Jesus turned water into wine. I understand that alcohol has been around and is legal for people of a certain drinking age established by the individual states. I take issue with the prevalence of alcohol abuse.

And so I decided long ago that since I could not see any way that it was going to help me and it wasn't something I would miss, I would choose not to drink. Besides, if I don't drink with a friend who has a problem keeping his drinking under control, I might influence him in a positive way to get help.

Another thing I have tried to choose carefully is my speaking venues. It's a concern my friend James Brown shares with me as a fellow believer. We both get quite a few requests to speak at corporations and have debated to what extent we should look at the values of the company or its products to determine where to speak or evaluate the impact we might have by speaking there. In certain instances, speaking at a particular company might be permissible, but might cause someone who doesn't know Christ to question our witness or values, so in those situations we've each declined.

We all need to be conscious of areas where we can be a positive influence. We also need to be aware of our behavior or lifestyle choices that could have a negative and potentially destructive influence on others around us. We don't need to make decisions on the basis of legalism, but rather what might help or harm someone else or have no effect at all.

We are allowed broad freedoms to live as we choose, and God grants us the free will to make decisions for our lives, but we need to understand that everything we do is observed by others.

Each day, you are sending a message to the people around you and some of them are extremely impressionable. Is your message one you are proud to deliver?

UNCOMMON KEY > *Be careful to choose what is good for you as well as those around you. The choices you make can greatly influence others. Remember that before you make any decisions.*

February 11

Easy as Breathing

> Are any of you suffering hardships? You should pray.... Are any of you sick? You should call for the elders of the church to come and pray over you.... Such a prayer offered in faith will heal the sick, and the Lord will make you well.... Confess your sins to each other and pray for each other so that you may be healed. The earnest prayer of a righteous person has great power and produces wonderful results. JAMES 5:13-16

Do we actually believe that we can be effective in prayer? Prayer not only impacts us, it has an impact on those for whom we are praying. I don't pretend to know how God makes it all work, but somehow there are tangible benefits when we pray in accordance with God's will.

Can we truly expect to have the miraculous results that the biblical heroes had when they prayed? Or are those days past?

I can't speak for anyone else, but personally, I have experienced that, as I'm sure many of you have as well. Duke University's divinity and medical schools even did a joint study a few years ago to assess how a patient's health—in conjunction with medical treatment and with continued treatment—was affected for a patient who believed in God and prayed and was prayed for, as opposed to a patient who didn't claim to have faith in God or a consistent prayer life. Sure enough, the patients who prayed or were prayed for had better outcomes.

Prayer is one discipline you should never get tired of. Read some of the miraculous answers to prayer that God gave in the Old Testament, to ardent praying men like Daniel and Elijah and others.

And there are countless stories of men and women where God's answers to their prayers could not be explained in worldly terms because they were so unbelievable. When evangelist George Müller was asked how much time he spent in prayer, he was said to have replied, "Hours every day. But I live in the spirit of prayer. I pray as I walk and when I lie down and when I arise. And the answers are always coming."

Do you live in a spirit of prayer? It's as easy as breathing. Breathe a prayer often today.

UNCOMMON KEY > *There is one means of communication that has never changed between God and human beings from Old Testament times to now—prayer. What do you need to pray about right now? Commit that you will spend more time praying.*

February 12

Loving the Sinner

> | Continue to show deep love for each other, for love covers a multitude of sins. 1 PETER 4:8

I don't know about you, but I imagine it will take a lot of love to cover not only my past sins, but also the present sinful situations I have created. And the future? Well, that's a story all its own. I can't even begin to fathom that, since my other sins have already put me well behind making up and catching up. And before you get too smug or start to feel sorry for me, remember that all of us are miserably behind in making up for our sins.

But here's the great thing: when others love us despite our sin and we can graciously extend love to those who have wronged us, we receive support and friendship, forgiveness and encouragement. We know that our struggles with sin will continue on earth, only ending in eternity with God. Jesus is the only person who lived a sinless life, but He also knows what we face and has compassion: "He faced all of the same testings we do, yet he did not sin" (Hebrews 4:15). Even if we've accepted Him as Savior, even if we're doing everything we can to keep from sinning, we simply can't avoid sin. But thankfully, God's loving forgiveness is ours for the asking. And love given from those we have wronged and extended to others who have wronged us will go a long way toward binding up wounds and helping us overcome any crisis we face.

It's the very nature of love to do that. Solomon writes that "love makes up for all offenses" (Proverbs 10:12). And Paul, in 1 Corinthians 13:5, says that love "keeps no record of being wronged." Then there was the woman whose tears washed Jesus' feet in Luke 7. Jesus said, "I tell you, her sins—and they are many—have been forgiven, so she has shown me much love" (verse 47). We are assured that Jesus' sacrificial love and forgiveness covers our sins. That assurance provides us with a fresh starting point when we've fallen short of God's standards. This is something to remind each other of.

UNCOMMON KEY > *Sin is part of our human nature. So is love. Hate the sin, but love the sinner. Love given or received is the best agent for change and forgiveness.*

February 13

It's Never Too Late to Say Thanks

| Honor your father and mother. Then you will live a long, full life in the land the LORD your God is giving you. **EXODUS 20:12**

My parents did a lot of things that didn't make sense to me. I knew my best interests and those of my brothers and sisters were paramount to them, but like any child, I didn't think my parents were always fair. I was allowed to disagree with them, but I had to accept their decisions and learn to deal with them. Sometimes that wasn't easy, and it didn't always make me happy.

But I knew I could trust my parents. Their decisions were for my benefit, whether I understood them or not. I learned at an early age to respect them, and they made it clear that they expected my respect. They believed children should honor their parents and abide by the decisions their parents made for them. They made it clear that their decisions were rooted in God's Word and that we were being raised on biblical principles. As a family, we were going to follow the Bible as our guide. Their strong convictions and their obvious love for us children earned my respect.

Parents play a huge role in shaping us into who we are. My parents certainly shaped me. Some who grew up in a difficult family situation may wish their parents had shaped them differently, but nearly every parent has done something right—something worthy of honor and respect. In our culture it has become more expected to criticize parents than to honor them, but God's command to honor them is more important and reaps more benefits than we might think. As adult children it's important to respect our parents for the role they have played in our lives.

Have you thanked your parents lately for the life they gave you? For providing food, clothes, and shelter for you? For taking care of you as well as they knew how? If so, that's great. Do it as often as you can. If not, consider letting them know that you appreciate what they did for you. And if they have already passed on, thank God instead—and ask Him to pass it on.

UNCOMMON KEY > *Respecting parents has almost become a lost art form. Let your parents know how thankful you are, honoring them for the good they have done for you.*

February 14

A Valentine's Message

> Let there be no sexual immorality, impurity, or greed among you. Such sins have no place among God's people. EPHESIANS 5:3

I don't know if you celebrate Valentine's Day or not. Lauren and I try to do something special, like go to dinner—I always wear a red dress shirt, which most people don't seem to expect from me. While we enjoy it, many people consider this a day specifically created for florists, jewelers, and candy and card companies. I don't think I could argue too much with that. After all, it is often a day when we spend money to let someone close to us know that they matter to us—something we can do, and should be doing, every day with our words and actions. What concerns me is how romance and love is marketed today, as strictly a physically charged relationship.

I've heard reports that there is an increase of abstinence among young people.[1] I applaud that. The "old-fashioned" ideal of girls staying sexually pure so they can wear white on their wedding days is growing. What I've never quite understood is why there isn't the same emphasis on boys remaining sexually pure. For some reason, there is a stigma on women who have a lot of sexual partners, but society seems to look at it differently when it comes to men. We've allowed ourselves to be fooled into thinking that it's acceptable because "that's what men do."

I've seen it too many times with some of the players I have been around through my years in football, players who were not told that sex outside marriage has consequences. The proof? Many of them are fathers who didn't plan to be at the time.

Valentine's Day aside, television and films seem to fuel inappropriate and sensual messages designed to jeopardize the sexual purity of our children and young adults. I think we need to talk to them about the danger of these messages and help them see that God created them as sexual beings, with the best parameters to abide by.

UNCOMMON KEY > *Don't buy into the world's definition of love and romance. If you are sexually active outside of marriage, stop. Think seriously about what you are doing.*

February 15

The Message That Changes Everything

> God did what the law could not do. He sent his own Son in a body like the bodies we sinners have. And in that body God declared an end to sin's control over us by giving his Son as a sacrifice for our sins. ROMANS 8:3

God's grace versus our own merit—it's a universal struggle.

Why do we make it so hard to accept His grace? Our inability to accept such an overwhelming gift—either directly from Him or through the actions of others—can sap us of energy and potential like few other things can. Instead, we opt to pursue merit on our own, which leads us on a never-ending cycle of yearning and earning—love, worth, esteem.

That's not God's way. Thank You, Lord.

I suppose we could blame it on society. After all, we are continually bombarded with messages contrary to the message of grace. We are told to work harder, earn more, be thinner, look prettier, acquire more stuff, build bigger, be better, and on and on. Messages infused with the vocabulary of doing and earning and merit. Messages that say we have to accomplish this list of things before we can expect to be fully loved and fully accepted. Messages contrary to God's empowering promise of grace.

Here's God's message of grace: "I love you!"

Really. He says it to you and to me. Every day, many times over. He says it to the person who society says is overweight, not very smart, not cool, not this, and not that. Bottom line? He says, "No matter what others tell you, no matter if you don't fit their idea of perfection, I love you." His grace is a promise He will never retract.

Once you receive that gift of grace, you join countless believers whom "God can point to . . . as examples of the incredible wealth of his grace and kindness toward us, as shown in all he has done for us who are united with Christ Jesus" (Ephesians 2:7). He has done it all.

UNCOMMON KEY > *When society pummels you with messages that make you feel defeated and worthless, listen to the Person who loves you more than anyone else, and receive His gift of grace. Thank Him for it right now.*

February 16

No Fanfare

> Don't do your good deeds publicly, to be admired by others, for you will lose the reward from your Father in heaven. When you give to someone in need, don't do as the hypocrites do—blowing trumpets in the synagogues and streets to call attention to their acts of charity!
> MATTHEW 6:1-2

Tim Tebow received just about every award that a football player can get in college—a Heisman trophy, the Maxwell Award, and two national championships with the Florida Gators, to name a few. His father, Bob, told Nathan that at the end of one season, he was helping Tim pack up his belongings in the locker room when Tim asked his father if he would carry a box to the car.

Tim's dad peeked inside the box, packed full of trophies, plaques, and certificates, most of which his dad never knew his son had won. Tim's just quiet that way. His parents are also amazed at the number of people who come up to them, unsolicited, mentioning a phone call or visit they have received from Tim. "He simply doesn't tell us," his dad says. "He doesn't tell anyone."

Like the weekly hospital visits that often last hours as the nurses lead him to room after room, and the countless phone calls to people who need a word of encouragement. Done for the right reasons, without fanfare or publicity.

Nathan unknowingly saw it firsthand when he was with Tim in Denver, working on Tim's book, *Through My Eyes*. Tim excused himself to make a phone call, returning ten minutes later. The next evening, Nathan was back in Florida visiting with a friend battling cancer, who said that he had gotten the most remarkable call the previous night.

"Apparently someone gave Tim Tebow my number, and he called to encourage and pray with me. A friend of a friend asked him to call. But why am I telling you? You probably were there!" True, but it was a surprise to Nathan, too.

God wants all of us to live lives of impact, but not in order to receive accolades or recognition. We should touch lives with virtuous acts done for their own sake. For the sake of others. For the sake of our relationship with the Lord. Simply because it's the right thing to do.

UNCOMMON KEY > *Be a person who finds ways to be selfless, to do something quietly and unexpected for someone else. You are more than your career or accomplishments, especially the things that are lauded publicly. The bulk of your impact, either here on earth or eternally, will be from those things that you do in private.*

February 17

Artificial Categories

> You are all children of God through faith in Christ Jesus. And all who have been united with Christ in baptism have put on Christ, like putting on new clothes. . . . You are all one in Christ Jesus. GALATIANS 3:26-28

God sees all of us through a different lens than the world uses. That should not come as a stunning revelation. God has always seen us and the world itself in the context of His vision and plan, beginning with Creation and through His return and ultimate victory over evil, and to the time when He will reign victoriously over all. God doesn't see us as black or white, big or small, fast or slow, or any other separate categories—categories the world sets up and that ultimately act as barriers between us. Instead, God sees every one of us as full of potential and purpose, each His children, one and all.

When Nathan was born, his parents decided they would be more proactive about knocking down some long-standing societal barriers. They had grown up seeing segregation and separation firsthand—"whites only" water fountains, public bathrooms, restaurants, and hotels. They wanted Nathan to grow up as accepting as possible, to see life from a different viewpoint—the way they felt God saw things.

And so they implemented a family rule: no one in the Whitaker family was allowed to describe a person by his or her skin color. For example, if there were three boys standing together and Nathan wanted to point out one of them, he had to say something other than "the black boy." He could say "the boy in the middle" or "the boy with the red shirt on" or "the one who is smiling."

How about you? It's easy to fall into the habit of describing people by skin color or nationality. I don't think I am being overly sensitive when I say that I most often hear skin color being used as a descriptive adjective when the "white person" is referring to an African American or black person. May I suggest that the next time you hear that description used, politely ask the person if that description is relevant to the point they are trying to make. It usually isn't.

UNCOMMON KEY > *If you "color" your language when talking about other people, be diligent about changing that. View people through God's eyes—we are all His children.*

February 18

The Fun of Faith

> I don't know what awaits me. . . . But my life is worth nothing to me unless I use it for finishing the work assigned me by the Lord Jesus—the work of telling others the Good News about the wonderful grace of God. ACTS 20:22, 24

I'm not one of those guys who handles massive doses of uncertainty well. I can do all right when I look at the big picture and—remembering my past experiences with God—know I can handle it. There have been a number of times when I wasn't at all sure how things would turn out, like whether we'd win a game or even whether Lauren would say yes when I asked her to marry me.

There have been many times where it would have been nice to know the answer before the question came to mind. To know the result before I tried something. The outcome before we kicked off. At least I think so.

But then where's the fun and challenge in that? Where's the faith that things may turn out as I had hoped? Faith. It should be an essential part of our lives. The writer of Hebrews says that "faith is the confidence that what we hope for will actually happen; it gives us assurance about things we cannot see" (Hebrews 11:1).

Here's the bottom line: just as the apostle Paul experienced, I may not know what awaits me around the next bend, but I have the faith to know that God is not only with me before I get to the bend, but also around that next bend. I also know that I must go because, like Paul says, it is part of finishing the work that God gave me to tell the world about the Good News and the wonderful love of God.

Are you willing to move ahead on something, even if all the ducks don't seem to be in a row? Or are you afraid to jump in? Life is full of uncertainty; God wants you to be bolstered by faith in Him.

UNCOMMON KEY > *Every time you turn to the left or right while driving today, thank God that faith in Him and His purposes for your life will get you around the next bend.*

February 19

Courage to Follow

> They brought the apostles before the high council, where the high priest confronted them. "Didn't we tell you never again to teach in this man's name?" he demanded. "Instead, you have filled all Jerusalem with your teaching about him, and you want to make us responsible for his death!" But Peter and the apostles replied, "We must obey God rather than any human authority." ACTS 5:27-29

Eventually, we'll all face it. Someone will ask us to do something we know is wrong in the sight of God or want us to take a shortcut that compromises our integrity or the integrity of what we are involved in. In either situation, if we agree, we'll dishonor God.

What would you do if you were faced with a decision to either honor God and His laws or submit to the unrighteous laws established by a human authority? This can manifest itself in a variety of ways—everything from official or unofficial persecution of Christians in China, Pakistan, or elsewhere around the globe, to instances that make us uncomfortable or that might threaten our occupation or calling.

I felt fortunate that I was in professional football and could speak about my faith in a way that other coaches at public colleges and high schools are not permitted to do. There's a rule of law that they must follow; if they break it, it could jeopardize their jobs and careers. And I appreciate that. After all, Romans 13 tells us to obey those in authority. And then, who knows what God may do? Either way, God may open other doors to share His story.

I find it interesting that in the situation described in Acts, Peter is one of the first to reply to the high priest—the same Peter who not too long before had denied he even knew Christ. So take heart—if we fail to put God's law first, we can find comfort in the rest of Peter's story. After denying Christ, Jesus reinstated Peter into his band of followers and ambassadors when He asked him this question three times: "Simon son of John, do you love Me more than these?" And three times Peter answered, nearly the same each time, "Yes, Lord, You know I love You." Christ responded each time by directing Peter to "feed My sheep."

There is one rule of law greater than all the rules that man creates—the rule of law of the God who created us. Where God's law and man's conflict, God's law always prevails. Followers of Christ simply must be discerning and obey His authority.

UNCOMMON KEY > *Obedience to God applies to all matters of authority. Have you played it safe because you didn't want to deal with the consequences? You have to answer to God first and foremost, not man.*

February 20

Basketball and Redemption

> The Lord isn't really being slow about his promise, as some people think. No, he is being patient for your sake. He does not want anyone to be destroyed, but wants everyone to repent. 2 PETER 3:9

I love the movie *Hoosiers*. The emphasis basketball coach Norman Dale places on fundamentals reminds me of my time with Chuck Noll when I was both a player and a young assistant coach with the Pittsburgh Steelers. And, of course, we all like stories of an underdog because we want the underdog to win. *Hoosiers* is one of the best underdog stories ever told.

There's certainly the classic moment when Coach Dale (played by Gene Hackman) takes his team from Hickory, Indiana, into the Butler University field house for the first time (Butler, of course, being a great underdog story in their own right!). They can't believe what they see. So Coach Dale has his players measure the height of the rim of the basket from the floor and the distance from the free throw line to the front rim of the basket, to demonstrate that the distances are the same in the big arena as they are on their court in the small gym back home.

The real beauty of the story, however, comes through the redemptive efforts of the coach toward Shooter, the town drunk and father of one of the players, who himself had been a star basketball player for the school. Coach Dale asks him to be his assistant. It always reminds me that God is still in the business of redemption. Isn't that something to cheer about?

In the movie, the drunk's son discloses to Coach Dale that he doesn't understand what the coach sees in his father. "I'm not seein' it. I mean, he's a drunk. He'll do somethin' stupid."

Coach Dale stops him. "When's the last time anyone gave your father a chance?"

The boy's response may be all too familiar. "He don't deserve a chance."

It's understandable, really. The boy has good reasons. He has been hurt too many times before by his dad's behavior and deceit. He's been embarrassed too many times. He wants him to change, but experience tells him that his dad will never change—there's no hope. Of course, the end of the movie proves him wrong.

God is in the business of redemption. He will stand there with open arms to receive us as many times as we turn to Him to repent and try again. A pretty amazing God.

UNCOMMON KEY > *Do you—or someone close to you—need another chance with God today? He's in the business of redemption and miracles. Ask Him to not give up. Maybe the ending will be nothing short of a miracle.*

February 21

Spotlighting the Best in Others

| As iron sharpens iron, so a friend sharpens a friend. **PROVERBS 27:17**

Several years ago, the Colorado Rockies baseball team re-signed a former player and asked for his input. This player had enjoyed a sixteen-year career with six different major league teams and in the process had been a teammate of hundreds of different players.

Before jumping into that year's free agency market, the Rockies organization was looking at potential players to sign to their roster. The insights from the former player they had just rehired could be invaluable to them in the process.

"The most indispensable player in this year's market will be Jamey Carroll. If we don't get anyone else, we need to get Jamey," he said.

To say that the others in the meeting were surprised is an understatement. Jamey was a 5-foot-9-inch, 170-pound middle infielder who had batted .251 with no home runs and three stolen bases the prior season.

But the wise consultant divulged Jamey's real talent: "He makes everyone around him better. He does the little baseball things, like hitting behind runners, bunting, and other personal sacrifices that won't show up in box scores, but in the process everyone around him rises to a higher level. He's the best teammate I've ever had."

We can all be like that—if we choose to be. We are around people every day whom we can either serve by helping to make them better or dismiss and focus on our own needs. We can help them by being a positive example and doing things for them that may go unnoticed, or we can drag them down.

We get to choose what type of teammate we want to be.

We also get to choose whether we want to be around people, such as Jamey, who lift us up or people who might drain us. If given the choice, wouldn't we want to be around the Jamey Carrolls of the world every day?

I would.

We all have the opportunity to have quite an influence on those around us on a daily basis, making others stand out and shine.

And a postscript to the story about Jamey Carroll. His own game improved with the Rockies, and in 2010, his current team—the Los Angeles Dodgers—awarded him the Roy Campanella Award for outstanding leadership.

UNCOMMON KEY > *Are you a good teammate, office mate, roommate? Be intentional in finding ways to bring out the best in those you are with on a regular basis.*

February 22

Energized by Failure

| I can do everything through Christ, who gives me strength. PHILIPPIANS 4:13

Thomas Edison made many attempts at inventing a working lightbulb with setback after setback. Yet he was confident he hadn't failed even once. He had simply found ten thousand ways not to make a lightbulb. That's a great perspective when you face adversity. In the effort toward any worthwhile goal, failure has to be considered part of the process. Failure in achieving a particular result isn't really failure if it's another step on the way toward the goal. It can be a vital part of the journey.

I wish I had learned more about failure when I was young—how to handle it and even appreciate it. I just didn't realize how often it would rear its ugly head. Twenty-eight years of coaching with one Super Bowl and twenty-seven years not so super. I saw successful people and didn't even consider the struggles that might have been part of their journey to get where they were. But I've since learned that failure—in sports and in every area of life—happens regularly. It's part of everyone's experience. And if we're afraid of it, we won't step out and try very much. We'll never accomplish our dreams if we're afraid of what might happen when we try.

Don't get discouraged when you fail. In fact, consider it a normal part of learning. I hope you fail less than I have, but you can count on failing sometimes. The most successful people I know are those who have handled failure the best. Though many people treat it as a dirty little secret and wear masks to cover it up, successful people have learned to be comfortable trying something that doesn't work out. Success isn't about never failing; it's about persevering through mistakes and adversity. If you persist, even your failures can turn into a valuable part of your success story.

UNCOMMON KEY > *Remember that failure isn't part of your identity; it's simply part of your journey. If you have failed at something recently, jot down some of the lessons you learned from it and use them to persevere toward your goals.*

February 23

Sharing Our Stories

> God is our merciful Father and the source of all comfort. He comforts us in all our troubles so that we can comfort others. When they are troubled, we will be able to give them the same comfort God has given us. 2 CORINTHIANS 1:3-4

God uses what we have been through to help us empathize with others—I have seen this in my life as well as in the lives of others. As a matter of fact, that is one of the reasons Lauren and I partnered with Nathan to write *Quiet Strength*.

However, when Nathan first approached me with the idea for a book that God had revealed to him while he was sitting in a church worship service, my response was far from enthusiastic.

"No!" I just couldn't picture myself walking into a bookstore and seeing a display of books with my name and face plastered on the front covers. I couldn't imagine that I would have anything to share that anyone would want to hear. And so we put the idea of a book about me aside.

And then my team, the Indianapolis Colts, won the Super Bowl. Suddenly, the pressure was enormous from everyone who wanted to write "my story." It had been three years since Nathan and I had first talked, so we revisited my reluctance, and I changed my mind. It was the right decision for many reasons—but the one that was the main impetus turned out to be the most gratifying.

Going into it, we felt that if one life would be blessed and made better because of something we shared, it would be worth the effort. I never imagined what God was going to orchestrate. We heard story after story of people who had been blessed, comforted, and whose lives had been made better because they read *Quiet Strength*. In many instances, people shared that they were challenged to make a difference in the world because of something we had written. I was humbled by many things through the process, including seeing the book become a *New York Times* bestseller. It was remarkable to see what God was able to do with my willingness to share.

What about your own story? It may never appear in print, but that doesn't mean it won't touch someone's life, the person God specifically wants to hear it. God has given you a unique story to share with at least one person—one that will bless his or her life.

UNCOMMON KEY > *Look for opportunities to share a word of comfort and grace with someone today—perhaps through a story of what God has done in your life.*

February 24

Compound Impact

> **Instead, God chose things the world considers foolish in order to shame those who think they are wise. And he chose things that are powerless to shame those who are powerful.**
> 1 CORINTHIANS 1:27

As I stood on the platform for the trophy presentation after we won the Super Bowl, I thought about the many people who had built into my life, who had given me an opportunity to speak about the Lord to millions of people watching. One of those lives that God had used more than three decades earlier to set the trajectory of my life on the arc He had planned was Leroy Rockquemore.

Mr. Rockquemore, the assistant principal at my junior high school, remained involved in my life years after I left the school. He once mediated a solution between my high school football coach and me after I had quit the team. No one asked him to get involved, but he cared enough about his students to take the time to get to know them. He was concerned for my well-being, and his concern shaped the rest of my life. Who knows what career I would have chosen if I hadn't followed his advice to hang on to my passion for football?

God has given everyone a platform. Some of those are broad and highly visible, but others are small—or at least they seem that way. A "small" platform is huge when it impacts even one other person who goes on to impact many. God is the author of our platform, and He gives us the privilege of using it to influence others. Sometimes we don't see the results of our investment in other people's lives for years to come, if at all. But everyone's platform is unique, and God has a plan for it.

You may not be a Heisman Trophy winner or a Super Bowl champion, but you have influence. A platform that may seem small to you can have lasting impact that you will only discover in eternity. That's why it's important to never sell your platform short. God is a master of doing big things with small beginnings. And He has put you where you are—and surrounded you with the people you know—for a reason.

UNCOMMON KEY > *You are in an exclusive position to have lasting influence on the people in your life. Use your platform. No matter how inconsequential it seems to you, it is greatly significant to God.*

February 25

Precious Commodity

> I tell you not to worry about everyday life—whether you have enough food and drink, or enough clothes to wear. . . . Look at the birds. They don't plant or harvest or store food in barns, for your heavenly Father feeds them. And aren't you far more valuable to him than they are? MATTHEW 6:25-26

A few years ago, we had a terrible three-month stretch of homicides in Indianapolis, the city's worst string of killings on record. Most of the suspects were young men, many of whom don't understand the value of life. Maybe they see human beings as cosmic accidents and life as a series of random events. Maybe they don't care about other people's lives because no one has ever really cared about theirs. Maybe they believe everyone is out for himself because that's what the people close to them have demonstrated. I don't know their individual stories. But I do know that when a young man feels no one really cares about him and his life has no value, it's easy for him not to care about anyone else. Then taking someone else's life doesn't seem like that big of a deal.

It bothers me that our society devalues life the way it does. It's devalued in our video games, music, movies, and TV shows. Unless kids have people in their lives who teach them that life should be respected, nurtured, and protected, they may not get that message because it too rarely comes through their entertainment. The world has gone too far in its casual approach to human life. And that approach opposes what God says.

Think about what Jesus taught about the value of human life. God knows each of our needs and desires before we can even tell Him about them. He cares about every aspect of our day-to-day living. He shares our excitement and our grief, He's with us in our ups and our downs, and He tells us we have no need to worry.

Whatever you've experienced in life—and whatever you're experiencing today—you need to know that God cares about you in every circumstance. He highly values you and considers your life precious. It only makes sense to agree with Him.

UNCOMMON KEY > *Life is more precious than you think, and God cares more deeply than you can ever know. When you really believe that, it changes everything. Dispel your self-doubt and believe.*

February 26

Humility Speaks Louder

> Those who exalt themselves will be humbled, and those who humble themselves will be exalted. **MATTHEW 23:12**

How often have we seen someone blowing his own horn—or trying to—only to have it blow up in his face?

It happens on a regular basis in the world of sports. There's the player who brags before the game about a sure victory because his performance alone will make it happen, and then he has one of his worst games ever. Or the player who is showboating in the middle of a play, high stepping it toward the end zone after badly beating the defensive coverage on a long pass play, and he drops the ball just before he crosses over the goal line into the end zone. No touchdown.

As former University of Texas football coach Darrell Royal said, "Act like you've been there before."

Even though my sport has been football, I respect how difficult the game of baseball is—especially deciding in about a quarter of a second whether to swing at a ball being hurled at ninety-five miles per hour toward your head. I can appreciate someone who just hit a home run running around the bases cheering himself with fist pumps. But you show more respect toward the pitcher if you implement Coach Royal's motto and express humility.

In Luke 18:9-14, Jesus describes an incident of showboating in the story of the praying Pharisee and tax collector. Both men were in the Temple. The Pharisee, a religious leader, thanked God that he wasn't a sinner like the other people around him. The tax collector, on the other hand, lamented his sins with regret to God. To the astonishment of his listeners, Jesus says it is the tax collector who is justified before God, not the Pharisee. Then He concludes by saying, "Those who exalt themselves will be humbled, and those who humble themselves will be exalted" (verse 14).

Have you caught yourself saying or doing something with an intentional "look at me" attitude? It can happen to anyone. And so can falling flat on your face and eating humble pie.

UNCOMMON KEY > *Is there something you want to pat yourself on the back for? It's okay to do it privately—even to share it with God. But striving to remain humble is the sign of a person seeking God.*

February 27

Choose Your Words Well

> We all make many mistakes. For if we could control our tongues, we would be perfect and could also control ourselves in every other way. JAMES 3:2

I don't know about you, but controlling my tongue is quite a task. Whether the words are said in haste or in anger or in an attempt to be funny, speaking without thinking seems to be a fairly common problem today. In fact, I think we live in the midst of an uncivil and thoughtless society.

Locker rooms seem to be particularly rife with verbal bashing, becoming breeding grounds for sarcasm and biting words. Players, coaches, or staff try to rationalize such remarks by telling themselves they wouldn't say those things out loud if they actually meant them. But more and more, people will say things and then later claim they were misunderstood or were simply joking. I think the real misunderstanding was *their* lack of understanding of how their words would be received.

I don't think locker rooms are any different than workplaces, classrooms, homes, or any other settings where we spend time with people. Careless words abound everywhere. The danger is that saying careless words is habit-forming—these unguarded moments become patterns for normal interaction with family, friends, teammates, coworkers, and others. And it's tough to break the habit, to flip the switch and say encouraging and uplifting words to the same people we've been mean to.

I used to be careless in my speech and quick to become angry when I was on the sidelines. Part of why I tried to become more stoic was to give myself a split second to think before my words came flying out unchecked. Trying to stay calm and quiet helped me keep my words deliberate and under control.

UNCOMMON KEY > *Watch your words. What might seem harmless or funny in one setting may be completely inappropriate in another, and probably isn't harmless or funny in the first place. Especially if what you say is not encouraging others.*

February 28

Responding to Stirrings of·the Heart

> Our lives are a Christ-like fragrance rising up to God. . . . And who is adequate for such a task as this? 2 CORINTHIANS 2:15-16

Warrick Dunn's mother, a Baton Rouge police officer and single mom, was shot and killed when he was eighteen, so Warrick took it upon himself to raise his siblings. All of them were younger; the last left the house years later, when Warrick was playing for the Tampa Bay Buccaneers.

Because of his experience, Warrick had a passion to ease the burden of single mothers. He came to Tampa Bay as one of our first-round draft picks in 1997, and since then he has helped single mothers purchase homes by providing the down payments for scores of houses in four cities. He has mobilized companies and other organizations to help furnish those homes. Using the gifts God has given him, he has helped many people who were struggling to get by, giving them a hand and providing opportunities they wouldn't have otherwise had. He has looked beyond himself to make a huge difference.

You probably have a passion for certain people in need too. Maybe you are sensitive to some needs more than others, but if you are like most people, your experiences have helped you notice the struggles other people face. Learn to see those passions or that awareness as God's prompting to help you look beyond yourself. You may not have the resources Warrick has, but you can certainly have the heart he has. And that is enough of a reason to act.

When you see a need that stirs your heart, act on it. It doesn't have to be a momentous action; it can be a small gesture that helps someone out. God has wired you to serve this way. Any step you take to meet someone's need is a step in the right direction.

UNCOMMON KEY > *Whether you start big or start small, act on your desire to help and see where it takes you.*

March 1

The Bright Side of the Road

> **A cheerful heart is good medicine, but a broken spirit saps a person's strength.**
> PROVERBS 17:22

In his marvelous book *The Soul of Baseball*, Joe Posnanski chronicles a series of road trips with Buck O'Neil, the venerable Negro League player and first African American coach in the major leagues. Buck took these trips when he was ninety-three. Joe was fascinated by Buck's youthful resilience and more important, his positive outlook on life.

Here was a man who, despite great ability, had been thwarted time and again, on the field and off, by what Buck referred to as "my beautiful tan." Relegated to playing in the Negro Leagues because of his skin color, Buck didn't let that and a lifetime of other slights prevent him from marveling at the small joys of life every day.

Posnanski opens with a story of a game in Houston that he and Buck attended. At the end of one inning, Houston's right fielder, Jason Lane, tossed a ball into the crowd, presumably intended for a young boy in the stands. Immediately, a man lunged in front of the boy, snatching the ball. The crowd booed, and Joe seethed.

Buck smiled and turned to Joe, telling him not to be too hard on the man. "He might have a kid of his own at home." Joe relaxed for a moment but wanted to stay irritated at the man. After a moment, he turned back to Buck. "Why didn't he bring the kid to the game?"

Buck smiled and said, "Maybe his child is sick." Try as he might, Joe knew he would never get Buck to say a negative word. Here was a man who refused to be a victim, to ever see life in any other way than as a gift, a marvelous occasion.

Take it from Buck. At every opportunity, be joyful and look at the bright side.

UNCOMMON KEY > *You only go around once in this life. You can spend it looking for the negative, or like Buck O'Neil, you can use God's gift of life as an opportunity for joy and grace.*

March 2

God in the Brackets

> The Lord will deliver me from every evil attack and will bring me safely into his heavenly Kingdom. All glory to God forever and ever! Amen. 2 TIMOTHY 4:18

Every spring, it happens—March Madness. The NCAA basketball tournament. A collection of extraordinary teams and games where the watchword is simply "survive and move on." Most years it seems as though the eventual winner had at least one game where they simply escaped with a win, allowing them to move on in the single-elimination tournament. The more you think about it, this basketball tournament is a lot like life, which I suspect is why people get so passionate about it. Sometimes, in basketball tournaments and in life, it's just about hanging on.

I don't know what you're facing today. I don't know how long you've been facing it. I don't know the disappointments or heartaches you are holding close in your heart. I don't know the failures or shortcomings you've experienced and can't seem to get past to move on with your life. I'll bet there are times you can't even see past the glare of problems blinding your eyes, when you don't feel like you deserve to see the light of a brand-new day. But I do know that for you—as well as for me—there is someone who cares and whom God will use to open up a hole for daylight to shine on all the turmoil you are facing. Somewhere there is someone God will use to help you hang on to what may seem to be the end of your rope.

So no matter what's going on in your life, wait just a moment longer. Look around and you'll see them—people who are there for you. Like a "Cinderella team" in the Final Four, it may be those you least expected. But they are sent by Someone who is always there for you: "I know the LORD is always with me. I will not be shaken, for he is right beside me" (Psalm 16:8).

Indeed, He is.

UNCOMMON KEY > *God will not leave you alone, no matter what you are going through. Believe it, hang on, and watch what He will do for you.*

March 3

Never Too Late

> The Lord said to her, "My dear Martha, you are worried and upset over all these details! There is only one thing worth being concerned about. Mary has discovered it, and it will not be taken away from her." LUKE 10:41-42

Nathan's uncle Gene is quite a character, always engaging his church, community, and family in fun and unexpected ways for as long as Nathan has known him. Gene's grand-children especially delight in whatever "Poppy" has in store for them, whether it's wood-working, home improvement projects, or playing board games on the floor. They never know what to expect.

His latest undertaking? Gene played the bugle when he was in the Marines, but he played by rote and never learned to read music, so his repertoire of songs has always been fairly limited. But, in the last year, he has started to take trumpet lessons so that he can learn to read music and expand his playlist.

Uncle Gene is eighty-six.

No matter—he's still engaged in what is important in his life.

And there he sits for over an hour each day, practicing his fingering on the three valves, working on his breathing, and learning to read music while his family watches in wonder.

Uncle Gene figures this is as good a time as any to work on expanding his musical repertoire. True, he's been battling cancer for a decade and has had a variety of other health ailments, but as he says, "If I don't start now, a year from now I'll be eighty-seven and still won't know how to read music."

Certainly we can all learn something from Gene—how thrilling it is to learn a new skill, to challenge ourselves, to make the most of our surroundings at any age. Will Gene learn to read music? I expect he will.

Is that the biggest point? I'm not sure that it is. It strikes me that Gene is doing something better than before. He is learning to do something important, like using and enhancing the gifts God has given him and in the process, leaving a legacy to his family and inspiring others to tackle new adventures. All they have to do is start.

UNCOMMON KEY > *What have you put off doing or learning? It's never too late to do something you should do or want to do—do it now.*

March 4

Spiritual Giants

> Physical training is good, but training for godliness is much better, promising benefits in this life and in the life to come. 1 TIMOTHY 4:8

Whenever I read this verse, I think back to our locker room. We had some absolute physical specimens, guys who looked like they came to life out of a college anatomy textbook. They spent hours and hours in the weight room exercising, building strength and flexibility to be able to do their jobs better. They didn't get to their position as some of the best athletes in the world by accident, but rather through exhausting physical training, strictly structured nutritional diets, and a generally careful approach to anything they put in their bodies.

If these guys had spent that kind of time and effort on their spiritual life, there would have been no spiritual body fat, and we would have had a locker room full of spiritual giants, not just physical ones. And think of what that would mean for our youth, who hold many sports figures up as role models. Not only would they aspire to properly condition their bodies to better play the games they choose to play, but it could help them develop their minds and hearts by encouraging them to grow in their faith—a discipline with eternal consequences.

The same is true with any follower of Christ. We need to become spiritual giants. It begins with a commitment to Bible reading, prayer, and joining a Christ-centered church as well as being accountable to at least one other trusted believer. We must also take care of the temples—our bodies—that God has given us. As more and more news comes to light concerning the harmful and illegal substances being used in professional sports to gain an edge to perform better, we need to make sure we and our children are kept safe. We should always watch what we put in our bodies—eating healthy food and drink and eliminating harmful or potentially harmful substances.

Do you need to increase your spiritual training? Set some goals and begin today.

UNCOMMON KEY > *Grow in the knowledge and wisdom of God through a regular, consistent training regimen. If possible, find a training partner with whom you can be accountable.*

March 5

Background Check

> King Darius sent this message to the people of every race and nation and language throughout the world: "Peace and prosperity to you! I decree that everyone throughout my kingdom should tremble with fear before the God of Daniel. For he is the living God, and he will endure forever. His kingdom will never be destroyed, and his rule will never end." DANIEL 6:25-26

When I was appointed to the President's Council on Service and Civic Participation, the FBI did a background check on me and the other appointees. We had to answer a lot of questions, but the last one really made me think: "Have you ever done anything that would be embarrassing for the president of the United States to be associated with?" It's an interesting thought—that my behavior throughout the course of my life could have an impact on someone else's reputation. It made me wish I had worked a little harder in the area of integrity.

Daniel served as an adviser to the Persian king Darius, and some of the other nobles were jealous of him. But they couldn't find anything to condemn or criticize in Daniel's behavior. He was known for being faithful and trustworthy. In other words, he had the kind of integrity that would be an asset to the reputation of people who chose to associate with him. And his integrity represented God well. Darius knew Daniel was a true servant of the true God.

What would your enemies find if they searched your life for something to criticize? What would the FBI find if they ran a background check on you? Is there anyone who would choose not to associate with you because it might harm his or her reputation? How does your integrity reflect on God and impact the people around you? None of us are perfect, but we can be authentic, grow in character, and live in a way that causes people to trust us and want to associate with us. Whether we have integrity or not may be a very personal decision—actually a constant stream of decisions—but it always affects others. Our minor choices when no one is watching can have major effects when people are watching. Our integrity makes an impact.

UNCOMMON KEY > *People who compromise their integrity because it's a "private matter" often end up having public troubles. Live with integrity to impact the world around you positively.*

March 6

Home, Peaceful Home

> "Don't sin by letting anger control you." Don't let the sun go down while you are still angry, for anger gives a foothold to the devil. EPHESIANS 4:26-27

Sometimes discretion is the better part of valor. I get that. There are times when my anger is such that it's better to simply walk away than to respond in a heated moment. Rash words at excitable moments can be deadly.

At the same time, however, especially in our marriages, it can get awfully tempting to simply brush things aside to "deal with them later." Especially if it's the same thing we've dealt with before. Who wants to go back over the same ground? It's discouraging. Better to sweep it under the rug. It'll go away, right?

Let me urge you not to do that. Don't let the sun go down on your anger. Find a moment to let the emotion pass, and even if it can't all be resolved then, try to find a way to take the edge off the moment. Find common ground. Agree to come back to it later. But don't stay angry and put it off until another time.

And don't simply write it off as the "same thing we've dealt with before," or that "he (or she) will never change." God gives us second chances, and while He's the God of transformation, sometimes these things don't happen without work on our part.

Believe it or not, conflict isn't always bad. It's a way of identifying the differences we have. Couples all have conflict in their lives—it's how we deal with the situations that make the difference. Will we be charitable and understanding? Or harsh and hardened? The choice is ours.

Some people say that if you get through the first year of marriage, it's smooth sailing from there. I think every day in marriage presents opportunities to practice patience, understanding, and compromise. Talk things out and don't force your opinion. Listen to each other instead of resorting to the silent treatment.

One final caveat: sometimes strict adherence to this isn't healthy either. Sometimes you or your spouse is too tired to rationally deal with something. I know I've made things worse sometimes by thinking that we'll "get it all straightened out" before bed. Sometimes a good night's sleep puts everything in perspective.

Be wise. Don't provoke, and don't brush things aside.

UNCOMMON KEY > *God wants you to live in harmony, to protect your marriage, to be salt and light for the world. Part of that begins with how you treat others and how you deal with conflict in your own home. Settle your disagreements as quickly as you can, by listening to each other and coming up with an amicable resolution.*

March 7

Tough Standard

> Love is patient and kind. Love is not jealous or boastful or proud or rude. It does not demand its own way. It is not irritable, and it keeps no record of being wronged. It does not rejoice about injustice but rejoices whenever the truth wins out. Love never gives up, never loses faith, is always hopeful, and endures through every circumstance. 1 CORINTHIANS 13:4-8

The multilayered facets of love. Are these as tough for you to put into practice as they are for me? I have a feeling that they are, or the apostle Paul wouldn't have challenged us with them. Everything he says about love is an action directed toward others and in particular, how a person is to treat other people. I suspect Paul had me in mind when he wrote these words.

And then if reading this now weren't striking enough, we probably hear this passage read in at least half the weddings we attend. Maybe God knows He needs to remind me—that eventually I will get it right. Don't get me wrong—this is a beautiful passage of Scripture. But for me to put it into practice and live up to what Paul is describing—well, that's a different story altogether.

Love is patient and doesn't demand its own way. Those two actions alone often disqualify me and would be difficult enough, since that requires me to put someone else's needs ahead of mine. I (or should I say we?) tend to filter most of life through the lens of what's in it for me (or us). Let's face it, we have many things we need and want that don't always allow time for patience. And "keep[ing] no record of being wronged" is just about impossible in any relationship—with friends, family members, coworkers—for any length of time. I know I'm guilty, so I'll ask you, how are you doing with not keeping a record of being wronged? How are doing on your list of people you need to forgive and not hold a grudge against, no matter what they may have done to you?

Of course, here's the good news. Through Christ all things are possible, and we can love others through the grace that He provides rather than following our own self-centered instincts.

What about your love in action? How does it measure up?

UNCOMMON KEY > *Breaking down the different traits of love into separate actions may be a way to make them become a habit. Work hard on ones that seem to describe you. And pray for God to help you discern the steps you need to take to live them out daily.*

March 8

Ready for What May Come

> **Wise people treasure knowledge, but the babbling of a fool invites disaster.**
> PROVERBS 10:14

I have always enjoyed watching college basketball, and listening to Bill Raftery broadcast games is a particular pleasure. His passion for coaches and players, as well as for the game itself, makes his commentary an enjoyable and entertaining play-by-play.

However, a recent article on Bill revealed a side of him that we don't see during the broadcasts: his meticulous preparation. Now that I am in the broadcasting world myself, I'm not surprised at that aspect of Bill, but it was still interesting to learn about the extensive background research that goes into his job.

He watches hours of video each week, poring over previous games played by each of the teams he is covering. He talks to coaches and players and others around the sport, looking for insights on what teams and players will be doing during the game and why, their strengths and weaknesses, and their injury status.

And over 90 percent of all the information Bill gathers doesn't get used.

That's part of preparation, being ready for whatever may happen. It is applicable to coaching and business, as well. Rehearsing your answers, your play calls, your negotiating stances, knowing that some might be used, but most won't. It's not wasted time if it helps you prepare, for now or for the future. And it also provides a level of comfort knowing that no matter what comes up, you are ready to deal with it.

Of course, it has to be part of a larger balancing act in your life. Some coaches I know go too far preparing for any and every contingency, spending valuable practice time fine-tuning plays they don't anticipate ever running. At the end of the day, however, it's important not to cut your preparation short. Know that what you are learning now is part of a foundation that will help you in the long run.

UNCOMMON KEY > *So much of what people devote their time to is "urgent"—those fires they put out on any given day. Spend time preparing now for life—your job, your family, what you'd like your* next *job to be. Your effort won't be wasted.*

March 9

Shades of Blue

| Share each other's burdens, and in this way obey the law of Christ. GALATIANS 6:2

In the spring of 2008, Eve Carson, student body president at the University of North Carolina, was murdered in Chapel Hill, North Carolina, just days before the North Carolina Tar Heels were scheduled to play a basketball game against archrival Duke. Located only eight miles apart, the University of North Carolina and Duke University are fierce competitors in athletics and academics, but especially in basketball. But even in a rivalry as fierce as this one, this was a time for compassion and caring.

Duke's basketball staff contacted North Carolina for permission to hold a joint moment of silence before the game. In the stands, Duke fans wore their customary royal blue, but also wore light blue ribbons on their shirts in tribute to Carson, who had been an enthusiastic Tar Heel. The players and coaches stood, not on the sidelines, but stretched across the foul lines, facing each other on opposite ends of the court. Their gesture said we stand together, united on the things that are really important, more important than a basketball game.

That's how we all should be: aware of and ready to share each other's burdens. As sad as that shooting was, it reminded a large crowd of basketball fans to focus on the important things in life. Tragedy tends to put life in perspective. It often causes us to reflect and even reprioritize our lives. There is a compulsion to reach out to others in need, doing what we can to share in whatever they are going through, maybe to alleviate some of the pain. We hug our spouses and children longer; we make phone calls to family and friends we haven't spoken to in a while. Things that were "important" now seem trivial, and things that had slipped to the bottom of the "important" stack are put on top.

Sports has its place. Sometimes it's more than revelry and rivalry. Sometimes it redirects us to the more important things.

UNCOMMON KEY > *Be aware of people who could use help with a burden they are carrying. Whether you are part of a united effort or implement something yourself, be a willing participant.*

March 10

Waiting for Miracles to Happen

> Be patient as you wait for the Lord's return. Consider the farmers who patiently wait for the rains in the fall and in the spring. They eagerly look for the valuable harvest to ripen. You, too, must be patient. Take courage, for the coming of the Lord is near. JAMES 5:7-8

In early 2001, rumors began swirling that the Buccaneers were considering replacing their current head coach if the team wasn't sufficiently successful in the upcoming season. People kept asking what I thought about those rumors, since I *was* the current head coach. My response was always that my job was to coach, and God's was to figure out the rest. Plus, a lot could happen in a year. . . .

The story is told of a man who was caught stealing in a far-off kingdom. As he was brought before the king, he was informed that the penalty for stealing is death. Despite the stress of the inevitable, the man seemed relatively calm. He knew that the king had a beloved, prized horse that was treated like a member of the family. And the thief planned on playing a hunch.

When the man was brought before the king to be judged and sent to his execution, the thief asked if he could say a few words. The king agreed.

"Your Majesty, I know you have a wonderful horse. If you will give me one year to work with him, I will teach your horse to talk. If I am successful, you will spare my life." The king thought over the man's offer for a moment and agreed.

On the way out of the king's chamber, one of the man's friends said, "Are you crazy? You can't teach the horse to talk! You'll be dead in a year." To which the temporarily reprieved man replied, "You may be right. But you know what? A lot can happen in a year. I may die of natural causes, the king may die, or . . . the horse may talk."

Sometimes life looks bleak, especially when we think we know what tomorrow will bring. The reality is that we don't know, either for better or for worse. Tomorrow is but a fog. Not panicking, but instead letting God work things out isn't a bad thing. We're aware of the situation, but our faith is in God, not in what we can do to work it out.

Don't count yourself out too early. Sometimes things work out in unexpected ways. Sometimes action is the best course in assisting God, but sometimes sitting back and letting God work is best.

Because sometimes, the miraculous happens.

The horse may talk.

UNCOMMON KEY > *Take care of today's business today, rather than being mired in what you think will happen tomorrow. The Lord is already working on that.*

March 11

Truth in Storytelling

> When the Spirit of truth comes, he will guide you into all truth. He will not speak on his own but will tell you what he has heard. He will tell you about the future. JOHN 16:13

Over the years, Nathan's family has enjoyed reading C. S. Lewis's stories together. The Christian apologist wrote many serious expositions on faith. But his fictional works tell about our individual journeys of faith and the nature of our relationships with God as well as his apologetics do. Lewis's Chronicles of Narnia series is a great teaching tool for children when they reach an age when some of the lessons of faith will begin to take hold. After all, truth is truth.

Sometimes we create artificial barriers to learning more about God's truth where there are none. We'll read nonfiction books because we want to learn, or we read fiction because we want to "escape the real world." In *The Voyage of the* Dawn Treader, Lewis describes the main character, Eustace, as a boy who was so unimaginative that he "almost deserved [his name]."[2] And then he runs up against a dragon. Like so many of us, Eustace was unprepared for the adventure, for the danger, for the challenges that encounter entailed:

> *Something was crawling. Worse still, something was coming out [of the cave]. Edmund or Lucy or you would have recognized it at once, but Eustace had read none of the right books. The thing that came out of the cave was something he had never even imagined.*[3]

God's truth is all around us, and stories can teach us more of it. Great movies can move us and inspire us. Great books can give us reason to keep pressing on, to show kindness to another person, to recognize the frailty of a coworker or family member.

God is present all around us, showing us His truth in art and literature and many other places, if we are open and sensitive to His presence and workings. Don't expect Him to be confined solely to a "serious" source.

UNCOMMON KEY > *God's truth is all around you—and He will use whatever way He chooses to try to reach you with it. Look for it, and keep a weekly list of the surprising ways you discover His truth. (And read—or watch—The Chronicles of Narnia.)*

March 12

A Simple Creed

> O Lord, who may abide in Your tent? Who may dwell on Your holy hill? He who walks with integrity, and works righteousness, and speaks truth in his heart. PSALM 15:1-2, NASB

Keeping your word and living with integrity.

Simple enough. A clear, admirable, and noteworthy mission statement for anyone's life. A commendable creed to live by, and one that you and your family will be respected for if you commit to it in all aspects of your lives.

But the trouble is that we typically live in a give-and-take, tug-of-war world that makes that creed very difficult and sometimes seemingly impossible to implement consistently.

Keeping your word and living with integrity.

Two elements that are essential to living with character and instilling trust in those around you.

No doubt when you read that creed, certain faces come to your mind. Faces of people who have been an intimate part of your life or associated with it enough to have had an impact on you—people whom you believe lived that creed throughout their lives. Faces of people who have spent years building into your life. People you could count on when they said something or promised you something. You always aspired to be like them, in more respects than just keeping your word and being a person of integrity.

But how were they able to maintain that creed in a world that often asks a person to compromise his or her word or integrity, a world that often pulls a person in the wrong direction? One thing my mom always stressed was the importance of staying close to the Lord. Whenever she felt tested or pulled to do something that might compromise her integrity, she asked for God's help; she knew it would be a struggle without His strength. She abided in Him when things got rough. It was a lesson I learned and have taught my own children because it is as relevant today as it was for me growing up.

Do people know they can count on you? Have you proven that you are trustworthy and that you approach life with integrity? Don't leave them guessing.

UNCOMMON KEY > *Keeping your word and living with integrity. Make that your creed, put it into action, and God will honor you.*

March 13

Real-Life Role Models

| A friend is always loyal, and a brother is born to help in time of need. PROVERBS 17:17

When I was growing up, my uncles and aunts were a big part of my life. We visited them often in Detroit. We watched movies together, played sports together, and they talked to me all about their jobs, the good aspects and the bad. They took time to interact with me and in the process influenced and enhanced my life. I can't thank them enough for what they did for me.

So I pass on this advice: think of your extended family often and the important role you have in their lives.

A study by The Barna Group illustrates how key that role may be. The survey asked teenagers to list their role models. The teens were specifically told not to include parents, since it's often an automatic response, whether it's true or from a feeling of obligation. A majority of participants named other family members as role models—uncles, aunts, brothers, sisters, and grandparents. In fact, family members outnumbered celebrities by a wide margin.[4]

Who would you put on your list of role models? And would you be on another family member's list? All of your siblings, nieces and nephews, and grandchildren are watching you. And listening, too, even if you are not aware of it. They may not take your words to heart yet, but if they're anything like I was, they are listening to how you approach life, work, and relationships and are filing it away for future reference. I learned so much from my family; their impact on my life was immeasurable.

As you go through today, think of a family member whom you might not have spoken with in a while. Pick up the phone or drop by to see them. Think of some way to connect and then make it happen.

UNCOMMON KEY > *You are a role model to your extended family members as well as those you may interact with on a daily or weekly basis. Make a conscious effort to be an active part of their lives as much as you can.*

March 14

Edging off the Path

> Don't do as the wicked do, and don't follow the path of evildoers. Don't even think about it; don't go that way. Turn away and keep moving. PROVERBS 4:14-15

Turn away and keep moving.

Sometimes we act as if it's the large things that trip us up—as if we merely need to avoid big pitfalls. But it's actually the small things that so often make us stumble. Joe Marciano, an assistant coach for me in Tampa, had a saying that always resonated with our team: "Death by inches." When a team is winning, coaches have a tendency to let little details slide by because things are going well. Then suddenly we're in a losing streak and can't figure out why. It's because those small, infrequent mistakes that didn't get corrected have become the norm, and the team can't get that sharpness back.

Death by inches.

It can happen in life as well. We know that the life God calls us to is straight ahead, that making a ninety-degree detour is clearly off track. But that's not how we get off track. We get off track when we take a five-degree turn off the straight path. Suddenly we're just a little bit sidetracked from where Christ wants us to go, not living as Christ wants us to live.

We know the rules to keep ourselves out of trouble. But it's the gray areas, the things that "aren't that big of a deal," that cause problems. First there's one compromise. Then something else. Before we know it, we're so far off course, we can't imagine how we got there. Of course, looking back, we can trace the path: one small step at a time.

How do we keep from getting off track? How do we fend off temptation that is lurking nearby, trying to pull us off the path God wants us to travel? Martin Luther warned that temptation was like hovering birds, and we should never let them begin to build a nest in our hair. Pastor Greg Laurie has fought temptation by envisioning Christ answering the door for him whenever temptation was knocking. That visual image helped him to turn away and to keep moving where God wanted him to go.

You need to do the same. Turn away and keep moving.

UNCOMMON KEY > *You know where God wants you to go. You know the life He wants you to live. Be aware and wary of the small things that can lead you off track.*

March 15

Get Your Eyes Checked

> Your eye is a lamp that provides light for your body. When your eye is good, your whole body is filled with light. MATTHEW 6:22

Vision.

We talked generally about it from day one as we gathered in the spring for meetings and workouts, and then more specifically and intentionally as we began minicamps and headed toward training camp in July.

Vision makes a critical difference in the outcome of games. Do we have a clear picture and understanding of where we are going? And even if it is clear, are distractions and misdirections muddying that clear vision of where we are going and what we are trying to achieve?

Think of the times you've seen a basketball team play better at home than on the road. Certainly, the support of the fans plays a big part, but so do the sight lines, particularly around the basket. When the opponents shoot, the fans waving frantically behind the Plexiglas backboard can be a huge distraction. A few years back, the NCAA Men's Final Four was held at the New Orleans Superdome, and some of the players never got used to seeing the giant video screens while they were shooting, clearly visible through the backboard.

Similarly in baseball, hitters can be affected and distracted by the background in center field behind the pitcher or with any shadows creeping across the infield as the sun sets on late-afternoon games.

What about our godly vision? How difficult is it for us to keep it clear and focused? Do we see the impact God intends for us to have, and are we following the vision He has placed before us?

Our vision is influenced by how we see the world. Do we see it through the lens of the hope and joy that our faith in Christ brings? Do we see it through the lens that knows we'll be in heaven for eternity, that our potential in God's hands is unlimited, and that the challenges of the moment are but a blink of an eye in eternity? Or do we see the world through a lens of fear and despair and see our potential as limited? I pray not.

What is your vision? Can you see the clear path God has set before you? Can you see past the distractions to where God is directing you? May your answers be yes, but make sure you have regular checkups.

UNCOMMON KEY > *Write down what you believe God's vision for you is. Then write down the distractions you already know or that you anticipate hindering your achievement of the goal. Work to shorten the list of distractions and expand the vision.*

March 16

Providing What You Need

> The LORD told Gideon, "With these 300 men I will rescue you and give you victory over the Midianites. Send all the others home." JUDGES 7:7

We've all been there before at one time or another. We're facing a deadline, feeling incredibly shorthanded in time, ability, supplies, or resources to get the job done. Perhaps we remember all too vividly some days in high school or college when we faced a fast-approaching final exam and were certain we hadn't studied the right material. Or we're frustrated that we've been so easily distracted by a host of other things that made us less disciplined than we need to be to assure success in our endeavors. We feel like our only chance is with an army's power behind us.

That's what Gideon was thinking as he prepared to march on the Midianite camp. This reluctant warrior surmised the only possible way to defeat the enemy was with numbers—thirty-two thousand men strong. But God instructed the leader to begin paring down the army; first, asking them to own up to their bravery and then through a unique test beside a stream. When three hundred men were left, God gave the green light to Gideon who, with his troops, emerged victorious.

Could Gideon have won with the huge army? Certainly. But God wasn't testing Gideon on his military strategy. He was giving Gideon a humility check. Rather than relying on a mighty force of men and boasting afterward, God wanted Gideon to rely on Him and be humble.

What mountain are you facing right now that you are sure you can't scale? What problems are mounting that you know you can't solve by yourself? Before you throw your hands in the air and heave a sigh of resignation, stop for a moment and remember something about the God who created you.

Remember this: He is there—right by your side. If He was able to secure a victory for Gideon over the Midianites with only three hundred men, He can help you with the insurmountable things you face. Humbly seize that assurance. The peace that brings will help you with the deadline, the test, or whatever seems formidable.

UNCOMMON KEY > *Whatever you are facing today, allow time to get ready, prepare as sufficiently as you are able, and do as well as you can—all to glorify Him. Humbly rely on His strength to help you finish victoriously.*

March 17

Changing Demands into Desires

> That is why I am boldly asking a favor of you. I could demand it in the name of Christ because it is the right thing for you to do. But because of our love, I prefer simply to ask you. PHILEMON 1:8-9

Asking someone to do something, rather than demanding they do it or else, is a good lesson and starting point for anyone who wants to be an effective leader.

I knew I could tell my players what to do and they'd do it. But what if I wasn't around to tell them? What would they do then? It was better to have them do things instinctively.

We see great examples of this kind of leadership in some of our great coaches—none better than Billy Donovan, the head basketball coach for the University of Florida. Coach Donovan emphasizes fundamentals and techniques—shooting, rebounding, picks, ball movement, defense, pressing, transition game, free throws, out-of-bounds plays. He works with players over and over on handling every possible game situation they could encounter. In practice players learn to recognize defensive and offensive patterns and make appropriate adjustments. Everything is designed to help them develop their basketball abilities.

But Coach Donovan takes what he teaches them about playing the game at the highest level and prepares them for other settings. He does this by continually casting the vision of where he wants them to be. He gives his players space to find their way, to succeed and to fail. He directs them less and inspires, challenges, and encourages them more. Coach recognizes that he can make them do what he wants them to do, but the mark of a true leader is that he can get his players to want to do it on their own with energy and passion.

Usually that autonomy works out—the overall results for Coach Donovan's teams have been more than satisfactory, including back-to-back national championships in 2006 and 2007. Sometimes, however, that autonomy brings criticism if the results don't work out. He accepts the trade-off and can take pride in his teams' achievements because he believes an even greater accomplishment is his part in building into his players' lives.

UNCOMMON KEY > *Review any recent "demands" you made to someone. You may owe that person an apology or a thank-you. Great leaders persuade rather than make demands to those they lead—and often achieve extraordinary results.*

March 18

I'm a Believer

> A man with leprosy came and knelt in front of Jesus, begging to be healed. "If you are willing, you can heal me and make me clean," he said. Moved with compassion, Jesus reached out and touched him. "I am willing," he said. "Be healed!" MARK 1:40-41

The leper got right to the point. "If you are willing, you can heal me and make me clean."

The leper had it. He had no reason to, based upon how he was treated in those days. But the leper had it.

Jairus had it as he left the side of his sick daughter to find Jesus in the crowds far from his home. While he was gone, his daughter died. But Jairus still had it.

Mary and Martha—as different as two sisters can be—both had it as they wept over their brother, Lazarus, lying stone-cold dead in the tomb not far from their home in Bethany. And even though they felt Jesus was slow to come to their aid, they had it.

Had what? Belief. They all believed. They all believed that Jesus was who He said He was. They all believed that He was the Christ, the promised Messiah, and the Son of God. They all believed that He could do what He said He could do—and they believed that He cared for them and others. They heard what He was saying and about the miracles He was doing, and they believed.

If you're like me, this next point is important. Don't confuse understanding with believing. None of them understood—most things about Jesus were far beyond their limited minds and capabilities to understand. Count me in that group. But I don't feel bad. There are biblical scholars who have spent their lives studying the Scriptures who can't understand all that Jesus did and continues to do for us as the Son of God.

But believe? That's something we all can do. Believe that Christ can heal that loved one who is sick. Believe He can provide that job that seems impossible to find. Believe He can change people's hearts. It's not necessary to understand how He is going to do all those things, but believe that He *can*! There is so much evidence of His life, His death, and His resurrection, it's hard not to.

UNCOMMON KEY > *Simply put: Jesus said it. Jesus did it. Believe it! What do you need to believe that Jesus will do in your life today? Talk to Him about it.*

March 19

Stand Your Ground

| Be on guard. Stand firm in the faith. Be courageous. Be strong.   1 CORINTHIANS 16:13

When it comes to sports, I'm not sure there's anything more unnatural than taking a charge in basketball. It's been years since I played basketball competitively, but I still vividly remember the drills during my freshman year at the University of Minnesota as the coach tried to prepare us to take a charge.

For those who don't know what it means to take a charge, it's simple: If an offensive player runs over a defender who has established his position on the court, a foul is called on the offensive player. A defender establishes his position by having his feet set and not moving prior to impact.

In other words, you have to stand still and allow yourself to get run over by another player who is running full speed at you.

That's not normal. Flinching is normal. Moving aside is normal. Covering up is normal.

I think that's why the crowd cheers so excitedly when someone takes a charge, because they recognize how courageous it is to stand still . . . and firm.

God calls us to stand firm in His Word and in the life He wants us to live. No flinching. No moving aside. No finding a path that's safer.

That's easier said than done, because life will run us over at times. When other people aren't living by the same rules we are, we might be unpopular, scoffed at, or not taken seriously. And oftentimes it hurts. The same is true for our children as they try to stand firm in a world that wants them to conform.

Be there for your family and friends as they establish their positions. Help to soften the blow when others run them over with criticism or peer pressure. Draw upon God's strength—He promises a never-ending supply.

UNCOMMON KEY > *Stand firm today as life comes flying at you, asking you to conform. Stand your ground. Stand with God and in His Word.*

March 20

Muscular Faith

> Faith is the confidence that what we hope for will actually happen; it gives us assurance about things we cannot see. HEBREWS 11:1

"Keep me safe while I'm asleep, okay?" my daughter Jade whispered. She hugged my neck and pulled me close as I bent down to give her a kiss and tuck her in.

"Of course I will, sweetheart," I told her. And I meant it. I will always do everything in my power to keep my children completely safe. Any good parent would. But the truth is that we don't have control over things that happen in this world. We have to live with a certain amount of trust in God and faith that He is watching over us.

That's not as easy as it seems. We like to think we're in control, even when we know deep down that we aren't. We often try to manipulate the outcomes of our circumstances. We try to manage every variable of every situation. We find ways literally and figuratively to insure our possessions and lifestyles against loss. We seek as much control as we can get.

But we know there are dangers and risks in this world and that God is ultimately in control over all of them. So we give up our sense of control and choose to live by faith—not counting on our own plan but on His. We have no choice but to live by faith—we do it all the time. We believe gravity will bring us down every time we jump, or that the plane will fly from point A to point B, or that the traffic light will be a red signal to cross traffic when it lights up green for us. But God is even more worthy of our trust than these things. If we can put our faith in people and machines and natural laws we can't see, we can certainly put our faith in Him.

Choose to trust God with every detail of your life and that of your family. You can't insure against every kind of danger, but you can place your faith in the God who guides you through every situation in life, even the hard ones. Know that when God says He is watching over you, He isn't just expressing His best intentions as a finite parent. He is the infinite Father who really does have control over every variable. And He wants you to live with the assurance that He is taking care of you all the time.

UNCOMMON KEY > *Add muscle to your faith through prayer and Bible reading. Faith is the key that empowers you to live confidently and securely—even while you are sleeping.*

March 21

Tapestry of Color

> I will also bless the foreigners who commit themselves to the LORD, who serve him and love his name, who worship him . . . and who hold fast to my covenant. I will bring them to my holy mountain of Jerusalem and will fill them with joy in my house of prayer . . . because my Temple will be called a house of prayer for all nations. ISAIAH 56:6-7

Sports have long been one of the leading agents for social change. While some coaches were slow to embrace the change that was coming to the nation in the area of race, other coaches were leading the charge. Eventually, once the recalcitrant coaches realized they could be more successful if they didn't artificially limit their talent pool by race, even they joined in. Sometimes a myopic focus on winning can do some good.

If you've never been to a college conference tournament, it can be a fun experience. Fans show up from the various schools, dressed in their school colors, singing their fight songs. And because the format is usually a nonstop succession of games with different teams participating, quite often fans' allegiances are formed and reformed. You might find a Wake Forest fan in their black and gold cheering alongside Clemson fans in their orange and purple, and then see them switch sides when the two schools finally face off. Or even Oregon Duck fans cheering for Oregon State . . . well, maybe not.

I think that's probably what the Kingdom of God is supposed to look like. We all look different and have different passions and things that excite us. We live in different areas with different customs and languages, but as Christians, we all should stand together, singing praises and cheering for God.

Too often that's not the case in our congregations. In fact, in many ways we may be *less* diverse than the rest of society. We need to make an intentional effort to change.

In making that effort to change, we show the world our true allegiance to Jesus and demonstrate that the superficial differences among us don't carry the day—Jesus does.

But maybe we don't have to cheer for Oregon State.

Who are you cheering next to in the arena of faith?

UNCOMMON KEY > *Think of an intentional step you can take to help the church live up to being a "house of prayer for all nations."*

March 22

Reaching Deep Within

> Whatever is true, whatever is noble, whatever is right, whatever is pure, whatever is lovely, whatever is admirable—if anything is excellent or praiseworthy—think about such things. Whatever you have learned or received or heard from me, or seen in me—put it into practice. And the God of peace will be with you. PHILIPPIANS 4:8-9, NIV

"What's down in the well will come up in the bucket," says my friend Ken Whitten. That fits with what Jesus taught about our mouths speaking whatever overflows from our hearts (Luke 6:45) and what James, when writing about the power of our words, said about fresh water and salt water not flowing from the same spring (James 3:11-12). The things that come out of our mouths or that flow into our actions come from whatever is inside of us. The potential in our lives comes from the things that are hidden in our hearts.

Hebrews 11 describes the faith of numerous people in the Bible—how their strength came from God, how they set out in obedience to Him without being able to see the end of the journey, and how they focused on Him, His purposes, and His faithfulness. They lived by His Word, envisioned His Kingdom, and followed His ways. They believed in a future painted by the hand of the one who had proven Himself to them time after time. That's what they thought about and established in their hearts. That was the well they were drawing from.

It's important not to just deal with what "comes up in the bucket" in your life—the way you live. You can try to change your behavior and discipline yourself to change, and you can do it with some success. But real change happens deep down inside—from the well. Your life will be governed by the truths that guide you and the relationship with God that fills your heart. If that's not in your well, the actions will just be actions. That's like putting a fresh coat of paint on a house with major foundation problems. Real life is lived from the inside out.

What's in your well? What is the source of your strength and direction? Where do you find your values? Look to the God who created you and planned a future for you. Your faith will influence everything about you. Your relationship with God will govern your thoughts, and your thoughts will move you where you need to go. Fill your well with Him.

UNCOMMON KEY > *Keep a bottle of water with you today to remind you to fill your well with God Himself. When you do, what flows out of your heart will be good, true, and satisfying.*

March 23

Entertaining Angels

> Keep on loving each other as brothers and sisters. Don't forget to show hospitality to strangers, for some who have done this have entertained angels without realizing it!
> HEBREWS 13:1-2

Hospitality is something anyone can offer to someone else. I know people can fill out spiritual gifts inventories to assess their spiritual gifts, matching them with specific ministries that seem to fit them best. Although the concept is worthwhile in identifying people's gifts, I wouldn't want to be labeled as only having this or that particular gift, especially when my life is always changing. And an inventory list may give me the excuse not to do something because I am not "gifted" in that area—like evangelism, for instance. That kind of thinking overlooks that Christ calls us to live our lives as He did, and even though we may not be as gifted in one area as another, we all have a duty to try to live in all areas as Christ did.

Hospitality included.

Nathan had a longtime friend who embodied this sense of hospitality every day of his life. He met Hal Ingman Sr. and his wife, Ann, at the University of Florida in Gainesville.

Hal was an engineering professor there for years. Their home was a landing place for anyone who needed it, including their children's friends; a gathering place for the college-aged Sunday school classes long after their own children were gone; and a haven for several adult friends with intellectual disabilities who would spend hours there each week. In addition, Hal and Ann filled their home with foster children, giving them a place to live, alongside their own four children, where someone cared about and loved them. Hal died from a heart attack while he was helping his granddaughter's classmate jump-start the dead battery in her car, another manifestation of meeting the needs of others.

Hal never saw a need that he could turn away from, hoping someone else would take care of it. And he never lost his childlike sense of wonder in all of God's creation and people around him. This no doubt gave him the perspective that meeting people's needs were wonderful opportunities to serve God.

Hal's response touched and changed lives. And his example is worthy to follow.

UNCOMMON KEY > *Practice hospitality by opening your home and your life to others. Be aware that you may be entertaining angels, unaware.*

March 24

You Are a Person of Influence

> But Moses pleaded with the LORD, "O Lord, I'm not very good with words. I never have been, and I'm not now, even though you have spoken to me. I get tongue-tied, and my words get tangled." Then the LORD [said], . . . "Go! I will be with you as you speak, and I will instruct you in what to say." But Moses again pleaded, "Lord, please! Send anyone else."
>
> EXODUS 4:10-13

Too often we tend to think of our platform as something that is tied to our position or occupation. We influence the people who work for us or who have a direct relationship with us. Certainly we don't have a platform to influence others outside our areas of authority, we think.

Nothing could be further from the truth.

When Dean Smith retired after thirty-six years as the head coach of the University of North Carolina, a number of sportswriters dusted off stories from his days as a young coach in the 1960s. Most people had forgotten or had never known the side of Dean revealed in the events that happened thirty years prior.

It was a tumultuous time in our nation, and Smith put himself in the middle of it, repeatedly. As stories go, he would invite an African American member of the community to lunch. They would head to the most segregated place in town, whether it was in Chapel Hill, Durham, Greensboro, or other places in North Carolina or other Southern states.

People would stare and become angry at his audacity to do that in public. Smith didn't care and would blithely eat his meal, knowing they weren't about to throw him out, as much as they might want to.

"He was a basketball coach," some critics might say. "What he did, well, that was outside his coaching platform. He overstepped his bounds."

Wrong. We all should be expanding our platforms, looking for ways we can influence others and situations for good. This doesn't have to involve civil disobedience. We can volunteer to tutor, carpool to soccer practice, or start a book discussion group. Have a cheery disposition for everyone we come in contact with. The list of options to make a difference is endless.

UNCOMMON KEY > *Everyone has a platform, in different settings, with small groups or large. What is yours? Use it to make a difference in the world around you. Don't wait for God to send someone else.*

March 25

Amazing Grace

This is a trustworthy saying, and everyone should accept it: "Christ Jesus came into the world to save sinners"—and I am the worst of them all.   1 TIMOTHY 1:15

There are two aspects to this verse. First, remembering Christ's mission in coming to earth—"Christ Jesus came into the world to save sinners." It's like a basketball player late in a close game who is called for a foul that could have gone either way. The hostile crowd roars at him, and he's got a choice—remember the mission of winning the game, gather himself, and move on, or get caught up in the emotion of being "wronged" and lose his focus, and perhaps even get called for a technical foul that will probably cost his team their ultimate goal of winning. Throughout His life among us on earth, Christ never lost sight of why He came.

The second aspect is realizing our shortcomings. If the apostle Paul thinks he is the worst sinner of all—"I am the worst of them all"—then where do I fit in that measurement? Rather than taking it literally, however, Paul is recognizing how far he has to go to match the level of Christ. Here Paul reminds us that our measuring stick is not compared to others, but to Christ. That we might be able to say, "Well, I know I'm better than that guy" or "I'm certainly not as bad as her" may make us feel better, but it is not the standard against which Christ is measuring our walks as His disciples. According to that standard—Christ Jesus—we all fall short.

In the movie *Amazing Grace*, chronicling the life of British statesman and antislavery spokesman William Wilberforce, there is a scene where Wilberforce meets former slave ship captain turned clergyman John Newton, who makes the powerful statement, "Although my memory is fading, I remember two things very clearly: I am a great sinner, and Christ is a great Savior."

Both of those self-professed thoughts became part of Newton's greatest hymn, "Amazing Grace."

Can you say the same for yourself? Do Newton's words ring true for you?

UNCOMMON KEY > *Sing or read the words to John Newton's most famous hymn, "Amazing Grace." And thank God that He gave that gift of grace to you!*

March 26

Trash Talk

> If you claim to be religious but don't control your tongue, you are fooling yourself, and your religion is worthless. JAMES 1:26

Trash talk has been accepted in sports culture as "part of the game," but there's no such thing as trash talk in God's view. You are responsible for everything you say, and what you say goes a long way in defining who you are. A certain coach disagrees with me on this and says, "You judge me unfairly when you make a determination about me as a person by my words." We'll just have to agree to disagree, I guess.

For the rest of us, this verse should hit home. Any stray word or comment can undermine our witness for Christ to people who hear what we say firsthand or who hear it at a later time. It is especially true in this age of electronic communication with the ability anyone has to record the audio or video of a moment and instantly send it around the world using a number of social networking media. Even if they don't right away, it's often saved for perpetuity.

Too often we casually think in terms of "walking the talk," which is important. But even more important, we should be modeling through what we say. We have to be careful about speaking rashly, about using words that aren't clearly thought out. But the bigger issue is why we are saying those words at all. Could it be that it is coming from what is within and that we have just been doing a good job of hiding that from the world? Why is it coming out now?

Speak with measured words. That admonition is not necessarily embraced in the middle of a football field on game day. We fans, players, and media defend "trash talk" as part of the game, helping get everyone "psyched up" to play. The reality is that it points out to everyone else what is inside us. And anyone who looks to those players who are "trash talkers" as role models is being led down a wrong path.

Your witness is demonstrated in many ways, by what you do for others and in the way you live your life, but it is also by the words that come out of your mouth. Make those words a witness worthy of the one whose story you are telling.

UNCOMMON KEY > *Plain and simple—what people hear you say will tell them, accurately or not, a lot about who you are. Make sure there is no question in their minds.*

March 27

Full Identity

> Because God's children are human beings—made of flesh and blood—the Son also became flesh and blood. For only as a human being could he die, and only by dying could he break the power of the devil, who had the power of death. . . . Since he himself has gone through suffering and testing, he is able to help us when we are being tested. HEBREWS 2:14, 18

It must have been a tough assignment to go from being the Son of God on His Father's right hand to being a regular guy on earth. Being next to the Father had to be a much more comfortable setting than Jesus experienced here. Having to deal with those who heard Him and still didn't believe and regularly squaring off with the Pharisees and Sadducees had to have been hard.

But think how much more helpful Jesus' human experiences were for us. I've seen that to be certainly true in the football world with players. When my teams had former players come in and talk about some of the challenges players would face when they were done playing, it resonated more than if I or another coach were telling them. The fact that those guys had walked in their shoes really carried weight.

Jesus had to endure so much more than simply becoming human and walking in our shoes. Beatings, scourging, a crown of thorns, spittle, cursing, and then being hanged on a cross. Three days later He would rise out of a damp, dirty, and stone-cold tomb.

The truth is that if someone other than Christ had come and done all of that and more, it wouldn't have had the same impact. We would have been eternally lost if He had not done all of that. The argument that says "if He had just done this or if they had just done that, Christ would not have had to die for us" doesn't hold water.

Wrong theology.

God's plan was to save His people. Following the law of Moses couldn't do it; the practice of animal sacrifices in the Old Testament had to be done on a regular basis because they didn't provide *eternal* pardon from humanity's sin. The only way God could eternally pardon us was through His Son—Jesus Christ.

Jesus became a flesh-and-blood man, a human being with similar desires and passions to us, except for one difference: He was without sin. In His humanity He identified with us, but more than that, we identified with Him. And that drew us closer to Him—a blessed place to be.

UNCOMMON KEY > *God can have a relationship with you because of what His Son, Jesus Christ, was willing to do. Jesus became a human being who suffered and died for your sin. Thank Him today for what He endured to make that happen.*

March 28

Staying True

| Cling to what is good. ROMANS 12:9, NIV

When I was traded from the Pittsburgh Steelers to the San Francisco 49ers in my third year of professional football, I wasn't just changing teams; I was changing cultures. I left a relatively small, blue-collar city to go to a relatively large cosmopolitan area, and in the late 1970s, that new city offered more temptations than I had ever experienced. I felt out of place.

Although I wanted to be accepted in San Francisco, I never really considered adopting any bad habits or using drugs. My beliefs and upbringing, as well as my athletic training, dictated against it. But I felt like an outsider because of that, and I wondered if people were watching me.

I later discovered that some guys *were* watching me, but not because they thought I was strange. One of my teammates had gotten into the drug culture in San Francisco because he thought that was what pro athletes did. But because I had come from a Super Bowl team and didn't do drugs, it made him feel that he didn't have to either. He later told me my example may have saved his life.

The familiar line from *Hamlet* is an important reminder: "To thine own self be true." Not only will that advice protect us against negative peer pressure, it will also put us in position to affect others through positive peer pressure. We sometimes forget that peer pressure works both ways—that we not only are affected by others, but others are also affected by us. Many people will exert pressure on us to conform, whether they realize that's what they are doing or not. But we are also in a position to influence them. We can help others make better decisions simply by making decisions that are true to our own convictions.

To do that, you have to know who you are. You need to have a strong sense of your identity and your purpose. When you do, you become an influence on others for good.

UNCOMMON KEY > *Peer pressure works in both directions. If you approach things positively, you can grow into a position of influence simply by remaining true to who you are.*

March 29

Lantern on the Stern

> Be strong and courageous, for you are the one who will lead these people to possess all the land I swore to their ancestors I would give them. Be strong and very courageous. Be careful to obey all the instructions Moses gave you. . . . This is my command—be strong and courageous! Do not be afraid or discouraged. For the LORD your God is with you wherever you go. JOSHUA 1:6-7, 9

Samuel Taylor Coleridge, the English poet, is usually a little deep for me. I hate to admit that; I can almost hear my English-teacher mother sigh as I do. But I at least understand this quote: "The light which experience gives is a lantern on the stern, which shines only on the waves behind us." That truth hits home for me.

That's why football coaches like me review the film after each game or practice. Most of our focus every week is on our upcoming opponent, but on Mondays we examine the previous game. It isn't that we want to focus on what players did wrong, although it may feel that way to them sometimes. No, we look at what they have done so we can correct the mistakes and play better next time. The review is a teaching tool. We study our experiences so we know not to repeat certain parts of them.

I suspect that the courage and insights which Joshua gained standing alongside Moses proved invaluable to him as he was tapped by God to succeed Moses in leading the Israelites. He had seen the experiences of Israel in the wilderness. I'm sure he benefited from the reservoir of research and experience not only for the knowledge he would need, but also for the confidence and courage he would have to muster as he focused his attention on the task before him.

The same is true in our lives too. Our experiences give us a reference point from which we can learn and grow. They may feel to us like yokes we can't escape from, dragging us down with regret and guilt. But they are really opportunities for growth. As with Joshua, they are an invaluable resource from which to draw confidence and courage for the task ahead.

UNCOMMON KEY > *Don't dwell on the past, but don't be afraid to examine it either. Looking back is often the best way to shine a light on the path ahead.*

March 30

Like No One Else's

> Those who trust their own insight are foolish, but anyone who walks in wisdom is safe.
> PROVERBS 28:26

My brother Linden was a pretty good athlete. Unfortunately for him, he was cursed with an older brother—me—who received a great deal of athletic accolades, making difficult comparisons for him. He didn't particularly love any sport but enjoyed several. He was an adequate student, but there was nothing about school that excited or motivated him. His specialty was carving out a role as the class jokester.

Making his classmates laugh was a greater accomplishment to Linden than anything he did in the classroom or the sports arena, much to my parents' chagrin. Both teachers, they searched high and low for the key to unlocking his potential, especially academically. Finally he discovered what ignited his passion—dentistry.

A whole new world opened up for Linden when he discovered what God had placed on his heart. After being an average student in high school, he blossomed into an outstanding student at Grand Valley State University and then in dental school at the University of Minnesota. His abilities took off once he had a dream to pursue. He had finally connected with the passion that God had placed within his heart.

Today Linden owns his own dental practice, and I'm extremely proud of him. He uses his God-given talents to help a variety of clients, including those not able to pay. His potential was not in following in my footsteps, fulfilling his teachers' expectations, or in any well-worn path in our family. It was in following the passion God had given him and pursuing the joy God had put in front of him. He continues to fulfill his purpose simply by being himself.

That's how it should be for all of us. We need a dream to follow, a passion to pursue, and a calling to recognize. We don't fulfill our purposes by following others' paths. We fulfill them simply by being ourselves. When we discover who we really are and what we are designed to do, it opens up a whole new world.

UNCOMMON KEY > *Find out what God has put in your heart and follow it. The passions He has placed there not only fulfill your needs but also His purposes.*

March 31

Intimate Instructions

> From the heart come evil thoughts, murder, adultery, all sexual immorality, theft, lying, and slander. MATTHEW 15:19

We can't talk about integrity, character, and values to the extent we have without also applying those attributes to our sexual lives as well. After all, the subject of sex occupies quite a bit of time in our thoughts. It's a vital part of how we were made; God created it and intended it for our pleasure and for procreation.

When we understand His purposes in creating us as sexual beings and respect the boundaries He put around our sexual behavior, it ultimately glorifies Him. And when our sexuality is misused and abused, it can cause heartache, conflict, and destruction on a surprising scale, affecting not only ourselves but even future generations. This deeply personal aspect of our humanity has powerful effects.

Many husbands and wives are afraid to talk about this with each other, and are even more reluctant to talk about it with their children. That's understandable; it can be awkward. But the alternative is to settle for misunderstandings and let our children learn through the media and from friends—with all the vulgarities and innuendo that come through those channels. As awkward as it is, we need to be more up-front about sex and its effect on our lives.

God certainly isn't afraid to talk about it. I believe what the Bible says about both the blessings of sex and the boundaries God gave us for it. I believe that any sex outside of marriage, whether during or before, is wrong. Most people would agree that infidelity while you're married is wrong, but not a lot of people think that sex before marriage is wrong. Regardless of what you think of biblical perspectives on sex outside of marriage, I'm sure you can agree that it's an important issue and can be a source of a lot of conflict and pain.

Our sexual purity is important to God. What He designed as a picture of unity, intimacy, and love is easily turned into a selfish act with little or no commitment involved. He wants sex to be as satisfying as possible. And the only way for it to be satisfying is for us to follow His instructions for it.

UNCOMMON KEY > *Integrity and character should extend to every area of our lives—including our sexuality. God designed us for both passion and purity.*

April 1

A Refuge Anywhere, Anytime

| **God is our refuge and strength, always ready to help in times of trouble.** PSALM 46:1

Is it just me, or have you noticed there are a lot of verses in the Bible that mention God comforting us, giving us peace, or helping us?

Sometimes life seems to buffet us. It's almost like God knew those days would come, and so to help us deal with them, He inspired the psalmist to pen the words of Psalm 46.

He knew there would be days when employees abandon us. When family members let us down. When friends are nowhere to be found. He knew there would be days when we were within a whisper of a breeze of losing all hope, where the clouds had set in and the sunshine no longer seemed to shine on our lives.

And the psalmist dares to proclaim, "God is our refuge and strength, always ready to help in times of trouble. So we will not fear when earthquakes come and the mountains crumble into the sea. Let the oceans roar and foam. Let the mountains tremble as the waters surge!" (verses 1–3).

The world has certainly seen its share of surging waters, roaring oceans, and crumbling mountains lately. Whether we have been in the midst of a natural disaster or not, I think that if we reflect upon our own lives, we'd have to admit that we have experienced plenty of tumultuous and raging storms of all kinds. And yet, we went through them knowing that God is there to be our refuge and strength, an ever-present help in all our times of need.

Do you believe it? What have you been in the midst of this past week? What are you facing that you are certain you cannot overcome or get around or through? What tragedy has hit that you never saw coming? What will you do with your child who seems to have lost his or her way?

Let me suggest that today and every day you turn to the one who truly is your refuge and strength and always ready to help in times of trouble—God the Father Almighty! He will free you from all your fears (Psalm 34:4).

UNCOMMON KEY > *Don't worry about wearing out the promise of Psalm 46:1. God is and will be our refuge and strength—no matter what we face. Claim that promise today!*

April 2

We Are What We Practice

> Those who are dominated by the sinful nature think about sinful things, but those who are controlled by the Holy Spirit think about things that please the Spirit. So letting your sinful nature control your mind leads to death. But letting the Spirit control your mind leads to life and peace. ROMANS 8:5-6

Football coaches are notorious for repetition. We show our players game film repeatedly, even if it shows the same situation or play. We outline the same play on a whiteboard day after day. Even more than viewing things repeatedly, however, we love to practice them over and over.

The "walk thru" was developed for just this purpose—muscle memory. We talk to our players about what we are going to run, and then we go on the practice field and actually do it—at half speed. No pads, no intensity, just a chance for the players' bodies and brains to perform the action. Later, during practice, we'll do it again, faster and with pads.

The goal is that when game time comes, the players will be ready to simply react without thinking when confronted with situations. They will have been filled with proper movements and reactions and won't have to stop and think through the proper response— it will simply pour out.

In the same way, what we fill ourselves with day in and day out will spill out whether we want it to or not.

God's divine plan to save the world was set in motion when He sent His one and only Son to die on the cross for our sins and our salvation. When Jesus Christ rose from the dead, He promised to send the Holy Spirit to fill His followers. And when we come into a relationship with Jesus Christ—when we accept Him as Savior and Lord in our lives—we get all the Holy Spirit we will ever need.

The problem comes when we don't allow the Holy Spirit—our Helper, our Advocate, our Comforter—into every area of our lives to help us with the journey and to help us live up to the absolute ideals of God's Word. Salvation is available because of what Christ did for us on the cross. Help for becoming all we were created to be and power for living up to God's directives for how we should treat others come through the Holy Spirit.

Is the Holy Spirit filling you? Are you ready to react?

UNCOMMON KEY > *Pray for the Holy Spirit to fill you now, and allow yourself to be filled on a daily basis so that when life rushes at you, you can merely let your "Spirit-controlled mind" take over.*

April 3

Cards on the Wall

Encourage each other and build each other up, just as you are already doing.
1 THESSALONIANS 5:11

Jim Caldwell, who coached alongside me in Tampa Bay and Indianapolis and then succeeded me as head coach of the Colts when I retired, began writing cards to his daughter Natalie when she left home to attend college. She was several states away, and their schedules—his as a football coach and hers as a basketball player—made times together and even phone calls very sporadic. So every time Natalie needed money, Jim not only sent a check, he also enclosed a note of encouragement and affirmation. "I wasn't sure how much mail she received," he said. He didn't think he had much to say that was particularly profound, or even that she was hoping for notes from him. He just wanted to encourage her.

When Jim was finally able to visit her apartment, he saw all of his cards taped to the living room wall at eye level—every one of them. "All of a sudden, I realized I hadn't written her nearly enough," he said. And he realized how much a father's words can mean to his child.

Encouragement is powerful. It has the potential to change people's attitudes, which can change how they react to situations, which can change the course of their days, their weeks, or even their years. There are plenty of forces in the world that discourage us, but not many people go out of their way to be encouraging. Be one of them. The people around us—especially our family members—are in need of encouragement every day.

Don't get so caught up in the day-to-day issues of life that you forget to pause and say encouraging words. Your effort to do that will not only benefit those you're encouraging, it will also benefit you. Your positive words, especially if they are repeated often, are an investment that will pay off in people's lives for years to come.

UNCOMMON KEY > *Your encouraging words have more power than you think, and people need to hear them more often than you think. Take a moment now to think of someone whom you can reach out to today and then follow through and make that connection.*

April 4

Enemy Territory

> You who are willing to listen, I say, love your enemies! Do good to those who hate you. Bless those who curse you. Pray for those who hurt you. LUKE 6:27-28

C'mon. Seriously?

If Jesus told me I could choose which of His teachings I didn't have to follow, this one would easily make the list. And I'll bet that if you're honest with yourself, you would feel the same way.

I'm supposed to be praying for the New England Patriots? I have plenty of results over the years that will demonstrate enough reasons why that shouldn't have to happen. To pray for them—after the whipping they put on us in the snow and ice in Foxboro during the playoffs? I think I still have some ice crystals in my hair, or what's left of my hair. That seems a little hard to swallow, frankly. It's one thing to love my friends—that seems reasonable. But to love my enemies? To pray for my enemies?

The truth is, how many of us have problems loving the people who love us all the time? We hold grudges against them, fail to forgive them, get angry, and refuse to pray for them. So if we can't even love those who love us, do good to those who do good to us, or pray for those who pray for us, how in the world are we going to love, do good to, and pray for those who don't do any of those things?

Christ is exposing the root of the problem: our self-centeredness. The reason we're unable to extend any of those loving gestures to others without His help is because we are the centers of our own universes. For many of us, it is all about us. Yet Christ reminds us over and over that life is about God, about others, and about loving the world with and for Him. That's why He hung on the cross—for you and me and all those "enemies" of ours.

Thank goodness *He* wasn't self-centered. No, thank God!

UNCOMMON KEY > *Make sure Christ is at the center of your universe, not you. You can't forgive, do good, and love fully without Him, but He never asked you to. He showed you through the cross how to do all of that—with and through Him.*

April 5

Clear as Mud

> **Father, if you are willing, take this cup from me; yet not my will, but yours be done.**
> LUKE 22:42, NIV

I can't tell you how many times I've asked myself, *What does God want me to do in this situation?* Sometimes it's a real challenge to see God's will. Even when you're walking with Him by reading His Word on a regular basis, by being around other believers and bouncing ideas off of them, by going to God in prayer . . . sometimes it's just a real challenge.

While I was an assistant coach for the Pittsburgh Steelers organization for nine years, I received offers to coach from four other teams. I was trying to decide between completely different areas of the country, different size cities, coaching offense or defense, and working for head coaches with completely different management styles. Two of the teams had just finished playing in the Super Bowl, while the other two were rebuilding.

And nowhere was there any writing in the sky. My wife, Lauren, and I were sorting through our options, trying to figure out where we should go. What did God want from us? Where was He leading?

Sometimes it's obvious what decision to make and still stay in God's will. Sometimes it's more challenging, and you have to prayerfully follow your heart—after all, He's the one who created you and gave you the passions you have.

In today's verse, of course, Jesus knew where it all was heading. The plan had been determined long before. Even when we know where God is leading, there are times when we can only do it in His strength, knowing that He is walking with us.

How about you? Where is your challenge today? It may be understanding where He is leading—it may not be clear at all. Or maybe it's clear, but it's something that is difficult and makes you uncomfortable—forgiving a friend who has wounded you, taking a step in faith to pursue another career, relocating to another city, or other stressful decisions of life.

Know this: clear or not, the Lord is leading . . . and is with you.

UNCOMMON KEY > *What challenging decision do you need to make while following His will today? Pray for His guidance and comfort as you move forward.*

April 6

Empowering the People above You

> But among you it will be different. Whoever wants to be a leader among you must be your servant, and whoever wants to be first among you must become your slave. For even the Son of Man came not to be served but to serve others and to give his life as a ransom for many. MATTHEW 20:26-28

Leadership isn't always about having the right answer or about telling others what to do. As a matter of fact, leadership is not about either of those things—there are plenty of smart, aggressive people who are very poor leaders. Instead, leadership—particularly the kind of leadership Christ exemplified and calls us to—is all about serving others. It's about helping them become better at whatever we are leading them in and helping them ultimately fulfill their potential in whatever setting they find themselves.

Mentor leadership calls us to focus on a point outside ourselves, because such leadership must be *others* directed and *others* inspired. It's not always easy, and it's certainly not our natural tendency. Mentor leadership runs contrary to the prevailing wisdom of the world, which focuses on personal success, achievement, and advancement.

We have all seen organizational flowcharts with the primary leader at the top and everyone else in the department or company flowing down from there. Mentor leadership flowcharts invert standard organizational charts. The leader appears at the bottom of the chart, serving and lifting those above, modeling servanthood to all. The emphasis is not on the leader but is focused on those the mentor leader leads. Our world insists on "looking out for number one." Mentor leaders do not follow that directive. Instead, they look out for others.

When I was coaching, I never asked anyone to do anything that I wasn't willing to do. I always made sure to clearly cast and keep the vision of where we were going and the mission of how we were going to get there before the team. And I provided the resources the other coaches and players needed to get there.

But most important, I did everything I could to let them know I was there to serve them.

UNCOMMON KEY > *How can you implement a mentor leadership approach in your life? The example of leadership is clear—"I came to serve and not to be served." Why would you think you should do it differently?*

April 7

Where the Rubber Meets the Road

I am leaving you with a gift—peace of mind and heart. And the peace I give is a gift the world cannot give. So don't be troubled or afraid. JOHN 14:27

It's impossible to grow up in Michigan, as I did, and not know who Henry Ford was. I had relatives working at the Ford plants in Detroit and all around southern Michigan. In the 1960s and 1970s, the automobile industry was a major part of Michigan life.

Developing the first car wasn't accomplished without challenges, not least of which was convincing people they needed it. Think about it for a moment. Generally speaking, people had no idea what Ford had created. It wasn't in their wildest imaginations. As Henry Ford was heard to have said, "If I'd asked people what they wanted, they would have said a faster horse." Little did folks know that what he had created would be such a benefit to them and their lifestyles.

It can be like that in business, where we don't see the opportunities before us for progress or growth or an improved product, process, or way of doing something that could be a benefit to many. People make a living helping businesses with strategic planning and thinking outside of the usual boxes to improve what they do.

It can also be like that with God's Word. So many people are blissfully ignorant of the abundant life that Christ is offering. They go through life, often going through the motions of church and worship without ever fully connecting to the source of power that is truly available to them, not thinking they are missing the peace, abundant life, and promises that flow from that power.

They know they need something, but can't pinpoint what it is. That's why so many people settle for merely getting a faster "horse"—more possessions, more free time, the things they think will make them happy. Why not share with them what a relationship with Jesus Christ has added to your life? The benefits are more valuable than a new car. Reignite a fire in their hearts.

UNCOMMON KEY > *Sometimes you don't know what you need to help you live each day better and more productively. When that something is Jesus Christ, the difference is exponential. Share Him with someone today.*

April 8

Taking Care of Friday

> Just as each person is destined to die once and after that comes judgment, so also Christ died once for all time as a sacrifice to take away the sins of many people. He will come again, not to deal with our sins, but to bring salvation to all who are eagerly waiting for him. HEBREWS 9:27-28

This is so straightforward and simple, it almost seems unnecessary to say.

Jesus died to make things right between us and God—a sacrifice to serve as our punishment for the sin in our lives that separates us from God.

You can imagine what it must have been like during those horrific events surrounding Jesus' crucifixion. On Friday Jesus is still hanging on the cross. Mary Magdalene is weeping; the disciples are distraught, running around in every direction like sheep without a shepherd; Jesus is spit upon and mocked on the cross; people uncaringly walk by Him as He hangs on the cross. Pilate has washed his hands of the whole thing, the Pharisees are running the show, and the Roman soldiers are strutting around with their spears in the air. It's Friday, and there seems to be no hope left in the world.

Mary and the disciples have forgotten all that Jesus said would happen three days later. She stands there defeated, unable to see that Sunday has come.

What about for us today—is it Friday for us in some part of our lives? Is it Friday for some friend we know or a family member we hold dear? Are we struggling to make ends meet? Do our career paths no longer seem fulfilling? Are there relationships that need restoring in our lives? Are there areas or habits in our lives that we can't seem to change? Do we still carry baggage from our pasts that we can't let go of and forgive ourselves for? Do our regrets for all we wish we had done in our lives hold us back from becoming all that God created us to be today and every day? Are there hurts, pains, and scars that just won't heal?

Has it been a while since you've spent time with the risen Lord or been in His church? Is it time to meet Him again? Through His sacrifice, your sins have been dealt with. He doesn't have to die again or do anything else except come back for you.

UNCOMMON KEY > *The Lord of lords came to earth as a man, died on the cross, and rose from the dead to assure the eternal salvation of everyone who believes in Him, particularly one special person: you! Believe it!*

April 9

A Bedtime Story

> Have the same attitude that Christ Jesus had. Though he was God, he did not think of equality with God as something to cling to. Instead, he gave up his divine privileges; he took the humble position of a slave and was born as a human being. . . . He humbled himself in obedience to God and died a criminal's death on a cross. Therefore, God elevated him to the place of highest honor. PHILIPPIANS 2:5-9

Nathan has always loved the story of my getting into a debate with my brother-in-law, Loren, the night before my first game as a head coach with the Tampa Bay Buccaneers. We were at a Tampa hotel, and after dinner and team meetings, I went up to the room to go to bed. Loren was downstairs hanging out with some of the coaches and players who were still unwinding after a long day in anticipation of an exciting opening game on Sunday. Loren, of course, was as excited as anyone. When he finally got to the room, he discovered that I was trying to fall asleep on the pullout sofa bed, leaving the bed in the bedroom for him.

The way he tells the story is that he didn't dare face his sister—my wife, Lauren—in the morning if I had been deprived of a good night's sleep because of the sleeping arrangements. In his mind, there was no way that could happen with me sleeping on the sofa bed. I told him I was fine and continued to try to fall asleep. But Loren persisted. We debated for a while who should take the bed in the bedroom. Honestly, I was fine sleeping in either place. It never crossed my mind that because I was the head coach, I should have the real bed. Loren was my guest, and I thought he should have the real bed. All I wanted was for us to stop talking and get to sleep. Finally, Loren got the message: he took the bed.

Whether we're talking about beds, positions, roles, or other things, we need to remember to approach every situation with humility, not with an attitude of entitlement that says, "I'm better than you, so . . ." We don't need to elevate ourselves; God will elevate us, if that is His will. And I can affirm that an attitude of humility always makes for a good night's sleep.

UNCOMMON KEY > *Examine where you stand on the humility scale. Is there a specific way you can cast aside your status or position today and humble yourself as Christ did?*

April 10

In the Business of Eureka Moments

> Mary Magdalene came to the tomb and found that the stone had been rolled away from the entrance. She ran and found Simon Peter and the other disciple, the one whom Jesus loved. She said, "They have taken the Lord's body out of the tomb, and we don't know where they have put him!" . . . Then the disciple who had reached the tomb first also went in, and he saw and believed. JOHN 20:1-2, 8

Mary Magdalene, Simon Peter, and John, "the one whom Jesus loved," were in desperate need of something other than the final vision they carried of Jesus hanging on a cross and then laid dead in a stone-cold tomb.

All their hope was gone. They had watched three days earlier when Jesus was nailed to the cross and left to die, they had watched as His limp and lifeless body was taken down and laid in a tomb, and now they stood before an empty tomb and wondered where His body had been taken.

In their despair they had forgotten His promise that He would rise three days later.

In Mary's mind, the one in whom she had put all her hope was dead and gone. It shattered her world and dashed her hopes, along with the others standing nearby. That's what they thought; that's how they felt.

And then John walked in and saw . . . and believed. It was his eureka moment.

I've seen that moment with children time and again when they are learning their multiplication tables. There's always that early period when they are memorizing a set of number combinations, but everything is still foggy, still just a lot of numbers to remember.

Then you see the light go on, that moment of recognition when it makes sense—five times three *is* fifteen and always will be. That's the kind of moment John had. That's the kind of moment we all need to have. That's the kind of moment our family members— our spouses and children—need to have.

A eureka moment with Jesus Christ—when a person realizes who He is and what His death on the cross means for him or her—clicks for different people at different times. Do you have someone you've been praying for? Have you been praying for your spouse or a child or a parent?

Don't grow weary in praying for their salvation, even if it hasn't clicked yet. Different people have that eureka moment with Christ at different times.

UNCOMMON KEY > *Have you had any recent eureka moments? How about the ultimate one—fully understanding who Jesus Christ is and deciding to follow Him? Don't keep it to yourself—pray for others to have a similar experience.*

April 11

This Is Something to Conquer

> But the person who is joined to the Lord is one spirit with him. Run from sexual sin! No other sin so clearly affects the body as this one does. For sexual immorality is a sin against your own body. 1 CORINTHIANS 6:17-18

Maybe they're only anecdotal. Maybe they're only a few isolated stories that don't reflect the everyday pressures our youth are facing. Maybe they're just a few bad apples tainting the image of the rest. Any way we cut it, it seems we're reading about too many cases of sexual assault involving athletes. Whether it's the same percentage as the rest of the population, I don't know. What I do believe is that it's too many—even *one* is too many—and it's in no small part happening because of the unhealthy attitude our society has about sex and the roles that we expect people—men and women, boys and girls—to play.

Men are expected to be the aggressors, the initiators. Women are expected to hold out and maintain purity. Good for the women, but whatever happened to men maintaining purity as well? Or was it ever a concept within our culture or any culture? Do we still live by the "notches" on the gun belt or in this case, the bed rail? Since when is sexual conquest of people who are often friends or acquaintances a positive development? Come on, really?

Whatever happened to valuing the innocence and purity of our young women and men—at any age? Maybe it's time to reclaim that for our society and for the sake of our children.

And what about honoring each other? You should never coerce a date in any way—or anyone else for that matter.

If you are a young person, make sure that other young people understand the stand you are taking. Too many times people shine a light on the negative behavior but are slow to recognize positive behavior and attitudes. Let your light shine.

UNCOMMON KEY > *If you are guilty of sexual conquests, stop right now. And stop hanging with people who consider this their right. You are one in spirit with God, so honor Him with your body. Don't hide that you stand up for purity!*

April 12

A Worthy Example

> Imitate God, therefore, in everything you do, because you are his dear children. Live a life filled with love, following the example of Christ. He loved us and offered himself as a sacrifice for us, a pleasing aroma to God. EPHESIANS 5:1-2

Chuck Noll told me often that it's better to invest yourself in something you can put your heart into rather than earning a living just to earn a living. He also knew that a career doesn't define who you are; it's simply what you do. Who you are is defined by something much deeper.

When I played professional football, the average salary was $47,000 a year, and a lot of guys made much less than that, so many of us had off-season jobs. I worked for Mellon Bank, Heinz, and the Dayton-Hudson department store. In fact, I tried a lot of things, but I never really found the job I loved—until I started coaching football. I'm thankful I was able to do something I enjoyed for so long. But that career doesn't define me.

If you've ever thought about what you want to be doing next year, in five years, or even in ten years, you've probably thought about it in terms of what will be fulfilling and satisfying. Yet too many people find themselves pressured to make decisions that take them away from their goals rather than moving them toward them. Sometimes it's for financial reasons, sometimes it's due to family issues, and sometimes it's just the logistics of making a change. And while all of those are real factors, it's important to keep your goals in focus and remember that what you do should be an overflow of who you are. You were designed for a satisfying life.

You may not find a career path that gets you excited right away, but wherever you find yourself, you can be who you were designed to be. Remember that the key is not what you do but who you are. You were meant to live as an imitator of Christ, sacrificing yourself for others as He did for you. More than anything else, that should drive your decisions about careers, relationships, and other commitments. Evaluate every opportunity not by how much money you can earn but by how effectively you can reflect Christ and live for Him in that situation.

UNCOMMON KEY > *Whatever situation you find yourself in, allow your life to be a reflection of Christ to others.*

April 13

Mouse-Sized Steps

> **I have fought the good fight, I have finished the race, and I have remained faithful.**
> 2 TIMOTHY 4:7

In the film adaptation of C. S. Lewis's *The Chronicles of Narnia: Voyage of the* Dawn Treader, the chief mouse Reepicheep is a master swordsman, er, swordsmouse. He proves to be a valiant ally to the children, who find themselves thrust into Narnia, and battles evil at their side, often leading the charge with his valor and bravery.

At the end of the movie, however, they have sailed so far east that they are at the edge of Aslan's country (the Narnian equivalent of heaven). Aslan has met them and is headed back to his country beyond the boundary of the giant wave when Reepicheep calls out, asking if he may go too. Aslan agrees, and Reepicheep turns to say good-bye to the children. They have been through so much together, and Reepicheep has fought the good fight extremely well. But his time in Narnia has come to an end; now, with great joy, he looks forward to his future with Aslan.

I pray we all reach that day in our lives when we are able to say that we have fought the good fight. We have finished the race.

We have remained faithful.

For most of us, our faithful journey isn't a fantastical adventure as much as a series of small, daily steps. How do we treat our family? Our friends? Our coworkers? Our employees?

Do we stand up for justice and the dignity of others? The dignity of people who do not have a voice?

Do we tell everyone of God's grace, freely offered to us and to them?

Fighting the good fight is less about the moments of grandeur that we often dream of and more about daily taking up our cross and sacrificing ourselves and our own wants and desires for those around us.

Your journey is still in progress. Make it a faithful one.

UNCOMMON KEY > *Fight the good fight today—put someone else's interests ahead of your own.*

April 14

The Possibilities Are Endless

> Again he said, "Peace be with you. As the Father has sent me, so I am sending you."
> JOHN 20:21

I visited ESPN's headquarters in Bristol, Connecticut, when my book *The Mentor Leader* was released in 2010. The network was hosting me for what they called the "car wash"—appearing on a wide variety of shows in a short period of time. With so many hours of original programming to fill, it's a great way for ESPN to get the most out of a guest, running the person from one show to another.

Producer Jason Romano took me around the set, from *Mike & Mike in the Morning* to *SportsCenter* to *SportsNation* and finally *First Take*. I had met Jason a couple of years earlier but hadn't had time to get to know him. This time, we had a chance to talk about a lot of things, including matters of faith and about using the platforms God gives us.

Among other outlets, Jason is taking advantage of social media with several thousand followers on Twitter. Fans check his updates @JasonRomano to keep track of what's happening at ESPN. And every morning, Jason posts a Bible verse. Those who don't want to read it don't have to, but Jason is letting them know what his priority is—front and center. The rest of the day, he'll add news about the sports world. And the next morning, he does it all over again, including a new Scripture verse.

There are many areas that can be used to impact others for the Lord, whether through social media, other technology, or face-to-face interactions. Because God has made each person unique, you don't have to do it someone else's way—God has sent you into the world to impact others, wherever you are, in whatever way fits you best.

UNCOMMON KEY > *Think creatively as you look for ways you can impact the world for God. It may be using nontraditional platforms. Or sometimes not. But don't stop exploring possibilities.*

April 15

What Is Finished?

> You were dead because of your sins and because your sinful nature was not yet cut away. Then God made you alive with Christ, for he forgave all our sins. He canceled the record of the charges against us and took it away by nailing it to the cross. COLOSSIANS 2:13-14

Those who were there that day knew something was different, that this was more than just another execution by crucifixion on Golgotha. The sky had darkened quickly and unexpectedly. The one hanging on the cross in the middle began to raise His head, peering upward and looking for something, and then focusing into the darkness, He seemed to roar, "It is finished!" The words came forth with authority and finality—a cry of victory.

The Greek word *tetelestai* means "it is accomplished," "it is fulfilled," "it is paid in full," "it is finished." Anyone who was standing close enough to hear Jesus may have wondered, *What is finished?* Perhaps one day they would learn that God's eternal plan of redemption for all of humanity was completed in that moment. Perhaps one day they would know that Jesus' death was the atonement for our sins, that He stood in our place before God to allow us to have a personal relationship with a holy God and that the tearing of the Temple curtain in two signified that access. That all the promises and prophecies of Scripture were fulfilled in this moment of history.

Jesus Christ was the ultimate sacrifice for us. Sinful human beings are simply unable to stand blameless before a holy and just God—our own merits fall short all the time—and so God sent His Son to stand in for us. And in that one act of love we were assured of our salvation—our eternal place in the presence of God. It was finished on the cross that day for you and for me—through Jesus Christ, the same man who walked the countryside for three years sharing, touching, eating with sinners, healing the sick, and calling disciples and others to the side of God.

He hung on the cross for you and for me. No more sacrifices are needed—His death on the cross was all that it took.

It is finished. And a new life is just beginning.

UNCOMMON KEY > *Read the crucifixion story in John 19:17-30. Jesus took your sin upon Himself at the Cross, assuring you eternal life with Him. Believe it, and commit your life to Him.*

April 16

Little Things Count

> You must remain faithful to the things you have been taught. You know they are true, for you know you can trust those who taught you.   2 TIMOTHY 3:14

Don Shula, who coached for the Miami Dolphins and the Baltimore Colts, won more games than any coach in the history of the National Football League. Although Don was a little more animated on the sidelines than I was, our coaching styles had a lot in common. Don played for Paul Brown in Cleveland, and later hired Chuck Noll, my future mentor, as one of his assistants with the Colts. So, in essence, Coach Shula and I both came from the Paul Brown school of football.

It's a school that emphasizes teaching alongside practicing. Coach Brown was one of the first coaches to put players in the classroom, requiring them to study the game before they ever stepped on the field.

I can tell you how Coach Shula won 347 games: one at a time. One game at a time. One play at a time. One stance at a time.

All coaches talk to their players about fundamentals. Coach Shula, however, believes that the details are the building blocks to success. I heard the same thing from Coach Noll and carried that idea into my own coaching experience.

I especially remember the 2003 season. We had won twelve games in the regular season but had lost a game to the Patriots, unable to score from the one-yard line. The loss cost us home-field advantage in the playoffs and the AFC Championship Game victory over the Patriots.

At the following season's camp, I wanted to make sure that our guys were immediately focused on the details. "We are not, at least now, one yard short of home-field advantage and a Super Bowl berth," I told them. With zero wins to our credit, we would start heading toward the first one with that day's practice.

One detail at a time.

UNCOMMON KEY > *Whatever goal you are trying to reach, break it down to the details and focus on them one at a time. Don't get sloppy and overlook the little aspects of life, because they add up to big things.*

April 17

A Bold Statement

> Since we have a great High Priest who has entered heaven, Jesus the Son of God, let us hold firmly to what we believe. . . . So let us come boldly to the throne of our gracious God. There we will receive his mercy, and we will find grace to help us when we need it most.
> HEBREWS 4:14, 16

Do you consider yourself a bold person? Whether you are a naturally timid person or someone who is not afraid of anything, you can come boldly before God's throne. Boldly, the way children feel confident they can approach their father or mother—usually in a negotiation for a snack, but sometimes more (like my ten-year-old, Jordan, who recently asked me if I could advance him his allowance money so he could buy a car)—who they know loves them and can be trusted with their feelings. We can have an even greater self-assurance as we stand boldly before the God of the universe. The family starts there, and from that bold and trusting relationship—or not—all other family relationships flow.

What do you think about that? Do you feel that way in your prayer life and in your daily walk wherever that takes you? That you can approach the God of the universe as if He is your Father, your Daddy?

I've got to be honest with you. I believe it, but it is still a bit intimidating for me. However, I know that what Christ did for me on the cross provided me, and you, with direct access to the heavenly Father. Prior to the moment when Christ died on the cross and the Temple curtain was torn in two, the only one allowed into the "Holy of Holies," where God resided in the Temple, was the priest. No one else had direct access to God except the priest.

But when Christ said, "It is finished" and breathed His last breath on the cross, the curtain covering the "Holy of Holies" was immediately torn in half, signifying that we now had—through Christ's death—direct access to God the Father.

It's still hard to fathom. But the picture of Him standing with open arms waiting for me, rather than being unapproachable behind a curtain, is a welcoming vision.

Someone said it this way: God has your picture on His refrigerator.

Father. Daddy. God.

UNCOMMON KEY > *Be bold and start bonding with your heavenly Father, who makes Himself readily available. It was how God wanted it, and it's part of His plan for you—to have an intimate, direct relationship with Him starting now and lasting for all eternity. Your earthly family will be blessed as a result.*

April 18

The Healthiest Partnerships

> What harmony can there be between Christ and the devil? How can a believer be a partner with an unbeliever? 2 CORINTHIANS 6:15

I've been fortunate in my life to be partnered with people who have shared my core beliefs. Let's face it: people were created to be in relationships. Whether it is a marriage relationship, a dating relationship, a business relationship, or any other relationship we find ourselves in, we should understand the risks of being partnered with someone who doesn't have the same faith and values that we do as followers of Christ.

Life is difficult on its own, even when clearly and unequivocally undergirded with a relationship with Jesus Christ. Why would you want to pile on relationship baggage that might pull you away from the life Christ wants you to lead? I certainly wouldn't. Paul begins chapter 6 of 2 Corinthians with the words "As God's partners . . .", a description of a very close working relationship. If a believer partners with an unbeliever, there is the real possibility of tension being created between your relationship with God and your relationship with the unbeliever because of the unbeliever's disregard for any relationship with God.

Talk about complications. Now you have three relationships—all with differing systems of values influencing decisions—being jammed together. The relationship between you and God. The relationship between you and the unbeliever. The relationship—or lack of relationship—between the unbeliever and God.

Your relationship with God is characterized by light and truth, yet the unbeliever's relationship with God is nonexistent or—at best—characterized by a relationship existing in darkness and lies. Even if you consider your partnership workable and pretty satisfactory, it will not stand up against the storms of differences, misunderstandings, or disputes that may happen. Darkness and light cannot coexist. And when the storms come—and they will—the relationship between you and an unbeliever will not prevail and could very well be destructive and a hindrance to your relationship with God.

Sure, we are to witness to and interact with nonbelievers. God certainly doesn't want us to withdraw from the world. But that doesn't mean we need to enter into an intimate, close relationship with those who don't share our core values.

UNCOMMON KEY > *Be choosy about the people you decide to partner with in your relationships. Is it time to make some hard decisions? If you are partnered with a believer, tell that person how much you value what he or she adds to the relationship.*

April 19

Picturing the Possibilities

> Trust in the LORD and do good. Then you will live safely in the land and prosper. Take delight in the LORD, and he will give you your heart's desires. PSALM 37:3-4

Bobby Thomson's famous home run—"the shot heard 'round the world"—lifted the New York Giants over the Brooklyn Dodgers in 1951 and has become one of the most dramatic moments in sports history. Legend has it that the guy who threw the pitch, Ralph Branca, had just been told by a teammate, "Whatever you do, don't throw it up and in." So where did Branca throw it? Up and in.

That happens often. Whatever we focus on, whether it's positive or negative, tends to come true for us. That doesn't mean if we expect to win, we'll always win. Or that everything we fear will eventually happen. But there's a general pattern: when we focus on what not to do, we often end up doing that. But if we can envision what we want to do, we have the motivation and the faith to see it through until it happens.

We need to discipline our thoughts to accomplish the things we dream of and the things God has called us to do. He wants us to do our best and use the gifts He has given us to achieve extraordinary results. In order to do that, we have to believe what He believes—that we can. It's hard, if not impossible, to achieve what we dream while focusing on all the reasons we can't. When we focus on the obstacles in front of us, they seem to grow larger and larger until we give up. But if we focus on what God can do through us—and on His promise that if we delight in Him, He will give us the desires of our hearts—we become confident and able to achieve whatever we were designed to achieve.

Start each day by focusing on what needs to occur that day. Set your mind on what you are attempting to achieve and where you want to go. If it's a God-honoring goal and you are following His leading, believe that He wants you to achieve it. And you will begin to see your heart's desires fulfilled.

UNCOMMON KEY > *Your beliefs shape your experience. Believe that you can reach your goal.*

April 20

A Little Latin

> Let us hold tightly without wavering to the hope we affirm, for God can be trusted to keep his promise. Let us think of ways to motivate one another to acts of love and good works. And let us not neglect our meeting together, as some people do, but encourage one another, especially now that the day of his return is drawing near.   HEBREWS 10:23-25

We have no idea what tomorrow will bring. Or even if it will come at all.

In one of Nathan's favorite movies, *Dead Poets Society*, Robin Williams plays a boarding school teacher trying desperately to convey one simple concept before his students get too jaded by life.

You probably remember the scene. The teacher, Mr. Keating, walks past a row of students in his class and beckons them to follow him into the hallway. Standing before the trophy case, he asks one of the students to read a page from their poetry text.

> *Gather ye rosebuds while you may,*
> *Old time is still a-flying;*
> *And this same flower that smiles today*
> *Tomorrow will be dying.*

That scene builds on an earlier scene, when Keating gathered the boys around him in the classroom and began the fully intended process of unsettling their nerves by making them stop to think about the import of their lives with the statement: "The powerful play goes on, and each of us can contribute a verse. What will your verse be?"

With that thought floating through the hallways of their minds, the boys stand transfixed, gazing into the faces captured in old photographs of basketball and football teams. Faces, now with hollow stares, which once reflected the same hopes and beliefs as theirs—dreams that probably went unfulfilled.

Keating's students realize that they don't know anything about the people behind the faces, except that they are gone. "Fertilizing daffodils," Keating muses. As the students continue to lean into the faces before them, Keating plants a life-changing paradigm shift for the boys, and for those of us watching from our seats, who have now been drawn into the scene, when he whispers:

"Carpe . . . carpe . . . carpe diem . . . seize the day, boys . . . make your lives extraordinary."

Carpe diem.

UNCOMMON KEY > *God has given you one life to live—make it count for Him. Carpe diem—seize the day! Today and tomorrow and the next day . . . as long as He determines.*

April 21

Our Part in God's Plan

> When the Lord Jesus had finished talking with them, he was taken up into heaven and sat down in the place of honor at God's right hand. And the disciples went everywhere and preached, and the Lord worked through them, confirming what they said by many miraculous signs. MARK 16:19-20

After Jesus had left them to go and be with His Father, the disciples were compelled by His instructions to be His witnesses all over the world with their words and lives.

It's the way He planned it and how it has happened.

I've heard it said that if Pontius Pilate had only listened to some of the voices of reason (like his wife's) whispering to let Christ go, rather than being swayed by the hysterical voices of the mob and religious leaders demanding that he turn Christ over to be killed, that Jesus Christ would not have had to die.

But that wasn't God's plan. The most significant part of His plan to save humanity was to send His Son to die for our sins, be raised from the dead to assure us of the hope of eternal life, and return to the right hand of the Father, leaving the Helper— the Holy Spirit—to instruct and guide us in our lives. That's how it had to happen. Pilate might have seemed to have a choice, but in reality, he had a predetermined role as part of God's plan of redemption for humankind.

When Jesus returned to the Father, the next part of the plan was launched—the expansion of God's Kingdom through the spreading of the Good News of the risen Christ. How was that going to happen? Through the disciples He had selected to train, equip, and encourage, sent throughout the world with the message of God's love for each of us through His Son, Jesus Christ.

Do you suppose we are a part of that plan? What role do we play?

My dad was quiet by nature, and so am I. About things of importance, however, I've learned to speak up, just as he did. And my faith in Christ is one of those things. Being a witness to how He has changed my life is part of His plan, a role I get to play.

It's that simple.

UNCOMMON KEY > *God's loving plan to save sinners started with Jesus' death and resurrection. The influence God calls you to have for His Kingdom is very simple: just tell the world what He did for you.*

April 22

The Pull of Heaven

> The Lord himself will come down from heaven with a commanding shout. . . . First, the Christians who have died will rise from their graves. Then, together with them, we who are still alive and remain on the earth will be caught up in the clouds to meet the Lord in the air. Then we will be with the Lord forever. So encourage each other with these words. 1 THESSALONIANS 4:16-18

At times when it all feels a bit bleak, when we have suffered the loss of a family member, when our jobs seem to be in danger or are already gone with no prospects on the immediate horizon, or when our children are making bad and dangerous choices . . . we should be encouraging one another with the promise of the Resurrection.

Over and over and over!

It seems to me that the more bits of information we have about how our own resurrection will occur and how and when Christ will return, the more assured we are of its happening. That's how our minds work—seeing tends to enhance believing. For a lot of us, that's how it worked when we trusted God for our eternal salvation. The more information and historical or scientific facts we had at our disposal to substantiate what the Bible says, the more likely we were to take that leap of faith into the waiting arms of God.

That's only natural. Or should I say, that's only human nature. Someone tells us it's raining outside. Depending on our level of trust and faith in that person as a reliable truth teller, we believe that person and get an umbrella or we simply don't believe until we look out the window ourselves. But in either case, when we eventually see for ourselves that it is raining, we add an extra level of conviction to the source of the information for future reference.

The whole subject of Jesus' return has sparked much debate, and it's something that people seem to have more than just a passing interest in. Books about someone's near-death experience continue to be published, and some even make bestseller lists—someone sharing a story about an encounter with God and a claimed early glimpse into heaven. The books sell because they provide one more source of information that fills that void of human understanding and serves to bridge the gap that requires a leap of faith.

At the end of the day, it still requires faith, but faith is all you will need.

UNCOMMON KEY > *Read the last two chapters of the book of Revelation in the Bible and any other books about heaven that interest you. When and how Christ will return will continue to be debated; the thing you need to remember is that He will. Amen.*

April 23

People Who Get Things Done

> Work with enthusiasm, as though you were working for the Lord rather than for people. Remember that the Lord will reward each one of us for the good we do. EPHESIANS 6:7-8

We all know them. We don't see them every day, but we still need them. They are the people in the background who take care of the things that wouldn't happen without their help. Great coaches and good leaders recognize their importance—those essential members of the team who get things done, often quietly working in the backrooms and behind the scenes. They are invaluable and indispensable people.

At church, the services aren't quite as effective when the sound technician isn't behind the board, adjusting the microphones and speakers. Often the only time you're aware that someone is running the PowerPoint display for a worship service or for a business conference is when it stops working. But your praise and worship service might have less impact without the technician's contributions. The evaluations at the end of your business meetings might fall short of expectations if the material and presentation relied solely on you to pull it off.

In football we watch cornerbacks and safeties make spectacular plays to break up passes, and we revel in their abilities. We miss the great job the unnoticed cornerback on the other side of the field is doing because the quarterback never throws to the wide receiver on that side. The excellent work that cornerback is doing often goes unnoticed by the average fan, but the coach notices and knows the team cannot win without him.

Even more than some of the players, I always loved our equipment men, the guys who work fifteen hours a day to make sure players are safely equipped for practice and games. The fans don't know them, and they never get their names in the paper, but teams appreciate them.

From time to time, thank the unheralded people on your team, in your work environment, at school, or even at home. Maybe they intentionally avoid the spotlight, but you'd be lost without them. Their skills make you the best you can be. Never take them for granted. God appreciates those who do their work for Him without seeking any glory.

UNCOMMON KEY > *Nothing you do, whether it is behind the scenes or not, is hidden from God. He wants you to approach your job as if you were doing it for Him. Don't worry about the world's perception. Do what you do to get God's approval.*

April 24

The Greatest Complement You Can Have

> Do not be yoked together with unbelievers. For what do righteousness and wickedness have in common? Or what fellowship can light have with darkness? 2 CORINTHIANS 6:14, NIV

The Bible gives a great illustration about marriage. The people who first read Paul's words about being "unequally yoked" would have envisioned two oxen yoked together to pull a plow. If one ox pulls in one direction and the other pulls in another direction, there's a problem. They won't pull in straight lines, and they won't be productive. When you're attached at the shoulder, you need to be going in the same direction at the same speed. You have to work together.

That has big implications for those who aren't married yet—and even for those who are. Ideally, people are designed to be married to someone whose basic philosophy in the essentials of life is the same as their own. If you aren't married, be patient until you find someone with the same source of faith, the same values, and the same sense of direction. And if you are already married, work toward finding that common ground in every area of life. Don't just go through the motions. Your marriage deserves all the focus and energy you can give it. Just as with the oxen, you have to be pulling together to be effective.

That doesn't mean you have to see eye to eye on every issue. You don't have to like the same color, vote for the same candidate, or pull for the same team. Even a Colts fan and a Patriots fan can have a great marriage. (Well, theoretically.) If love is at the center of your marriage and you can move forward harmoniously on the important, foundational issues of life, your life will be richer. God has a marvelous ability to complement your life with someone who can make you even more complete than you already are.

If you haven't yet made a decision about whom to marry, take your time. Don't settle for less than what God has designed you for. You deserve a loving, caring spouse who is on the same page with you—pulling in the same direction you are.

UNCOMMON KEY > *Your decisions about marriage will impact everything in your future. Be patient, and you'll find the person God has created for you. Never settle for second best; He will guide you to His first choice for you.*

April 25

Being There

> Two people are better off than one, for they can help each other succeed. If one person falls, the other can reach out and help. But someone who falls alone is in real trouble. Likewise, two people lying close together can keep each other warm. But how can one be warm alone? ECCLESIASTES 4:9-11

When Nathan's wife, Amy, was a little girl, her family lived in the Netherlands, where her father was stationed in the Air Force. The family returned home with a saying: "Shared joy is a double joy; shared sorrow is half a sorrow." What a great thought.

Lately it seems like I've been to so many visitations at funeral homes and subsequent funeral services that I've lost count. You know what I mean—you no doubt have experienced the same thing. You want to be there for the family and offer comforting words. So as you are getting dressed, then driving over to the funeral home or church, you are searching for just the right words to say, just the right sentiment to console the family in their time of loss. Surely there must be something you can say that will help fill the gaping emptiness they feel, suspended between life and death, between joy and crushing heartache.

Through years of being in those settings with family and friends—whether I've been on the receiving or giving end of the moment—I'd like to pass on a couple of things I've learned. First, there are seldom any words you could share that would fill the void that now exists or alleviate the pain that now has filled every fiber of those who are suffering this loss most deeply. I have heard feeble attempts to do so, and maybe have offered some of them myself, but so often they come out as trite and ineffectual. Don't get me wrong. I'm not saying that cards aren't appreciated, but there's something even more meaningful you can do.

What means the most is your presence, your touch, the warmth of a hug—just being there to help the person who is grieving. Just being there—without any magical words— to share their sorrow is a gift that will sustain them in that moment and in the days to come. That's what Christ calls His followers to do in moments of sorrow and brokenness, whether it's death or other difficult moments in the lives of family or friends.

Just be there.

UNCOMMON KEY > *You don't need to deliver a rehearsed speech to a grieving person. Share his or her sorrow by simply showing up and being there. Who needs you to be there for them today?*

April 26

An Antidote for Worry

> Don't worry about anything; instead, pray about everything. Tell God what you need, and thank him for all he has done. Then you will experience God's peace, which exceeds anything we can understand. His peace will guard your hearts and minds as you live in Christ Jesus. PHILIPPIANS 4:6-7

Worry—it's what we do. No matter how brave a face we put on in certain situations, worry still nags at our hearts. I wasn't sure what college to attend and then, when that was finished, where I would get a chance to play quarterback. Worry. Would Lauren marry me? Worry. Raising our children. Worry. It seems like a day doesn't go by without it.

Worry, or trust God and reside in the peace He provides?

This issue of worry is mentioned numerous places in the Bible, so obviously it is important to God. And for good reason. Worry not only saps us of passion and energy, but it also drains us dry of our hope and trust in the God who created us.

In Matthew 6:25-26, Jesus says, "That is why I tell you not to worry about everyday life—whether you have enough food and drink, or enough clothes to wear. Isn't life more than food, and your body more than clothing? Look at the birds. They don't plant or harvest or store food in barns, for your heavenly Father feeds them."

What's a good antidote for worry? The apostle Paul reminds us to stop and thank God for all He has done for us. It's the "count your blessings" perspective. If we remember what God has already done for us, we can hold on to the assurance that He will continue to provide and make a way through the uncertainty of tomorrow. It's lying back in the strong arms of God and basking in the peace that time with Him provides.

Worry. We all do it. But we need to stop.

God will relieve you of worry if you ask Him. It doesn't always mean that instead of worry He will give you success or the outcome you think is best. What He does promise to give seems unfathomable to the world: peace.

UNCOMMON KEY > *How has God shown His faithfulness to you? Reflect on that for a moment, maybe even jotting down some specifics. That exercise each day is a sure cure for worry.*

April 27

From the Inside Out

> The LORD doesn't see things the way you see them. People judge by outward appearance, but the LORD looks at the heart. 1 SAMUEL 16:7

Everybody in eighth grade had a pair of Chuck Taylor basketball shoes. *Everybody.* They were a canvas high-top, the Converse All Star, the company's most popular shoe. With all the shoes out there today, the popularity of a canvas high-top may be hard to imagine. But at that time, those were the shoes to have—if you were somebody. And I wanted them.

I had that opportunity when my father took me to Kmart. The Chuck Taylors were in stock, retailing for $7.99. Right next to them was the Kmart version of the same shoe for $3.99. My dad showed me that the shoes were made of the same material and were of the same quality, and he didn't want to pay twice as much for the marketing hype. He told me that for playing basketball, the Kmart shoes would do just fine. I tried to explain how important it was to have the cool shoes—that my friends' opinions mattered to me and I wanted to be part of the group. He didn't tell me I couldn't get the Chuck Taylors, but he did say he wasn't going to spend the extra money for them. His job, as he saw it, was to provide what I needed. If I wanted more than that, I could pay the difference. It was quite a dilemma—my first lesson in style versus substance.

That's a hard lesson to learn, and as we go through life, the stakes get much higher than shoes. Ironically, Converse later had the slogan, "It's what's inside that counts," and they were right. Valuing style over substance can force us into a lot of unwise decisions, not only with minor purchases but also big ones, and not only with what we buy but with the goals we pursue and the people we choose to associate with. It can become a lifelong pattern that leaves us disappointed in the long run.

God chooses substance over style, and He wants us to do the same. While the world looks at the outside of people, He's concerned with the inside: who we are becoming. He wants us to have substance ourselves, to be able to see the substance in others, and to value it above outward appearances. After all, styles change. Substance can last forever.

UNCOMMON KEY > *What's on the inside matters more than what's on the outside. Commit to the things that have deeper value than what the world says. Always choose substance over style.*

April 28

Failed Leadership

> "Your brother is back . . . and your father has killed the fattened calf. We are celebrating because of his safe return." The older brother was angry and wouldn't go in. LUKE 15:27-28

It's one of the most familiar stories in the Bible, the parable of the Prodigal Son. A father has two sons. One day the younger son asks for his inheritance on the spot, essentially saying to his father, "You're dead in my mind, and I'm out of here." Most of the time, the younger son gets star billing in a discussion about this story; after all, he makes a mess of his life, then comes to his senses and returns home.

Equally significant is the father's response when the younger son returns, a picture of God's response to us as our heavenly Father. The father is filled with compassion, patience, and grace—even for a son who, frankly, doesn't deserve it. Sound familiar?

But what about the older brother? Was his anger justified? Sometimes I wonder if he may have been partially responsible for his younger brother's rebellion. No one was in a better position than the older brother to mentor his younger sibling. Where was his leadership? We don't know if the older brother reinforced his father's goals and ideals or if he tried to counsel his younger brother and stop him from running out on the family. But I wonder what might have happened if he had truly taken his brother under his wing.

Fathers aren't the only possible mentors in a child's life. And it isn't up to teachers, coaches, and supervisors to always be responsible and take the lead. Sometimes it falls to older siblings because they are in the best position. All of us can fill that mentoring role at some time. All of us can step up and offer leadership. We all can nurture lives of value and create "coaching trees" of people whose lives we have affected.

And it doesn't have to be a biological sibling, either. I spoke to the Minnesota Vikings at their chapel service before a game, making just that point. Too often we wait on coaches or others in "authority" to lead, but leadership opportunities are all around us.

Act on them.

UNCOMMON KEY > *Have the right attitude about being a "big brother" to someone and mentoring them. When you touch the lives of the people right around you, you increase the number of potential leaders exponentially.*

April 29

Watching the Plan Unfold

> This foolish plan of God is wiser than the wisest of human plans, and God's weakness is stronger than the greatest of human strength. . . . God chose things the world considers foolish in order to shame those who think they are wise. And he chose things that are powerless to shame those who are powerful. 1 CORINTHIANS 1:25, 27

Want to make God laugh? Try making plans—your own plans. How often do you make plans, deliberately evaluating your options, praying for wisdom, and trying to figure out where God wants you? Later, of course, those plans are often sidetracked by something you didn't see or expect, something even better than what you had planned.

I think Garth Brooks's song "Unanswered Prayers" typifies this whole relationship with God and prayer as we plan and try to figure out what the God who created us wants us to do. As he sings, "Some of God's greatest gifts are unanswered prayers."

So often we pray seeking a yes to something we've already mapped out. We have it figured out and know what we want, so we don't spend time consulting God through the Holy Spirit. And consequently, what we find is that very often the answer is not yes, but no or not now.

When I was hired as the head coach of the Tampa Bay Buccaneers, I was certain that if we coached in a way that honored God, God would reward our efforts. And I believe we did that in Tampa Bay. Our reward? We were fired.

That was not the answer to prayer I was looking for when things became tense during that last year. God's answer obviously was different from what I thought I should be seeking and was also not an option I was aware of. I'm not sure if anyone, even God, was laughing. Instead, God was putting the finishing touches on the plans He had for me and my family in Indianapolis.

To this day, He faithfully continues to unfold His plans for me, and it's exciting to watch.

UNCOMMON KEY > *You may not be able to see it, but God has a distinctive plan that He is unfolding for your life. Pray for wisdom and clarity to understand it, but more than anything, pray that God will continue to show you how to serve Him wherever you are.*

April 30

Be Draftable

> Who may worship in your sanctuary, LORD? Who may enter your presence on your holy hill? Those who lead blameless lives and do what is right, speaking the truth from sincere hearts. PSALM 15:1-2

When I was coach of the Indianapolis Colts, we evaluated a lot of draft prospects coming out of college. Sometimes a player would have plenty of experience, talent, and skills—and would perfectly fit a need on our team. But in spite of all those qualifications, we still wouldn't draft him if we had written DNDC next to his name on the evaluation form. That's because DNDC stands for "Do Not Draft [because of] Character." No matter how qualified a prospect was, spending a draft pick on someone with a lack of character could be a costly mistake.

Not everyone realizes the importance of character. In the NFL and in American culture, there's often an undue emphasis on results. To many, it doesn't matter what kind of person you are as long as you can get the job done. It doesn't matter whether you follow the rules or break them, as long as you come out on top. Moving up is more important than the *way* you move up. And in that environment, it's easy to think that if everyone else is trying to get a competitive advantage at all costs, then you have to join in or lose out. After all, in a results-oriented world, results matter most.

But an emphasis on results over character, even if it pays off in the short term, usually creates long-term problems. In the NFL, this kind of mistake in the draft process can eventually disrupt a team, impacting its work ethic and stability. And this applies to much more than competitive sports. In any area of life, the character of a few affects the well-being of many.

You will never lose by emphasizing character over results. Everyone wants success, but if it comes at the expense of integrity and honor, the cost is too high. Choose what truly matters most: to be successful not just in what you do, but in who you are.

UNCOMMON KEY > *Reaching your goals is important, but the way you reach them matters more. God is interested in your success, but He is more interested in your character.*

May 1

Knowing True Balance

> "Because of his grace he declared us righteous and gave us confidence that we will inherit eternal life." This is a trustworthy saying, and I want you to insist on these teachings so that all who trust in God will devote themselves to doing good. These teachings are good and beneficial for everyone. **TITUS 3:7-8**

After sixteen years in the major leagues, Yankee pitcher Andy Pettitte retired in early 2011. He had talked about the 2010 season possibly being his last and spent much of the winter wrestling with the decision.

Andy and I spoke about it at length because he was struggling with many of the same things I had been during my career—striking the appropriate balance between work and family.

First, he really loves pitching. What a great place in life, to do what you love. Second, he's had remarkable success: the most postseason wins in baseball history, never having a win-loss record lower than .500 during his career. And his 2010 season ranked the highest winning percentage by a pitcher in the final year of his career (minimum twenty starts).

Over his career, God gave Andy quite a platform, as millions watched every move he made on the field. His contribution to the Yankees was significant, and I'm sure they thought he should pitch as long as he could.

I'm not so sure. There is no doubt that God wants us to use the platform we've been given, and we are to develop that platform in a way that impacts others for Christ.

At the same time, Andy has teenage children who will be going out into the world soon to impact others with their own platforms, whatever those may be. And they need their dad as they find their way.

Sometimes the size of our platform isn't what matters—it's the quality of it.

UNCOMMON KEY > *Sometimes striking the appropriate balance between work and family is a difficult decision, such as changing jobs. More often, however, it's achieved with small changes, like having lunch with your kids at school or being intentional about spending time with a friend, spouse, or child. Don't measure your platform by its size, but by its depth and impact.*

May 2

Fishing Lessons

> Stay away from all believers who live idle lives and don't follow the tradition they received from us. For you know that you ought to imitate us. . . . We worked hard day and night so we would not be a burden to any of you. . . . We wanted to give you an example to follow. 2 THESSALONIANS 3:6-9

This is a tough subject in any setting. The reasons are many, not the least of which are that people tend to make political hay when the discussion of how much and how long and to whom to give arises. But the reality is that when people are continually given things, they tend to lose a sense of personal responsibility for their lives.

I think it goes beyond the political realm to the social as well, whether people perform good deeds poorly or well. *How* we impact those around us is just as important as the act itself, in most instances. And how we view them—as objects of our largess or friends in need—is also important in how they view themselves while we're there and when we leave.

Certainly, after a natural disaster, people's immediate concern is where their next meals are coming from—that's clear. But is providing food the best and most complete resolution? Once the crisis situation is past, we must be focused on allowing people to maintain dignity and helping them to grow their sense of accountability and self-worth. It's the difference between giving a man a fish and teaching him to fish. It's how we would help our friends.

That's part of what I respect about World Vision. It is an enormous organization, providing humanitarian aid around the globe both in crises and in other times, but it is always done with an intentional focus on leaving the recipients not only immediately valued, but better able to deal with the world moving forward. They try to assist but leave intact—or help build—an infrastructure or economy that provides for opportunity going forward. Their goal is to never provide assistance and then leave a vacuum behind.

We do people a disservice when they begin to believe that—aside from God's plan and involvement in their lives—they don't have to take personal responsibility for their lives. We need to ensure that our assistance equips them to thrive in the future and that we don't force people to abdicate their responsibility for their own well-being. Friends help friends get to a better place in their lives by lifting them up as needed along the way but allowing them to set the course for themselves.

We all need a helping hand at times; we all need someone to come alongside and walk with us at times. If you are able to contribute a gift to someone who needs it, by all means, do so. Just make sure that you are not applying a temporary fix but empowering people to become more responsible once they are on their own.

UNCOMMON KEY > *It's wonderful to be able to immediately alleviate needs in a crisis. But think of ways you might be able to offer something that has a long-term payoff. God created everyone uniquely for a purpose—you must help others fulfill their purposes as well.*

Connected to the Vine

> I am the vine; you are the branches. Those who remain in me, and I in them, will produce much fruit. For apart from me you can do nothing. **JOHN 15:5**

Have you ever been in a forested area where myriad trees are fighting for space and light and nutrients and water from the soil? Within many of those areas, you might see enormous vines hanging down from tree limbs.

If you inspect them more closely, you can see that each one of the vines sends off branches, or smaller vines, which wind their way up out of the ground and around the trunk of a tree until they reach a point where the vine's weight is too much to sustain the upward growth. So the branches turn and continue to grow downward to the ground.

Once the vines are within reach, they make a swing sturdy enough to hold the weight of an adult. However, if you located the taproot, or main vine from which the smaller vines were shooting off, and cut it, eventually those branches would die and your swing would be weakened. Its life-sustaining force—the vine rooted in the nutrients and water from the ground—no longer feeds the branches, and they begin to wither and eventually die.

Just as the branches are connected to the vine, our lives are connected to our Lord. Our ability to live and thrive comes from the vine—our Lord and Savior Jesus Christ. We have to stay connected to Christ not only to live but to become for others in this world all we were created by Him to be.

UNCOMMON KEY > *The next time you prune or pick up a branch in your yard, keep a small one as a reminder of this verse. You are the branch—He is the vine. The continued connection is an eternal lifeline.*

May 4

An Attitude of Frogged Persistence

> So let's not get tired of doing what is good. At just the right time we will reap a harvest of blessing if we don't give up. GALATIANS 6:9

One of my favorite scenes in *The Muppet Movie* is when Kermit the Frog and his friends are stuck in the desert. He has been on a long journey to Hollywood, trying to fulfill a promise to himself and achieve a dream: not to become rich and famous but to "make millions happy." But when the Studebaker he and his companions are driving breaks down, Kermit gets discouraged. His dream and his promise seem broken, and his integrity begins slipping. He believes he has let everyone down, including himself, bringing misfortune to his traveling companions: a lady pig, a comedic bear, a piano-playing dog, a quiet chicken, and a thing—whatever Gonzo is. All seems lost.

A second Kermit shows up on the scene—his conscience, perhaps—and helps him get some perspective. Kermit realizes that his initial promise wasn't to his friends, it was to himself. He had set out to accomplish something bigger than himself, and the others had joined him because they believed in the dream. His dream—to make millions happy—is still a good one. And if he stays the course, he can still accomplish it. He needs to keep the dream in front of him and persevere. All is not lost.

That's a pretty good picture of what it's like to pursue a God-given dream. We often find ourselves stuck in the desert, discouraged when we hit a bump in the road and think we've let ourselves or others down. In those moments when our morale is slipping away, our integrity can begin to slip away too. We want to compromise our commitment. And it takes a new perspective to regain the motivation we need to stay the course and fulfill the dream.

When you're pursuing a dream that God would honor and it seems that all is lost, it isn't. Maintain your integrity toward the promises you've made to yourself, to others, and to God. Keep pressing ahead on a straight path toward the goal. Listen to the voice of conscience that keeps you grounded and reminds you that you can still accomplish what you set out to do. Renew your commitment to your calling, and don't give up.

UNCOMMON KEY > *The missing ingredient for accomplishing most dreams is perseverance. When you're wrestling with doubts, stay the course. Don't be persuaded to give up; if those ideas of quitting persist, talk yourself out of it.*

May 5

Not Buying the Hollywood Version of Love

> Because there is so much sexual immorality, each man should have his own wife, and each woman should have her own husband. 1 CORINTHIANS 7:2

In most television romantic comedies and dramas today, an unmarried couple sleeping together is a natural step in the growth of the relationship. The story lines create a strong emotional connection between the viewers and the characters, so we're happy for the lovers when they finally get physically intimate. In most cases the addition of sex to the relationship is depicted as a step forward. It doesn't create more anxiety and complications for the characters; it's normal, expected, and problem free.

I think this portrayal does us a disservice. That's not how it works in real life. Sex is powerful, and the depth of such intimacy can have a negative impact on a relationship if it happens too soon and before a permanent commitment. A relationship that might otherwise grow from a friendship into a romance and then into a marriage is often derailed when a couple rearranges the order of things. Sex before marriage moves an act of commitment into the earliest stages of the relationship, long before a commitment is appropriate. The result is a very distorted and idealized picture of how relationships work.

The goal of dating should be friendship first. Then, when you've found your soul mate, comes marriage and then sex. But this progression is often sabotaged for a few moments of pleasure. And unlike in television shows or the movies, there are often long-term consequences that come with this short-term pleasure in real life. The pressure added to the relationship can result in unwise commitments. I agree with George Bernard Shaw: "Not only are our adolescents not taught the physiology of sex, but [they are] never warned that the strongest sexual attraction may exist between persons so incompatible in tastes and capacities that they could not endure living together for a week much less a lifetime." Sex does not cure anything in a relationship or take things to the next level. It more often adds complications and masks other problems.

If you are unmarried, learn to delay gratification. If you are a parent, teach your kids the importance of waiting. God teaches you to remain sexually pure for your own benefit—so you'll experience the best and most fulfilling sex life possible. Sexual purity requires daily diligence in your thoughts and actions, and it isn't easy. But it is definitely worth it.

UNCOMMON KEY > *The art of delayed gratification, especially in the area of sexual purity, is well worth learning. Make changes in this area in your life if you need to.*

May 6

Answering the Call

> As Jesus went on from there, he saw a man named Matthew sitting at the tax collector's booth. "Follow me," he told him, and Matthew got up and followed him. MATTHEW 9:9, NIV

That's it? *Follow Me.*

So Matthew got up and followed Him. Really? He had a business, didn't he? Not many friends, I suppose, since he was the tax collector. But still. *Follow Me.* Two words? That's all it took? I wish it were that easy.

You see it every night in baseball, when the manager calls to the bullpen for a relief pitcher. "Let's go! I need you—now!" As intense as some of those situations can be, it's still a far cry from a call to abandon the life you knew for the potential one promised. And unlike the relief pitcher, Matthew didn't know exactly what he was getting into.

There must have been something special in that call for Matthew to choose to leave all the money, power, position, and affluent lifestyle to follow this man who looked like just another guy. Before that moment Jesus was nobody to Matthew. What do you think got Matthew's attention?

Maybe Matthew asked around and found out what Jesus did for a living—ah, He was a carpenter. Not that impressive. Jesus was a former working man who was walking around the countryside telling stories and saying things that were getting the religious rulers of the day riled up. A guy who ate locusts and wore clothes made from animal hair—John the Baptist—claimed Jesus was the promised Messiah. Really? *Follow Me.* Matthew would later learn that this *Follow Me* scenario happened over and over again.

But that's the way God does it. That's the way God's call on your life can be—powerful. You may turn your back on it. You might ignore it for a while. Maybe you laugh at how ridiculous it all sounds. Me? You want me? And you can run from it—for a while. But only a while. Because if it truly is a call of God on your life to follow Him, it will never go away.

That was the case with Matthew and Peter and the other disciples. They immediately recognized God's call on their lives as something irresistible.

And because they did, the world has never been the same.

What about you? What is God calling you to accomplish for Him?

UNCOMMON KEY > *Remember this: when God calls you to follow Him, He will keep reminding you until you take some kind of action.*

May 7

Trust Account

> A truthful witness saves lives, but a false witness is a traitor. PROVERBS 14:25

"Your word is your bond." My mom said it so often that I can never forget it, which is probably exactly what she wanted. She couldn't stand the thought of someone thinking she was unreliable. She believed a person's character reveals what he or she really believes. My parents were very clear about the importance of character and taught us to choose friends we could trust.

That lesson must have stuck with me, because my closest friends today are people of high character. I have friends of all ages, races, and backgrounds, but I don't hang around people I can't trust. I also look for character in the people I work with. I hired coaching staffs with that in mind. My style has always been to hire talented people and let them do their jobs, so they had to be trustworthy, because I wouldn't spend my time checking up on them. I always wanted coaches and players who would represent the team well, both on and off the field.

As far as I'm concerned, this is the only way to have a successful team. Ability and talent can't make up for a lack of character. And that applies not only to sports, but to every area of life. In any joint effort—family, work, church, or any other aspect of life—we have to have unwavering trust in each other. I have to be able to depend on you to follow through on what you say, and you have to be able to depend on me to do the same.

We are far more effective in life when we believe it's important to be honest all the time, not just to avoid getting caught in a lie; when we realize winning at all costs isn't worth it when the cost is our integrity; and when we understand that there really is a God who rewards good character.

UNCOMMON KEY > *People will respect your character more than they respect your accomplishments. And a key element of character is trustworthiness. If others can trust you, it challenges them to be just as honorable. Everything you do flows out of who you are and whether you can be counted on.*

May 8

For the Beauty of the Earth

> In the beginning the Word already existed. The Word was with God, and the Word was God. He existed in the beginning with God. God created everything through him, and nothing was created except through him. JOHN 1:1-3

Sometimes I think children are wiser than adults. They understand life better than many of the rest of us. They see an exotic animal or a beautiful flower or a colorful sunset, and they marvel at what the Lord has created. Sometimes we adults get too busy or jaded to appreciate what is around us and realize that God created it all.

Nathan's father, Scott, told me about spending an afternoon with his six-year-old granddaughter. They were outside in the backyard, looking at the flowers and letting the breeze blow through their hair—or in his case, what was left of it. It was fall, and there were small piles of raked leaves in the yard, and so the two of them were kicking leaves as they walked around, making memories that would last them forever.

After a while they went into the house to get a drink, then returned outside to sit and survey more of God's creation. All of a sudden, Scott's granddaughter shrieked, "Granddaddy, granddaddy, look, look! A butterfly!" Sure enough, flitting around them was a beautiful bluish-white butterfly. They kept staring for what seemed like forever, and then the butterfly floated on the breeze toward a patch of pansies.

As the butterfly disappeared from sight, Granddaddy thought, *It's been years since I've seen a butterfly.* Then he realized that he had actually seen many of them but had never noticed them as he did that day with his granddaughter by his side. God's creation had been all around him for years, and it took that moment—that day with his precious granddaughter—for God to get him to stop long enough to notice.

That day not only changed his perspective on life—it changed his life.

Is it time for you to experience that too?

UNCOMMON KEY > *God's creation is all around you, whether in nature or the child who shows you that nature. Stop to notice them, and your life will never be the same.*

May 9

Reach Out and Touch Someone

> Don't be selfish; don't try to impress others. Be humble, thinking of others as better than yourselves. Don't look out only for your own interests, but take an interest in others, too.
> PHILIPPIANS 2:3-4

Communication is easier now than it has ever been. Whenever we need to get in touch with somebody, we can call, e-mail, or text, regardless of where we are and where they are. Geography isn't an issue; we can instantly send a message to somebody halfway around the world. Some people even text each other while they are in the same house—just because they don't want to get up and go to another room. Without much effort, we are almost always "connected" if we want to be.

But have you thought about what we may be losing when we depend more on electronic contact and less on face-to-face communication? Our deepest, most meaningful relationships develop in one-on-one time and extended conversation. When we're with others, we understand them much better. We can read facial expressions, pick up on emotional responses, and communicate our own feelings very clearly. The result is more interaction, more depth, and more substance.

I believe that if Jesus had all the communication tools of today at His disposal, He would still choose to spend His time face-to-face with His disciples. He would still heal people by touching them physically and be close enough to them that when He spoke to them they could hear the compassion in His voice. His presence in itself would be meaningful. God designed relationships to be developed and strengthened through personal, face-to-face interaction. That's how we really bond with other people.

The communication tools available to us today are wonderful. It's great to be able to get in touch with people anywhere, anytime, and I wouldn't want to go back to being unable to contact someone easily when I'm out of town or need a quick response on an urgent matter. I like being able to keep in touch with my kids regardless of where they are. But when we start to depend on technology as a substitute for one-on-one time with each other, we are missing an important key to relationships. In forming virtual bonds, we may be forsaking the benefits of true human interaction. We need to make sure we're not so connected with everything out there that we miss the chance to connect with the people directly in front of us.

UNCOMMON KEY > *Being connected means thinking of others and reaching out. Make that happen as often as you can.*

May 10

Asked to Run

> Don't you realize that in a race everyone runs, but only one person gets the prize?
> So run to win! All athletes are disciplined in their training. They do it to win a prize that
> will fade away, but we do it for an eternal prize. So I run with purpose in every step.
> 1 CORINTHIANS 9:24-26

I remember playing Little League baseball in Jackson, Michigan, and one of the first lessons in baseball that I was taught and that I carried with me my entire baseball career—we run off! When the team who was hitting made three outs and we got to come in to hit—we *ran* off the field. Every time.

Of course, when the ball was in play, we also hustled, but it was expected that everyone would do that.

The apostle Paul says to run to win, which is important too. It's such a fine line to help children learn to enjoy sports, but then in the next juncture to help them understand that there is a point to the games we are playing—to win. God has given them talents and abilities, and never asked them to be soft or passive once they became Christians. Paul says we are running for "an eternal prize," not a prize that will fade away like the laurel wreath awarded to an athlete in his day. What better place to put our talents and abilities to use and to passionately pursue victory than in the name of the Savior and within the Kingdom of God, no matter what age we are?

But what does it require? We are to "run" not just by attending an occasional worship service on Sunday with maybe a Sunday school class thrown in, participation that I would consider the equivalent of just a couple of laps or a jog around the park; we are to run with discipline and perseverance, faithfully obeying Him, serving those who need our help, accepting people who are different from us, loving those who disagree with us, and never compromising the one we are following. Running until it hurts, giving of ourselves sacrificially every step of the way. And not just at the expected times, but during the little times that show our character, when others aren't watching.

We run off!

The Greek word for *race* is *agon*, from which we get our word *agony*. It signifies a match or a race in which endurance and determination must overcome those moments of difficulty that come in any race. We may experience spiritual cramps or pains, but it's critical to push on and run . . . to win. With excellence.

UNCOMMON KEY > *If you are going to get into the game for the eternal prize—run with purpose as if your life depended upon it—it might!*

May 11

Putting "Civil" Back into Civilization

> I appeal to you, dear brothers and sisters, by the authority of our Lord Jesus Christ, to live in harmony with each other. Let there be no divisions in the church. Rather, be of one mind, united in thought and purpose.   1 CORINTHIANS 1:10

Civility is important for our society to function.

I recently read an article in the *New York Times* about a friend of mine, Mark DeMoss. Mark runs a prominent public relations firm in Atlanta that specializes in helping evangelical Christians navigate American culture. Mark, a conservative, started CivilityProject.org in 2009 alongside his friend Lanny Davis, a Jewish Democrat who worked for President Clinton, and ran the website for a couple of years. They mailed 585 letters, asking every sitting governor and member of Congress to sign a pledge that said:

> I will be civil in my public discourse and behavior.
> I will be respectful of others whether or not I agree with them.
> I will stand against incivility when I see it. [I'm always reminded of the baseball "arguments" between manager and umpire. We have accepted it as part of the game in baseball; in other sports it is not tolerated. It was one of the reasons I tried to hold myself to a higher standard—Christ's standard—when I disagreed with an official's call.]

Mark reported that only three legislators initially signed the pledge: Senator Joe Lieberman of Connecticut, Representative Frank Wolf of Virginia, and Representative Sue Myrick of North Carolina. He expressed surprise that so few would have risen to what he saw as a "rather low bar."

We seem to be living in a world that needs a refresher course in how to "act civilized." I believe we have become a society that either encourages or turns a blind eye to uncivil behavior, whether in public, in legislative chambers, or sadly, even in churches.

God's Kingdom is being held in check by any church that is quick to criticize and disrespect others. Some have justified their actions by comparing themselves to Jesus, who challenged the Pharisees, Sadducees, and other religious leaders of His day. I think that's just an excuse to be mean and self-important; it's serving Satan instead of God. And if Satan is allowed to get his way, he will keep us distracted, disrupted, and in constant dispute, making the church lose its power, influence, and appeal in the world.

UNCOMMON KEY > *Civility has a lot to do with the words you choose and how you present them. You may disagree with others about a lot, but how you disagree has the ability to draw you together or drive you apart. Make sure to aim for a "higher bar" in your interactions as much as possible.*

May 12

A Lasting Gift

> True godliness with contentment is itself great wealth. After all, we brought nothing with us when we came into the world, and we can't take anything with us when we leave it.
> 1 TIMOTHY 6:6-7

It's not a new phrase with me, and we've all heard it many times before, but it makes the point clearly: you'll never see a hearse pulling a U-Haul. Why? *Because you can't take it with you.*

"You can't take it with you" is actually a biblical truth. Okay, Paul, if I can't take it with me, what lasts beyond myself? Memories. A legacy.

A friend of Nathan's recently died of cancer, and in his own obituary, which he helped prepare, Rob Eubanks concluded with what he wanted his family and friends to do as they pressed on: "to care about each person with whom you come in contact, to be a friend to children, to donate bone marrow to a match, to make a person's life better where you have the power to do so, to forgive easily, to make a choice each day to be positive, and to allow God to work through you."

I like where he was headed with that list—thinking about others and the memories and impact you can create while you are living.

In order to leave memories with the ones you love and who love you, you have to make some. To leave memories for your spouse of your time together, you have to take time to be with your spouse. To raise your children as good and godly people who love and respect you, you have to be a viable, real, and caring part of their lives. To make a difference in the lives of your friends, your coworkers, and those in the church and wherever you find yourself, you have to take time to care. To forgive easily.

Take time to build those memories by taking time to care. Don't take yourself too seriously, but take those around you whom you love and who love you very seriously.

UNCOMMON KEY > *Spend the days of your life making memories in the lives of those you love, beginning today.*

May 13

Keep Going

> Let's not get tired of doing what is good. At just the right time we will reap a harvest of blessing if we don't give up. Therefore, whenever we have the opportunity, we should do good to everyone—especially to those in the family of faith. GALATIANS 6:9-10

How many times do we quit something just before we have the opportunity to experience whatever blessings we have coming to fruition? We don't know. But I suspect it's more than we realize. I know as a team we were reminded of this every year at the end of a bitter playoff loss, realizing that to get to that point again we had to pick up the pieces and start back at the very beginning. I had to remind myself not to get tired of doing good, but rather to persevere in doing good.

The story is told that the great Polish pianist and composer Ignace Paderewski was scheduled to perform in Philadelphia. While the audience was arriving and making their way to their seats, unbeknownst to his mother, a young boy disappeared down the aisle to the foot of the stage.

The spotlights shone on the beautiful piano, positioned center stage for the long-awaited concert. The young lad was fascinated by the piano, so he climbed onstage and onto the piano bench and, to the shock of everyone in the concert hall, played his own version of "Chopsticks." Immediately, some shouts started:

"Who is that boy?"

"Where are his parents?"

"Get him off the stage and away from that piano!"

Offstage, Paderewski had heard the commotion. He walked onstage behind the young boy, and leaning over him, he began to play the most beautiful melody around the simple tune the boy was playing. As he did, Paderewski whispered in the boy's ear:

"Don't stop; keep going. Don't quit; I'll stay right here by your side."

That's what the Master, Jesus Christ, is saying to you as you awake to a brand-new day in your life. Yes, the day may be weighed down at times with discouragement, disappointment, a sense of defeat, and uncertainties, but listen for Jesus' promise:

"Don't stop; keep going. Don't quit; I'll stay right here by your side."

Talk about motivation to persevere! Let the harvest of blessing roll in.

UNCOMMON KEY > *Have you ever read the beautiful prayer called "St. Patrick's Breastplate"? Find a copy. With Jesus Christ beside you, behind you, and ahead of you, you should have no reason to ever stop doing good!*

May 14

The Benefits of Discipline

> As you endure this divine discipline, remember that God is treating you as his own children. Who ever heard of a child who is never disciplined by its father? . . . But God's discipline is always good for us, so that we might share in his holiness. No discipline is enjoyable while it is happening—it's painful! But afterward there will be a peaceful harvest of right living for those who are trained in this way. HEBREWS 12:7, 10-11

This view of discipline should be obvious to any of you who are parents or bosses or in some position of authority with others who should look to you for direction or guidance. What if you had to provide feedback to those individuals without being able to establish discipline and enforce it with consequences? For example, say your child darts into the street or comes home after curfew or pulls the dog's tail. Without discipline and consequences for the violation of the rules, you'd be stuck trying to reason with your son or daughter with little satisfaction or opportunity to change the child's behavior.

And for those of you with children, you know that at times discipline can be an arduous, uphill battle. You know that children don't seem to process things and experiences the same way adults do. Lauren and I have seven children between the ages of two and twenty-six, children at all stages of development. I can tell you from experience that children are always precious, but they can be trying sometimes.

Therefore, we have to create consequences for them. Consequences that are a part of a system of discipline that sets up parameters and guidelines of what is and is not acceptable behavior. Otherwise chaos ensues; behavior potentially worsens as they continue to defy the rules.

It may be painful at the time when the Lord directs us to discipline our children, but as He shows us when He disciplines us, it is necessary for their health and well-being.

In the same way, it's no fun when the Lord disciplines you, but as the verse says, He's doing it for your good. Actions have consequences. Just like a parent teaches a child.

UNCOMMON KEY > *What discipline needs to be enacted in your life? Discipline helps you be the very best you can be and helps others to be the very best they can be. Whether it's human or divine, it's not always fun, but it helps you grow.*

May 15

Curbing the Urge to Ask Why

> As Jesus was walking along, he saw a man who had been blind from birth. "Rabbi," his disciples asked him, "why was this man born blind? Was it because of his own sins or his parents' sins?" "It was not because of his sins or his parents' sins," Jesus answered. "This happened so the power of God could be seen in him." JOHN 9:1-3

It would be so nice to understand why things happen to us at times, but sometimes there isn't a reason other than God's being glorified. And even then we may not be able to see that unfold until God's plan is fully evident in eternity.

The "why" of life has become a bit more prevalent in my life since I retired from coaching football. I now have the opportunity to become much more akin to those affectionately and respectfully called "stay-at-home dads." I am not at home full-time, but I do have a number of days each week when I help Lauren around the house with the activities and all the school-related responsibilities of our family—and they are many.

I never fully appreciated what a popular word *why* is with our children. It is most often used in response to my asking them or telling them to do something. When I don't have a good answer, I will get a "but why?" And then after a while I will simply resort to something fairly clever like, "Because I said so." This back-and-forth exchange happens most often when I'm trying to get everyone to buckle their seat belts while other parents are waiting in line for me to move my car.

When I was coaching, trying to make sense of something by answering the why question would often present me with longer teaching moments—for which sometimes I had time and sometimes I didn't.

But sometimes the answers for a coach—and always as a parent—come down to a matter of trust. The ones who are asking why will simply have to trust me that my solution is the best way—this is the way the play works best or you need to do your homework as soon as you get home from school.

It's the same in our relationship with God when we don't know why. Sometimes the answer will come later. Sometimes it won't become clear until eternity. What we need to do now is trust that it is all part of the plan of our all-knowing, all-powerful God. And in the end He will be glorified, and we will understand how what we were questioning was for our eternal good.

UNCOMMON KEY > *The question "Why?" doesn't always come with a ready answer you can understand or know here on earth. But just as you want your children to trust you, you can always trust God, who knows the answer. Keep that in mind the next time you're about to ask the question.*

May 16

Encounters of the Civil Kind

> **God blesses those who work for peace, for they will be called the children of God.**
> MATTHEW 5:9

I'm a big proponent of standing firm for what I believe, including important issues that we as followers of Christ are facing today. What I'd caution is that we don't throw too many "rocks" at each other in the process, by being strident or intolerant or intentionally sowing seeds of discord. It's easy to get caught up in an attempt to prove we're right and someone else is completely wrong.

It's clear that Jesus didn't bend on the essential truths He instructed us to live by. But when others disagree with us on those points, do we automatically put up walls or instead try to find common ground for discussion, without compromising the essentials?

When we dig in and become immovable in our views, even belittling another person's belief in order to win the argument, aren't we really undermining Christ's Kingdom?

I've heard it said this way: conflict is unavoidable, but combat is a choice. Are we choosing combat? Are we dealing with conflict in a constructive manner? Conflict can illuminate differences and in the process actually help us. But pushing it to the next level of combat is rarely, if ever, productive.

And sometimes it seems like our response is more strident if it's a Christian who takes a position contrary to ours. Or if the church takes a position we believe to be wrong. Rather than striving for peace, we automatically wage war, moving into combat before we have provided an opportunity to understand the differences.

God wants us to bring people together, to build bridges, not walls, wherever possible. Especially within His church.

UNCOMMON KEY > *Without compromising what you believe, the next time you face a conflict, instead of heading into combat and throwing "rocks," find a way to build bridges with them. That gesture of civility will change you and possibly the entire direction of the discussion.*

May 17

Making Failure Work for You

> Let us run with endurance the race God has set before us. We do this by keeping our eyes on Jesus, the champion who initiates and perfects our faith. . . . Think of all the hostility he endured from sinful people; then you won't become weary and give up. HEBREWS 12:1-3

Part of what set Michael Jordan apart was his philosophy about being willing to take a risk. As Jordan said:

> I've missed more than 9,000 shots in my career. I've lost almost 300 games. Twenty-six times, I've been trusted to take the game-winning shot and missed. I've failed over and over and over again in my life. And that is why I succeed.

Babe Ruth struck out almost twice the number of times that he hit a home run, yet he is still considered one of the greats. Abraham Lincoln lost almost every political race he entered, until he was finally elected president of the United States.

We'll fall short. We'll fall down. We'll fail. That's one piece of life advice that we seem to forget to tell young people. So often they are confronted with failure in ways that they didn't expect.

You could tell them the story of Thomas Edison, who went through thousands of experiments before inventing the lightbulb. You'd think that Edison must have felt like quitting, giving up on the idea altogether. Instead, he pulled himself out of whatever discouragement that seemed rightly his and pressed on.

When things happen to us that aren't exactly what we had hoped for, there are a number of ways we can respond. But there's only one response that will help us to move on toward the promise of a new day full of opportunities.

Get over it, get up, and try it again.

Olympian Eric Liddell once said, "In the dust of defeat as well as the laurels of victory there is a glory to be found if one has done his best."

Get over it, get up, and try it again.

UNCOMMON KEY > *Is there something you have failed at in the past? Revisit it and try again. Maybe enough time has passed that you have learned a new approach or technique that will help you succeed with this attempt. If you fall into a mud puddle, there isn't much you can do to make matters worse—unless you stay there.*

May 18

You Don't Need a Passport to Make a Difference

> O LORD, hear my plea for justice. Listen to my cry for help. Pay attention to my prayer, for it comes from honest lips. Declare me innocent, for you see those who do right. PSALM 17:1-2

I probably should stop doing it so much, since too often the result is the same. When I read the newspaper in the morning, it makes me angry. It's hard for me to believe what people are capable of doing to each other or even worse, to children. And then there's the people around the globe who eke out a meager existence with backbreaking work and live in deplorable conditions—well, it's hard for me to even imagine.

We caught a glimpse of that several years ago when we traveled to South Africa to visit our daughter Tiara, who was in graduate school in Johannesburg. There we were introduced to squatter villages, where the landscape was filled with houses made of corrugated cardboard and tin. It was certainly sobering, but as much as I support short-term mission trips or long-term ministries to third world countries, we don't have to travel halfway around the globe to find areas of need. Most of us can find plenty of hurting people right in our local communities.

Where do we begin to make a difference in the heartache all around us? Perhaps here: let us be instruments of God's justice on earth. How? Where do we start when faced with a world in such need? Start where we are.

Perhaps you can do something to help young children in the community where you live. There are children who go to bed hungry, afraid, and abused not too far from your front door. Volunteer to be a guardian *ad litem* for abused and neglected children at the local courthouse. They could use an advocate speaking out on their behalf and in their best interests.

Find the nearest children's home where you can help. There are a number of denominations that have developed and operate homes where disenfranchised children live and learn and heal from difficult home environments where they have been neglected, abused, or abandoned. They could use your help.

Locate a spouse abuse center where abused spouses and their children can find a safe and secure place to heal and get their lives together.

There are many things you can do that may make reading the morning newspaper a little easier. And maybe what you do will help change the headlines.

UNCOMMON KEY > *You can make a difference in this world right where you are. Find a place where you can plug in and help.*

May 19

A Fresh Look

> The LORD doesn't see things the way you see them. People judge by outward appearance, but the LORD looks at the heart. 1 SAMUEL 16:7

Seeing is believing, right? So often it seems that way. We've become a society that jumps to conclusions—instantly—based on an endless stream of information. Twenty-four-hour news coverage, blogs, tweets, e-mails, and texts seem to fly around nonstop, giving us immediate access to information that plays into the decisions we make.

Football coaches make lots of decisions too, most often determined by watching lots of film. Lots and lots of film. During my career, the only difference over the years has been that I went from watching videotapes to watching DVDs.

It's customary for coaches to watch every play in a game at least two times: once from the sideline camera's angle and once from the end zone camera's angle. You may have seen the sideline camera on television, located up in the stands around the fifty-yard line. The end zone camera shoots the action from between the goalposts at one end of the field. For the coaches' viewing purposes, the films are spliced together so that each play is seen back-to-back from both camera views, first sideline, then end zone.

Why? Added perspective.

From the sideline camera shot, you can't see the spacing of the offensive and defensive linemen, but it becomes very clear from the end zone camera. On the other hand, actual yardage is lost on the end zone camera angle but is apparent from the sidelines.

Life is like that as well. So often we'll view someone through our single-lens life experiences. But that's a skewed view. A person who may seem arrogant to us actually could be extremely shy, or a person who doesn't speak openly about their faith or has concerns about faith may have past experiences that make that understandable . . . if we try to understand.

God wants us to avoid making snap decisions about people without getting to know them. Our initial perspectives may be inaccurate pictures of who they are.

UNCOMMON KEY > *Be slow to form opinions about others without getting additional input—either from them or from someone who knows them well. Always look at people with God's eyes, because He can see straight to their hearts.*

May 20

The Heart of All Things

| God blesses those whose hearts are pure, for they will see God. MATTHEW 5:8

We hear the term used a lot in reference to athletes: "He has a lot of heart." It's not only important to coaches, but also important to God. Just not in the way we think of it. It was the reason God wanted to replace Saul with David. It was the reason He called Moses to lead His people. It directed the fortunes of Joseph in Egypt. Esther was guided by it in all she faced. And for Jesus, it's where everything begins.

The heart. It reflects to the world who we are—the inner character we display outwardly. It's the quarterback of the soul, guiding the decisions we make and dictating what we choose to leave behind or take with us on the journey. Our heart sets the course of every day of our lives.

Jesus talked about the heart a lot. He told the religious leaders of His day that the prophet Isaiah had described them perfectly: they honored God with their lips but their hearts were far from Him (Matthew 15:8). Another time He was even harsher: "You brood of snakes! How could evil men like you speak what is good and right? For whatever is in your heart determines what you say. A good person produces good things from the treasury of a good heart, and an evil person produces evil things from the treasury of an evil heart" (Matthew 12:34-35).

In our relationships, the state of our hearts will reveal how we view those around us. Do we see people in terms of their roles and responsibilities, or do we deal with their hearts as special creations of God? Can we look past the externals and see them as they really are? Do we see the burdens of friendships or the blessings of friendships? Do we really believe that we and others were uniquely created by a God who loves us and walks with us?

The condition of our hearts will set the tone for all our relationships—including our relationship with God. It's the lens we look through. Our perceptions of God and others are based more on ourselves and our expectations than on our hearts. No wonder Jesus said a prerequisite for seeing God is having a pure heart. And no wonder Proverbs 4:23 tells us to guard our hearts above all else. In the Kingdom of God and in all our relationships, the heart matters.

UNCOMMON KEY > *Do you want to see God? Pursue what only He can give you: a pure heart.*

May 21

What God Has Given You

> Remember this—a farmer who plants only a few seeds will get a small crop. But the one who plants generously will get a generous crop. You must each decide in your heart how much to give. And don't give reluctantly or in response to pressure. "For God loves a person who gives cheerfully." 2 CORINTHIANS 9:6-7

God wants what is in our hearts.

But more than that He wants our hearts.

He says that if we plant sparingly, we will reap sparingly, and if we plant generously, we will reap generously. We should view all that we have—treasure, gifts, abilities, and family—as being things that are God's and on loan to us, His stewards, to use for His glory. There is a tendency to "plant" without honoring or glorifying God. We think of it as an obligation, a drudgery, and feel pressured to do it, and secretly we don't trust God for any results from our hard work. On the other hand, when we plant cheerfully, God sees our sincere hearts that believe His plans are good for all our tomorrows and that honor Him when those plans are fulfilled day by day.

Therefore, we should be willing to give back to God all that He has given us, because everything we have has simply been entrusted to us. It is His to begin with. And that creates the tension: we say that's true and seem to know it, but we don't really embrace that truth enough to act upon it. I empathize with pastors and church leaders who must talk about finances and the financial support of God's church. But we all need to remember that money or any other gifts are necessary to expand the Kingdom of God, to reap that generous crop. It's a privilege that should encourage us and give us a sense of boldness because, in the end, it is all about God.

If we are about the work of God, God will provide the resources for that work. If we are proclaiming the Word of God with our thoughts, words, and actions, God has the resources to help us do that. When we connect God's mission to change the world with the heart of a cheerful giver who trusts God and understands everything is His, we have the potential for an exponential advancement of His Kingdom.

UNCOMMON KEY > *Have you been holding out on your giving? Or do you give with an attitude of ingratitude, believing that the person who has more of everything needs to step up and be responsible, not you? Look at your own heart today and commit to giving cheerfully and generously. The payoff is watching what He does in your life and the world.*

May 22

The Importance of Showing Up

> Jesus returned to the Sea of Galilee and climbed a hill and sat down. A vast crowd brought to him people who were lame, blind, crippled, those who couldn't speak, and many others. They laid them before Jesus, and he healed them all. MATTHEW 15:29-30

Woody Allen is quoted as saying, "Eighty percent of success in life is just showing up."

I think that's an overstatement, because a lot would be riding on that other 20 percent. But there's a truth in that saying that I resonate with. Today's verses give an account in one of the Gospels of people showing up to be with Jesus. As word of Jesus' ministry spread, crowds gathered, some with high expectations and some just wanting to see Him for the first time. Jesus was accessible, maybe even more than they thought possible. Jesus showed up.

That is one of the things that Clyde Christensen, Mark Merrill, and I have discovered with All Pro Dad over the years: some of the best times with family are unplanned, the times just when you're present.

When you show up.

I'm not an expert on the subject, and certainly I have my share of regrets for not showing up for my family during my coaching career. Too often the demands of my job stole time from my family. Sometimes it was unavoidable; other times I simply scheduled too much of my time at the office, coaching and preparing for the next game, rather than at home with Lauren, watching our children grow. The expectations of the team and coaching staff were too great for me to—I hate saying the words now—"waste time" at home by simply being there. When there was nothing scheduled or no particular occasion to show up for, like a birthday or school play, work took top priority.

As time passed and the children got older, I changed. Do you need to change? When I retired and got to spend even more time at home, I couldn't believe how much fun I had doing simple things with my family. I was blessed to be able to "retire" at age fifty-three, but many of us never get to be home enough. You never know what you might miss when you're not there—a baby tooth falling out, a word spoken for the first time, the look of excitement after swimming across the pool without help. Small miracles, but miracles everyone can see together.

UNCOMMON KEY > *Spend time with your family and loved ones—for no reason at all but to be there. You will witness miracles you might otherwise miss forever.*

May 23

Unorthodox Approach

> Remember, O LORD, how I have always been faithful to you and have served you single-mindedly, always doing what pleases you. ISAIAH 38:3

Clint Hurdle can't be accused of doing everything by the book.

He certainly got attention when his Colorado Rockies made their 2007 run to the World Series by winning twenty-one of twenty-two games to close out the season, making the playoffs, and eventually facing the Boston Red Sox, in the franchise's first World Series appearance. Clint often avoids traditional approaches to the opportunities God places within each of his days.

His recent choice to become the manager of the Pittsburgh Pirates rather than explore other jobs in bigger baseball markets stemmed from two things: what he thought would be best for his family and the attraction of a city like Pittsburgh with its young and improving ball club, the Pirates. It was a decision that surprised many people, especially since the Pirates hadn't had a winning season since 1992.

One of Clint's less-than-traditional ideas is a "text ministry" that he began a few years back, shortly after he was fired by the Colorado Rockies. Each day, he types a text message— usually spanning several messages, actually—and sends it to a list of more than five hundred people. The list has grown through the years, as it has spread through word of mouth with other teams, as well as with many people both in and outside of baseball.

The seeds for several of the entries in this book even came from Clint's devotional texts.

It's a challenge for him to type on his phone, and the daily regimen takes time. He even considered quitting at one point. But Keli McGregor, the Colorado Rockies' late president, encouraged Clint to stick with it. "If that's where God has you helping people, maybe that's something to weigh in favor of continuing it," Keli suggested. Keli had had to make the difficult decision to fire his former manager, but they were still close friends. After thinking about Keli's words, Clint agreed.

And today, over five hundred of his texting friends (at last count, but growing) are grateful.

UNCOMMON KEY > *Be innovative or traditional, but find a way to serve God and lift the lives of others. But be prepared. God often works in the strangest ways, through folks like you and me. All He asks for is commitment.*

May 24

Attitude Worth the Headlines

> Stop condemning each other. Decide instead to live in such a way that you will not cause another believer to stumble and fall. ROMANS 14:13

It happened June 2, 2010, in Comerica Park in Detroit. You may remember that the call and signal by American League first-base umpire Jim Joyce was emphatic and immediate. "Safe!" And it was wrong.

Cleveland Indian shortstop Jason Donald was out by a half step for what should have been the final out to a perfect game pitched by the Detroit Tigers' Armando Galarraga. It would have been just the twenty-first perfect game pitched in Major League Baseball history, and the first ever by a Detroit Tigers pitcher.

Yet watching Galarraga's reaction after the call, you would never have known that he had just been unfairly denied a place in baseball history. Jim Joyce, reviewing the play after the game, admitted he blew the call. "I just cost that kid a perfect game. I thought [Donald] beat the throw. I was convinced he beat the throw, until I saw the replay."

Officially, it will not be recognized as a perfect game.

Unofficially, it always will be a perfect game.

And how the aftermath was handled by the two central figures in that Wednesday afternoon's "non-perfect" game may very well always be recognized as one of baseball's perfect moments. A "non-perfect perfect moment."

Armando Galarraga and Jim Joyce will be remembered, not so much for their role in the game or the missed call, but for how they handled it—Joyce, a respected twenty-two-year veteran umpire, for tearfully and apologetically admitting to everyone, but most importantly to Armando Galarraga, that he made a mistake; and Galarraga, for the calm, classy, and forgiving way he handled the situation and respectfully and forgivingly treated Jim Joyce, from the moment it happened through every moment thereafter.

It's almost as if both men were showing us how to behave in circumstances where things don't go our way. They didn't resort to judgment or criticism of the other person, even though one was clearly in the wrong. They demonstrated that we need to forgive, apologize, admit that we've been there and may be again, and move on. They showed that a person can handle moments of conflict and disagreement with class and grace.

Stop passing judgment, even if you believe you have the right to do so. It only escalates the situation and makes it more difficult to achieve harmony. And among Christians, less judgment means better relationships and more accomplishments for His Kingdom.

UNCOMMON KEY > *If you disagree with a decision that affects you, instead of condemning the person, forgive. Instead of rendering judgment, offer grace.*

May 25

A Small-Ball Mentality

> That night Paul had a vision: A man from Macedonia in northern Greece was standing there, pleading with him, "Come over to Macedonia and help us!" So we decided to leave for Macedonia at once, having concluded that God was calling us to preach the Good News there. ACTS 16:9-10

Baseball players are often rewarded for their stats. Batting average, extra base hits, and home runs are markers often reviewed when contract negotiations begin. How are they rewarded? Through the terms, particularly compensation, of their next contract when they hit free agency. The problem? It's still a team game, and the team needs them to do things that don't show up on the stats sheet—things like bunting, taking an extra base, and hitting behind the runner even if it causes them to make an out. Things that people in baseball refer to as "small ball."

In 2007, the Colorado Rockies finished the year on a remarkable run and headed to the World Series, even without the depth of talent many other teams had. How did the Rockies do it? By an emphasis on the overall team, with the individual team members working together for the overall good of the organization. The Rockies' president, Keli McGregor, and manager, Clint Hurdle, built an organization on team concepts and people with character. Not necessarily "choir boys," but the kind of character that puts the organization first—character that follows the vision and direction the leadership sets forth because it has been clearly and compellingly communicated.

That idea of working together for a common purpose should be taught from the first time a child picks up a ball in the youth leagues to high school and college. Too many athletes are looking to move up and get the best opportunity they can—at the expense of the overall good of others and the common purpose and success of the team. And not just athletes. We all tend to analyze things by "what's in it for me."

When the apostle Paul shared his vision with the people who accompanied him, there was no argument about packing up and heading to Macedonia. They left with him immediately. They displayed character, trusting in Paul and knowing that if they aligned with him in the common purpose, they would achieve the greatest good for God's Kingdom.

UNCOMMON KEY > *You don't have to be a marquee player for God. Join with others and play some consistent "small ball" to help build God's Kingdom. Your common purpose reveals your true character.*

May 26

Examined Actions

> "A man with two sons told the older boy, 'Son, go out and work in the vineyard today.'
> The son answered, 'No, I won't go,' but later he changed his mind and went anyway.
> Then the father told the other son, 'You go,' and he said, 'Yes, sir, I will.' But he didn't go.
> Which of the two obeyed his father?" They replied, "The first." Then Jesus explained his
> meaning. MATTHEW 21:28-31

In sports, talk is cheap. It's not what you say that determines if you will be a champion or an also-ran. It's what you do on the field that counts. The same is true spiritually. What reflects your heart more to God—your words or your actions? Anyone can say the right thing. But it's the person who puts it into practice who pleases God.

In Jesus' parable, the second son had the right response when his father told him to go work in the vineyard, but he disobeyed his father by not following through. It was just the opposite with the first son. Even though he had started out badly by refusing to go, he eventually obeyed his father.

Usually we view verses like this as being about our faith and how we demonstrate the way our relationship with Christ has changed our lives, which is an accurate way to view them.

I also think it shows the way we need to model our lives for others. We've all heard that we should "walk the talk," but do we actively try to live that, knowing others are watching?

When he first started his law career, Nathan clerked for a US district judge. Judge Hodges had been given a cell phone by the government, and each month Nathan watched the judge review his cell phone bill for personal calls. Inevitably, Judge Hodges would write a check to the United States, reimbursing the taxpayers for those personal calls. The judge never commented on the procedure to Nathan, but his clerk saw it in action.

Finally Nathan asked Judge Hodges about it. "Judge, isn't it because of your job that you even need to make personal phone calls?"

"That may be true, Mr. Whitaker," the judge replied, "but sometimes it's the appearance of impropriety that matters most. I think I should be paying for my personal calls whether that's actually correct or not. Following that course will never lead to criticism of me or my position. Plus, it's the right thing to do."

UNCOMMON KEY > *How are you demonstrating the principles that God has placed in your heart? How can you do even better in that area? Keep in mind that people are watching, whether you know it or not.*

May 27

For Us

| If God is for us, who can ever be against us? ROMANS 8:31

How many times have we prayed for a certain outcome, imagined that a problem has only one solution, and lost heart when that outcome or solution didn't occur? How many times have we seen that happen in our lives at home, at work, in sports, or with financial investments?

And then we learn, of course, that God has something much better in store.

That's what the apostle Paul proclaims in today's verse.

For me, 2001 was a monster of a difficult year in Tampa Bay. First, as a team, we had all gone through the uncertainty of 9/11 and the aftermath together with the rest of the country. But we rallied from a slow start to make the playoffs again, only to lose to the Philadelphia Eagles in Philly—again. Off the field, the media was having a field day speculating whether I would be fired and if Bill Parcells would be the guy to replace me. My staff and I just kept coaching, believing that the Lord requires us to do our jobs and He will take care of the rest.

And then, despite much prayer, we were fired. That was not the answer or outcome we were looking for, but it was the answer we got. And so in the midst of much disappointment and uncertainty for the future, we packed up, not knowing what doors the Lord would open tomorrow, but still believing He would provide.

And He did. The Indianapolis Colts called with a mission statement they wanted me to fulfill. *If God is for us.* How could I have forgotten that promise? *Then who can ever be against us?*

Once again I was reminded that in every outcome—whether it was the one I had been praying and hoping for or not—God had a good plan in place, something whereby He would be glorified.

And the amazing thing about that plan? It was just one of many in my life.

UNCOMMON KEY > *Unsure of what God's plan for you right now is? Remember: "If God is for us, who can ever be against us?"*

May 28

Committed to the Fight

> A time is coming when people will no longer listen to sound and wholesome teaching. They will follow their own desires and will look for teachers who will tell them whatever their itching ears want to hear. They will reject the truth and chase after myths. But you should keep a clear mind in every situation. . . . Work at telling others the Good News, and fully carry out the ministry God has given you. 2 TIMOTHY 4:3-5

One of the great, courageous leaders of the twentieth century was Sir Winston Churchill. His first speech as prime minister was delivered in the face of insurmountable odds as Hitler's Nazi forces were rampaging through Western Europe during World War II. On May 13, 1940, on radios heard round the world, Churchill addressed the British House of Commons:

I have nothing to offer but blood, toil, tears, and sweat. . . . You ask, what is our aim? I can answer in one word: It is victory, victory at all costs, victory in spite of all terror, victory, however long and hard the road may be; for without victory, there is no survival.⁵

On June 4, Churchill's words helped weld the iron pillar of commitment, courage, and hope of his great nation against Hitler:

We shall not flag or fail. We shall go on to the end. . . . We shall fight on the beaches, we shall fight on the landing grounds, we shall fight in the fields and in the streets, we shall fight in the hills; we shall never surrender.⁶

Two weeks later, at the end of the aptly named speech "Their Finest Hour," Churchill said, "Let us therefore brace ourselves to our duties, and so bear ourselves, that if the British Empire and its Commonwealth last for a thousand years, men will still say, 'This was their finest hour.'"⁷

England's worst times were turned ultimately into its best. The people refused to give in and in that commitment overcame tremendous obstacles while being handicapped at every turn. They believed they could prevail and refused to give in or give up, staying the course and achieving victory.

Let's face it: we will run into trials and tribulations. Many people will try to pull us in different directions that are not the way we know God wants us to go. And yet, we need to keep a clear head in the middle of all of that and hold on to His Word.

Do you need to momentarily clear your head about something that has made you question whether you are committed to things that honor God? Do so now.

UNCOMMON KEY > *The best way to maintain a clear mind is to know the mind of Christ by meditating often on His Word. Ask yourself that familiar question: "What would Jesus do?"*

May 29

What Fathers Should Know Best

> **Fathers, do not aggravate your children, or they will become discouraged.**
> COLOSSIANS 3:21

My father was always a part of my life, always involved in what his kids were doing. And though I doubt I've done that for my kids as well as he did for his, I've tried to follow his example. I strongly believe in the importance of a father's role.

I worry about the vacuum left in our culture by absentee fathers. I know the obstacles can be enormous; a lot of men are divorced or have jobs that keep them on the road much of the time. It's hard to balance meeting the family's financial needs with meeting their emotional needs. I've had a lot of conversations with men recently, asking about how to determine God's will for them in balancing jobs that provide for the family with responsibility to be around and involved with the parenting. As you know, I struggled with this for a few years myself.

And even when a man is in the home, he can become an "absentee father" by turning his kids over to the TV set or video games, or to other people. The children often get the leftovers of dad's time. His goals are often good—to advance a career or to enjoy a social life. But an even better goal—to support and encourage his kids or simply be there at bedtime—goes unmet.

Those of us who are fathers need to be careful to not become absentee dads—at any level, whether by being away from home too much or by being unavailable when we're there. Too many kids, especially young men and boys, are growing up without a male role model in the house. Our society often equates fatherhood with financial support, but it's so much more. A father's relationship with his daughter strongly influences her relationships with men, her sexual behavior, and her marriage. And a father's relationship with his son strongly influences how the son behaves as a man. He learns to be a good husband and father by observing his own father.

If you're a father, be there for your children. There is no better way to make a mark in this world, to shape the next generation, and to leave a lasting legacy than to show love and acceptance to your own kids. Be there as much as you can.

UNCOMMON KEY > *Never underestimate the importance of your role as a parent. Your involvement today can impact the course of your kids' lives forever.*

May 30

The Rewards of Patience

| **Be patient with everyone.** 1 THESSALONIANS 5:14

Patience. In our world of constant connectivity, instant gratification, and immediate results, patience seems in short supply. A cursory look at cable television news seems to show a rush to judgment from a lack of listening and little time or room for a fair and full airing of differences of opinion.

That was always a challenge when we were building a football team. There were times when we had to fill needs quickly on our team when there were holes on the offensive or defensive side of the ball created by free agency or retirement or injury.

Consequently, there were many times we had to act quickly. However, our preference was always to approach meeting our present and future player needs patiently, thoughtfully, and corporately with as much input as possible. It required a lot of trust and demanded patience. It required time for others to offer their input—contributions I always valued and often embraced. This preparation all lent itself to building our team and filling our needs through the draft.

There were other teams who would trade high draft picks for players who were disgruntled elsewhere because the organization felt they had to rush to a decision. We never wanted to do that.

Even though in the NFL there is the ever-present pressure to win the Super Bowl, we found that our slow, careful method was a better way to build for the future. It provided a longer-term satisfaction and joy within our organization. And since everyone had an opportunity to contribute in some way, they claimed ownership in the decisions and direction we undertook.

How well do you score on the patience scale? When you make one snap decision after another, it could affect your health, your family, and even your job or business. If possible, take time and seek additional input from others before something is set in stone. From my experience, I believe a person always benefits from different perspectives.

UNCOMMON KEY > *Watch your patience meter today. Having a patient attitude toward life means you focus on God, not on the things of this world, which can so often drag a person down. And there's a side benefit when you keep your eyes on Him: personal joy.*

May 31

Getting in the Race

> We can rejoice, too, when we run into problems and trials, for we know that they help us develop endurance. And endurance develops strength of character, and character strengthens our confident hope of salvation. And this hope will not lead to disappointment.
> ROMANS 5:3-5

I have a lot of friends who are racing fans. They are as devoted and passionate to the sport as the drivers and racing teams themselves. And their devotion carries them through all the qualifying heats, the practice laps, and the details of getting ready. It carries them through all the moments of planning and preparation all the way up to the race.

But unlike the crew and driver they follow, they never get in the race. We may be a lot like that—planning for this and for that but never actually jumping in because we are concerned with the trials and problems we may face, concerned with the very real prospect that we may not be able to finish the race. And so we never give ourselves a chance to develop that endurance the apostle Paul refers to—endurance that develops a person's character and leads to hope.

Remember the last project at the office you were sure you could never do or get done on time, even if you figured out how to make it happen? You were defeated from the start. Every time you made an attempt, some childhood admonition played through your mind, one that broke your spirit and put you on a downward spiral. Things like, "You've never been a good test taker," or "I wish you were more like . . ." or "You'll never amount to much." Statements that colored your view of your abilities. Or how about the time you weren't sure which life-changing fork in the road to take . . . and so you sat in the corner waiting for a sign? Frozen in the planning stage and afraid to jump in.

God calls us to something beyond the planning stage. Planning is beneficial, but we have to take the next step and get in the race with God. He will be pacing us to the finish line.

UNCOMMON KEY > *Planning is necessary and will help you, but there comes a time in everything when you have to step out and get in the race. God is waiting for you at the starting line.*

June 1

Not Questioning the Plan

> King Herod Agrippa began to persecute some believers in the church. He had the apostle James (John's brother) killed with a sword. When Herod saw how much this pleased the Jewish people, he also arrested Peter. . . . Then he imprisoned him. ACTS 12:1-4

James is killed by Herod, while Peter is miraculously spared. God's providence and plans are not easily understood. He uses us in different ways and allows different scenarios to play out in our lives in ways we cannot fully understand. He allows good and evil to exist together, often side by side in settings where that is uncomfortable. Things that you or I may never fully understand until we stand face-to-face with Him in heaven.

I had one of those experiences when I was in Indianapolis, coaching the Colts against my former team, the Tampa Bay Buccaneers. It was a *Monday Night Football* game. On prime-time television. On my birthday.

It was my first time returning to Tampa after being fired, and I was sure it was going to be a night of redemption for me. That had to be God's plan. Instead, with just over four minutes to go in the game, we were behind by *three touchdowns*, and I found myself thinking, *What kind of plan is that, God?*

Next thing we knew, we had won the game in the largest comeback in *Monday Night Football* history. It was unbelievable, and I was so grateful for the way we won that night—miraculously! But as I look back now, I often ask myself, *What if God hadn't allowed us to come back? Could I have accepted that as His will?*

We may not like to admit it, but our minds are finite and limited in their ability to understand everything that happens to us. As much as we would like to and often try to, we can't predict the future. And as much as there are people who try, they cannot understand the infinite mind of God. We cannot see the scope of God's plan for our lives and the lives of others inextricably woven together for good. And, to be perfectly honest, would we really want to see all the details?

There's really only one thing we need to know: "God causes everything to work together for the good of those who love God and are called according to his purpose for them" (Romans 8:28).

UNCOMMON KEY > *When God unfolds His plans in your life that you don't understand, don't ask why, ask what.* What do You want me to take away from this, Lord? *Trust that God will show you one day how it all fits together.*

June 2

Be an Encourager

> Let everything you say be good and helpful, so that your words will be an encouragement to those who hear them. **EPHESIANS 4:29**

We all remember the old joke, "How do you know if a politician is lying? His lips are moving." A serious twist on that classic is this quip: "How do you know if someone needs encouragement? She is breathing."

In his letter to the church in Ephesus, Paul shares the importance of encouragement among them and in the world they have been called to reach. He encourages the believers to remember this responsibility of their faith in Christ.

Paul's letter is as relevant and pertinent today as it was when he wrote it. The world of people both inside and outside the church is vast and growing. Day-to-day living is tough and getting tougher. The economy always seems to be one bad stock market plunge away from trouble. And somewhere out there someone needs a lift to get through the trouble. The number of people who need a word of encouragement and a lift in their lives is growing. It is our duty to be that voice and hand of encouragement to everyone we meet.

To get us started, let me suggest that we do something together in the next few weeks. Think about all the friends and extended family you haven't seen or talked to in a while. Make a list of ten of those people. Then, within the next week, call each of them to catch up on each other's lives and in particular to find out how they are doing.

As you close the conversation, ask if there is anything you can do for them or anything you can pray about for them. I've become more intentional about doing that lately. If they are bold enough to mention something, be ready to do it. Then check in with them again in a month.

Once you begin with people you know, expand your sphere of encouragement. Get to know people you run into on a regular basis: the grocery store cashier, the server at your favorite restaurant, your hairdresser or mechanic. Begin with a smile and small talk, but be prepared if God wants you to do more. You can also volunteer with organizations whose primary purpose is to minister to people in need such as food pantries, programs for the homeless, and relief missions.

UNCOMMON KEY > *Everyone, everywhere, needs encouragement on a regular basis. Start with people you know and add to your list.*

June 3

Letting God Fight

Moses told the people, "Don't be afraid. Just stand still and watch the LORD rescue you today. The Egyptians you see today will never be seen again. The LORD himself will fight for you. Just stay calm." Then the LORD said to Moses, "Why are you crying out to me? Tell the people to get moving!" EXODUS 14:13-15

Sometimes we get too caught up in the moment.

Or, more precisely, we get too caught up in our supposed ability to *control* the moment.

Mike Martin, the head baseball coach at Florida State, has been wildly successful in his four decades at the school, becoming one of the three winningest college baseball coaches ever. He has gone to the College World Series thirteen times, even though he would note that he is still looking for his first championship.

Not too long ago, on a recent trip to the College World Series in Omaha, Nebraska, he texted this response to a well-wisher: "Exod. 14:14. Letting God fight for me."

We always strive for what's best. Coach Martin pushes himself and his team for whatever is over the next horizon, and that's the right response. After all, you're where you are for a reason. Don't quit or mail it in. God doesn't ask Christians to be soft, weak, or passive. If you're a great saleswoman, close the deal. If you're a great attorney, win the lawsuit. If you're a great coach, win the game.

But don't leave the earth scorched behind you in the process. Don't let your stress level grow. You can't control everything. You can prepare only up to a point, as Moses did, and then you have to step back and say, "I've done enough. The Lord Himself will fight for me. Just stay calm."

Just stay calm. It's tough to do, but how liberating it is when we realize that it doesn't ultimately fall on us. When Coach Martin runs up against those tough moments, those bad calls, he takes a deep breath and looks for God's peace. A peace that comes from knowing that God walks alongside us, through good times and bad times.

And that He will always fight for us.

UNCOMMON KEY > *Jot down the words from Exodus 14:14: "The LORD himself will fight for you. Just stay calm." Believe that the ultimate outcome in whatever you are facing is in the Lord's hands.*

June 4

His Irresistible Fragrance

> Live a life filled with love, following the example of Christ. He loved us and offered himself as a sacrifice for us, a pleasing aroma to God. . . . You can be sure that no immoral, impure, or greedy person will inherit the Kingdom of Christ and of God. . . . Don't participate in the things these people do. EPHESIANS 5:2, 5, 7

Have you ever walked into a greenhouse full of beautiful, fragrant flowers—orchids, gardenias, roses, and other aromatic blooms? Immediately, the air seems heavier than it is outside, densely perfumed with the flowers' scents, so much so that if you spend a few minutes inside the greenhouse, the fragrance of the flowers clings to your clothing long after you've left. You know that's true because when you come into a different room filled with people, they know where you've been just by the fragrance you give off.

Flowers aren't the only things that have a penetrating fragrance. People do too. Those who have the aroma of Christ have a pleasing fragrance, but people who intentionally sin give off a sickening stench to God.

When we follow Christ's example and imitate Him, we should be able to easily distinguish when someone is following their own sinful desires. We shouldn't partner with people who fall into the traps of the world, who deem ungodly behavior both acceptable and commendable. We should be in the world and yet careful of our associations within the world. We need to be so immersed in Christ and God's Word that our pleasing aroma is stronger than what the world offers.

Paul says not to be fooled by people who try to make excuses for their sins (verse 6). Peer pressure and inappropriate associations will try to throw us off track and even cause some of the fragrance of Christ to dissipate in our lives. But when we return to the greenhouse each day, it will restore us and bathe us once again in Jesus' aroma so that people will know where we have been. They will glimpse Jesus in our faces, hear Him in our voices, and see Him in our actions; they will catch the aroma of Christ—His presence in our lives—emanating from us.

UNCOMMON KEY > *Buy a rose today as a reminder of how strongly the aroma of Christ can permeate your life. Diligently spend time with Him and follow His example so people will undeniably know whom you are imitating.*

June 5

Fully Committed

> A man leaves his father and mother and is joined to his wife, and the two are united into one. **GENESIS 2:24**

Over half of couples today are living together before they get married, if they get married at all. Why is that? What happened to the sense of commitment necessary to form a strong marriage partnership?

I believe the answer lies in what we think about the marriage vow. The common approach today is to consider this vow to be nothing more than a tradition or, at best, a statement of good intentions. Instead of meaning what it says, to many people it means, "We'll try this relationship out. As long as my spouse is doing what I expect, as long as he or she is fulfilling my needs, then I'll show love and respect. But if not, I'll move on." And many people grow apart, chalk it up to "irreconcilable differences," and go their separate ways.

I don't know how no-fault divorces came about, but they turn the whole commitment idea on its head. Christ, on the other hand, encourages the uncommon approach: "Let no one split apart what God has joined together" (Matthew 19:6). The marriage vow is a commitment, and when we make that vow, we have a duty to make the marriage work. If we are men and women of our word, we will.

Commitment isn't only a marriage issue. One of my children once asked if he could quit the team he had joined. It wasn't as fun as he thought it would be, and down in Florida, the practices were hot. Once Lauren and I made sure that there weren't any other reasons for his desire to quit that we needed to address, we said no. He couldn't quit. He didn't have to play the following season if he didn't want to, but he had made a commitment to his teammates.

If commitment matters with temporary relationships like playing on a team, how much more does it matter with a relationship like marriage? It's important to hang in there. When you say "for better or worse," understand that sometimes the better comes after the worse. But it's always worth working and waiting for.

UNCOMMON KEY > *Moving in and out of "commitments" is common today. Be uncommon: never enter them or break them lightly.*

June 6

Going to the Mat for You

> Epaphras, who is one of you and a servant of Christ Jesus . . . is always wrestling in prayer for you, that you may stand firm in all the will of God, mature and fully assured.
> COLOSSIANS 4:12, NIV

What a fantastic picture. Someone who is devoted to Christ, "wrestling in prayer" for us so that we "may stand firm in all the will of God."

When I was a freshman at the University of Minnesota, I lived in the same dorm as two of our NCAA wrestling champions, Larry Zilverberg and Pat Neu. They were two of the toughest guys I have ever known. Wrestling is such an involved, intense sport. The matches are composed of three two-minute periods of one wrestler pitted against the other. It's a sport that can't be done halfway—you're either all in, or you're defeated.

Now think of that in terms of prayer. What a wonderful gift to have someone "all in" like a wrestler has to be, praying fervently on your behalf that you may stand firm in the will of God, mature and fully assured! Do you have any friends like that? Is there anyone you pray for like that? Maybe a family member or a good friend? You've probably heard those stories of mothers or grandmothers who have prayed and prayed and prayed for their children and grandchildren until they turned to Christ, basically praying them into heaven.

That you may stand firm in all the will of God. There is an ebb and flow to life, times when things are going more smoothly, and other times when you're battling and struggling. Did you notice the word *may* is used rather than *will*? Standing firm remains a choice—regardless of the number and intensity of the praying saints out there. It is undergirded in prayer, but it remains a choice.

Where do you stand in living out the will of God?

UNCOMMON KEY > *Thank the people you know who are continually wrestling in prayer for you. And consider doing the same for them and others.*

June 7

Dousing the Flame

> The tongue is a flame of fire. It is a whole world of wickedness, corrupting your entire body. It can set your whole life on fire, for it is set on fire by hell itself.   JAMES 3:6

On October 8, 1871, two great fires occurred in the Midwest. The Great Chicago Fire killed 250 people and left one-quarter of Chicago homeless. The other one, the Great Peshtigo Fire in the forests of northern Michigan and Wisconsin affected 1.5 million acres and killed approximately fifteen hundred people.

Fire can be devastating and incredibly fast-moving. In the movie *Backdraft*, I was startled at how quickly a fire can go from seemingly under control to raging out of control and consuming a building. I remember thinking that if I ever faced such a force, I would never think of it in the same way. Fire unleashes terrible power and can result in total devastation.

So when the writer James compares the tongue to a fire, it makes perfect sense. I've seen it happen way too often. What seemed to start out as a friendly conversation becomes a major disagreement with hurtful, damaging words and lingering consequences. How often have we seen a simple disagreement smolder ever so slightly and then combust and ignite the situation into an incredible inferno of anger? Our words reflect what is in our hearts.

According to Proverbs 23:7, "As [a man] thinketh in his heart, so is he" (KJV). And Jesus says something similar: "Whatever is in your heart determines what you say" (Matthew 12:34).

Be slow to speak, especially when you're angry or your emotions are racing; it only takes a few inflammatory words to destroy a relationship forever.

UNCOMMON KEY > *Put out the fire of angry words before saying them. If someone is angry and screams at you, maintain your cool. Do your best to douse the situation with your silence.*

June 8

I Love to Tell the Story

> God has not given us a spirit of fear and timidity, but of power, love, and self-discipline. So never be ashamed to tell others about our Lord.   2 TIMOTHY 1:7-8

These verses describe my dear friend Donnie Shell perfectly. We were teammates during the two years I played for the Pittsburgh Steelers. Donnie was named to the Pro Bowl five times and won four Super Bowls during an NFL career that spanned fourteen seasons. But the first thing I noticed about him was not his athletic ability; it was his Christian lifestyle.

That's the thing Donnie is most proud of in his life: his relationship with Jesus Christ.

And he's quick to tell you about that relationship. He won't hammer you with it, but he is always ready to share the importance of it in his life. You can see his relationship with Christ in his manner, in his talk, in the way he treats and engages people, and in the decisions he makes in his family life as well as in business. Donnie lives out the idea of "power, love, and self-discipline," and of "never be[ing] ashamed" of the gospel. Donnie always has Jesus on his heart and wants to talk about Him to anyone he meets.

How about us? When it comes to telling others about Jesus, you and I should follow Donnie's lead, always ready to share what Jesus Christ has done in our lives. There may have been times in the past when we tried but were hesitant. And that has intimidated us, so we haven't attempted it since. Maybe we're timid to share because we don't know how it will be received. Maybe we feel inadequate to share—after all, we haven't memorized the entire Bible yet.

Here's the bottom line: God, through what Jesus Christ did for you, changed your life forever. You are not today who you were before God changed your life, and you are becoming more of the person He wants you to be each day. Share *your* story—don't worry about knowing all the Scripture verses or about teaching the Bible to someone. Just share your story. If you want just one verse to use, use John 3:16—"For God loved the world so much that he gave his one and only Son, so that everyone who believes in him will not perish but have eternal life."

UNCOMMON KEY > *The world is waiting to hear about Jesus Christ—from you. Just share your story of how He changed, and is changing, your life.*

June 9

Abundant Crops

> Other seeds fell on fertile soil, and they produced a crop that was thirty, sixty, and even a hundred times as much as had been planted! MATTHEW 13:8

We get lots of weeds in Florida. I think I have seen every kind invading my yard at one time or another. I'm told that the best way to keep weeds out of our yards isn't to focus on eliminating the weeds, but rather to keep the grass thick and lush; strong grass chokes out the weeds and keeps them from gaining a foothold. In yards full of weeds, there are probably also thin, poor patches of grass.

Remember the parable of the farmer and the seeds in Matthew 13? As the farmer scattered the seeds across the field, they landed in several places. Some seeds fell on the path and were gobbled up by birds; some seeds fell on shallow, rocky soil, and the shoots, because of their shallow roots, withered in the hot sun; other seeds were choked out by nasty weeds. But thankfully, some seeds fell on fertile soil, grew beautifully, and produced an abundant crop.

We put "seeds" into our lives every day. Whether it's our thought lives, the friends we associate with, or the things we allow to influence us, all of these things can either make us stronger or weaken us. The more good things and good people, the more positive influences we associate with in all areas of our lives, the more likely those things will choke out the bad—that's just how it works. The more we spend time with good influencers and think on things that are good and pure, as the apostle Paul suggests in Philippians 4:8, the better the chance the weeds of temptation and evil will not gain a foothold in our thoughts and lives.

Sometimes it's just a single weed. One weak spot opens itself up to a weed and leads to an uncontrollable amount. But it doesn't happen overnight. Make sure your relationships aren't encouraging weeds to crop up in your mind, your attitude, or in the things you do. Surround yourself with positive influences, and be a positive influence for others.

UNCOMMON KEY > *If you spend a lot of time keeping your yard weed-free, do the same for your life. It's much more important. Add good, positive, and godly influences, attitudes, habits, and associations to your life to grow strong roots in Him.*

June 10

Hard-Hat Faith

> The God of heaven will help us succeed. We, his servants, will start rebuilding this wall.
> NEHEMIAH 2:20

If he were alive, I wonder what Nehemiah would think of some of the recent football stadium building projects that have been completed throughout the United States. Stadiums like Lucas Oil Stadium in Indianapolis, Reliant Stadium in Houston, or Cowboys Stadium in Arlington, Texas—the largest domed stadium in the world. He probably would be impressed, especially when he learned how quickly they went up. It was a different story for him. He didn't have blueprints or heavy equipment to make things easier. But that was God's plan.

Have you ever wondered how Nehemiah did it? He wasn't an architect or a stone mason. He hadn't grown up in construction. And to be honest, when he was given the assignment, Nehemiah didn't know how this crucial building project would turn out. He had left his role as the official cupbearer/food taster to King Artaxerxes of Persia and donned a hard hat as he undertook to rebuild the wall around Jerusalem. The city was in constant danger from troublemakers, and it needed to be done.

Nehemiah stepped out to rebuild Jerusalem's walls without any idea how it would go or how he would accomplish such a daunting task. He could not see the end of the project, but he knew that God could. And since he was doing this for God, God would lead him every step of the way. Nehemiah did have control over some things, and he carefully brought those aspects to the project. He surveyed the ruins and resources, laying out careful plans and gathering and equipping committed people to build the wall, and then assigning each group a section of the wall to complete.

Everyone took ownership over their sections, and even though they were doing something they had never done before, they knew this was a labor of love for the God they served and that He would lead and bless their efforts.

Have you ever been in a position like Nehemiah? You feel certain that God has called you to take charge of something, but you may have a lot of questions in the back of your mind. Let it be a faith-stretching experience for you.

UNCOMMON KEY > *Whenever you know God is calling you to do something, be confident that He will guide the process, even if a successful outcome is hard to imagine. He will get you to where He wants you to go.*

June 11

Out of the Spotlight

> The way you live will always honor and please the Lord, and your lives will produce every kind of good fruit.... You will grow as you learn to know God better and better.... You will be strengthened with all his glorious power so you will have all the endurance and patience you need. COLOSSIANS 1:10-11

Muhammad Ali's signature line was "I am the greatest." The more he said it, the more people watched him—even if they were only watching to see him get beaten. He had supreme confidence in his ability, and he knew his attitude sold tickets. And because he fought in an era when not many black men had been able to stand up and be bold, he became an icon in the African American community. His swagger was a novelty.

That was somewhat true of Joe Namath, too, when he guaranteed a win in Super Bowl III, delivered on his promise, and became a larger-than-life star. The idea of the humble athlete—the guy who let his skills do the talking—was on the way out. The media loved the sound bites because they made good highlights and attracted attention. A big mouth became cool.

Today this "look at me" attitude isn't uncommon at all. Maybe it's an ego trip for some players, but for most it's driven by a need to survive in a world where so many others stand ready to take their places. The more *SportsCenter* moments they have, the more viewers they will draw and the more valuable they will be to their team—and the more they will be paid. At least that's what they think. They feel they need to blow their own horns because no one else will. And it seems to work.

This "look at me" attitude used to make a player unpopular—and in some ways it still does—but the culture has shifted to the point that now it pays off. But while that attitude gets a lot of attention, it still isn't very appealing. Nobody really believes us when we blow our own horns because we're biased. And our focus on ourselves comes across as self-centered and prideful.

Scripture tells us not to praise ourselves but to let others speak about us. Whatever field we work in, our job is to do the best we can and let our attitude, work ethic, gifts, and skills speak volumes. When we do that, others will eventually notice, and that will mean much more to us and to them than if we had to make them notice with our mouths. A "look at me" attitude may get attention in the short run, but it doesn't pay off long-term. God honors humility, not pride.

UNCOMMON KEY > *Remember that it's His "glorious power" through which we operate. Humility is more impressive than accomplishments. It will earn respect without words.*

June 12

Testing the Truth

> The people of Berea were more open-minded than those in Thessalonica, and they listened eagerly to Paul's message. They searched the Scriptures day after day to see if Paul and Silas were teaching the truth.   ACTS 17:11

When he was growing up in Tampa, Nathan had a Little League coach who told him, "Put your feet and knees together when fielding a ground ball so it won't go through your legs."

Brought up to respect people in authority, Nathan did as he was told, even though it felt very awkward. I guess it would. Stand up and try bending over to field an imaginary ground ball, moving from side to side with your feet and knees together. Not easy, is it? Nathan was pretty sure this wasn't what he had been taught at home by his dad, a future baseball coach in the Southeastern Conference. So when he arrived home, Nathan asked his father, Scott, if the coach's instructions were correct.

No, his father confirmed. The coach's way wasn't the correct way. But even though the coach didn't know much about baseball, he was a good guy giving up his time to help the kids with baseball, so Scott advised Nathan to follow his coach's method at practice, and then come home and work on it correctly so that in the game he would do it the right way.

Like Nathan, we need to test and approve what we are told, especially when it comes to something more critical than fielding ground balls. It's hard to believe anyone would need to verify the apostle Paul, but here we're told that's what the Bereans did. We don't need to enter and confirm things with a spirit of skepticism, but we should be open to discernment from the Holy Spirit as to what is right and what is God's truth.

Have you been given conflicting instructions? Sit down with the person who is asking you to do something that doesn't seem exactly right.

UNCOMMON KEY > *Practical matters aside, you should always be ready to test what you hear against the Word of God, to be certain that there is no conflict.*

June 13

Sound Advice in a Noisy World

> The LORD passed by, and a mighty windstorm hit the mountain. . . . but the LORD was not in the wind. . . . There was an earthquake, but the LORD was not in the earthquake. . . . There was a fire, but the LORD was not in the fire. And after the fire there was the sound of a gentle whisper.   1 KINGS 19:11-12

The world is full of loud voices trying to get our attention. Usually the loudest are the ones least worth listening to. When God spoke to Elijah, He did so with "a gentle whisper." That's how wisdom usually comes to us. Whether it is God's voice or the counsel of a friend, the words we most need to hear are the ones we actually have to make an effort to listen to.

No matter how many friends you have, you probably only turn to a few when you need advice. Number one on my list of confidants is my bride, Lauren. She has been a voice of encouragement, love, character, and godly wisdom as long as I've known her. And I have a few other voices of wisdom in my life as well—friends I can count on to give me honest feedback and sound advice when I need it.

But most of us let a few other voices affect us too. The opinion of the crowd sometimes weighs more than it should. There's no shortage of internal voices either: ambition, power, wealth, revenge, greed, pleasure, compromise, and self-centeredness. In one respect or another, all of these voices—whether internal or external—are simply expressing the ways of the world. And they can be noisy and relentless. In order to hear true wisdom, we have to ignore some pretty loud words and listen to the subtle ones.

Learn to tune in to the quiet voices that consistently speak truth to you. First and foremost, that's God. Practice hearing His gentle whisper. But also listen to the counsel of those you trust: your spouse, your parents and other family members, your close friends. These people know you well, they have been with you in the valleys and on the mountaintops, and unlike many other voices, they want what's best for you.

UNCOMMON KEY > *Listen to the voices of those who have earned the right to be heard. The words of those who have been faithful to you—who are speaking God's words—are worth far more than the words of the world.*

June 14

Strength for the Weary

> He gives power to the weak and strength to the powerless. Even youths will become weak and tired, and young men will fall in exhaustion. But those who trust in the LORD will find new strength. They will soar high on wings like eagles. They will run and not grow weary. They will walk and not faint. ISAIAH 40:29-31

I didn't always do it when I was coaching in the National Football League. Not every day, anyway. But if I ever get back into coaching, I think I will be sure to make these verses from Isaiah a part of my daily reading—out loud—beginning at least midway through the toilsome training camp and then continuing halfway through the season. And I'd share them with the team at various times during those stretches as well. Because those are the times when the journey we are on seems to be all uphill. Those are the times when every limb seems weak, there is no desire to go on, and the body is faint and the spirit weary. Very weary.

We've all been there. For me, it's been on the football field or lately riding my bike up a long, tough hill. For you, it may not be in an athletic environment, but we all know and have experienced enough to know that the uphill climbs are found everywhere in our lives.

We all get weary sometimes. Even "youths" and "young men" will grow tired—it's a part of the human condition. Maybe it's Mondays or at the end of the month or the quarter. Maybe it's after something has happened in your life to sap you of that last ounce of energy and "able to" that you were saving to get through the week. Sometimes week after week just gets to you.

It's easy to get worn down, emotionally and physically. We need to look to the Lord for rest and rejuvenation, which He promises.

Read the verses again—out loud this time.

"He gives power to the weak and strength to the powerless."

UNCOMMON KEY > *This prophetic promise is worth committing to memory. Or do what I suggested: read it aloud during those times when you are especially weary. God is your source of power. Plug in to Him.*

June 15

Always Connected in Him

> I am the vine; you are the branches. Those who remain in me, and I in them, will produce much fruit. For apart from me you can do nothing. JOHN 15:5

When I was with the Tampa Bay Buccaneers, we started a staff Bible study. We met weekly because we knew we needed to support each other and provide a time to be accountable and in fellowship with the Lord. We also needed to continue to build the foundations in our lives that would help us withstand the storms we knew would come as the season wore on. And those of us who began the study and encouraged participation realized that to be productive in this world—despite this world—we would need to be more closely attached to and growing in our relationships with the Lord Jesus Christ.

As you can imagine, the group was fairly fluid in its membership as coaches came from and went to other teams and opportunities. But we continued with the Bible study and prayer times, and when we added new coaches to our staff, we'd invite them to join us. The coaches and other staff members who had gone to other teams would check in from time to time with specific questions about something we had talked about in those weekly sessions. In 2002, when a large group of us moved together from Tampa to Indianapolis, we started our weekly Bible study again with the Colts and pressed on.

Even though there has been a constant flow of changes in our lives, we have remained committed to what we started. To this day a group of us continue to get together by phone on Tuesday mornings during the season and have been getting together once a year in Minnesota to fish and fellowship and continue to grow together.

Jesus is right. He is the vine, and we are His branches, wherever we happen to be located. In order to be healthy and produce fruit, we must be attached to Him. I have also learned through the help and encouragement of many others, and especially through that growing and diverse group started from a Bible study in Tampa, that it helps us stay connected to the Vine when we stay in fellowship with fellow "branches."

UNCOMMON KEY > *Encouraging each other and lifting each other up together always helps to point you back to the Vine from which you receive what you need to grow. Stay in fellowship with fellow "branches."*

June 16

Price Check

> Oh, how great are God's riches and wisdom and knowledge! How impossible it is for us to understand his decisions and his ways! ROMANS 11:33

Time and again God's ways prove different from our ways. Those eternal things upon which He places great value we often treat with scorn. And those things we treat as treasures are temporal, fleeting possessions to Him.

Why does Jesus always seem to be switching the price tags on our values? Clearly His values don't match those of a society bent on success, achievement, and winning for the sake of winning. His price tags are the right ones; we've switched them and misplaced our values. One of the most obvious areas in which we've done that is education and sports. We pay athletes and entertainers much more than we pay teachers. Many of us would rather have a son who grows up to be a starting shortstop for the Yankees than a social worker who helps hundreds of people get their lives back on track.

We see this when children are pushed to compete in sports by overzealous parents. Sometimes parents and coaches try to live vicariously through their children's achievements, and they can take every umpire's call personally or treat the other team as the enemy—even though the kids are only playing a game. Athletics is not the only arena in which we sometimes try to achieve our dreams—on our own or through our children. But these dreams won't really satisfy us. We often put our highest price tags on things of much lesser value.

Do you feel the stress and strain of misplaced price tags in your life? If so, maybe it's time to remember what's most important and focus on that. You'll notice that Jesus and society have two different value systems. He emphasized humility, hunger for truth and righteousness, and things that have eternal rather than temporary importance. Society emphasizes power, status, awards, fame, and wealth. Whose values would you rather follow? Stay focused on God's values, and help others see the folly in many of the world's values.

UNCOMMON KEY > *Values are a choice, and some of society's price tags cost too much. What are you paying for today? Choose what's good, true, and lasting.*

June 17

True Identity

> When Jesus came to the region of Caesarea Philippi, he asked his disciples, "Who do people say that the Son of Man is?" "Well," they replied, "some say John the Baptist, some say Elijah, and others say Jeremiah or one of the other prophets." Then he asked them, "But who do you say I am?" Simon Peter answered, "You are the Messiah, the Son of the living God." MATTHEW 16:13-16

Peter was spot-on. This was the same Peter who would later deny Christ on three different occasions. But at least for this moment, Peter was right on track.

We are often tempted to turn from Christ and who He calls us to be.

During the course of a season, at various times in team meetings unrelated to the football side of things, I would ask the guys to consider who they were. Many of them had never taken time to think that question through, especially when I said they needed to take football out of the equation. They had never thought of themselves except in the context of football. Everything they were, had done, and were about to do—to them, at least—was related to football.

So for them to stop and think for a moment about themselves unrelated to that environment—well, it was uncomfortable, to say the least. For some of my players, it seemed impossible to think in those terms. For many it was a totally new concept: to begin to think of who they were and of who God made them to be. To look at their interests and passions outside of football. To notice certain people in their lives—family, spouse, children—in a different way. To see their potential and purpose in other things besides being a football player was a bit unnerving. And also to stop and think for a moment where God fits into all of that.

"But who do you say I am?"

Who do *you* say He is?

UNCOMMON KEY > *Ask yourself the question Jesus asked His disciples, and jot down what comes to mind. Do you believe that Christ is the Son of God? Ask God to make your belief even stronger.*

June 18

Listening First

> You must all be quick to listen, slow to speak, and slow to get angry. Human anger does not produce the righteousness God desires. JAMES 1:19-20

My father, Wilbur Dungy, always worked hard to impress this scriptural teaching upon me. He was a man of few words by nature anyway, but I know he believed that the more he listened, the more he learned, which benefited him as a teacher and pleased him as a life-long learner. In addition, he wanted to give himself an opportunity to process information before he spoke. And so the more he listened and thought through what he heard in any setting, the more likely he could bring wisdom to the situation by responding intelligently and thoughtfully, rather than simply reacting in the emotion of the moment.

I think I learned well from my dad. People told me that when they saw me on television during games, I was rarely the animated coach they were used to seeing. The fact is, most of the time on the sidelines I was *listening*—to coaches, players, and even to officials—trying to take in information to plot our next move.

As for getting angry, I tried to keep that in check as well. As one coach shared with me, he once got so angry he was yelling at the officials and ran out of time to call his next play, let alone give any thought to what play to call before calling it. My dad always asked me, "What can you do to make the situation better?" On the football field, I could remain angry about what just happened, but the game goes on. I needed to use the information I had to make the next outcome better.

Do you need to improve your listening skills? It's one of the least-used skills that people have. Learn to know when you should stop talking and start listening.

UNCOMMON KEY > *Communication is made up of talking and listening, listening and talking. Do less talking—and more listening—today.*

June 19

"I Spy" Blessings All around Me

> Then God looked over all he had made, and he saw that it was very good! . . . So the creation
> of the heavens and the earth and everything in them was completed. On the seventh day
> God had finished his work of creation, so he rested from all his work. And God blessed the
> seventh day and declared it holy, because it was the day when he rested from all his work of
> creation. GENESIS 1:31–2:3

It's another day. How is it shaping up for you? Does it look like a good one? Maybe all
you can see are a calendar full of appointments and a day full of challenges. We've all had
those days, and they'll happen again. Still, here's a suggestion. As important as your scheduled time may be, take time each day to look around and acknowledge your blessings. It's
an exercise guaranteed to rejuvenate you as you think of all that God has given you and
say thanks. And as you do, start looking up close—within the gift of your family.

Before you exclaim, "I don't have time," look at your computer. Do you have a screen-
saver picture of your family at your favorite vacation spot? A snapshot of your pet? Your
children's favorite teams?

Now look at your desk. How about that framed photo of your family? Do you consider them a blessing in your life? The blessings of God are all around you, and every day
is the perfect time to celebrate them. Why? Because He created them especially for you.

It's the blessings we find in a hope-filled sunrise filtering through our windows or the
wrinkled red face of a newborn baby. In a grandmother's gentle smile or the trusting laugh
of a child.

We find the blessings of God in a table full of food and in those members of the
family we share it with. In the opportunity to watch our sons' baseball games or to love
our adult children, because we missed the opportunities to fully love them as they grew.
Maybe we get the "second chance" in the blessing of our grandchildren, to love them
no-holds-barred.

Speaking of kids: their sense of awe and wonder has to make God smile. They can
rattle off big and small things that can be considered a blessing from God, like dolphins
unexpectedly breaking the surface of the bay, or the twinkle of stars millions of miles away,
right where we left them the night before. Take a cue from them, and I think you'll come
up with an endless list.

So no matter what you may be facing right now, take a few minutes, look around at all
that God has created, thank Him, and savor the gift.

Don't get so wrapped up in today's worries or tomorrow's "urgent" priorities that you
miss the beautiful things right in front of you.

UNCOMMON KEY > *Don't let a day go by without naming at least one of God's
blessings in your life. The evidence is all around you. Start with His creation, then move on to
your family; it won't take long for you to lose count.*

June 20

The Friends Who Matter

> So Jonathan made a solemn pact with David, saying, "May the LORD destroy all your enemies!" And Jonathan made David reaffirm his vow of friendship again, for Jonathan loved David as he loved himself. 1 SAMUEL 20:16-17

In the work that I do, I've had plenty of opportunities to rub shoulders with people of high status. I could easily have chosen to be friends only with those considered by society to be "important." But that's not how I choose my friends. I look for people of character whose company I enjoy. Some of those people are famous and influential, others are not. I appreciate the people in my life for the ways they live according to their character and values and in the process, shape and reinforce mine.

My parents always discouraged us from hanging around people who didn't share our values. We knew to be friendly to everyone but not to become friends with everyone. Instead, we were encouraged to hang out with people whose inner cores would build us up. And I still look for that today.

That's why I always enjoyed attending the coaches' camps put on each year by the Fellowship of Christian Athletes. No one cares about status at those camps. NFL coaches interact with high school assistant coaches. Division I college coaches aren't distinguished from small-school coaches. You wouldn't be able to tell who's who simply by listening to their conversations because they are all just guys who enjoy football, helping young men, and living for Christ. Their achievements and their status take a backseat to the more important things.

The short week spent together at these camps gives me much-needed encouragement. I share the same values with the friends I've met there, and they build me up. Just being with them reminds me of the important things in life and reinforces the values I've chosen to have.

When you choose your friends based on their values and not their status, being with them will recharge your batteries and help keep you grounded in a world in which status is much too highly valued.

UNCOMMON KEY > *Choose your friends because you enjoy their company, not because their company makes you look better. Spending time with those who share your values creates an environment for solid friendships to grow.*

June 21

Don't Let Your Guard Down

| Be on guard. Stand firm in the faith. Be courageous. Be strong. 1 CORINTHIANS 16:13

There is so much that the apostle Paul packs into this warning to the church at Corinth. In his final words to the Corinthian believers, he urges them to be vigilant: always on guard and watchful. And as they do so, to also be courageous and strong.

The cautionary words are rendered "be on the alert" in other translations. *The Message* says to "keep your eyes open." No matter how it's phrased, the bottom line is that as we attempt to live the way Christ calls us to live, we need to expect a constant attack from the forces for evil. Satan will be continually out to get us, to create doubt in our personal faith, and to destroy us physically, emotionally, intellectually, and spiritually—in any way, by any means that he can.

The more closely aligned we feel with God in our walk of faith and the more we seem to be doing for His Kingdom, the more severe the attacks will be. Attacks challenging our integrity and our personal faith. Attacks that dangle temptation in front of our eyes, appealing to the areas of our greatest weakness. Satan has a mission: to destroy not only our lives, but also our credibility.

Do you know where Satan is doing his work most frequently? In Christ's church. If he can cause destruction and chaos in Christ's instrument for spreading the gospel throughout the world—by causing dissension, pride, self-centeredness, biblically incorrect teaching, and loss of passion—then he knows he will affect the influence of God's Kingdom.

Be on guard.

UNCOMMON KEY > *Satan is always on the prowl, looking for people and settings to destroy. And there is no more likely target for his evil ways than the church of Jesus Christ. Be on your guard and stand firm against his cunning, insidious, and evil ways so you can influence others for good.*

June 22

Substance and Style

> Don't worry about these things, saying, "What will we eat? What will we drink? What will we wear?" These things dominate the thoughts of unbelievers, but your heavenly Father already knows all your needs. MATTHEW 6:31-32

Our search for significance shows up in a lot of misdirected ways. We've talked about the trappings of status, style, wealth, and the appearance of success as pursuits that will not satisfy us in the long run. There's nothing wrong with enjoying life, but when having the right car, the right clothes, the right neighborhood, or even the right partner becomes part of our identity, we're attaching our significance to things that won't last very long. That's why so many football players have trouble when they leave the game. When they lose their status, they lose their sense of significance and feel worthless. Clearly that isn't a problem unique to pro athletes; it's common in all walks of life.

I don't know anyone who says his or her mission in life is to choose style over substance, but that's how many people live. And that keeps them from valuing the things that really do have worth. It shapes their decisions about relationships, careers, where to live, how to raise their kids, and virtually everything else. A lot of people want to be good parents, loyal and committed spouses, mentors to others, and good friends to all, but many don't actually do what is necessary to become those things. They are too busy trying to impress others, establish their lifestyles, and add to their possessions. The result is that the ideal of being people of substance takes a backseat to being people of style. They try to serve two masters, and the things important to the true Master get neglected.

If we really want to live lives of significance, we need to value what God values and choose to live according to those values above all else. That means daily making conscious choices between substance and style: using money to meet someone's needs rather than catering to our wants, spending time encouraging and strengthening someone else's life instead of wasting time on some less important activity, and so on. Either substance or style will come first in our lives—we can't serve both equally. One of those masters will undermine our sense of significance; the other will lead us directly to it.

UNCOMMON KEY > *True significance comes by not only knowing what's worthwhile but also choosing it. Where do money and material things rank on your significance list? What about helping a friend in need or surprising your family with a day focused completely on them? If you need to make changes to your list, do it now.*

June 23

Meekness Is Not Another Word for Weakness

| God blesses those who are humble, for they will inherit the whole earth. **MATTHEW 5:5**

The Jews who lived in Jesus' day had been eagerly anticipating the Messiah as the fulfillment of Isaiah's prophecy of "the Spirit of the Sovereign LORD" being upon God's servant, a message spoken more than four hundred years earlier. They assumed that the Messiah would rule and deal gently with them and harshly with their oppressors.

None of them anticipated the Messiah Himself would be a humble and meek person and would suggest their lives would be blessed if their behavior displayed meekness too. They understood military and miracle power; they even understood the power of compromise, but they did not understand or agree with the power of meekness.

Meekness wasn't a common trait found in a powerful leader. And then Jesus was born in a manger. Suddenly something special turned the mundane into the majestic.

And that is often how God does what God does, through the ordinary and the common—transforming it into the majestic and eternal. Simple tools, through gentle and pure lives, like the baby born in Bethlehem; simple moments, like that moment when God came to earth in a dingy, dank stable.

Meekness, gentleness, and humility are not the first words you might encounter in trying to characterize the professional athlete who often relies on strength, speed, toughness, and confidence—even cockiness, perhaps, at times—to be able to excel.

But meekness is the very character quality that we all should have.

Meek people realize their position before God and gladly live it out before their fellow human beings. They do not look down on themselves, but they do not think too highly of themselves either. Their focus remains on God. They know their gifts and abilities come from God. They remember that where they want to be is standing before a Holy God, available to Him, allowing Him to flow and work through them for His glory, not for self or societal adulation. They don't carry a microphone around with them to tell others of their deeds.

The spirit of meekness before God is found in the Spirit of Christ, who gave His life as a sacrifice for you and for me. Clearly, the meekness Jesus displays is not weakness, but a strength to aspire to make our own.

Do you know anyone who is meek and humble? Can you see where their strength lies?

UNCOMMON KEY > *What do you need to be more humble about today? When you are meek and humble, you are acknowledging that it is all about God, not you. That's where the power to live each day will come from.*

June 24

Faith That Dispels Doubt

It is impossible to please God without faith. Anyone who wants to come to him must believe that God exists and that he rewards those who sincerely seek him. HEBREWS 11:6

Do you have moments of doubt? Doubt always seems to stick its destructive head into all we are trying to do. That's where faith comes in. Faith isn't the absence of doubt, but it reaches beyond doubt and toward that which we believe to be true. Or as the writer of Hebrews puts it, "Faith is the confidence that what we hope for will actually happen; it gives us assurance about things we cannot see" (11:1).

On the football field, I'm sure our guys had occasional moments of doubt before the game got started, especially when we played the New England Patriots. Since we'd lost to them so many times in a row, the Colts had to push that aside and replace our doubts with information we knew to be true. By creating a vision of what the desired outcome would look like and focusing on those things that we knew we could accomplish, there was little room left for doubt.

In the 2006 AFC Championship Game, I was convinced it was our time to end our losing streak. I had faith it was "our time." However, when we fell behind 21–3 in the first half, I confess that I had serious doubts. Thankfully, our guys held on to the vision long enough for those doubts to pass.

I like the story of the perpetual optimist. He fell off the roof of a ten-story building and still had a smile on his face when he passed the fifth floor on the way down. When someone yelled out the window, "How are you?" he answered, "Okay so far!" That may seem to be an unrealistic faith that flies in the face of scientific knowledge—gravity. But it's still faith. Many of us don't know how a plane takes off, stays in the air, and lands, yet we step on the plane in faith that it will fly.

Doesn't it make even more sense to believe the promises of the Creator of the universe, whose work is visible all around us?

UNCOMMON KEY > *The moment you feel doubt overtaking you, pray for an extra measure of faith. Then reevaluate the situation with God's guidance.*

June 25

Well-Executed

> A person standing alone can be attacked and defeated, but two can stand back-to-back and conquer. Three are even better, for a triple-braided cord is not easily broken.
> ECCLESIASTES 4:12

I have some very good friends who coach or play baseball at many different levels, including within the major leagues. I don't pretend to know much about baseball—they do. I enjoy baseball, but I don't know it as well as I know football, so I don't appreciate all the nuances of the game that occur inning by inning.

Even though it is a team sport, it seems to the casual observer that baseball is a game played by nine individuals on the field together—until you watch closely and realize that like other team sports, it really is all about the *team*.

The classic case is demonstrated in the cutoff play. Ninth inning with the tying run on second. On a sharp single to left, the pieces begin to move: an outfielder moves to get the ball and throw it, while infielders move to various places to receive the ball; still others, who aren't directly in the play, move into position to catch overthrows. In the meantime the batter, who now represents the potential winning run, is rounding the bases. The first baseman yells, "Two! Two!" signaling to the catcher that the runner is heading for second.

This is where a perfectly executed cutoff play comes into action. The catcher sees that the runner from second will beat the throw and yells, "Cut two!" a few times to the third baseman, who has moved onto the infield grass in line with the throw from left. The throw—properly made—is low enough so the third baseman can catch it and throw to the second baseman to tag the batter out as he tries to slide in the bag.

No one could have done it by himself. Nor with two of nine players. Instead, it took the left fielder, shortstop, pitcher, first baseman, catcher, third baseman, second baseman, center fielder, and right fielder. All nine.

All nine players involved in a cutoff play executed after a base hit. That's what community and teamwork should look like in the Kingdom of God. We shouldn't do it alone—we *can't* do it alone.

UNCOMMON KEY > *Life is meant to be lived in community, with people whom you trust and can count on. Are you part of a faith community? If not, start looking for a place to make your contribution to the team.*

June 26

The Promise of a New Day

> You are a chosen people. You are . . . God's very own possession. As a result, you can show others the goodness of God, for he called you out of the darkness into his wonderful light.
> 1 PETER 2:9

I don't know if you have ever been at a crossroads like the one I faced. I vividly remember the moment in my life, in August 1980, when I had reached the end of my career as a football player. I remember standing in the locker room after my final release with an enormous amount of concern for the uncertainty I was facing, wondering what was next.

I had always played football, and now that seemed to be over.

I had been blessed to receive a football scholarship to the University of Minnesota out of high school and after playing out my eligibility and getting my degree, to play for three years in the National Football League. Those opportunities seemed to easily follow one after the other, and now I faced what definitely seemed to be a new phase in my life—and I wasn't at all sure what path I was to follow. It had all been so easy up to that point. Each opportunity had seemed almost preselected for me—I would continue to play football.

And then it was over. Needless to say, it created a couple of anxious and sleepless nights for me. In my better moments, I knew God was in control and had a plan. For the first time in my life, though, I didn't know what it was. Little did I know that God had twenty-eight years of football *coaching* in store for me.

Young people confront this dilemma a lot. They finish high school and then college—but what's next? It's hard for them to see beyond the uncertainty of the next day. After a major disappointment or setback, it's hard for them to see the bright side. The future may seem murky, or at worst bleak, but tomorrow's a completely new day.

God promises that He has each of our days firmly in His hands.

UNCOMMON KEY > *Write "God has it covered" on your calendar for today and tomorrow. Your present and your future are in His hands. Have you made your reservation with Him for eternity?*

June 27

Lonely at the Top

> Zacchaeus stood before the Lord and said, "I will give half my wealth to the poor, Lord, and if I have cheated people on their taxes, I will give them back four times as much!" Jesus responded, "Salvation has come to this home today, for this man has shown himself to be a true son of Abraham. For the Son of Man came to seek and save those who are lost."
>
> LUKE 19:8-10

We have all heard the term "down and out." We have probably used it ourselves to refer to people who are having a tough go of life and need a lift. Churches and other ministries develop programs to reach folks down on their luck: soup kitchens, homeless shelters, community food and clothing ministries, housing assistance. All sorts of things have been developed through the years to reach those who are "down and out," including sharing the love of Christ with them.

I have a friend who has coined the phrase "up and out," referring to another group of folks who seem to have it all together: the wealthy, well-off, and respected people, in terms of worldly things. Luke 19 introduces us to one such man—the wealthy tax collector Zacchaeus, who was lost and out of touch with the living God. People like Zacchaeus may seem to have it all together, but when all the fanfare subsides and the day's activities are done, they are empty and all alone.

They may seem unapproachable from a distance, but getting up close and personal may reveal that they are in desperate need of someone who really cares for them and of the touch of God. Some, like Zacchaeus, respond to Him with unbridled gratitude. So don't shy away from someone because of their "untouchable" status. Maybe your attempt at connecting with the person will turn into a friendship that goes somewhere, maybe not. But it's certainly worth a try.

Unfortunately, I saw this all too often in my thirty-one years in the NFL. People the world assumed had everything—wealth, notoriety, and public adoration—were lonely and hurting inside. I was often reminded of Christ's question, "What do you benefit if you gain the whole world but lose your own soul?" (Matthew 16:26).

We should all strive to stay connected to the good things around us—our family and friends who have been with us throughout our journey—and seek to add other friends who will have a positive impact on us. In addition, we need to be proactive in seeking out and encouraging others, helping to keep them from becoming disconnected themselves.

Don't ever assume that someone doesn't need an encouraging word or your friendship, no matter what that person's status might be.

UNCOMMON KEY > *If you work for a large company, ask someone at the top if there is anything in his or her life that the person would appreciate prayer for. That simple request often breaks down walls and may eventually lead to more spiritual discussions.*

June 28

Work in Progress

> I am certain that God, who began the good work within you, will continue his work until it is finally finished on the day when Christ Jesus returns. PHILIPPIANS 1:6

It certainly has happened to me, and I'm certain it has happened to you. Life hits us with something unexpected, unplanned, and unpleasant, and we're clueless as to why it has happened or for what purpose. And even though I don't welcome those types of circumstances, I have been around long enough to know that there is a godly purpose—Christ will continue to work in us through those situations until His work is complete. What happens in the journey of faith may seem unfair or even painful at times. But I truly believe it is all part of God's overall plan for my good and the good of others who love Him.

I've gone through professional heartaches—numerous losses in the playoffs and being fired from my position. I've been greatly disappointed by players who have let me down off the field. What I have experienced isn't really any different from what anyone else has experienced; it's just a different set of challenges in life to deal with and overcome.

I've also gone through personal heartaches, including the deaths of family and loved ones. I have experienced real struggles from time to time that made no sense. Thankfully, most days aren't like that. But the challenges in all parts of my life sometimes seem to be never-ending.

In April of 2010, a good friend of mine died suddenly and unexpectedly—Keli McGregor, the president of the Colorado Rockies. Keli was only forty-eight years old and the picture of health. In fact, friends who knew about his stint as a player in the National Football League would joke that Keli looked like he could still play if he wanted to. Keli's wife and family and friends could make no sense of their untimely loss and questioned how something so tragic could be part of God's overall plan for the good for those who love Him.

We don't always know the answers—we only know that God is working on our behalf, for our good, through it all.

UNCOMMON KEY > *Philippians 1:6 is a verse worth memorizing, if you haven't done so already. There will be so many times in your life when you will be holding on to the promise that God is working on your behalf if you follow Him.*

June 29

Well Done

> The master said, "Well done, my good and faithful servant. You have been faithful in handling this small amount, so now I will give you many more responsibilities. Let's celebrate together!" MATTHEW 25:23

As the clock ticked down at the end of our Super Bowl win over the Chicago Bears in February 2007, we hugged each other. It was such a spectacular moment for the Indianapolis Colts to finally finish a season the way we had hoped. All the details we had worked on for so many months, all the way back to the off-season conditioning in February 2006. All the meetings and game preparation, all the film the coaches watched for months up until just two days earlier. The rehabilitation of injuries for so many guys. Fighting through illnesses. On and on. All of it had culminated in this celebratory moment.

"Well done." "Congratulations." "You finished what we set out to do," I told the players.

It was glorious. But it was only a fraction of what I anticipate we'll see when we finish this life and participate in the ultimate celebration.

I anticipate a scene in heaven when God tells us, "Well done, my good and faithful servants. Well done."

It was special to share that feeling of accomplishment with each other after the Super Bowl victory, but I can only imagine how spectacular it will be to hear those words from God!

But don't get me wrong—His "well done" comes in large part through grace. I can never overcome my sin and have Him say "well done" on my merits alone. I can remain faithful and stay on course as best as I can, knowing that Christ will present me to His Father as "blameless" and "without a single fault" (Colossians 1:22; Jude 1:24). I will strive to show Christ's love for me through my compassion for others and my faithfulness to Him, even though I know my attempts will always fall short.

But I will keep trying and will look forward to that glorious day—well done, indeed!

What have you celebrated recently that makes you think, *It couldn't get any better than this*? It certainly does. And how you live your life makes the difference.

UNCOMMON KEY > *Keep striving each day to stay in God's will and accomplish things for Him. And know that one day you will stand before Him and hear the words, "Well done."*

June 30

Naturally Sharpened

> Therefore I, a prisoner for serving the Lord, beg you to lead a life worthy of your calling, for you have been called by God. **Always be humble and gentle.** EPHESIANS 4:1-2

When I was growing up, I was mesmerized by the talk that went on inside our local barbershop, and I especially enjoyed listening to my barber, Mr. Hampton. He was another of those people in my life who probably didn't realize the platform he had but used it to impact many people anyway. I often got my hair cut on Fridays before football games, and Mr. Hampton would always wish me well.

But he did much more than that. He talked with me about sports, classes, girls, and anything else that was going on in my life. He would encourage me, offer advice, and show that he cared. In some ways, it was like the stereotypical barbershop you see in movies, with practical wisdom flying around as freely as the freshly cut hair. But it was real and honest, and it made a difference to guys like me. Whether he was aware of it or not, Mr. Hampton had an audience with men, especially young ones, and used it to influence and impact our lives. Many of us would come in thinking we were getting a haircut, but we left with so much more.

Mr. Hampton didn't seem concerned with impressing people with status or fulfilling a certain role. He believed that if he simply listened and showed that he cared, God would sort out the rest. As he faithfully did the best he could at cutting hair, he was able to be involved in the lives of those who came into his shop. And everyone who walked in the door would leave feeling a little better about life than when they came in.

That's a wise way to live. God has put each of us in a place where no one else stands. There are people around us who will look up to us, listen to us, and follow our example for no other reasons than because we are available, have shown that we care, and have offered whatever wisdom we have. That's a role worth appreciating—and using to build into the lives of others.

UNCOMMON KEY > *You stand where no one else stands in the lives of those around you. Make a point to engage in conversation as often as you can, sharing lessons from life experiences. You can make a positive difference.*

July 1

I've Got Friends in Praying Places

> When you pray, don't be like the hypocrites who love to pray publicly on street corners and in the synagogues where everyone can see them. I tell you the truth, that is all the reward they will ever get. But when you pray, go away by yourself, shut the door behind you, and pray to your Father in private. Then your Father, who sees everything, will reward you.
>
> MATTHEW 6:5-6

We pray as a family before every meal, even in public. I've had people watch us do so and comment later that they appreciated our boldness. Their comments have been affirming for me and I hope for them, but we don't do it for the comments.

So which is it? Is public prayer a witness or an act of pride? Or is it something else—like an act of love and affection?

Could it be all of the above or any one of the above? I suppose it could. I think it depends entirely on the state of our hearts as to why we pray—whether it is in public or private. If we as a family thank God for our blessings on a regular basis, I don't think we need to, or should, stop doing that when we're out in public. If, however, our motivation for praying in public is to be seen and to demonstrate to others that we are a family who prays to God, then maybe we've got a problem. Because then it seems to be about us. And if it's about us—well, then, it probably is not about God.

After all, praying is merely speaking with God, spending time with Him. But praying to God is also, and most importantly, an act of love and affection. Praying to God is an act of trust in the one who gives us life. Praying to God is an act of humble surrender to the one who is in charge of it all and who created it all. If that's where our focus stays, then these other thoughts shouldn't matter. If we're worried about what others are thinking of our words or whether we are being watched, then our focus has changed.

UNCOMMON KEY > *Praying to God is a matter of the heart—wherever and whenever you pray—a heart that loves, trusts, and surrenders to Him. Make sure your heart is right before bowing your head or closing your eyes.*

July 2

Keeping Your Wellspring Clean

Listen carefully to my words. Don't lose sight of them. Let them penetrate deep into your heart, for they bring life to those who find them, and healing to their whole body. Guard your heart above all else, for it determines the course of your life. PROVERBS 4:20-23

Living in Florida makes a person very aware of water. Lakes, rivers, the ocean. Droughts, hurricanes, and thunderstorms. One of the things impressed upon residents is that we've got to be careful about our water supply—how we use and conserve it and how we care for it. We always need to be vigilant against overuse. And although homeowners are permitted to use chemicals to treat lawns, any chemicals used too close to wells or the Floridan aquifer—the main supply of our drinking water that sits beneath all of Florida, as well as parts of Georgia, South Carolina, Alabama, and Mississippi—can taint that supply, creating serious danger for everyone.

It's not unlike the flow of negative influences into your heart. People today don't guard their hearts carefully. The analogy in today's verses is like a sentry standing at his post to guard your heart from evil influences, invasion by ungodly thoughts, and for your children, things that could rob them of their innocence.

No matter how old we are—young, middle-aged, or older—I believe we give our hearts away too quickly. We open our hearts too readily and easily to inappropriate influences—things like television shows where characters use inappropriate language or behave suggestively, especially in front of our children and youth. Perhaps it's simply inappropriate associations with others who strip the innocence from us or penetrate our lives, minds, and hearts with ungodly thoughts, words, and deeds and in the process begin to create in us a heart no longer aligned with God. All these things contaminate the "wellspring" of our lives—our hearts.

Think about your emotions that have been damaged—or could be in the future—by allowing the wrong person into your heart. Children and young people are especially vulnerable in this area and need to rely on godly parents to advise them, and to protect their hearts and their innocence. They need direction in the choices they make.

It's time for you to check the doors of your heart. What safeguards do you have in place? Do you need to increase your protection?

UNCOMMON KEY > *Guard your heart and the hearts of the children in your life. Keep a sentry at the door. Your heart is the "wellspring" of your life, the place where God dwells and from which He works through you. Keep it pure and godly.*

July 3

A Cure for Low Self-Esteem

> You made all the delicate, inner parts of my body and knit me together in my mother's womb. . . . You saw me before I was born. Every day of my life was recorded in your book. Every moment was laid out before a single day had passed. PSALM 139:13, 16

So much of what we do as human beings—so many of the mistakes we make and desires we have—flows from having very little self-esteem. It often begins to happen when we are young. Many of us wear masks, strive for unworthy goals, get into bad relationships, compromise our integrity, or just blend in with the crowd because deep down inside we're wounded and needy. We forget who we are: children of God in the family of God.

One of the most important truths I want to impress on you is this: You were created by God. You've probably heard that before—maybe so often that it has lost its meaning. So take a minute to let it sink in. You were created *by God*! Before you were ever born, He knew who you would be. You are designed with a unique combination of abilities, interests, and passions that has never been before and will never be seen in anyone again. He knows every detail of your life and carefully planned the way you were made.

Not only that, you are created for eternal impact. Your one-of-a-kind design was intended to last. He guards over your purpose and destiny, He is aware of all your needs, and He watches you even while you sleep. Jesus told a crowd that God takes care even of the birds of the air and the lilies of the field. If He does that for them, how much more does He do that for you? You are an intentional part of His plan. You are family, and He is your Father; He designed you for incredible purposes.

If that sinks into your heart—really becomes a part of who you are at your core—you will never have problems with low self-esteem. Your heart and mind will be filled with a healthy sense of self-worth that enables you to know your purpose in life and to fulfill it.

UNCOMMON KEY > *God knew you ahead of time and chose to make you. Keep reminding yourself of that truth because it will impact every other area of your life.*

July 4

The Greatest Commandment

> The man answered, "'You must love the LORD your God with all your heart, all your soul, all your strength, and all your mind.' And, 'Love your neighbor as yourself.'" "Right!" Jesus told him. "Do this and you will live!" LUKE 10:27-28

"What is my purpose in life?" It's a question many people ask but few really answer. Some people constantly strive for ways to satisfy themselves—in relationships, careers, possessions, and much more—but that focus on self always ends up being unsatisfying. God created us for something more focused on others and more fulfilling. Jesus made it clear that our purpose is to love God and love others.

What does that look like in our lives? As we pursue God's purpose for us, it helps to ask what kind of world we want to live in. When we look beyond ourselves to see what needs to be done, we will have a much better idea of what God wants us to do. We find fulfillment not only in pursuing ways to improve ourselves but in enriching other people's lives. We've all seen people less fortunate than ourselves, people who seem to have little hope for change unless someone intervenes. We've seen communities and nations go through difficulties and wrestle with problems like starvation or disease that we may never have to worry about. We may not have a full solution to any of these problems, but we can affect lives one at a time. Loving God will fill us with a desire and a vision to improve our homes, our towns, our countries, and the world.

I believe our purpose is to serve God and use whatever He has given us to help others. When we focus on that, we find the joy and abundant life Jesus promised. We find that we are much more fulfilled when we use our passions and abilities to make a difference in someone's life.

You may not reach every goal in life—in fact, you probably won't—but you can fulfill your purpose. When you love God, you are doing what He made you for; and when you love others, you are expressing His own attitude toward them. You can find peace and happiness in the knowledge that you are satisfying your purpose and honoring Him.

UNCOMMON KEY > *Loving God and others is not only the best thing you can do for them, it's the best thing you can do for yourself. As you begin, look first to your friends and how you can serve them.*

July 5

Believe This

> Since you have been raised to new life with Christ, set your sights on the realities of heaven, where Christ sits in the place of honor at God's right hand. Think about the things of heaven, not the things of earth. COLOSSIANS 3:1-2

We know the feeling of being all alone. I certainly know the feeling. We've all been there—at any and every age in life. We find ourselves facing something we hadn't planned on and don't think we can get beyond, hoping a word of wisdom will fall from above. Instead, the clouds continue to swarm, and the sky darkens.

We have found ourselves walking through life, not sure which way to turn for help, not knowing whom to trust, let alone who could possibly help. Too many times we've looked down a long, dark, and winding road stretched out before us, uncertain of where it leads, but knowing we have no choice except to proceed.

And then we read the apostle Paul's words to the Colossians, and that urges us to embrace heavenly thoughts that will guide our actions. All of this is possible because we have a new life and a fresh start in Christ. Because He is risen!

In the darkest moments, the stone was rolled away, and we found that the tomb was empty! We are not alone. In the midst of all the stuff of life that overwhelms us, we know we have been raised to a new life in Christ—and we are not alone. Knowing that provides us with the motivation to press on, to punch through the gathering clouds—knowing that He will provide a way through into the sunshine of a brand-new day.

He is risen! For you and for me.

That's the message of Christ as He connects to each of us and, in particular, to that one person among us who is in need. That one person struggling to take just one more step.

Have you been there? Have you felt all alone, with hopelessness circling around you for the final descent? The message of Christ today and all the way to the end of your life and into eternity is that hope reigns. Hopelessness has been defeated.

UNCOMMON KEY > *Feeling all alone? Look again—it's not so. Do yourself a favor and never believe that again. Christ is risen.*

July 6

Left to Speak

> Mordecai sent this reply to Esther: "Don't think for a moment that because you're in the palace you will escape when all other Jews are killed. If you keep quiet at a time like this, deliverance and relief for the Jews will arise from some other place, but you and your relatives will die. Who knows if perhaps you were made queen for just such a time as this?" ESTHER 4:13-14

I had the opportunity to visit the United States Holocaust Memorial Museum in Washington, DC, when I was in the nation's capital. The moment you enter the building, you can't help but be swept back in time—to a horrifying time in world history. Not only does the museum tell the wrenching story of the Holocaust, but through leadership-training programs, it helps people in many walks of life to commit to preserving the core value of fighting against hatred and genocide and promoting human dignity.

The book of Esther relates a story of ethnic hatred that started with one man, Haman, an official in the court of King Xerxes of Persia. At first, Haman's seething rage was focused on one person—Mordecai, a Jew—but it soon escalated to a plot of annihilating all Jews. Esther, chosen by King Xerxes to be his queen, was Mordecai's cousin. Through his urging, she courageously uncovered the evil plan to the king and saved the Jewish people.

When we stop to think about it, our lives could be summarized just like the story of Esther. We were placed where we are for such a time as this. Just as God knew what Esther would face and what the world would be like then, He knows what the world will be like for us and how we can make a difference.

He requires that we respond to the call of duty on our lives. Indifference is not an option because it is the first step toward abdicating our personal and moral responsibility toward others. This call of duty is an innate sense created within us to aid others, to lift them up, and to fan the flicker of hope in them.

As you leave the main exhibit in the Holocaust Museum, you read the words by Pastor Martin Niemöller:

> In Germany, the Nazis came for the Communists, and I didn't speak up because I wasn't a Communist. Then they came for the Jews, and I didn't speak up because I wasn't a Jew. Then they came for the trade unionists, and I didn't speak up because I was a Protestant. Then they came for me, and by that time there was no one left to speak.

This will never happen again, you say. We know better, don't we? Take a look around and make sure.

Your life and mine—for such a time as this.

UNCOMMON KEY > *Never become indifferent toward people or how you treat them. Instead, consider how you might be able to help them. God may have put you in their paths for such a time as this.*

July 7

Preparation for the Battlefield

> Your eye is a lamp that provides light for your body. When your eye is good, your whole body is filled with light. But when your eye is bad, your whole body is filled with darkness. MATTHEW 6:22-23

Whatever is evil, vengeful, lustful, tempting, or otherwise ungodly tends to stick in our minds or hearts and grow. We need to be vigilant not to let that happen.

This applies to all kinds of inappropriate thoughts—anger, bitterness, vengeance, jealousy, criticism, negativity, and on and on. But this also applies to lust and pornography, which can turn into an addiction as real and as strong as an addiction to alcohol or drugs. Pornography is easy to access and is considered harmless by many, so it can take residence in your mind before you realize it's a problem. You don't have to be in an adult bookstore or an X-rated movie to be tempted by it. It gets into our lives in lots of ways. It's subtle. But it can be extremely damaging, and the best way to keep it from becoming a problem is to avoid it altogether.

As a father, I have to be sensitive to the ways our culture handles this issue. As easily tempted as we adults can be in this area, our kids are more so. And it isn't just a matter of pornography, but of decency. If I put that swimsuit issue of a familiar sports magazine on my coffee table, what message am I giving to my son about having a pure heart? What message am I giving my daughter about how women are perceived? And how am I allowing myself to be tempted? We have to protect our own minds and the minds of our kids. It often begins with those "small things" chipping away at the boundaries we should keep.

The best way to protect those boundaries is to pray early and often. Whenever you sense an inappropriate thought forming, ask God to take it from you and cleanse your mind of it. Envision your mind and your heart as God's treasured territory, and do whatever it takes to protect that territory. Whenever you're confronted with an impure thought, reject it and replace it with something much more positive. Teach your kids how to redirect their thoughts and discipline themselves in truth. Whatever it takes, prevent infiltration.

UNCOMMON KEY > *Your mind can be a battlefield. Protect it from impurities and fill it with truth. If that means changing some things that seem "innocent," do it today.*

July 8

Ready or Not . . .

> You know quite well that the day of the Lord's return will come unexpectedly,
> like a thief in the night. . . . So be on your guard. . . . Stay alert and be clearheaded.
> 1 THESSALONIANS 5:2, 6

We don't know the hour that Christ will return, but rather that He will sneak in "like a thief in the night." We should always be ready for that surprise arrival.

It's a lot like the opening kickoff of a game. Bum Phillips, the former head coach of the old Houston Oilers (now the Tennessee Titans) used to say in his pregame pep talks that the kickoff was coming shortly whether we were ready or not, so we shouldn't think about just warming up; we needed to get ready to play. Of course, when the kickoff came, we hadn't yet had a chance to see what the other team has planned for us, so we must be ready for anything—whether an onside kick or crafty return or a different blocking scheme.

When I was still with the Indianapolis Colts, we played the Chicago Bears in the 2007 Super Bowl in Miami, Florida, on a rainy night. It was the first time a Super Bowl had been played in the rain. The Bears had a dangerous returner by the name of Devin Hester, and I was convinced we had the right scheme to stop him on the kickoff. In previous games, other teams had decided not to kick off to him so they wouldn't give him a chance to burn them with a big return, but I was confident in what we had planned to contain him. Besides, on a wet field, he wouldn't be nearly as elusive, so we opened the game kicking the ball deep and right to him.

Seconds later, it was 7–0 Bears, as Hester ran the kickoff all the way back for a touchdown. I shouldn't have been surprised.

That was the last time we kicked the ball to him in the Super Bowl that night.

Similarly, Jesus' return may surprise you in a manner much like that. Therefore, you should always be ready.

UNCOMMON KEY > *Consider what you and your family need to do to be prepared for Christ's return. It might happen later today, tomorrow, or next week—you never know. Get ready.*

July 9

Breaking Free from Your Past

> No, dear brothers and sisters, I have not achieved it, but I focus on this one thing: Forgetting the past and looking forward to what lies ahead.   PHILIPPIANS 3:13

Press on, move ahead. Forget what is behind—whether it's good or bad, whether anything made any sense at all, yesterday is done and gone. That was one of the things I always tried to impress upon my teams. No matter what happened on Sunday—even if it was a devastating, last-second loss—by Monday night they had to let it go. Focusing on last week's game would not help them prepare for the next one.

We can't replay what's past or change what occurred. We want to think we can, we wish we could, often out of a sense of guilt or loss for whatever happened. It probably explains why so many popular movies have dealt with the subject, like *Back to the Future*, *Mr. Destiny*, or *Sliding Doors*. But as the apostle Paul recognized, we're just not going to change the past.

And that's why Paul makes the only rational decision he can make and offers the same to us, as well: he forgets the past and presses ahead. If there's anyone who could have clung to the past—the decisions he'd made, the people who'd wronged him—it would have been Paul. After Paul's conversion on the road to Damascus, he became hunted and persecuted with the same zeal with which he hunted and persecuted Christ's followers. Now Paul followed Christ and served the believers called by Christ to touch the world. Time and again Paul was wrongfully imprisoned or beaten nearly to death for his new life, witness, and uncompromising testimony for Christ.

Where are you today in your journey with Christ? Are you stuck in the past, holding on to regrets, remorse, or feelings of guilt for things you should have done or people you should have spent more time with? Are you still holding on to grudges against someone else for something they did to you, which they have long ago forgotten?

Forget it, and press on to reach the heavenly prize of a continuing relationship with the Lord Jesus Christ.

UNCOMMON KEY > *Release your past by giving it to Him, and press on to reach the heavenly prize of being in His presence forever.*

July 10

Complementary Gifts

"A man leaves his father and mother and is joined to his wife, and the two are united into one." This is a great mystery, but it is an illustration of the way Christ and the church are one. So again I say, each man must love his wife as he loves himself, and the wife must respect her husband. EPHESIANS 5:31-33

Talking about the roles of men and women in marriage can stir up a lot of controversy. The idea of well-defined roles makes many of us uncomfortable in this day and age, me included. What concerns me is that these discussions tend to focus on who gets to be in charge. But the Bible makes it clear that both husbands and wives are supposed to be looking out for each other's well-being, not concentrating on who has the power. That means, as a husband, I'm supposed to be doing everything for the good of my wife.

Look at it another way: God is not only my Father, He's also my spouse's Father. That means He's my Father-in-law. That's a pretty heavy responsibility. That motivates me to serve, not to figure out who's in charge.

One of God's gifts to us in marriage is the idea of roles— that each of us brings something unique to the partnership. Putting others first is never easy, and it can be especially taxing in the context of marriage—an up-close-and-personal, day-after-day relationship. In that kind of bond, you can't take a break from looking out for each other. Your spouse's well-being is just as important to you as your own.

Try this exercise to help you see how your partnership works. Take a look in the mirror and recall all the things you are good at—in your career, at home, with the children, at church, and around the neighborhood. Think about the things you love to do—those things you're passionate about. Then think about the things you aren't so good at or that you never look forward to doing.

Now take a moment to go through the exact same questions about your spouse. Do you see how you fit together? The picture that emerges will tell you a lot about your roles—and how you can put each other first. Remember above all that your role in marriage is for your spouse's benefit.

UNCOMMON KEY > *Your spouse's well-being is directly related to yours. Seek to fulfill your role in your home, not solely for your benefit, but for the benefit of everyone in your family.*

July 11

The Importance of Christian Community

> And let us not neglect our meeting together, as some people do, but encourage one another, especially now that the day of his return is drawing near. HEBREWS 10:25

William Rehnquist, the late chief justice of the United States, was so often alone in his opinions that his law clerks presented him with a Lone Ranger action figure. Similarly, William O. Douglas, an associate justice on the Supreme Court, authored more dissents than any other justice in the Supreme Court's history. Although they engaged and collaborated with their fellow justices, these men often rendered their own, differing opinions in the end.

We're really not that different in our relationship with each other as believers and followers of Jesus Christ.

As Christians, it's easy to fall into patterns where we aren't in regular fellowship with others. We go it alone a great deal of the time. Even when we're members who regularly attend church with a local body of believers, we still do little in the way of engaging others and growing together in our faith. God, however, knows that we need community, and we need to realize it as well.

Jesus surrounded Himself with a close band of believers and spent time with them—teaching, equipping, sharing with, and engaging them in the culture of the day. In the days soon after Christ ascended into heaven, people were repenting and being baptized and being added by the thousands to the number of those who were followers of Christ. The author of Hebrews urged the early church to "not neglect . . . meeting together" (Hebrews 10:25).

In Acts we read, "All the believers devoted themselves to the apostles' teaching, and to fellowship, and to sharing in meals (including the Lord's Supper), and to prayer" (Acts 2:42). They were empowered in their communion with each other and grew exponentially, building into each other's lives and strengthening each other, all in preparation for spreading the message of Good News and helping the poor, the widows, the sick, and those in need.

If your fellowship with other Christians has been lax lately because you don't think you need them or they need you, think again. Jesus wasn't a lone ranger in His ministry; His followers thrive the most in community.

UNCOMMON KEY > *God calls believers to be together as they journey in their relationship with Him. Don't become a lone ranger in your walk with Him.*

July 12

Attitude Instructions

> Always be joyful. Never stop praying. Be thankful in all circumstances, for this is God's will for you who belong to Christ Jesus. 1 THESSALONIANS 5:16-18

These verses are packed with attitude instructions. That's a good thing, because our attitude toward what life throws at us has so much to do with the outcome.

In his book *Man's Search for Meaning*, Viktor Frankl recounts the unspeakable horrors of his longtime imprisonment in Nazi concentration camps like Auschwitz and Dachau, where he was stripped of everything. His father, mother, brother, and wife had died in similar camps. Yet despite losing all his possessions; having all value destroyed; suffering from hunger, cold, and brutality; and expecting his own execution to come at any moment, Frankl still found that life was worth preserving.

In what little there seemed to be left of his life, he found value and hope. Despite his circumstances, he had not been stripped of one of the last human freedoms—"the ability to choose our attitude despite our given set of circumstances."

Frankl's experiences serve as a reminder that even though we can't always choose our circumstances, we can always choose our attitude in the circumstances. We can realize the capacity within each of us, with God's hand on our backs, to rise above those circumstances. Our choice reveals the depth of our inner character directing our lives and will shine brightly in the most dire circumstances, whether the outcome is life or death.

God has given each of us potential—to know Him, to receive Him, and then through Him to make a difference in this world, one person at a time.

UNCOMMON KEY > *Attitude is everything—or at least a great, big piece of everything! Check your attitude as you do small tasks and then take on greater things. Your attitude should be the same for both.*

July 13

Mistaken Identity

> What is the price of two sparrows—one copper coin? But not a single sparrow can fall to the ground without your Father knowing it. And the very hairs on your head are all numbered. So don't be afraid; you are more valuable to God than a whole flock of sparrows. MATTHEW 10:29-31

Children have a lot of dreams. Some want to be pro athletes, or Olympic gold medal winners, or famous singers or actors, or maybe great inventors or explorers. Some want to make lots of money, or live in big houses, or have more cars than they can drive at one time. They often have great dreams, but most of those dreams are related to *doing*, not *being*. They aren't focused on who they should be on the inside—their values and priorities—even though those inner attributes affect everything else. Who they are will shape everything they do.

In our society, this struggle between *being* and *doing* starts early and is often innocently encouraged. We ask our children what they want to be when they grow up much more often than we ask them what kind of person they want to be. And when we say, "What do you want to be?" they know what we really mean: "What job do you want to have?" It's a focus on what they do rather than who they are. And most will spend their lives identifying themselves by what they do.

I never heard Chuck Noll act as if his value as a person was lessened when we lost a game. He was the same person whether we were winning or losing because his self-esteem didn't depend on what he accomplished. And when he retired from football, he didn't lose his identity because his identity was based on something deeper than being a coach. His job didn't define who he was.

That's a great example. The most important thing about you is who you are, not what you do. You may think you'll be satisfied when you accomplish your goals or fulfill the role you've dreamed about, but if you have an unsatisfied heart now, outward accomplishments won't change a thing. Know who you are on the inside and what God has done to make you who you are. That's where your identity comes from.

UNCOMMON KEY > *Who you are is not a vocational question. Your identity is defined by the God who made you, and it doesn't change with circumstances. Remind yourself to not get so caught up in "doing" that you forget about "being."*

July 14

What JB Does Best

> Live wisely among those who are not believers, and make the most of every opportunity. Let your conversation be gracious and attractive so that you will have the right response for everyone. COLOSSIANS 4:5-6

My friend James Brown—JB—of CBS Sports is one of the best examples of someone who is gracious in every opportunity and moment God gives him. He is remarkable with people. The reasons are too many to list, but two things stand out the first time you meet JB: his love of Christ overflows from his life to everyone he meets, and he is absolutely sincere and genuine in all his interactions, no matter who you are.

Another friend of mine, Charley Casserly—now a television analyst but previously a longtime NFL general manager—once said that JB may be the most gracious person he's ever met in his life.

"I've been traveling for a long time and have met a lot of people," Charley says, "but I don't think that I've ever seen anyone treat every person they run across the way that JB does. Regardless of their position or what they can do for him."

Of course, we should all strive to be like that. The way JB treats others everywhere— no matter who they are—flows out of his deeply held belief that every person is a special and sacred creation of God. When we start there, as JB does, we will treat people as Christ treats them and expects us to treat them as well.

JB fancies himself a car guy—he loves restoring old cars. When you talk with him about it, however, you realize that his passion isn't just about the satisfaction of bringing a car back to its original splendor. He says that being around car people is invigorating because he's the one who knows the least about cars. He enjoys the "regularness" of car people sharing their knowledge with him at car shows and just having a chance to hang out together over a shared love of old cars. He may be a TV personality and Harvard-educated, but he knows that every person has something to teach him.

That's JB.

UNCOMMON KEY > *Be a gracious and authentic person for Christ—He can do wonders through your interactions with others for His Kingdom. Be ready to learn and possibly share your own knowledge.*

July 15

Gone Fishin'

> At dawn Jesus was standing on the beach, but the disciples couldn't see who he was. He called out, "Fellows, have you caught any fish?" "No," they replied. Then he said, "Throw out your net on the right-hand side of the boat, and you'll get some!" So they did, and they couldn't haul in the net because there were so many fish in it. JOHN 21:4-6

Fishing? That's what He calls us to do with Him?

Because fishing is my favorite hobby, I can appreciate these verses. Unfortunately, I have spent days on the water when my companions and I just didn't catch anything.

Here, some of the disciples are in a boat on the Sea of Galilee, still grumbling about a disappointing night of fishing. Blame it on luck or the tides, but they had caught nothing. This happened about a week after Jesus had been crucified, buried, and miraculously raised from the tomb and began to reappear to hundreds of people in the area.

Now it is early morning, and the disciples are back at it when they hear someone call out, "Fellows, have you caught any fish?"

"No," came the reply, the disciples not realizing who they were talking to.

"Throw out your net on the right-hand side of the boat, and you'll get some." And indeed they did, more than they could haul in by themselves. As soon as they saw a net teeming with fish, they knew who had given them the fishing tip.

Jesus is simply reminding the disciples of all He had tried to teach them when He was with them before He died. He had built into their lives—selecting and teaching them, equipping and encouraging them, and then sending them into the world. He forbade them to stay in the classroom; He wanted them to have hands-on experience in the field. That's what it was all about. He sent them out to fish for the souls of men, women, and children—as He had demonstrated with them by His side. He sent them out to make a difference in the world. To change lives. To love the unloved. To feed the hungry. To heal the sick.

It's something the Lord asks us to do too: if we faithfully cast out the net, He'll be responsible for what comes back in.

UNCOMMON KEY > *Are you ready to go fishing? Look for places where the "fishing" doesn't seem too promising and watch what God can do through you.*

July 16

Honest Endeavors

| You will know the truth, and the truth will set you free. JOHN 8:32

I thought my dad coined the phrase "the truth shall set you free" because he believed in total honesty. If I came home after curfew, it was much better to tell the truth and suffer the consequences than tell a lie and add that offense to the other. The punishment would always be less if I told the truth than if I had made up an excuse. And my parents would know if I made up an excuse—they seemed to have spies out in the streets reporting back to them about my every move. I learned to live by the concept of "no excuses, no explanations."

I eventually learned that Dad's words were actually a quote from Jesus—and that God is even more interested in my truthfulness than Dad was. Jesus was talking primarily about the importance of learning the truth—the eternal truth of His teaching—but the principle of speaking truth applies to our own words too. God knows that skirting the rules will always come back to hurt us, and our dishonesty will always catch up with us. Whether we're actually doing something illegal or simply cutting corners ethically, the short-term win is never worth the long-term cost. Honesty really is the best policy.

Of course, knowing that our dishonesty will catch up with us is poor motivation for telling the truth. It's better to tell the truth because it's the right thing to do—and because we want to be known as people of integrity. We want others to be able to count on us, we want to set a good example for the young people in our lives, and we want to be looked to for guidance and direction. Most of all, we should want to glorify the God who is the source of truth. We were designed to be reflections of Him. When we don't relate to Him and others in honesty, we're missing our purpose.

The truth really will set you free. Lies are hard to maintain. A pattern of lying can be exhausting. If you want to live in freedom, practice seeking truth in every area of your life—including your own words.

UNCOMMON KEY > *Truth—learning it from God and speaking it to others—is the key to living in freedom.*

July 17

Always by Your Side

> Then He appointed twelve, that they might be with Him and that He might send them out to preach. MARK 3:14, NKJV

Derek Redmond believed he could win a silver medal for Great Britain in the 1992 Olympics in Barcelona. After years of training and multiple operations on his Achilles tendons, he had already won two heats and was running in the semifinals of the 400 meters. But coming out of a turn, he heard a snap, felt a sharp pain in his leg, and dropped in a heap on the track. His hamstring had literally exploded. So had his dreams of a medal.

But Derek was determined to finish. He waved off the race officials running toward him with a stretcher. He slowly limped, even hopped, toward the tape. And he pressed through the pain trying to accomplish at least the goal of crossing the line.

On his way to the finish line, Derek felt a hand on his shoulder. He started to brush it off—no race official was going to stop him. But when he turned, he was looking not into the face of an official but into the face of his father. Jim Redmond had pushed his way through the crowd and onto the track to tell Derek that he didn't have to finish. When his son insisted, Jim decided they would do it together. They walked the rest of the course, Derek crying on Jim's shoulder all the way to the finish line. But he did finish.

That scene is one of the most memorable from that Olympics—or really from sports in general. Not only was it a poignant picture of the heartbreak of competition, it was also a poignant picture of a father-son relationship. Our children need to know we're with them—that we'll help them pick up the pieces of their dreams, that we'll walk with them through any painful journey, that we'll help them reach their goals however we can. They need to know they are loved and are not alone.

The only way to show them is to spend time with them—both quality time and quantities of time—and to be there when they need us. They need to know we would choose to spend our time with them over other interests. Even when we don't have all the right words to say, we can make ourselves available. We can be present. And presence is often all they need.

UNCOMMON KEY > *A child's ability to deal with hardship often depends on how the child's parents teach their son or daughter to deal with it. And the best way to teach a child is to walk with him or her through life.*

July 18

A Way out of the Snares

> If you think you are standing strong, be careful not to fall. The temptations in your life are no different from what others experience. And God is faithful. He will not allow the temptation to be more than you can stand. When you are tempted, he will show you a way out so that you can endure. 1 CORINTHIANS 10:12-13

It's easy to waver in the face of temptation. Leading up to these verses, the apostle Paul reminds the believers in Corinth about the Israelites, whom God personally accompanied during their journey from captivity in Egypt to the Promised Land. Along the way, however, they worshiped idols, succumbing to the lures of sexual immorality and putting God to the test. They even grumbled the whole way because things weren't just the way they wanted them, even though God had freed them from slavery.

It's easy to do the same today. We can be cruising along at times in life, doing what God has set before us . . . then *things* show up that distract us, dishearten us, and tempt us to stray. It's been said many times that Satan doesn't worry about throwing roadblocks in front of us if we aren't posing a threat to him. But if we are a threat to him—if we are doing things for God—then look out!

Want some practical advice? Stay rooted to people who are of similar mind and have a similar focus on God and Christ. I had weekly Bible studies with other coaches on our staff, guys I could talk with at any time about important things—things that didn't involve the X's and O's of a game plan, drafts, free agency, or other on-the-field stuff. I even had regular walks scheduled with another coach, both for the added exercise and also to deal with things that might come to mind as we were walking along.

Similarly, stay grounded in and connected to your family. Everyone gets busy, and it's easy to get disconnected a little bit at a time. Don't let it happen.

Finally, make sure that you stay tethered tightly to God through regular personal quiet time and fellowship with others through reading the Bible, prayer, and worship.

God, through the leading of the Holy Spirit within us, is unwavering and always absolutely right in where He leads us.

UNCOMMON KEY > *To guard against temptation, stay rooted to people of faith, God's Word, and the leading of the Holy Spirit.*

July 19

Doing Things for His Pleasure

> Train yourself to be godly. "Physical training is good, but training for godliness is much better, promising benefits in this life and in the life to come."   1 TIMOTHY 4:7-8

God gave you gifts that stir passions within you. They are intended to be used for godly purposes. They are intended to be used for God's glory. Don't be ashamed or afraid to fight for and defend what may be a more "godly" calling. In the movie *Chariots of Fire*, runner Eric Liddell was dismissed by critics who felt he wasted too much time on other pursuits—namely, godly pursuits—to ever be considered a world-class runner.

His critics suggested that Liddell needed to change his approach to training if he really wanted to successfully compete at high levels. His response was succinct and direct: "I believe God made me for a purpose, but He also made me fast. And when I run, I feel His pleasure."

For Eric Liddell, it was all about God. In the 1924 Olympic Games in Paris, he was forced to withdraw from the 100-meter race—his best event—because one of the qualifying heats was scheduled on a Sunday. Liddell kept the Sabbath holy; he would not run on Sunday. He knew the source of his athletic ability, and he knew he was running for God's smile and honor. His heart's desire was to honor God with the gift He had given him. Liddell went on to win the bronze medal in the 200 meters and the gold medal in the 400 meters for Britain.

After reaching that pinnacle of competitive running, Liddell left for China as a missionary, again simply to honor God. He would do that up to the day of his death in a POW camp.

Eric Liddell recognized that the two greatest passions the Lord had placed on his heart—running and reaching the lost—should both be used to his utmost for God's glory.

UNCOMMON KEY > *If you are disciplined about physical training, consider being as disciplined with "godly training" in your life. Use what you are passionate about to glorify God.*

July 20

Prepared for Anything That Comes Your Way

> If someone asks about your Christian hope, always be ready to explain it. But do this in a gentle and respectful way.... Then if people speak against you, they will be ashamed when they see what a good life you live because you belong to Christ. 1 PETER 3:15-16

We have all heard the Boy Scout motto, "Be Prepared," which has been part of the movement since its founding in 1907 by Robert Baden-Powell.

"Be prepared for what?" someone once asked Baden-Powell.

"Why, for any old thing," he said.

Think about that for a minute. "For any old thing"—that's a pretty broad spectrum of knowledge to store up to be prepared for whatever might come our way. And even though I still think that "I don't know" is a perfectly respectful and appropriate answer, I also know that the more we know about what we are doing, the more we can usually get people to listen.

I found that especially true in coaching. Players would listen because of the respect they needed to show initially to us as coaches. However, when it became apparent to a player that a coach didn't really know what he was talking about, the player tuned him out.

Coach Noll, our head coach when I was with the Pittsburgh Steelers, always wanted his staff to be sure that we understood what we were teaching the players. We were teachers first, and our goal was to prepare our players for as many situations as possible—to be able to think and be prepared for whatever might happen.

The same is true when God tells us to go out and speak about Him. He wants us to be ready when someone asks us why we believe what we believe. Why we accepted Jesus Christ into our lives. Why we follow Christ and try to live—hopefully it shows—as He wants us to live.

"Be prepared." Any moment could be a time when He works through you to change a life for all eternity.

UNCOMMON KEY > *You don't need to be a Bible scholar to tell someone how Jesus Christ has changed your life. Look for an opportunity to talk to someone today.*

July 21

Discernment Instead of Judgment

> You may think you can condemn such people, but you are just as bad, and you have no excuse! When you say they are wicked and should be punished, you are condemning yourself, for you who judge others do these very same things. ROMANS 2:1

My mom and dad always taught us not to judge other people. They encouraged us to try to get an understanding of what others were going through, to try to walk in the other person's shoes for a while. But even when all of that was done—which more than likely changed our perspective considerably—we were told not to judge.

Let me set up Romans 2:1 for you. In the first chapter of Romans, Paul introduces himself and then delves into the heart of the gospel—everyone has fallen short of God's standard; neither Jews nor Gentiles have lived perfect lives.

People who knew God didn't glorify Him or give thanks to Him; their hearts became darkened and filled with sinful desires. They became immoral and lustful, told lies, and were prone to all kinds of wickedness.

Paul wasn't done with cataloging human depravity. They have been envious, murderous, deceitful, malicious, gossiping, slanderous, arrogant, senseless, faithless, heartless, and disobedient people.

But here's the rub, Paul says in Romans 2:1. Don't be quick to point your finger at those wicked people and condemn them. "You are just as bad, and you have no excuse!" We aren't any more successful in keeping the law than anyone else. We all need God's mercy and forgiveness. So be slow to judge.

I suggest a better approach for the moments when you're ready to judge others. Discard judgment and use discernment, redirection, and encouragement instead. Be Jesus Christ's hands and heart to help others to get to the bottom of their problems, redirect them, and encourage them to change.

If nothing else, it will do wonders for your own heart.

UNCOMMON KEY > *Do you tend to rush to judgment about people? Leave the judgment to the Judge and instead find ways to help change your opinions.*

July 22

Seriously . . . Joy!

> We were filled with laughter, and we sang for joy. And the other nations said, "What amazing things the LORD has done for them." PSALM 126:2

Laughter. Excitement. God is a God of joy. And if I were heading into a nearby church for a first-time visit, that's exactly what I would hope to find—joy, laughter, excitement.

But way too often we don't find that—at least in the faces of some of His would-be followers gathered within the walls of some of our places of worship, our houses of God.

Christians can be some of the most dour people on the planet.

We claim to be different, but too often we look as joyless and angst-ridden as if we were unbelievers. We claim to be called to serve the God who was the architect of the beauty all around us; yet we act and appear at times as if we have nothing to wake up to. I don't think others would find it attractive or appealing to be part of that setting.

Here's the saddest part of the whole thing: it doesn't have to happen. Times can get tough. I know; I've been there. But as followers of and believers in Jesus Christ—if we have asked Him into our lives—we have the joy and hope of the Lord of lords and the King of kings in our lives. A joy that can overcome whatever we face. A joy that leads us into all the fullness of our futures with Him in eternity.

Let it out! Let the joy out! Let the source of your joy—Jesus Christ—shine through you to the world around you. Let the joy, love, and power of the God of the universe flow through you so that others see a twinkle in your eyes, a smile on your face, and laughter in your voice.

Then they'll see Him! And He is the one they'll be attracted to!

UNCOMMON KEY > *Consider yourself a PR person for Jesus. Your joy should be contagious and irresistible to unbelievers. Find a body of like-minded people who want to share God's joy with others and start an epidemic.*

July 23

The Golden Rule of Mentoring

> Do to others whatever you would like them to do to you. This is the essence of all that is taught in the law and the prophets. MATTHEW 7:12

We often think about this verse in terms of being nice to others because we want them to treat us nicely, but I wonder sometimes if there aren't other qualities we should consider as well. Do I think this way when I deal with people in other settings?

How about mentoring others? Throughout my coaching career, I had guys on the team making multimillion-dollar salaries. Anyone with the slightest interest in sports knows that professional players' salaries have skyrocketed in the past few years. So what do you think the response would be if players were asked to teach and "coach" other players in their particular positions for the overall good of the team?

Believe it or not, that's what happens on good teams. Veteran players help the younger players improve because it will help the team grow stronger. Defensive backs could show new defensive backs the techniques that took them years to learn. The end result? Sometimes the new guy eventually beats the veteran out of a position and the lucrative salary that comes with it.

How about honesty? How about helping someone see where they need to improve by being candid and forthright about it—rather than sugarcoating it or, worse, not pointing it out at all? Sometimes hearing no is painful, but we can pick ourselves up and move on much easier than if it were maybe. Sometimes getting a poor job review can give us the opportunity to work with what we have and learn. If we believe everyone was created by God with specific gifts and abilities—like no one else—then we have to believe they are equipped to do incredible things in some setting, some place. Maybe right now they are just in the wrong place.

What about helping someone grow in his or her faith? If we didn't know about Jesus Christ or had not asked Him to be our Lord and Savior, and someone we know did know Him, wouldn't we want that person to tell us about Him?

UNCOMMON KEY > *Do unto others as you would have them do unto you—there are many opportunities if you look for them. Start thinking about—and acting upon—them today.*

July 24

An Infectious Love

> I brought glory to you here on earth by completing the work you gave me to do. . . . I have given them the glory you gave me, so they may be one as we are one. I am in them and you are in me. May they experience such perfect unity that the world will know that you sent me and that you love them as much as you love me. JOHN 17:4, 22-23

You know the people who look at the world through rose-colored glasses? We've all been around people like that. They seem to bring a childlike passion to almost every setting they are in. Their enthusiasm is infectious and uplifting for everyone it touches.

Mike Flaherty is one of those guys in Nathan's life. Mike is the head of a movie studio and hangs around with celebrities and titans of business of every kind, every single day. As you can imagine, he has an incredibly busy schedule flying back and forth across the country from meeting to meeting, putting together the next project that will make a difference in the world. That's how he sees it, by the way. He's busy doing great and impactful stuff.

And yet whenever Nathan talks with him, it's as if he can't believe his good fortune to get a few minutes with Nathan. "What a blessing that you can find some time to talk with me." I already know what his reaction to today's devotional will be: "I can't believe you put my name in a devotional! That is so amazing . . . wait until I show my children!"

That's how God reacts to us. "Hey, Judy is praying, wanting to talk with Me! It is so great to hear from you again, Judy!" God loves us that much. Christ gave us "the glory" that God gave Him. He did that when He hung on the cross for us and when He sent His Helper, the Holy Spirit, to walk with us. He did that so He can have a moment-by-moment relationship with us.

Take a moment and thank Him. And listen to Him say, "What a blessing for Me that you called!" Now that is a pretty neat God.

UNCOMMON KEY > *God's passion for you is enthusiastic and real. What a blessing to have a God who loves you and wants to spend every minute with you. Keep that in mind when you talk with Him today, and let your passion for Him overflow.*

July 25

Disbanding the Me Generation

> For people will love only themselves and their money. They will be boastful and proud, scoffing at God, disobedient to their parents, and ungrateful. They will consider nothing sacred.   2 TIMOTHY 3:2

We are living in a time when people refuse to see where God is directing or listen to what God is saying. We are living in a day when many of us could be characterized as rebelling against God, even though that might sound ridiculous.

Think about it for a minute. Everything today is designed to isolate us, give us autonomy, enhance individualism, and emphasize being "self-made." The buzz words for today are "me—me—me!" The rebels of today's society are you and me, so full of self-indulgence at times.

And we perpetuate our focus on self through Facebook, Twitter, MySpace, and on our own individual blogs. They all reflect our insatiable desire to express ourselves, to tell others what we think, what we do, and where we go. They all highlight our desire to point the world to ourselves—to lift ourselves up and to somehow feel the world's affirmation. Of course, God's direction for us is toward Him and others—we should love God and love others.

At the core of our rebellion is our lust for self, to do things our way, to have personal success. Surrendering our "me" nature for an "others" nature is God's way of breaking the rebellion. God dislikes self-aggrandizement and self-centeredness.

I've tried to help my players through the years to understand this truth both on and off the field—that we will be successful only when *we* are playing the game. We will be successful only when we understand that what we do is not just about football. There are others around us who need our help and encouragement; our role is to try to impact them in a positive way.

UNCOMMON KEY > *There is an old children's chorus, "J-O-Y," that stands for Jesus, others, and you. God calls you out of "me" and points you to Him and others. To become all He intends for you to be, listen to that call.*

July 26

Advice for High-Anxiety Moments

> This is my command—be strong and courageous! Do not be afraid or discouraged. For the LORD your God is with you wherever you go. **JOSHUA 1:9**

I'll bet if you close your eyes you can almost see Joshua's knees knocking, feel his pulse racing, watch pools of sweat form on the ground beneath his perspiring palms. No doubt, this is a high-anxiety moment he is feeling as he realizes the position God has called him to take. Now that Moses has died, Joshua has been chosen by God to lead the Israelites into the Promised Land.

Listen closely and you can probably hear him nervously muttering, "Me? Are you sure, Lord? There's got to be someone else you could pick."

I wonder how many of us have felt at various times like Joshua felt so long ago. My hand is in the air.

Let's be honest. We have all been where Joshua was that day. And here's the news flash: what happened three thousand years ago is as relevant for us as it was for Joshua. God made a promise.

The promise is that God will go with you and ahead of you across your Jordan—into all He has planned for your tomorrow. Will it be easy? Not necessarily. Will it require staying close to Him and following His direction? Yes. Will the currents take you to a place on the other side you didn't intend to go? Maybe. But will He be with you wherever you end up? You can bet your life on it!

What's your Jordan River you are facing today? A family illness? A career change? A personal challenge? Perhaps a relationship has gone stale and you need help freshening it up. Or maybe there's something you know you should have done or tried long ago, and instead you've been sitting on the bank of the Jordan for too long, dangling your feet in the rushing waters. It's time to jump in and make a mad dash for the other side.

God calls you to be strong and courageous, to know that He is with you.

UNCOMMON KEY > *Be strong and courageous—God is with you!*

July 27

God's Scorecard

> I knew you before I formed you in your mother's womb. Before you were born I set you apart and appointed you as my prophet to the nations. JEREMIAH 1:5

In his book *Game Plan for Life*, Joe Gibbs talks about performing for an audience of one. The idea is that while we may think that we are acting at times with no eyes on us, in fact the pair that matters most—God's—are always watching.

God knew us before He formed us; He determined the path of our lives. He saw us before we were born, and He sees us now.

Sound daunting? I like to think of it as unbelievably liberating. It puts a different perspective on things. Who measures success? God does, not the world. Who measures impact? God does, not the world. God's standards are rock solid, not subjectively driven by the differing opinions and standards of other people's agendas.

Too often we get messages that we've got to be more, do more, achieve more. But God is looking at things differently. He is looking at the state of our hearts. He is looking at our desires. He is looking within us to see what we feel matters most. That's where His scorecard is applied.

It's a funny thing. The size of your house, your bank account, the number of cars you own, or how big your flat-screen TV is don't appear on that scorecard. Instead, the way you make your spouse feel each day is marked on the card. The time you spend with your children and whether you affirm or intimidate them is another mark.

Your success in following God's plan is based upon what you invest in the relationships with the people He brings into your life. I think you'll know whether He's smiling down on you or not.

UNCOMMON KEY > *God's scorecard doesn't monitor the size or amount of the things you have; it tracks the size of what comes from your heart. Constantly evaluate what you need to do for tallies that will please God. When you perform for Him, everyone reaps the benefits.*

July 28

Yours When You Earn It

> Give to everyone what you owe them: If you owe ... respect, then respect; if honor, then honor. ROMANS 13:7, NIV

Hardy Nickerson was a natural leader and one of our team captains in Tampa Bay. He had been an elite player with the Pittsburgh Steelers and surprised a lot of people by choosing as a free agent to play for the Buccaneers. He took a chance on us as we tried to turn the franchise around, and I was counting on him to use his leadership skills to influence the team culture and mentor some of our younger players who had never played for a winning organization.

In the first game of 1997, Hardy was called for a penalty for unsportsmanlike conduct at a critical moment while we were trying to protect a slim lead against the 49ers. I brought him to the sideline to find out what happened. "He disrespected me," Hardy said of the 49er who provoked his retaliation. I reminded him of the character of the team we were trying to build—that we were basing our character on poise and mutual accountability and that this was an important ingredient in becoming a winning team.

As a proven winner, Hardy knew more than most what kind of attitude we needed to have as a unit. I reminded him that he needed to stand for the team first as a leader and couldn't abandon our goal of winning simply because his individual honor had been challenged. His answer surprised me: "That's all fine until somebody disrespects me."

That was a revealing moment for me, one of my first glimpses into the psychology of respect. Hardy wasn't expressing an unusual thought. If one of our brightest, most experienced players felt this way—even if only in the heat of the moment—then many other players probably did too. We met during the next week, under calmer circumstances, to make sure we were on the same page, and we got everything straightened out. We were able to move forward with a common understanding of respect and his role on the team.

We all learned something from that incident. The Bucs went on to become a playoff-caliber team, and Hardy became one of our most respected leaders.

Respect isn't a right. We aren't entitled to it, and we can never earn it by demanding it. It's something we earn because of our character—and by giving it to others. If we want to be respected, we have to show ourselves to be worthy of it, not by our status, possessions, or accomplishments, but by honesty, integrity, and responsibility.

UNCOMMON KEY > *Respect can only be earned, not ordered. And character is the key to earning it. Maintain your character, and other people's respect for you will grow.*

July 29

Running Full Speed to Him

> Truly I tell you, unless you change and become like little children, you will never enter the kingdom of heaven. MATTHEW 18:3, NIV

Have you ever watched little children around a swimming pool? Whether they can swim or not, you need to watch them very carefully. So many of them have no fear whatsoever. Deep end or shallow end, it doesn't matter. Fearless and not fully aware of the consequences, they jump, confident that everything will turn out okay because Mom and Dad or Grandma and Granddad are there. A simple—but not simpleminded—approach to life.

It's the picture of the complete dependence Christ describes in today's verse, a dependence necessary to enter His Kingdom, to be great in His Kingdom, to be His servants for all the world. A dependence marked with a simple—not simpleminded—approach to life. A dependence using the knowledge, gifts, and abilities—the wisdom—He has created within us to make decisions that honor Him, not us. And then announcing, "God, here I come!" knowing He will be there to make sure everything turns out okay.

You may not believe that God stands ready to catch you in His arms. You may not have had the benefits of being raised in the secure and loving setting that you are providing for your children or grandchildren. Maybe instead of loving, protecting, and defending you, your parents, grandparents, and other family members did the exact opposite.

Let me suggest that you find someone to share with, someone you can begin to trust with some of the difficult moments of your life. Someone who by their example gives you a glimpse of the loving nature of the God you can trust to always provide and who wants the very best for you. Start there to catch the view of the God who waits for you. Start there to develop that eternal relationship with the God you can trust to catch you when you fall or when you jump, yelling, "God, here I come!"

UNCOMMON KEY > *Spend time with children to see their simple approach to life. And then try to adopt that approach in your own life. If things seem too complicated, find someone you can confide in. And pray that God will give you the faith of a little child.*

July 30

Why Does This Keep Happening?

> I have discovered this principle of life—that when I want to do what is right, I inevitably do what is wrong. ROMANS 7:21

If there was ever a verse that I could relate to, it's this one. How many times have I prayed for forgiveness, concluding with the promise that I won't lose my temper (or fill in the blank with plenty of other items) the next time around? I can clearly see my sin. I feel a deep sense of remorse, and I have an overriding conviction not to let it happen again.

I wish it were so easy.

Because before long, I lose my temper again and remember that heartfelt, sincere prayer and think, *What is wrong with me? What is wrong with me that I can't seem to stop doing the things I don't want to do and instead do the things I want to do?*

What's wrong with me is that I am a very flawed sinner, and very fertile ground for the subtle wiles, evil plans, and devious ploys of Satan. What's wrong with me is that in my humanness I am bound to fall short of the glory of God and the standard of His Son, my Savior, whose example I try to emulate.

I try to remember the myriad moments when I've fallen before, asking God once again for His grace. And when I find myself correcting the same behavior in my children, I think, *How can I expect them to be perfect when I—someone older, wiser, more experienced, and I would think more spiritually connected with God—have such a difficult time?*

Whoops.

Just to be clear, God's grace is not a ticket to get out of jail or a free pass to sin at will. But I must admit I find it liberating that the apostle Paul dealt with the very same thing in his life. That gives me hope.

What about you? Only God's grace will do.

UNCOMMON KEY > *Use a concordance to look up the word* grace *in the Bible, especially all the times it occurs in the New Testament. Then thank God for His unmerited favor to you when you sin. Don't be discouraged. Ask the Holy Spirit to guide you in the future.*

July 31

In It for the Long Haul

> Fix your thoughts on what is true, and honorable, and right, and pure, and lovely, and admirable. Think about things that are excellent and worthy of praise. PHILIPPIANS 4:8

Every year, football fans expect their teams to win. And if the previous season ended with a poor record or fans believe certain players have consistently played subpar ball (usually the quarterback), they want to see a change. The media often fuels the fire. Of course, what the fans and media see is not lost on the organization; management will look at free agents and the college draft as ways to shore up their team's fortunes for the coming season.

However, the best moves that teams make are often done without changing personnel. Sometimes the biggest improvement in productivity comes from players who are already on your roster, who have had a year to mature and grow, to learn your team's system and become further acclimated in their roles and responsibilities. Those teams never end up being the fan darlings in June or July, however, because they haven't "done enough to improve" their teams.

We're all like that. We think the grass is greener elsewhere, that the big splash is the best way to reach our goals. But sometimes the employees you already have will be the best fit for that new position in your organization. Give them a chance to prove themselves.

Oftentimes we find ourselves in settings where we don't need major changes; we merely need to readjust our thoughts and our focus.

This "greener grass" thinking can easily slip into a marriage, too—"I thought I married the right person, but I think so-and-so is better for me"—when the couple is going through troubled times. A husband or wife believes the answer lies outside their relationship when the real work needs to be done closer to home—with each other.

So next spring when the flowers bloom and the free agents switch teams, don't lose faith if not many names change on your team's roster. Sometimes the teams that focus on growing with the same personnel are the ones that make the greatest improvement and achieve lasting success.

UNCOMMON KEY > *It's human nature to look to the outside for improvement or growth, when often all you need is right in front of you. It may simply require refocusing on what is truly important. What do you need to refocus on right now?*

August 1

Encouraging Intercession

Pray for all people. Ask God to help them; intercede on their behalf, and give thanks for them. Pray this way for kings and all who are in authority so that we can live peaceful and quiet lives marked by godliness and dignity.   1 TIMOTHY 2:1-2

It's a powerful feeling to know that someone is praying for you. I've been in so many situations where I've had somebody tell me that, or pass me a note, or even yell it out to me from across a mall!

It's especially reassuring when someone does that for you at a challenging time in your life. I remember several instances when I was with the Colts when our punter Hunter Smith told me that he was specifically praying for me.

One time in particular was during cut day, a loathsome day for me. Every year during training camp we'd have to let go of about twenty players on one day and another ten players on a different day the following week. It was an excruciating decision because the difference between the skills of various players with others was so slight, yet that difference meant some guys would stay and the other guys would have to go. With that their dreams were dashed.

I felt it was only right to meet with every one of those guys individually, in person, on those days and speak with them as the head coach, which made it even tougher. To see the hurt in each guy's face . . . thirty times over.

That's why I greatly appreciated that Hunter said he was praying for me on cut day. He knew I hated that day and wanted me to have those extra prayers, plus the encouragement that he knew prayer would bring.

Similarly, at unexpected times, Nathan has gotten handwritten postcards from one of his Tampa pastors, Matthew, each noting that Matthew prayed for Nathan that day. What an unexpected blessing!

It's a good habit to put into practice. Prayerfully lift up friends, give thanks for the people in your life, and pray for leaders whether you agree with them or not. And take it a step further. Let them know that you prayed or are continuing to pray for them. What an encouragement that may bring.

UNCOMMON KEY > *Lift up someone in prayer today and drop them a note or an e-mail to let them know. Over time, make sure you do it for both people you know and people you don't.*

August 2

Unbelievable Resources

> "What can I do to help you?" Elisha asked. "Tell me, what do you have in the house?"
> "Nothing at all, except a flask of olive oil," she replied. And Elisha said, "Borrow as many empty jars as you can. . . . Pour olive oil from your flask into the jars, setting each one aside when it is filled." So she did as she was told. . . . Soon every container was full to the brim! 2 KINGS 4:2-6

Jeff Feldhahn, a friend of Nathan's, started a business called World2one. Nathan remembers how excited Jeff was when he first told him about it, especially about its prospects for allowing ministries to quickly, easily, and safely connect with the people they serve and who serve them.

And then the dot-com bubble burst, all sources of funding dried up, and 98 percent of the employees left, leaving Jeff and a part-time programmer to carry the vision. Companies were drying up right and left and filing for bankruptcy, but Jeff felt such a passion for the investors and for the concept itself that he believed he should stick it out.

"I'll just keep going for six months, and if it doesn't turn the corner, I'll move on." Several months later, Nathan asked for an update.

"It hasn't exactly turned the corner, but there is something that may happen that'll turn it for us." And so it has gone on.

Jeff is now almost ten years into it and finally has a product and website. Through it all, however, his attitude has remained unflagging: God will provide.

So often we fret from day to day, wondering how we will get to tomorrow. What we easily forget is that God has plenty of oil in an endlessly flowing flask. Plenty of resources. In fact, God has all of the oil, all of the resources. We are simply stewards of them.

How does the World2one story end? Right now, only God knows.

But I know that Jeff's story is unfolding in the way that it should, and that Jeff is growing through the process. And in the interim, he and his wife have coauthored bestselling books on marriage, the For Women Only and For Men Only series, which grew out of their shared experience in this uncertain time in their lives. It was an untapped resource that surfaced when it was needed.

UNCOMMON KEY > *When things aren't going the way you'd hoped, remember that the Creator of the universe has all the resources you could ever need. If you trust in Him and stick it out, you may end up being surprised by the outcome.*

August 3

Feeling Hounded

> God saved you by his grace when you believed. And you can't take credit for this; it is a gift from God. Salvation is not a reward for the good things we have done, so none of us can boast about it. For we are God's masterpiece. He has created us anew in Christ Jesus, so we can do the good things he planned for us long ago. EPHESIANS 2:8-10

I was asked to participate in a recent Willow Creek Leadership Conference held at the Willow Creek Community Church campus outside of Chicago. Craig Groeschel, an Oklahoma pastor whom I met there, described how in Ephesians 2:8-10 the apostle Paul was not emphasizing being saved by good works—it's by God's grace, the free gift of His Son, of course—but the need to *do* good works. And when we do, God has something in store for us.

Paul, before the Lord struck him with a blinding light on the Damascus road, was the same guy—then known as Saul—whose "doing" for years and years was the persecution and execution of the Lord's disciples.

In one dramatic moment, God got Saul's attention and caused him to be sightless for three days. Not only could he no longer keep doing what he was doing, he couldn't see to go where he needed to go. And the men traveling with him had to help him do everything.

From the moment he was converted, Paul's "doing" changed. God transformed Paul's to-do list in that experience when He demonstrated how much He loved Paul, who had openly defied Him. God sought Paul much like the "hound of heaven" described in the poem by Francis Thompson. And Paul, in that life-changing moment, went from being a Jewish zealot named Saul, who mercilessly persecuted the followers of Christ, to a fervent missionary and evangelist who would preach the gospel of Jesus Christ unashamedly to both Jews and Gentiles alike.

What about you? Has the "hound of heaven" caught you and offered you His free gift? Have you accepted it? The to-do list He will give you might just change the world.

UNCOMMON KEY > *Read Francis Thompson's poem "The Hound of Heaven." If you have surrendered to God, be ready to receive a new to-do list.*

August 4

Wherever You Go

> Do not be afraid, for I have ransomed you. I have called you by name; you are mine. When you go through deep waters, I will be with you. When you go through rivers of difficulty, you will not drown. When you walk through the fire of oppression, you will not be burned up; the flames will not consume you. For I am the LORD, your God, the Holy One of Israel, your Savior. ISAIAH 43:1-3

During the opening ceremonies of the 2008 Summer Olympics in Beijing, China, Lopez Lomong, one of the "Lost Boys" from Sudan and a competitor in the 1500 meters, carried the flag for his country.

The United States.

Taken from his parents during a church service at a young age and shipped off to a rebel camp, Lopez and three other boys escaped through a hole in the fence and ran west, back toward their home village.

Except that the six-year-old Lopez and his new friends were actually headed *south* and ended up in Kenya. Lopez spent the next ten years at a refugee camp in Kenya, and with the help of Catholic Charities, he was brought to the United States along with other "Lost Boys" in 2001. Once here, he lived with a family in Tully, New York, just outside of Syracuse.

In Tully, Lopez discovered that the Lord had blessed him with an amazing ability to run. And even though as a six-year-old he ran in the wrong direction and never made it home, God—just as He promises—was running with him. God protected him and directed him to a place where his gift could be developed for God's Kingdom. Since then, Lopez's running has opened door after door for him, but his focus has been beyond himself. Throughout it all, his goal has been to use his gift and his citizenship in his adopted country to influence change there and to raise awareness for the plight of Sudan and to encourage investment in the fledgling Republic of South Sudan.

Certainly that six-year-old boy on the run could never have imagined that God would be using him as a means of influence to raise awareness for an entire nation.

That may be the case with you as well. Hopefully you will never be caught in a situation as horrific as Lopez was, but no matter how difficult times become—and they will—know that God has promised that He will walk alongside you, through *all* of your days.

UNCOMMON KEY > *"I am the LORD, your God." Think of that promise often in the midst of the good and the not-so-good situations that come your way. He is there.*

August 5

The Redeemer's Gift

> We are made right with God by placing our faith in Jesus Christ. And this is true for everyone who believes. . . . For everyone has sinned; we all fall short of God's glorious standard. Yet God, with undeserved kindness, declares that we are righteous. He did this through Christ Jesus when he freed us from the penalty for our sins. ROMANS 3:22-24

Chuck Swindoll once noted that as humans, we seem to be addicted to doing something to earn our salvation. I am guilty as charged, along with a whole host of my friends.

It's really no surprise. We see it all the time in the world. We work to be paid. We study to earn grades. We plant to harvest. We've heard the phrase, "There's no such thing as a free lunch." Over and over there is a causal relationship between our efforts and our production and prosperity. Yet salvation is a free gift from God, contrary to everything we have ever known and been taught since birth.

Football is a lot like that. Our efforts in preparation—whether through our draft and player analysis, off-season practices and workouts, weekly practices and game planning, or play calling—lead directly to our results. We are publicly measured on those efforts every single week by a very clear marker: the score of the game. And usually, the harder we work, the more often we win.

However, our spiritual prosperity doesn't hinge on our efforts. The basis and foundation of our faith and the spiritual growth that occurs in our lives is in our relationship with Jesus Christ. That relationship is established not because we do something to earn the right to the relationship, but simply because we recognize what Jesus Christ did for us on the cross—He took all of our sins, and those of everyone, everywhere, upon Himself.

He stood in for you, the sacrificial "pinch hitter," and pardoned you so that now you can stand in God's presence, holy and blameless before Him. And as costly as that gift was for Jesus—it cost Him His life—you cannot do anything to earn it. It was given as a free gift—requiring you to simply accept it.

UNCOMMON KEY > *In the busiest moments of your day today, stop and thank God for giving you the precious, free gift of His Son.*

August 6

The Components of a Sound Structure

> You are members of God's family. Together, we are his house, built on the foundation of the apostles and the prophets. And the cornerstone is Christ Jesus himself. We are carefully joined together in him, becoming a holy temple for the Lord . . . being made part of this dwelling where God lives by his Spirit. EPHESIANS 2:19-22

For anyone who has built a home, you know that the foundation is critical. It must be built to fit the ground it will sit on—sand, rock, clay, or other types of soil—and support the weight of the house when it is finished. The foundation determines the structural integrity of the house, and the better it is designed, the longer the house will stand.

Nathan just finished building a new home, and between issues with the clay and sinkhole activity in the region, he spent almost as much time on construction *under* the ground as above it. It's not nearly as much fun to deal with root issues, but it's no less important.

Foundations apply to more than structures. As the apostle Paul says, the apostles and prophets form the firm foundation of faith—a long history of service and examples of people honoring God. The writer of Hebrews refers to the "great cloud of witnesses," the loved ones in our lives who have guided and directed us—parents, spouses, friends, pastors, and others who have helped to build the foundation of our lives and point us toward the cornerstone: Jesus Christ.

In a masonry foundation, the cornerstone is the first stone laid on the foundation, the stone that orients the building. The alignment of the cornerstone gives the entire building its proper dimension and alignment, and the other stones are set in reference to it.

We can have a strong foundation of faith, but we also need to have perfect alignment with the only person who truly matters—Jesus Christ, the cornerstone of our lives. When the storms come and beat against our lives, even if we are battered and knocked down, the foundation and cornerstone stand securely. With them still in place, we can rebuild again and be even stronger.

UNCOMMON KEY > *Don't scrimp on your spiritual building materials. Stay connected with people whose faith strengthens your foundation. And every day, align yourself with Christ, your cornerstone.*

August 7

Adding to the Memory Bank

> Don't store up treasures here on earth, where moths eat them and rust destroys them, and where thieves break in and steal. Store your treasures in heaven, where moths and rust cannot destroy, and thieves do not break in and steal. MATTHEW 6:19-20

Since my son's death in 2005, I have talked with hundreds of parents who have lost children to accidents, illnesses, or violence. Every one of those parents, including me, wishes they could spend even just a few more minutes with their child. Life is precious, and so are moments with our children. We have to make the most of our time together.

Think about how quickly time passes. How long until the playroom is empty? When will the window of opportunity for influencing your kids start to close? How long until your children have other interests or more demands on their time that limit the opportunities you have to spend the day with them and talk about things they need to know? The Bible says that tomorrow isn't guaranteed. You need to take advantage of today's opportunities today.

Whatever seems important to you right now is probably less important than spending time with your kids. They grow up quickly. No one wants to look back with regret, see missed opportunities, and wonder what might have been. Everyone wants to look back and see God's fingerprints in their lives and have wonderful memories of the people He has entrusted them to care for.

Listen to God's gentle whisper when He tells you to enjoy the sacred moments of life. When your kids—or your spouse, relatives, or friends—ask you to spend time with them, set aside "important" business and treasure the opportunity. Be with the people who love you, and make lasting memories with them. Invest yourself and your time in the things that really matter before you end up with regrets. Those are the investments that make a difference and that can last forever. Whatever is going on in your life right now, remember what is truly important.

UNCOMMON KEY > *The memories you will have tomorrow are made today. Live now in a way that will keep you free from later regrets.*

August 8

The Most Dangerous Emotion

> Anger is cruel, and wrath is like a flood, but jealousy is even more dangerous.
>
> PROVERBS 27:4

Have you ever been jealous of someone? Maybe your coworker got the position you legitimately felt was yours, along with the raise. Maybe your neighbor invited you over to see the new luxury car or elaborate home theater. Maybe your roommate got the newest iPad and keeps showing off all the cool apps.

Here's the thing: jealousy exacts a high toll on the person who embraces it. Because I know that, I've tried to be careful of it, but it's a challenge at times. Each year thirty-one teams watch the Super Bowl champion—the goal they also shared but fell short of. Contracts for coaches get extended at surprisingly high amounts, especially when compared to other occupations. But I always tried to guard against that emotion, because jealous people don't become embittered just against those who have what they don't; jealousy colors other relationships as well. Jealous people's hearts slowly become hardened toward what they know the Lord wants them to think and how He wants them to behave. Jealous people obsess about the object of jealousy, believing that if they get what someone else has, they will be fulfilled. Instead of building others up, jealousy wants to destroy them.

In the Bible, Esau and his descendants—the Edomites—lived and breathed jealousy. In the book of Genesis, Esau's brother Jacob stole Esau's birthright through a deceptive plan dressed up in a delicious meal. By the time Obadiah prophesied almost fifteen hundred years later, Esau's descendants had watched the ups and downs of the people of Israel for centuries—cheering, jeering, and hoping the worst would befall them. After all, that seemed sweet revenge for what had happened to Esau so many centuries before.

Things haven't changed over the millennia. People still struggle with jealousy. If left unchecked, it can escalate from a mere grudge to reveling in someone else's misfortunes to horrifying revenge.

UNCOMMON KEY > *The moment jealous thoughts run through your mind, ask God to take them away. Never let jealousy take hold. It always leaves a bitter taste in your mouth.*

August 9

The Word That Isn't in God's Vocabulary

> Beware! Guard against every kind of greed. Life is not measured by how much you own. LUKE 12:15

I have been richly blessed in my career. Wonderful people, wonderful positions, wonderful places. But when I decided to retire, people kept asking when I planned to go back to coaching, assuming I would miss it. Certainly, there are parts I miss about being with a team, but I didn't retire to inactivity. My life—and yours, when you reach that point—continues to have purpose serving God and using the gifts and abilities He has given me. God always has something else in store.

How many of us have material blessings and don't appreciate them or worse, don't use them to benefit others?

In his book *Don't Waste Your Life,* John Piper retells a story from a February 1998 issue of *Reader's Digest* as an example of not living your life with purpose. As a matter of fact, Piper calls it an American tragedy: a couple took early retirement and moved to Florida, where their life consisted of cruising on a thirty-foot trawler, playing softball, and collecting shells.

For this couple, that was the dream they decided to live. Piper muses sadly that a day will come when they are at the end of their precious, God-given lives. As they stand before Christ at the day of judgment, they will only be able to say, "Look, Lord. See my shells."

God has placed you here for a reason, even when you reach "retirement." Maybe to build up His Kingdom through another career or volunteer service or a mentoring opportunity He plans to keep you busy with.

UNCOMMON KEY > *Read the parable of the rich fool in Luke 12:13-21. What do you dream of doing for God's Kingdom? That dream may be realized. To live the life God created you to live, remember it is an "always" thing—there is no such thing as "retirement" in the Kingdom of God.*

August 10

His Choice

> You didn't choose me. I chose you. I appointed you to go and produce lasting fruit, so that the Father will give you whatever you ask for, using my name. JOHN 15:16

One thing I'm sure of: we're not going to get the whole debate about predestination and free will cleared up until the day we see the Lord face-to-face.

And another thing I'm sure of: no matter how the end times are designed and unfolded by Him, God is in control of everything. Doesn't that take much of the pressure off? We are not heading out alone. We are called by Christ to make disciples of all nations, but it's not all up to us. Maybe someone accepts Christ and is assured of eternal salvation through my invitation, nudging, or personal testimony. Or maybe I am a catalyst for that person's decision for Christ through my example of Bible study, prayer, or other actions. Maybe I simply encourage someone along the way who is struggling with issues in his or her life and faith.

But the remarkable fact is that God chose us. He isn't surprised by what happened to us, and He won't be surprised by what might happen to others through us. We are to make the most of our opportunities, to grow and stretch in our faith, and to influence others to come to Christ. And in all of that, we are to trust God, guided by His Word, to not only be there as we walk through doors He is opening, but to realize that He is leading us through and encouraging us along the way.

As Isaiah 55:11 says, "It is the same with my word. I send it out, and it always produces fruit. It will accomplish all I want it to, and it will prosper everywhere I send it."

God's Word is what is producing the fruit through the Holy Spirit, not our efforts. We are called to be God's messengers, God's ambassadors, while we are here. We are not called to be God. But He will use our humble efforts for good—His eternal good.

UNCOMMON KEY > *What can you—through God's power—do to bless others and impact them today?*

August 11

Reading a Lot into It

Direct your children onto the right path, and when they are older, they will not leave it.
PROVERBS 22:6

My parents were both educators within the public school system. My mother taught high school English and public speaking, and my father taught physiology at the college level.

They loved what they did and were good at it. And as a result they left a trail of lives changed for the better.

They were both planners, wise in how they went about teaching others and how they viewed the world. I think they would have appreciated this Chinese proverb: "When planning for a year, plant corn. When planning for a decade, plant trees. When planning for life, train and educate people."

I learned from the late Abe Brown, my longtime friend who mentored me about prison ministry and so many other things of life, that state governments today determine the need for future prisons based on the percentage of children in fourth grade who cannot read.

That's a trend that needed to change long ago, but now it's up to us to make sure it does. The problem seems to be the lack of people adding value in the lives of our younger children until we begin to lose them. Often these children come from homes where little positive intellectual stimulation and learning happens. Head Start programs were developed to stem that tide and increase the learning curve—but the tide still seems to be coming in. There are so many Old Testament admonitions for adults to teach the children—not only God's Word, but also to teach them other necessary skills as well—reading being one of them.

We each need to be a part of the solution. Get involved as a tutor in a local school or community program. Partner with the Dungy Family Foundation to read at area schools. Whatever it takes, help a child get an education.

UNCOMMON KEY > *Determine today that you will make a difference in the life of a child by being available and willing to help that boy or girl succeed.*

August 12

Accessible

> Since we have a great High Priest who has entered heaven, Jesus the Son of God, let us hold firmly to what we believe. This High Priest of ours understands our weaknesses, for he faced all of the same testings we do, yet he did not sin. So let us come boldly to the throne of our gracious God. There we will receive his mercy, and we will find grace to help us when we need it most. HEBREWS 4:14-16

We can approach God through Jesus.

When Christ breathed His last breath on the cross, the curtain that separated the Holy of Holies from the rest of the Temple area was torn in two from top to bottom (see Mark 15:38). The priest was no longer necessary to access the Holy of Holies, where God resided—Christ provided direct access into God's presence through what He did for us on the cross.

When I was coaching, both the Indianapolis Colts and the Tampa Bay Buccaneers had a phalanx of people to screen others who wanted to get through to me. It's not that I didn't want to be approached—I love being around people—but the sheer volume of people who wanted access didn't make many one-on-one moments possible, not if I was going to do the job that the team needed me to do.

Requests from reporters and other writers and broadcasters would be handled through our public relations department, who would then schedule my appearances as needed; yet they often found that their questions could be handled during general press conferences. Inquiries from the neighboring community came through the community relations department, who would also have input into my schedule. Finally, everything else was handled by my two assistants, Lora in Tampa and Jackie in Indianapolis.

You wouldn't believe the amount of mail and the volume of calls I received with fan suggestions about which players we should play and in what positions, which players we should draft and what plays we should run, and on and on. I don't think a day went by without someone sending us a diagram of a play that the person was sure would work against this particular team or that one—or all of them.

Thankfully, through Christ, you have been given direct access to God. You don't have to go through a certain protocol or a PR person to reach Him. You have the ability and confidence to go directly to Him.

UNCOMMON KEY > *How accessible are you to the people in your life? How accessible are you to God in your life? You have direct access to the holy God of creation through His Son, Jesus Christ. Think about what a gift and privilege that is.*

August 13

Crossing the Finish Line

> We are ignored, even though we are well known. We live close to death, but we are still alive. We have been beaten, but we have not been killed. 2 CORINTHIANS 6:9

In the 2008 Summer Olympic Games in Beijing, China, Michael Phelps was aiming to win eight events. If successful, he would break American swimmer Mark Spitz's 1972 record of seven gold medals in a single Olympic Games. To accomplish the feat, Phelps needed to win the 4x100 meter freestyle relay, which consists of four swimmers from each competing country's team each swimming one hundred meters of the freestyle, or two lengths of the pool, down and back.

The US team was well behind after the third leg, when Jason Lezak dived into the pool. No one watching in the crowd or glued to their televisions gave him any chance of overtaking France's Alain Bernard on the final anchor leg of the relay. It looked as though the United States would again lose this relay race—a race they had captured gold in seven times before—for the third straight summer games.

But the crowd and the millions watching weren't swimming that final lap, and they hadn't consulted one key person: Jason Lezak. At thirty-two, Jason was the oldest swimmer on the US team. He started the final leg well back of Bernard—the reigning world record holder in the 100-meter freestyle—and at the final turn, he was still a full body length behind. He had many opportunities along the way to concede and accept second place; everyone else had already assumed he couldn't overtake Bernard's enormous lead. But there was no quit in Lezak, and with one incredible last stroke he bested the world's best to win the relay for the United States by a fingertip and set a new world record. And Michael Phelps, with the help of his teammates, went on to achieve his goal.

As I recall hearing in an interview with Lezak after the race, he didn't think he would have caught Bernard in an individual race—the deficit was too big. However, because it was a relay, Lezak felt he was swimming for his teammates, so he couldn't just give up. We need to feel that same way—we're doing what we're doing for the Lord, so we can't just give up.

You may not be training for the Olympics, but you do have personal goals that you've set for yourself, goals that mean a lot to you, like spending more time with your children or attempting your first half marathon or starting a Bible study. The moment you find reasons to quit, think of Jason Lezak. And thank God that you have the opportunity to be in the race.

UNCOMMON KEY > *You will face many moments in your life when you want to throw in the towel. Decide right now that quitting is not an option. You may have been beaten this time, but you are still alive!*

August 14

My Least Favorite Day

> The LORD said, "Name him Lo-ammi—'Not my people'—for Israel is not my people, and I am not their God." HOSEA 1:9

My least favorite part of coaching in the NFL was the day we had to cut the roster. As I've said before, you'd almost be willing to work on game day for free, but they couldn't pay you enough to make cut day tolerable. Those cut players had become become family in a way. Watching dreams dashed was tough, especially when you—as the head coach—were doing the dashing. You'd tell yourself it wasn't the end of the line, but for so many guys, it actually was. Players who had been stars in high school and then college didn't even reach training camp unless they were in the top one percent of everyone playing football in the United States.

And often, even that wasn't enough. They simply couldn't be Colts any longer. Our roster size was limited, and they didn't measure up.

In Hosea, the Lord was in the same situation. He'd finally had enough of the people breaking the covenant He had made with them. In essence, He told Hosea, "I'm cutting them."

"They are not My people." They are not measuring up.

Of course, God is not talking about a continuing relationship with the Indianapolis Colts. He is talking about falling out of a relationship with Him, a break in the family ties. Pretty serious stuff to stop and think about.

But the great thing about our God is that if we read the Bible on a regular basis, we will see all the times God continued to open the door of redemption, to restore that relationship with Him.

When we fail to follow the light He shines on the path He wants us to walk on and go our own ways, God—like a good parent would do—keeps opening the door and inviting us to return to a daily relationship with Him.

Not too different from the player who was initially cut but returns as a member of the practice squad. Or the one who comes back as a member of the active roster, alongside the players that he thought would never be his teammates.

Our God is faithful . . . even when we don't measure up.

UNCOMMON KEY > *Face the truth that you don't measure up to God's perfect standard; no one does. But don't be discouraged. He hasn't cut you from the team. The two of you just have some work to do.*

August 15

Willing to Stand Alone

> I focus on this one thing: Forgetting the past and looking forward to what lies ahead, I press on to reach the end of the race and receive the heavenly prize for which God, through Christ Jesus, is calling us. **PHILIPPIANS 3:13-14**

Twelve Angry Men is one of my favorite movies (and Nathan's, too). Henry Fonda plays a juror in a murder trial, and the evidence seems so clear-cut that the other eleven jurors are ready to return a guilty verdict. But Fonda's character isn't satisfied with the evidence and wants to go through it again—and again and again. Every time a vote is taken, he stands alone. The other jurors are impatient and ready to move on, and some turn the disagreement into a personal battle. But he keeps his focus on the job, urges them to reexamine the case, and points out the gaps in the evidence. The votes begin to shift. Eventually all the jurors agree on a not-guilty verdict.

It's hard to stand alone against popular opinion. Most of us have experienced days when we seem to be on the other side of the fence from everyone else. We feel pressure to compromise, and it's easy at such times to lose perspective on what's important to cling to and what isn't. Sometimes we realize we were wrong about something, sometimes we still believe we're right but it isn't worth fighting for, and sometimes we stand firm on what we know is true and worth fighting for. But knowing the difference can be difficult.

Coach Noll said, "Stubbornness is a virtue—if you're right!" As a Christian, you need to be stubborn about the things God says are right. Always stand firm on essentials. Focus on the main thing, the truths that are most important and worth fighting for. Be single-minded about pursuing Christ, His Kingdom, and the things that are important to Him, and be persistent. Sometimes we have to stand alone for a long time. But be willing to compromise on nonessentials. Let go of what isn't important, and be comfortable admitting when you're wrong. Your convictions combined with your humility may even attract others to your viewpoint, and you won't be standing alone for long.

UNCOMMON KEY > *Stand your ground when you're right about something important, and be willing to admit when you're wrong. And keep your eyes on Christ and reflect on His Word so you can know the difference.*

August 16

Moving On

> I have called you back from the ends of the earth, saying, "You are my servant." For I have chosen you and will not throw you away. Don't be afraid, for I am with you. Don't be discouraged, for I am your God. I will strengthen you and help you. I will hold you up with my victorious right hand. ISAIAH 41:9-10

Life isn't trouble-free. Trouble often finds us, even if we're trying to avoid it. And for anyone who is pushing the envelope and maximizing their full potential, there's no guarantee that hardship won't show up too.

But so will the Lord, He promises. Life is hard, but God is good.

I thought when I became the head football coach with the Tampa Bay Buccaneers, it would be forever, or at least as long as I wanted. My family would finally have some stability. Our children could stay in the same school for a while. We could develop a relationship with a local church, allowing us to grow in our faith and to minister to the community through that body of believers.

And beyond that, it was for more than just our good. After all, I was encouraging our players to get more involved in helping the community, and they were coming through. Our club was trying to stand for the right things as well as be a good example.

Of course, things didn't quite work out that way. At the end of the 2001 season, I was fired. No, my time as head coach of the Bucs would not last forever, and it reminded me that at the end of whatever is the end for us, there is only one thing that is forever—a personal relationship with our Lord and Savior Jesus Christ. Praise God that I have made that choice with Him.

What about you? Each day seems to bring something new to each of us—sometimes we welcome whatever comes with open arms, and sometimes we do our best to hold it back. All of it can be used by God for our good and His glory; how it affects us depends in large part on whether we believe that or not.

God will always have a hold on us—no matter what we face.

UNCOMMON KEY > *Clasp God's hand today in faith, knowing that everything that comes your way is under His control. Nothing gets by Him.*

August 17

Rising to Each Occasion

> May our Lord Jesus Christ himself and God our Father, who loved us and by his grace gave us eternal comfort and a wonderful hope, comfort you and strengthen you in every good thing you do and say. **2 THESSALONIANS 2:16-17**

Mr. Magorium's Wonder Emporium is a wonderful movie from Walden Media, portraying the tale of a whimsical toy store and its equally whimsical 243-year-old proprietor. Maybe one of the reasons I enjoyed it so much is because it's not just a story of a magical toy store—it's a story about life, life and the richness it can contain if we strive to be all that God created us to be.

As the film begins, Mr. Magorium (played by Dustin Hoffman) is readying the store for his passing ("Lightbulbs die, my sweet. I will *depart*."). After all, 243-year-olds don't run toy stores forever, even magic ones. It turns out that his assistant, Molly Mahoney (played by Natalie Portman), is afraid to truly live her life as she really feels she should. Drawing upon his centuries of acquired wisdom, Mr. Magorium looks Molly straight in the eye and says, "Your life is an occasion. Rise to it."

So is yours. God created you for something distinctly suited for you. Maybe to stand before big crowds, maybe not. Maybe to obtain untold wealth and fame, maybe not. Maybe to become a world-renowned pianist or athlete or preacher, maybe not. Whatever it is, this much is clear—your life is an occasion that was created for you, and you alone, to live. You will impact the world in ways that only you can.

God created an abundant life for you and for me that is best achieved and fulfilled through living it in a relationship aligned with Christ. God intended for our lives to travel a pathway of immeasurable impact in the lives and world around us. He will not only walk alongside us but when necessary will help carry us where He wants us to go.

UNCOMMON KEY > *Take the message "Your life is an occasion. Rise to it!" as a positive reminder that God has made you quite unique and will use you in extraordinary ways. Embrace the wisdom of that message every day.*

August 18

No Limits

> How much more do I need to say? It would take too long to recount the stories of the faith of Gideon, Barak, Samson, Jephthah, David, Samuel, and all the prophets. By faith these people... HEBREWS 11:32-33

The list above is certainly not exhaustive. There are many more who have gone before us, making a long and unwavering fence line of influence for us. They have shown us that all things are possible through Him who gives us strength. The writer of Hebrews recounts through chapter 11 countless examples of people who achieved incredible things through their faith, but he has to finally give up on the list—the rest would simply "take too long."

We have similar people of influence around us today, few more inspirational than Dara Torres, an American swimmer and Olympic gold medalist. Torres became the first US swimmer to compete in five Olympic Games. She participated in 1984, 1988, 1992, 2000, and again in 2008.

At forty-one years old, a relatively advanced age for competitive swimmers, she became the oldest swimmer to swim on the US Olympic team. In the 2008 Summer Olympics, she competed in a number of events, including the 50-meter freestyle, 4x100-meter medley relay, and 4x100-meter freestyle relay. Dara won silver medals in all three events.

It is impossible to measure how far-reaching and long-lasting Dara's influence has been on others, and it was largely because she never saw retirement as a viable option. Now others see doors open that they may not have seen before and may see potential where they saw defeat.

People are quick to tell us that we're too old or that our "window of opportunity" has passed. God is always ready and willing to use us.

Make sure you're using your influence to help others see their limitless potential through Christ—what they can be, how they can grow, what they can do to impact others.

Through Him all things are possible.

UNCOMMON KEY > *At any age, and in any setting, there really are no limits on the potential we have to influence others for good. And that's how God intended it to be.*

August 19

Heading Back for More

> Some Jews arrived from Antioch and Iconium and won the crowds to their side. They stoned Paul and dragged him out of town, thinking he was dead. But as the believers gathered around him, he got up and went back into the town. The next day he left with Barnabas for Derbe. ACTS 14:19-20

Something nobody wants to see is a player down on the field. In fact, the training staffs of both teams are ready to run out and attend to an injured player, no matter who is hurt. I've seen trainers from the opposing team in the most heated of rivalries race onto the field to help a fallen player. Even fans wait in hushed silence to see that an opposing player is okay.

In this story from Acts, Paul's mission was almost life-ending. He was stoned, dragged outside the town limits, and left for dead. But then, miraculously, Paul got back up and headed back into town for a night, setting off the next day to finish the trip.

Some people would say that's perseverance. Others might call Paul crazy or obsessive. Still others might suggest that Paul was totally sold-out to what he was being called to do and to the God who called him to do it. And yet still others might say the apostle Paul was totally in love with the person who changed his life forever on the Damascus Road—God through His Son, Jesus Christ.

We might never have to experience what Paul went through as a result of the call upon our lives to follow Jesus Christ. There were many more painful moments, disappointments, beatings, imprisonments, and heartaches that Paul would experience in his service to the Lord. But Christ calls us to follow Him all the way to the cross if that is His plan. What we need to embrace, in addition to our relationship with Jesus Christ, is the passion, persevering spirit, and example of the apostle Paul in our journey to serve and touch the world for Christ.

We may or may not be beaten or jailed for it. We may or may not lose our life in the process of doing what we do for Christ. We may or may not know of any life that is different because we lived for Christ. What is important for us is that we are sold-out for Christ to the point where we are able to persevere through anything we face—until the last breath we take for Him.

UNCOMMON KEY > *Reflect on any difficulties you've encountered when you've shared Christ with someone. Then thank God that you were able to be a witness for Him. There is one and only one way to follow Christ—sold-out!*

August 20

Prayer Warriors

> You have been deceived by your own pride. . . . You should not have gloated when they exiled your relatives to distant lands. You should not have rejoiced when the people of Judah suffered such misfortune. You should not have spoken arrogantly in that terrible time of trouble. OBADIAH 1:3, 12

It's easy to rejoice in the misfortune of someone who has wronged us. Praying for and blessing those who persecute us, as we're called to do in Matthew 5:44 and Romans 12:14, certainly aren't the natural responses.

When you have a bitter rivalry in sports, it isn't natural to turn around and think you should now pray for the well-being of your adversaries. Rodney Harrison and I faced off several times in crucial games when he was with the New England Patriots and I was with the Colts. Now, however, we're on the same team, working on the show *Football Night in America* for NBC.

I wish I could look back and say I prayed for him then the way I'm praying for him now. It's natural now that I know him personally and see him regularly. We are part of each other's lives, and I have a much better understanding of him and who he is. But we've got to work hard to see that the people we disagree with have the same good qualities we do. I should have realized that was true about Rodney even when he and his teammates had the upper hand on the football field so many times.

In his twenty-one-verse book in the middle of the Bible, the prophet Obadiah clearly proclaims that even if we feel the situation warrants it, God does not want us to relish the misfortune of others. At the time Obadiah wrote this, the descendants of Jacob and Esau were still having disputes, and the Edomites (Esau's people) rejoiced in the fall of Jerusalem (Jacob's people). Obadiah sternly warned the Edomites that their own end was approaching because of their attitude—namely, their desire for revenge, their pride, and their rejoicing in the suffering of their enemies.

Have you ever found yourself relishing a person's misfortune, someone who has wronged you in some way? Think seriously about praying for a change in your heart and being able to ask that person how you can pray for him or her.

UNCOMMON KEY > *Are there people you aren't getting along with today? Is there something specific you can do to soften your heart toward them and then pray— meaningfully—for them?*

August 21

The Power of Your Platform

"Make sure you eat a good breakfast," I told my son Eric repeatedly. I wanted him to get a good, healthy start to his day, and his fondness for Froot Loops wasn't really accomplishing that. He would listen to me and try to change his breakfast habit, but it didn't seem to last—until someone else was able to get through to him.

That someone else was his football coach at his new school. On the second day of school, he went to an introductory meeting for the football team. Eric informed me that night that we would need to leave earlier for school the next day.

"Why?" I asked.

"Coach told us that we really need to be taking care of our bodies," he told me. "That starts with getting a good breakfast. The only thing we have here is Froot Loops, so we'll need to go early enough that we can stop somewhere for something more nutritious."

Apparently that's all it took—someone in a position of influence giving Eric a good reason for changing his habit. All of a sudden, he was motivated.

Whether you're a parent, coach, teacher, neighbor, or even just a friend, you likely have some degree of authority and influence over others in your life. The power of your platform is greater than you think. You have an opportunity to influence people for good. Teachers and coaches may have a more obvious role in motivating their students and players, but everyone can exercise influence in someone else's life. And you need to allow yourself to be influenced positively by others. Everyone needs to be aware of their platforms and the power they hold. And you need to learn to use that power effectively.

UNCOMMON KEY > *Never underestimate the potential of your authority and influence to impact others. Look for someone who could use a motivational push today. Emphasize the positive benefits of a change.*

August 22

The Company You Keep

| Do not be misled: "Bad company corrupts good character." 1 CORINTHIANS 15:33, NIV

Growing up, I wanted to hang out with the kids who seemed fun or were cool. I don't think that desire has changed much over the years with kids. But my mother had different criteria. Her primary concern wasn't whether kids were cool enough for me, but whether those kids had character. This verse from the apostle Paul's first letter to the Corinthian church (using a quotation from the Greek poet Menander) is one I remember her using. It didn't leave any wiggle room for further discussion from myself or my brother and sisters.

How can you impart that lesson to your children or other young people? It's true that you can't always choose the people you hang out with because of the environments you are in, but you can make some deliberate decisions as to who you will not hang out with. You should choose other couples or families who love God and who will help you to continue to become men and women of character. Folks who will help your family to grow in the encouragement and guidance of God.

Back to my parents. Whenever my siblings or I mentioned someone new, my mom and dad wanted to know if that person was a complainer, a gossip, or involved in things that he or she shouldn't be getting into.

You can apply the same questions to evaluate your own children's friends. Emphasize that it's important to have friends with the same positive qualities you are teaching to them. You probably will be able to assess someone's character pretty quickly after a few meetings. Learn about his or her family. Your input into the lives of your children's friends and their families can possibly be life-changing for them. Maybe you can be the positive influence they are missing. Befriend the entire family when possible and make a difference in their lives.

UNCOMMON KEY > *Think about your own friends. Is there someone you should be spending more time with? Someone you should be spending less time with? It may be time to make some choices in this area.*

August 23

Why Your Thoughts Are Important

And so, dear brothers and sisters, I plead with you to give your bodies to God because of all he has done for you. Let them be a living and holy sacrifice—the kind he will find acceptable. This is truly the way to worship him. ROMANS 12:1

It's one thing to model our behavior after other believers in the church and try to fit in, but it's another thing altogether to be transformed into the likeness of Christ. That transformation starts with our thinking, and then it moves to our hearts, where it begins to take shape and mold us more permanently into who God intends for us to be.

Proverbs 23:7 says, "As [a man] thinketh, so is he" (KJV). That Scripture is true in so many ways and settings. The glass is half empty or the glass is half full. In any given set of circumstances we face, our own view of them will determine and direct our response. Our thinking will illuminate what we feel inside—worry and despair or confidence and hope. James Allen, whom many consider to be the founder of the self-help movement with his inspirational writings, said, "A man is literally what he thinks, his character being the complete sum of all his thoughts."

A Harvard Business School study found that there are four critical factors in business: intelligence, information, skill, and attitude. The first three make up 7 percent of success, while attitude alone makes up the other 93.

Of course, we know character is a product of more than just our thoughts. The values we hold dear and how we implement them into our lives and relationships are key. The vision and mission and purpose we have for our lives and how they are guided and directed by God also build our character.

That's how the apostle Paul was describing character: it starts with our mind and flows from there into every aspect of who we are and who the world will see and be impacted by—for good or not. And that "character strengthens our confident hope of salvation" (Romans 5:4).

UNCOMMON KEY > *Thoughts lead to values of the heart, which lead to character and hope. Guard your thoughts.*

August 24

What Kind of Grace Do You Have?

> If any of you wants to be my follower, you must turn from your selfish ways, take up your cross daily, and follow me. If you try to hang on to your life, you will lose it. But if you give up your life for my sake, you will save it. LUKE 9:23-24

There is nothing about the verses in Luke that is appealing or part of any natural human inclination. Certainly we like the idea of following Christ and of having eternal life in heaven with Him rather than spending eternity in hell with Satan.

The Cost of Discipleship by Dietrich Bonhoeffer is a powerful book. If you haven't run across it, I suggest that you find it. Just as powerful is the backstory of Bonhoeffer himself, which was well chronicled by Eric Metaxas in his 2010 book *Bonhoeffer: Pastor, Martyr, Prophet, Spy.*

"Cheap grace," according to Bonhoeffer, a German pastor who stood up to the Nazi regime, is the forgiveness of our sins through what Christ did for us on the cross. But without more, the outspoken theologian says, it merely means the justification of the sin without the justification of the sinner. We begin to believe that since we are forever forgiven—past, present, and future—we're covered. Nothing needs to change. Life goes on as it always has, but we're secure.

But then Bonhoeffer presents the uncomfortable idea, the part about taking up our crosses daily. That part that sounds a little too much like what Christ did that got Him nailed to the cross for us. Does He really want us to hang there with Him?

Bonhoeffer says that is the "costly grace" that we don't talk about too much. It's the part of the relationship with Christ, through His free gift of eternal life bought with His blood on the cross, that requires complete obedience at all costs. That means in all situations, at all times of our lives, with all aspects of our lives—including all of our time, talent, and treasures.

It's the costly part of grace we try to avoid thinking about because it means going all the way—sacrificially and selflessly—to the cross with Christ.

Bonhoeffer was willing to do that, standing defiantly against the Nazis for his faith and the freedom of others, and he paid for it with his life.

UNCOMMON KEY > *Get a copy of* The Cost of Discipleship *and* Bonhoeffer *and spend time absorbing what God has done for you and what He is asking you to do. Taking up your cross also means hanging on it with Him.*

August 25

Vision Keepers

| Where there is no vision, the people perish. PROVERBS 29:18, KJV

Mean Joe Greene, one of my teammates on the Pittsburgh Steelers, told me about the time he was ready to quit. The team had been losing, so one day in 1972 he cleaned out his locker and headed for the airport. One of the Steelers' coaches persuaded him to return, but his story illustrates one of the challenges of leadership: keeping everyone on the team focused on and committed to the vision and mission through thick and especially thin.

It's easy to lose sight of the goal—or to lose heart in trying to reach it—but occasional reminders can help. When I was coaching, I met with the whole team before and after games and every Wednesday. I would remind our players of the big picture and help them set smaller goals within the larger mission. After a loss, I would often remind them that our short-term goals were still attainable and that we were still on track to reach our ultimate goal. When the team had been playing well, I would remind them not to fall in love with their own press clippings but to remember that both pride and complacency were enemies to our mission and would eventually lead to a fall. Whether we were winning or losing, we had to shake off the past and keep moving ahead. We just needed to focus on the task right in front of us.

Whether with our personal goals or as leaders of others, we must always keep the vision out front and readily accessible. It's easy to put our heads down and forget why we do what we do, but keeping our eyes on the prize can keep us going. This is especially important when circumstances are bleak and discouragement sets in, but it's also true when things are going well and complacency sets in. Both situations tempt us to lose our focus. But when we remember where we're headed, we tend to get there much more often.

UNCOMMON KEY > *When you lose sight of the goal, it's unlikely you'll reach it. Keep the vision in front of you and those around you—and always continue moving toward it.*

August 26

Grace Is Good

> "No," Peter protested, "you will never ever wash my feet!" Jesus replied, "Unless I wash you, you won't belong to me." Simon Peter exclaimed, "Then wash my hands and head as well, Lord, not just my feet!" JOHN 13:8-9

Have you ever taken that type of person to lunch? Or are you that person?

You know the one—either through the obstacle of pride or a feeling that he or she must earn everything, the person can't accept a gift. Even a small one. You invite them to lunch and have a great time, but when the check comes, the friend insists on being the one to pay it. Every time. You offer a bit of grace—and the person makes a deal for it.

In my experience, especially spending a lot of time among well-paid professional athletes, it happens.

You can see it with Peter: "You're not washing *my* feet. I should be washing yours." Then, when Jesus insists, Peter attempts to make it ridiculous and escape the moment. "Fine, wash my head, too!"

There's nothing wrong with occasionally accepting a gift. It's good for the giver—and it's good for the recipient.

I think that's part of why it's so hard for us to deal with grace. We feel we need to do something in return. Of course, then it's not grace, God's unmerited gift of love for us. God has given us eternal life and a relationship with Him through the gift of His Son Jesus Christ's sacrifice, which we "merely" need to accept. We can't do anything for it—it's already been done. We can't earn our way into heaven. He's not waiting for us to be "good enough." He'd be waiting forever. He asks us to live the life He has set before us, but the first step can't be earned, merely accepted.

The other difficulty we have in accepting God's grace is something Peter understood: what Christ demonstrates to us is something He expects us to follow and demonstrate to the world around us. Peter pushed back on the foot-washing offer because he also knew that Christ was telling him to go and do the same.

Do you struggle with the concept of God's grace, either because you don't feel worthy to receive the gift or because you know what He is asking you to do after you've received His grace? Humbly let Jesus wash your feet today.

UNCOMMON KEY > *Grace—God's merciful gift that promises eternal life in heaven, abundant life here, and the reminder of a world that needs your touch. Have you received it? Do you know someone else who needs to?*

August 27

Nothing but the Truth

| **Make them holy by your truth; teach them your word, which is truth.** JOHN 17:17

One of Nathan's daughters, Elise, loves to kid her dad and other family members, and when she isn't kidding them, she is trying to tell if the others are kidding or telling her the truth.

She continually asks everyone to "pinkie promise" that they are telling her the truth. To emphasize her seriousness, she extends her pinkie finger toward the person she is addressing. I suppose if she still isn't convinced, she will ask for a "double pinkie promise" to determine the truth tellers in her midst.

I don't know who introduced her to pinkie-promise truth telling. It's cute, in its own childish way. But the message it conveys to Nathan is troubling. He and his wife have tried to teach their children that they should always tell the truth. That whenever their mouths are moving and words are coming out, they should be truthful. And if the girls tell their family something about a particular matter or situation, and a nonfamily member tells Nathan or his wife something different about the same matter or situation, they will believe their girls. Period. No questions asked.

Using a pinkie promise doesn't necessarily demonstrate that the girls are stretching the truth, but it does introduce the concept of situational or relative truth that is rampant in our society today. It's the idea that things could be said and stories told, and unless someone pledged a "pinkie promise" to substantiate what they were saying, no one could rely on it as being true.

God teaches and demands absolute truth. A pinkie promise circumvents that. Although Nathan admits he's not crazy about throwing cold water on his daughter's game, the slippery slope of pinkie-promise truth will have to go.

UNCOMMON KEY > *Even if others can't tell if you are kidding, lying, or telling the truth, you and God know. Hold yourself accountable to tell the absolute truth. There is really no other kind.*

August 28

Challenged to Make a Choice

> Choose today whom you will serve. . . . As for me and my family, we will serve the LORD.
> JOSHUA 24:15

You want to get your priorities right, and you know what they are, but in crunch time, do you really follow them and live them out? You need to look no further than your family to find a myriad of crunch-time challenges to what you know are the right priorities.

Simply put, when times are good, when we're flush with cash, or when our careers are going well, it's easy to realize and embrace the truth that we are called to serve God and not things. But what about when times are tight? Who gets top priority then?

What about when you've just lost your job and you don't know which way to turn, and when you're sitting down to update your résumé, your younger daughter asks for help with some homework? What's more important? How about when you've been offered the opportunity you've been waiting for—a job with a big advancement and a larger salary—but it requires moving to another state just as your son begins his senior year in high school? Not an easy call. "As for me and my family, we will serve the LORD." Right? Easy?

What happens to your priorities when you're pulled at the seams? What happens to serving the Lord first, putting your family next, and bumping everything else farther down on the list?

Remember Joshua? He succeeded Moses as leader of the people of Israel after Moses' death, safely crossing the Jordan River with God's people into the Promised Land. It had been a long and difficult journey, to say the least. But immediately, there was dissension and grumbling in the ranks caused by a number of issues, not the least being temptations around them as well as the perceived lack of room and amenities in the new location. But Joshua was unwavering in his faith, knowing that if he faithfully served God, He would provide. Decades later, in his farewell speech to the assembled tribes, Joshua challenged them with the choice recorded in today's verse. And they responded, "We will serve the LORD!" (verse 21).

God still poses that challenge to you today. Think what you will choose. Then guide your family in that way.

UNCOMMON KEY > *Decide today whom you will serve: God or everything else. Make it God!*

August 29

Uncompromised

> **But even before I was born, God chose me and called me by his marvelous grace.**
> GALATIANS 1:15

Entertainers Isaac Hayes and Bernie Mac, who died within days of each other in 2008, blazed their own trails. They believed their originality—not their ability to market themselves or come up with commercially viable material—was the key to their success. Hayes said he and artists of his era looked for ways to express themselves without focusing on what sells and what doesn't. Mac said he was his own kind of comic, not trying to conform to the expectations of others. His way might have been a longer road to success, but it was also the key to his success. Both entertainers emphasized how important it is to be yourself, express who you are, and do what you love to do.

That's not only a key to success, it's a key to relationships. Too many people compromise themselves in order to live up to the expectations of others. Some are still trying to compensate for things they missed in childhood, or positioning themselves to get their careers on track, or making up for past failures. We have all kinds of ways of adapting ourselves to make relationships work, even when we know the relationships aren't healthy. In work, in relationships, in any area of life, we can tend to pose as someone we're not.

But each of us was created for a reason. No matter how we've messed up or what we've missed, the future is still ahead of us. We have choices about how to handle it. We've learned some things from our pasts that might make the journey better. If we know—deep down in our cores—who we were created to be, we're much more likely to make the most of the future. We can build our relationships authentically, basing them on who we really are, not who others want us to be. When we develop friendships, we'll know they are genuine because people will be relating to and accepting the real us. We can live our lives without compromising ourselves.

That's what Bernie Mac and Isaac Hayes did, and they were loved for their originality and creativity. They chose not to base their lives on superficialities but rather on the ways God made them and the expression of the genuine persons they were. You can too.

UNCOMMON KEY > *Be yourself. God had a purpose in making you the way He did. When you compromise yourself, you miss that purpose and weaken your ability to have genuine relationships.*

August 30

Surf's Up!

> In the same way, wisdom is sweet to your soul. If you find it, you will have a bright future, and your hopes will not be cut short. PROVERBS 24:14

Have you ever wondered why we often give greater weight to the advice of people who don't know us rather than to those who do? I've heard friends—or their wives—lament that their spouses, children, or friends will give greater weight to someone else's opinion than the opinion of a trusted member of the family. I certainly have seen that happen in my family.

Nathan remembers a good example of that from his college days. Two of his friends, brothers Robert and Hal, were waiting in the course drop/add line at the University of Florida, back when changes were still entered by hand. It was the final day to add the classes that they needed that semester to stay on track to graduate.

That evening their father, who was an engineering professor at the school, asked them how everything turned out.

"We went surfing instead," they told him.

Their dad nearly fell to the floor, but luckily he landed in a nearby chair as his sons continued what seemed a logical explanation of their change of plans. It seems that when they were in line, they struck up a conversation with a guy who offered his piece of advice: if Robert and Hal weren't particularly excited about any of the courses still available, maybe they should skip this semester and try to get the classes they wanted the following semester. It made perfect sense to Robert and Hal. So they drove to St. Augustine and surfed all day.

Their father was beside himself, partly because they decided to drop out a semester, but even more so because their decision making totally lacked wisdom. How could they value so highly the opinion of someone they had just met, who had no idea who they were or what was important to them or what they were trying to accomplish?

It was unthinkable and unbelievable. It would be quite a while before they could all laugh about it.

UNCOMMON KEY > *Be careful of listening to "the man on the street." God's wisdom can usually be found in trusted relationships and revealed during times spent with Him.*

August 31

No Excuses, No Explanations

> Jesus saw him and knew he had been ill for a long time. . . . "Would you like to get well?"
> "I can't, sir," the sick man said, "for I have no one to put me into the pool when the water
> bubbles up. Someone else always gets there ahead of me." Jesus told him, "Stand up, pick
> up your mat, and walk!" Instantly, the man was healed! He rolled up his sleeping mat and
> began walking! JOHN 5:6-9

How many times do you find yourself making excuses to God?

In John 5, Jesus encounters a man beside the pool of Bethesda near the Sheep Gate. The pool was trapezoidal and as huge as a football field. Beneath the pool there were underground springs that bubbled up and disturbed the surface of the water from time to time. Many believed the disturbances were caused by an angel, thus giving the pool curative powers, and that the first person who got into the pool after the water moved would be healed from any illness that afflicted them.

The man Jesus approached had been an invalid for thirty-eight years. One solitary human being in the midst of this vast throng of people, and Jesus saw him! The man had given in to his illness and become a prisoner of his own despair.

Jesus asked, "Do you want to be made well?" The answer seems pretty obvious, except that Jesus saw a person who was full of excuses and defenses nurtured over thirty-eight years. The man had given up and given in. He gave the excuse that he had no one to help him.

There he was, confronted with the Healer of healers, and instead of recognizing that renewing power in front of him, he squawked, "It's not my fault that I'm still this way; my friends have let me down." Instead of saying yes when Christ asked him to make a choice, he threw out more excuses.

I wonder if those words have ever been our words.

Don't let it be the case again. No excuses, no explanations. The Healer of healers is right there to help make you whole. Take Him up on the offer.

UNCOMMON KEY > *Decide today that the next time an excuse starts to come out of your mouth, you will confess it to God and ask for His forgiveness. Try to live excuse-free before God and your family.*

September 1

Dave Thomas's Greatest Successes

> Anyone who welcomes a little child like this on my behalf is welcoming me. But if you cause one of these little ones who trusts in me to fall into sin, it would be better for you to have a large millstone tied around your neck and be drowned in the depths of the sea.
> MATTHEW 18:5-6

What is Christ actually saying here? What does it mean to let the little children come to Jesus and to not cause them to fall into sin?

Let me suggest that it comes down to what kind of role model we are, especially to children. Are we setting a good example for them by how we live out our faith, in our lifestyle choices and in our behavior—both publicly and privately?

The late Dave Thomas founded Wendy's Old Fashioned Hamburgers in 1969, naming the chain after his daughter, Wendy. Thomas had left school in the eighth grade, and as a result of his upbringing and his inability to get the education he still dearly wanted, he developed two passions focused on helping kids.

One was his promotion of adoption, since he was adopted. Thomas wasn't just making a nice suggestion that he wanted people to consider. He raised multimillions of dollars to assist families who were willing to adopt but didn't have the money to afford the expenses that the adoption process entailed. Thomas's other passion was education. Every time he had the chance to grab the microphone before a room full of kids, he would not only encourage them but tell them to stay in school.

One day during a presentation to high school students, one of them asked, "If education's so important, why didn't you go back?"

Convicted by the question, Dave Thomas earned his GED in 1993 from Coconut Creek High School in Florida and was voted "Most Likely to Succeed" by his classmates. Well, of course.

Dave Thomas realized that it's not enough to say the right things. We've got to live them out.

UNCOMMON KEY > *You have a responsibility to be a role model for the young people around you. Check into ways you could help a child be adopted, or assist a girl or boy struggling with educational challenges.*

September 2

Deeply Grieved

> Mary . . . said, "Lord, if only you had been here, my brother would not have died." When Jesus saw her weeping and saw the other people wailing with her, a deep anger welled up within him, and he was deeply troubled. "Where have you put him?" he asked them. They told him, "Lord, come and see." Then Jesus wept. JOHN 11:32-35

It had been four days since Lazarus, the brother of Martha and Mary, died, and a fountain of grief still engulfed the sisters. They were in a valley they couldn't see their way out of. As Jesus approached the edge of town, returning from a journey, a disappointed Martha ran to meet Him.

"Lord, if you had been here, my brother would not have died." She stared into His face with confused eyes. This was the same Martha who had always been in control, always ready for everything, always on duty. But facing her brother's death hurt too badly. And she was angry because the one person who could have saved Lazarus wasn't there to prevent it. He seemingly didn't care, even though He always said He considered Lazarus and his sisters to be good friends. Martha had seen Him do miraculous things for so many others, yet when her family needed Jesus most, He was not there for them. Or so she thought.

And then Jesus wept. His heart was torn with grief. In one of the most sensitive moments in all of Scripture, Jesus displayed both His godliness and His humanity. He wept, not only for those suffering the loss, but also for the people who still didn't believe He was the Messiah, their Savior, "the resurrection and the life" (John 11:25). No matter how much they had seen Him do and how many times He had told them, they still didn't believe.

Death will come to all humanity, but death does not have to have the last word.

The story of Lazarus begins with the promise that those who believe in Jesus will never die. And it ends with a Savior who is with them in their time of loss. Just as He is with us.

UNCOMMON KEY > *Jesus wept with empathy and with sympathy—and in frustration at their unbelief. Is He weeping for you or someone you know? Read the entire story of Lazarus in John 11:1-45.*

September 3

Knowing the Right Thing to Do

| **Never get tired of doing good.** 2 THESSALONIANS 3:13

My first class on my first day at the University of Minnesota was a psychology class that met three times a week for large-group lectures and twice a week for small-group discussions. On my way into the lecture hall, I was met by a guy with a box of notes for the entire quarter. He was selling them for twenty dollars, and lots of people were buying them. The notes would make attending the three lectures each week unnecessary, I was told. But I wasn't sure this was a good idea.

I questioned the guy about the notes. What if they weren't complete notes? What if the professor changed the lecture since the last course? How could I know the notes were accurate? He answered all the questions well enough to convince me—or at least for me to rationalize the need for them. I bought the notes.

But I was unsettled in my spirit about the whole thing. As the course progressed, I couldn't bring myself to skip the lectures. I found that the notes were accurate, that the professor didn't deviate from one quarter to the next, and that I really could have skipped without missing much. But it felt like cheating. I wouldn't have been earning my own A if I hadn't attended class myself. And I kept hearing my mother's words: "It's sometimes easier to do the wrong thing, but it's always better to do the right thing."

I learned a lesson from that experience: don't waver from doing what you know to be right and true. I've found that the unsettled feeling in my conscience is there for a reason. It's a God-given warning signal that I'm about to cross a line and violate His character. When I ignore that signal, I end up regretting it. But when I pay attention to the truth He has instilled in me through the course of my life, even when it isn't easy, I'm glad I did. Many people say they regret doing the wrong thing, but I rarely if ever have heard someone say they regret doing the right thing. It's always worth it to do what's right.

UNCOMMON KEY > *It's more satisfying and fulfilling to do a difficult thing that's right than an easy thing that's wrong. When your conscience speaks, listen.*

September 4

A Two-Way Street

> Submit to one another out of reverence for Christ. For wives, this means submit to your husbands as to the Lord. . . . As the church submits to Christ, so you wives should submit to your husbands in everything. For husbands, this means love your wives, just as Christ loved the church. He gave up his life for her. EPHESIANS 5:21-25

The relationship between a husband and wife is a two-way street. If the wife is going to submit to her husband—a word that makes many people uncomfortable—it has to be in the context of the husband loving his wife as Christ loved the church, enough to give up his life for her . . . day after day.

Similarly, if the husband is expected to give up his life for his wife, she has to be submitted in love and devotion to him. The mutual responsibilities of the husband to the wife and the wife to the husband are complementary to each other. They fit together just as the differences between the husband and wife complement each other.

Lauren and I are as different as night and day in many things that are part of our lives. The reason is simple: we were each created unique, like no one else, with our own sets of gifts and abilities, different things that interest us, and varying objectives and goals we want to accomplish. And yet despite all those differences, God brought us together. Why? To complement each other. To leverage our gifts and abilities for His Kingdom purposes. The unique insights, passions, life experiences, knowledge, and wisdom have been given to us for the benefit of each other and our marriage—and for the beneficiaries of that relationship, family and friends and the many others God brings into our lives.

There is no doubt in my mind that God had that in His mind when we stood before each other at the altar. Both Lauren and I bring what God created in us to this marriage relationship, for this time, for each other, and for all whom we will impact together in the days, months, and years ahead.

And it starts with mutual love and submission.

UNCOMMON KEY > *If you're married, think of how your spouse complements you. If you're single, what complementary things do you think God wants you to look for in a future spouse?*

September 5

Kickers Know Best

> Fix your thoughts on what is true, and honorable, and right, and pure, and lovely, and admirable. Think about things that are excellent and worthy of praise. **PHILIPPIANS 4:8**

During my career as a player and a coach, I worked with some of the best kickers in the National Football League—guys like Adam Vinatieri, Mike Vanderjagt, Michael Husted, and Martín Gramática. One of the things they all had in common was the ability to focus on the positive. They always believed they were going to make the next kick. The really successful kickers are able to envision the ball splitting the uprights, dead center. They know from experience that negative thoughts doom their efforts.

Since a lot of a kicker's time is spent on the sideline waiting, each of them has a different technique to help maintain his focus until the crucial moment he is called onto the field. Some talk about other things with their coaches or teammates. Some kickers sit by themselves and relax. Some focus on the goalposts at the far end of the field that present a much narrower target, so that when they line up facing the goalposts that are their actual target, they appear much wider and inviting. Others pray.

Essentially, these kickers do what the apostle Paul suggests we do in whatever setting we find ourselves: focus on the positive; fix our thoughts on things that are good and right and pure. On the field or in our homes or at work, when we think of our spouses, our children, friends, employees, or coworkers—we should fix our thoughts on what is true, and honorable, and right, and pure, and lovely, and admirable. We should think about things that are excellent and worthy of praise.

Adopting a positive attitude, even when you're under pressure or the odds seem stacked against you, nearly always assures a positive outcome. And thinking of people in a positive light changes how you treat them.

UNCOMMON KEY > *No matter what you face in life, approach it with a positive outlook. Consider what's true, honorable, right, pure, lovely, and admirable about the situation or the person. And go from there.*

September 6

Job Satisfaction

My purpose is to give them a rich and satisfying life. JOHN 10:10

Work is good. Work is necessary. Work should be a reflection of our God-given talents, abilities, and passions. Work should be fun.

My good friend Tony Evans, a pastor in Dallas, says we were created to work. "Before Adam had Eve, he had a job," he says. Work is good. Adding value is positive. Using the gifts and abilities God designed within us is good. Being compensated for using them in a productive way that benefits others is not only good, but the means God gave us to be self-sufficient and able to help others.

"What am I going to do with my life?" is a question we all ask. A lot of times we think we're trying to figure out our careers when we're really trying to figure out our purposes. I've seen it often in high school and college students as they think about what they want to do in life. The bigger question isn't what we're going to do but why we're going to do it. And we need to answer it not in terms of activity but in terms of purpose, meaning, and fulfillment.

I've had at least seven different employers in the sports industry, and not all of them have hired me to do the same thing. I've been a player, a coach, and an analyst. You've probably performed different jobs too. What you're doing today probably isn't what you've always done and probably isn't what you'll always do in the future. People who have been in one line of work for their entire career are rare. But people who know their purpose in life will never become obsolete.

Before you decide what to do, figure out what your purpose is. Then decide what to do—how to accomplish that purpose—not on the basis of money, convenience, or availability, if possible, but on the basis of what you're passionate about. Sure, there are times when you have to just "get by." But make those times temporary. Use your gifts, pursue your passions, and work toward your purposes. When you do that, you'll find that work isn't a burden but a gift from God. And it can be a key to living a fulfilling life.

It's great to love your work and a blessing to enjoy it.

UNCOMMON KEY > *Work—make it an extension of who God made you to be.*

September 7

Witnesses Wherever We Are

> "But you will receive power when the Holy Spirit comes upon you. And you will be my witnesses, telling people about me everywhere—in Jerusalem, throughout Judea, in Samaria, and to the ends of the earth." After saying this, [Jesus] was taken up into a cloud while they were watching, and they could no longer see him. ACTS 1:8-9

Don't rush out to buy a ticket to Jerusalem, Judea, or Samaria. Jesus' directive to His disciples isn't a literal command for you and me. As Jesus ascended into heaven, the disciples were left with the Holy Spirit for guidance and assistance in following God's commands, especially the command to share His message everywhere they went. The same is true for us—wherever we find ourselves.

God knows where we are, both in physical location and in spiritual maturity. He sees what spheres of influence we have, the places we have access to, the people we know.

Those spheres of influence may include our family, both nuclear and extended, as well as our neighborhood, workplace, and nearby community (our "Jerusalem"). From there, we move into areas such as our cities and towns and among our friends, wherever they are located (our "Judea"); and then other extended areas of influence across our region and nation, within our universities, government, and other places of impact (our "Samaria") and well beyond.

We never know what God has in mind. People all over the world heard me mention my faith when we played in the Super Bowl, but I would say it's harder sometimes to share one's faith closer to home.

Christ's call on our lives is forever, and even if we don't have the opportunity to go to the ends of the earth, we are told to begin with every place and person within elbow's reach. We don't go alone; the Holy Spirit accompanies and counsels us. His power will help us to become bold witnesses for Christ.

UNCOMMON KEY > *Does the word* witness *scare you? You are commanded to share with others what Jesus has done in your life. Pray for the boldness you need to start today.*

September 8

Foundations of Stone

> I am planning to build a Temple to honor the name of the LORD my God, just as he had instructed my father, David. For the LORD told him, "Your son, whom I will place on your throne, will build the Temple to honor my name." . . . At the king's command, they quarried large blocks of high-quality stone and shaped them to make the foundation of the Temple.
> 1 KINGS 5:5, 17

Since she started middle school, Nathan's daughter, Hannah, has been bringing home more complex math homework. Remember word problems—taking abstract math concepts and applying them to real-world situations? "A train leaves city A at 11:00 at 17 miles per hour, while a bus leaves city B at . . ." When Hannah sets up the word problem correctly, she is one step closer to the answer. But if she rushes through the addition, subtraction, multiplication, and division integral to the solution, the answer will still be wrong. The foundational math skills she learned in elementary school are principles she is now building on and are crucial to her success.

Solid foundations are critical in all aspects of life, whether it is constructing a building, learning the fundamentals in a sport, or mastering another new skill. Did you notice that Solomon used "high-quality stone" for the foundation of the Temple? That high-quality stone would not be noticed by the people who came to worship, but it was critically important for the integrity of the building. It was also important to Solomon because he felt he was doing something necessary to honor the name of the Lord.

The same is true for you. You can strive to be the best role model possible by volunteering at the soup kitchen or participating in charitable events, but your real influence comes from the foundation of your character. People will see how you handle things when problems tackle you and notice the difference.

UNCOMMON KEY > *The fundamental things you've been told since you were young— to tell the truth, act courageously, stand firm for things that matter—form the foundation of any future influence that you may have, like it or not. Keep honing those traits so they become "high-quality stone."*

September 9

From Mercenary to Volunteer

> Sell your possessions and give to those in need. This will store up treasure for you in heaven! And the purses of heaven never get old or develop holes. Your treasure will be safe; no thief can steal it and no moth can destroy it. Wherever your treasure is, there the desires of your heart will also be. LUKE 12:33-34

Chester Taylor is an honest man. The running back was asked by Jim Trotter of *Sports Illustrated* why he had chosen to join the Chicago Bears in 2010 as a free agent. "First and foremost, it was the money," he said. Of course, he went on to give a variety of other reasons for selecting the Bears as his new team, but the first thing out of his mouth was sincere. He wanted a bigger paycheck.

I can appreciate his candor. He articulated what most of us suspect to be true, not only for pro athletes like Chester, but for anyone who changes jobs. In spite of all the reasons we give for a decision, money is often the most significant motivator.

Chuck Noll, my coach when I played for the Pittsburgh Steelers, used to tell us, "The mercenaries will beat the draftees, but the volunteers will crush them both." To me, that's not only a statement about motivation—that those who are there because they want to be will have an advantage over those who are there for the paycheck—but also a reflection of the heart. Where our treasure is, there will our hearts be also. For better or worse.

As human beings, our motives will almost always be mixed. That's okay. But in whatever we choose to do, at some point we need to make the shift from "mercenary" to "volunteer." Our "have to" needs to change into a "want to." And whether we're parents, coaches, or employers, we'll have to help others make that shift too.

How can we do that? For ourselves, I think we always need to hold the bigger picture in front of us—to step back, look at what's really important, and invest our lives in something that lasts. And we can help others through that process too. It starts with listening and understanding where someone is coming from, giving them a vision, and inspiring them to buy into something larger than themselves. The motives we start with don't have to be the motives we end up with.

UNCOMMON KEY > *Always check your heart when it comes to the motives behind your decisions. Is it following its "have to" or its "want to"? If necessary, make adjustments.*

September 10

No Room for Complainers

> Do everything without complaining and arguing, so that no one can criticize you. Live clean, innocent lives as children of God, shining like bright lights in a world full of crooked and perverse people. **PHILIPPIANS 2:14-15**

I'm sure you're not guilty of complaining about your boss or the owner of your company. But believe it or not, some people complain about a lot of things. I certainly have. And so have my children. They've gotten better about being obedient, but sometimes they feel the need to voice their displeasure before they do what they're told. Let's admit it: all too often, we live in a society of complainers.

The apostle Paul is right. We'd definitely stand out if we didn't complain about everything like everyone else does, whether it be rising gas prices or a mistake in our take-out order. We'd certainly be "bright lights." It's hard to hide or blend in or be part of a group of complainers when you don't think the same way. Who knows? If we stay focused on the positive, perhaps our energy and enthusiasm will change those around us. Perhaps we can remind them of some of the benefits they are overlooking—like being employed in a hurting job market, working in a comfortable environment, and getting a regular paycheck.

Maybe we could put our heads together to figure out how to make the current situation better, something my father always encouraged me to do. The key is to focus on the positives, not the negatives. I agree with Winston Churchill, who said, "For myself I am an optimist—it does not seem to be much use being anything else."

When I was coaching in Tampa Bay, I remember venting at the officials during a game with the New York Giants as we were heading into the locker room—I was totally frustrated at a call they made right at the end of the game. I commented on it afterward to the media.

The next day I apologized to the officials publicly. I knew that people watched me as an example of someone who didn't complain, and I'd totally blown it in that moment when I vented. I felt it only appropriate to apologize to the officials publicly, since my actions were public.

UNCOMMON KEY > *Rather than complaining about a situation, try to count the blessings in it, and then be a positive force to make things better.*

September 11

Bedtime Stories

> Do not let these memories escape from your mind as long as you live! And be sure to pass them on to your children and grandchildren. DEUTERONOMY 4:9

One of the great moments of raising children is the bedtime routine. There are those who have it down to a science. Within a brief span of fifteen minutes, their child is bathed, brushed, tucked, prayed over, and off to sleep. Then there are the rest of us. For an ever-changing set of reasons, we never fit within that time frame.

We like to think of ourselves as efficient, regimented; we've had plenty of practice. But once our kids learned that we are malleable, especially when it comes to bedtime stories and books, we are lucky if they're off to sleep within forty-five minutes or an hour. Meanwhile, we prepare our defense to our spouse for the extended bedtime ritual.

Just when we think things are all set and seem to be moving quickly, the words "Tell me a story" cut the night air. And off we go. Sometimes the stories are about a little girl or boy whose experiences are amazingly similar to those of Cinderella, Peter Pan, or Pinocchio, or about the little girl who grew up to become anything she wanted to be. At other times, the stories are about when they were younger and how cute they were. About the time the family went to the zoo and waved at the monkeys, howled with the wolves, or squealed when the dolphins splashed them. It's a time for children to hear something about their roots—where they were born, how Mommy and Daddy met, the country Granddad came from, when Grandma first heard about Jesus. All those stories matter and never grow old.

Through the spoken word, children learn about their personal history and how it has helped shape who they are now and will become in the future.

Take advantage of the opportunities to tell stories to your children, as much as possible. They are some of the sweetest times you'll ever have and a great time to plant spiritual seeds, tell your children about Christ, or include God in some of those bedtime stories.

UNCOMMON KEY > *We all need to remember who we are and where we came from, and eventually, Whose we are. Bedtime is an opportune time to do that.*

September 12

Following the Light Brings Hope

> I am the light of the world. If you follow me, you won't have to walk in darkness, because you will have the light that leads to life.   JOHN 8:12

There's not a lot of light when I go in there. Darkness seems to permeate the atmosphere. And yet I need to go.

I have had the sad yet hope-filled privilege of visiting the inmates in many jails and prisons in my life. My dear, departed friend Abe Brown was the man who called me into that outreach.

Coach Brown realized that too many men from all sorts of backgrounds end up behind bars and need some sense of direction and hope, not only for the time they are incarcerated but also for when they are released. Too many, he realized, had never found themselves, never seen anything worthwhile in themselves, and never seen where they could possibly fit in the world around them or the world outside.

I recently saw a movie by Walden Media, under the guiding hand of my good friend Micheal Flaherty, that offers that sense of hope. *I Am David* follows the life of a twelve-year-old boy, David, separated from his parents in childhood and sent to a labor camp in Bulgaria, part of the Communist system of camps of the former Soviet Union.

Set just after World War II, David knows little else than the evil he sees around him. Yet through an unexpected source of grace, David escapes and survives a treacherous journey to Denmark.

Because of his past, he doesn't seem to fit in anywhere and can only see the darkness in people and circumstances. Yet slowly, through some "chance" encounters, he begins to trust a few people in whom he sees a ray of light that finally brings him peace, comfort, and a place in the world.

That's what a life in Christ promises for each of us. In the midst of the darkness, He will always be a light guiding and illuminating our way in order for us to discover who we were created to be in this world and the next. And we, in turn, must reflect that light for others around us.

UNCOMMON KEY > *Support a prison ministry in some way, if you can—either through volunteering, writing letters, making a charitable gift, or in some other tangible way. Help bring Christ, the Light of the World, to the lives of inmates.*

September 13

You Are What You Absorb

> You are not controlled by your sinful nature. You are controlled by the Spirit if you have the Spirit of God living in you. (And remember that those who do not have the Spirit of Christ living in them do not belong to him at all.) And Christ lives within you, so even though your body will die because of sin, the Spirit gives you life because you have been made right with God. ROMANS 8:9-10

If you have hydrangeas in your yard, you may have heard of this. Some people swear that if you plant rusty nails with a pink-blooming hydrangea, the flowers will change to blue over time. Supposedly it has something to do with adding metal to the soil, but gardeners know that the hydrangea is the litmus test of the flower world—its color is affected by the pH level and the amount of aluminum in the soil.

Like all plants, the hydrangea absorbs nutrients through its roots that, for these showy blooms, benefits the final outcome.

We're like that as well. We absorb what is around us and reflect it back in different ways, good or not. Someone lets us pull out in front of them in traffic, and we wave someone else in a few moments later. Someone shares a word of encouragement or prayer with us, and when we return home, our spouse is the beneficiary of a kind word and a warm embrace.

What we take in often comes back in ways we can't anticipate. The key is to make sure that what we absorb is helpful to us and glorifying to God. It must demonstrate that we know our bodies and minds are God's temple, the dwelling place of the Holy Spirit.

That's why Coach Noll was always careful with the coaches and players he brought to the Pittsburgh Steelers. Because he was trying to create a positive atmosphere that would solidify the team, he had to carefully screen the attitudes of everyone who was coming in. He preferred not to trade for players who had been with other teams because he didn't want them talking in the locker room about how things were done with their old team. He was reluctant to bring in coaches from other clubs for the same reason.

What are you absorbing into your life today? Do you need to add more healthy things, eliminating things that compromise your witness and do not glorify God? The things that you take in often come out in your words, your attitudes, your habits. Make sure everything you bring in is worthy of being in the temple.

UNCOMMON KEY > *Your mind is like a sponge, absorbing everything it dwells on. Is it a soiled sponge or a clean one? Keep it clean and focused on what will bring glory to God.*

September 14

Eternity Is Wrapped Up in a Relationship

As to whether there will be a resurrection of the dead—haven't you ever read about this in the Scriptures? Long after Abraham, Isaac, and Jacob had died, God said, "I am the God of Abraham, the God of Isaac, and the God of Jacob." So he is the God of the living, not the dead. MATTHEW 22:31-32

God is eternal. He existed before anything else and will last long after we pass from this earth. That's what we hope. That's what we believe. It's what Scripture has taught us, and it is what provides us comfort as we live in this world and look forward to living in the next.

Nathan says he was saved at the age of twelve, but that it wasn't until he reached high school and heard the preaching of Ken Smith—longtime team chaplain at a variety of schools, including Florida State, Mississippi State, and Carson-Newman—that he realized Christ calls us to strive to live an exemplary life every day, long before we're in heaven.

Sometimes, though, our mind-set dwells on the temporary, the here and now. We tend to focus on the transient. Our waking moments are occupied by the things going on in our waking moments. Sometimes we think of our physical lives as all that defines us. But just as God is eternal, we are eternal—created by Him to spend an eternity with Him.

Have you ever heard someone say, "This is taking an eternity"? It's usually when the person is waiting—often impatiently—for something. The next time you catch yourself thinking of eternity in terms of time, think of Jesus and your relationship to Him. Christ's death and resurrection assures those who believe in Him of that ongoing relationship that spans and conquers time and place. For eternity—forever.

UNCOMMON KEY > *Live each day thankful for Jesus' death and resurrection. Not only was it a historical event, but it was the way God made it possible to have a relationship with Him—now and for all eternity.*

September 15

Critical Condition

> John the Baptist didn't spend his time eating bread or drinking wine, and you say, "He's possessed by a demon." The Son of Man, on the other hand, feasts and drinks, and you say, "He's a glutton and a drunkard, and a friend of tax collectors and other sinners!"
>
> LUKE 7:33-34

Some people are incessant critics.

The Pharisees and Sadducees in the day of John the Baptist and Jesus Christ fit within that group. They remind me of sportswriter Bob Kravitz of the *Indianapolis Star* and some other sportswriters I've known. These first-century leaders criticized John for not drinking wine or eating enough, and they criticized Jesus for eating and drinking with tax collectors, prostitutes, and other sinners. How about that for consistency! Actually, the underlying focus of their concerns was that both men continually exposed the hypocrisy of the complainers' "religion." They didn't like what John and Jesus stood for or put into action, and as a result they did all they could do to find things to criticize them about and damage their credibility in the eyes of the general public.

I faced that at times—we all do. Some sportswriters would take me to task for giving second chances to players, while others criticized me for emphasizing character too heavily. I received criticism for having a defense-led team in Tampa Bay and being too conservative, rather than developing a higher-powered offense; in Indianapolis, I was criticized for having an offensive-minded team that didn't have enough defensive stars.

Some will criticize NFL coaches for making the playoffs regularly but never "winning the big one"—the Super Bowl. Other coaches are criticized for selling out their future teams to attempt one year of greatness instead of sustained excellence and regular appearances in the playoffs, even though they don't have a Super Bowl–caliber team to work with every year.

Go figure.

That's what Jesus noted too. People criticized John the Baptist for not drinking wine and then criticized Jesus for drinking wine. Of course, the religious leaders of the day criticized both of them for other things as well—revealing the inconsistency in their complaints.

When people criticize you, it's not always for your actions but for what you represent. If they're really criticizing you for your faith, it's important to maintain your focus and continue on the pathway that God has set before you, even in the midst of criticism.

UNCOMMON KEY > *When you feel attacked by critical remarks, ask God and a fellow believer for wisdom on how to deal with the situation. See if you can get to the bottom of the criticism before it has a chance to snowball.*

September 16

The Gate That Leads to Victory

> You can enter God's Kingdom only through the narrow gate. The highway to hell is broad, and its gate is wide for the many who choose that way. But the gateway to life is very narrow and the road is difficult, and only a few ever find it. MATTHEW 7:13-14

When my son Eric was a freshman football player at the University of Oregon, I shared some thoughts with him and his teammates about entering through the narrow gate.

Eric is still irritated with me for that talk.

You see, there are two entrances to the football practice field on the campus. The one nearest to the locker room is the standard entrance, usually used by everyone to go to practice. However, down at the far end, much farther from the locker room, is a second entrance to the field, one with a much smaller entryway.

A narrow gate. Followed by a difficult road.

After hearing me share with the team, and I suppose to make the point that the team that year would be doing more than what was normally expected of them, Oregon's head coach, Chip Kelly, had them walk every day to the far gate as they entered the practice field. I guess this didn't make Eric very popular with his teammates.

But it seemed to make the point with the team, as day after day they would head down to the narrow gate, realizing that to be exceptional, to reach the goals they had set for themselves, it would take doing more than what was expected. It would take doing the little things better and more often. It would take entering through the narrow gate—which Christ teaches in this passage is the only way to eternal life. It would take walking on the difficult and hard road that followed—which Christ advises is the way of discipleship filled with persecution and opposition—and would lead to eternal life.

The analogy to their team was easy. And the lesson was clear.

By the way, they also went on to play in the national championship game. As for Eric? Hopefully he isn't upset with me any longer.

The path through the narrow gate is not always easy, but it's the most rewarding.

UNCOMMON KEY > *There is only one way to obtain eternal life—through the narrow gate Christ holds open to you. Walk through it and follow Him.*

September 17

Life's Landmarks

> Hear the instruction of your father, and do not forsake the law of your mother.
> PROVERBS 1:8, NKJV

Life is full of opportunities to take the easy way. I found that to be true pretty quickly when I left home to attend the University of Minnesota, and the temptations only increased after college. Doing the right thing seemed to involve many shades of gray—good reasons like convenience and saving time—so finding shortcuts always looked appealing. My mother's words—"It's sometimes easier to do the wrong thing, but it's always better to do the right thing"—came to mind more often than I could count. They applied to more situations than I imagined.

So much of what seems convenient and expedient at any given moment is really a distraction. Temptations to take the easy way will throw us off track and send us on the wrong direction in our lives. They are detours from the landmarks that should guide us. Even though we live in a world that considers values to be fluid, subject to change with circumstances or popular opinion, we know we can count on certain absolutes. We all have a sense of right and wrong. Some of us have a lot of practice ignoring that sense, but it's there. And we need to do whatever we can to rely on the landmarks.

Where do your landmarks come from? If you had good parents who instilled values in you, like I did, you have a great foundation. If not, you still know people of integrity who can serve as examples for you. In either case, we all have access to God's Word, which is the basis for the absolutes we believe and the values we are to live by. These absolutes and values don't change. They aren't a matter of popular opinion. They don't apply to some situations and not to others. They aren't negotiable. We can always count on them to keep us headed in the right direction—even when a more expedient or convenient shortcut tempts us.

The landmarks we should use to find our footing and direction will always be the same. The fundamentals don't change. And my mother's words will always be relevant: "It's sometimes easier to do the wrong thing, but it's always better to do the right thing."

UNCOMMON KEY > *Know your values and don't depart from them. Choose "right" over "easy" whenever life offers you a shortcut.*

September 18

The Choice

> I am the way, the truth, and the life. No one can come to the Father except through me. If you had really known me, you would know who my Father is. From now on, you do know him and have seen him! JOHN 14:6-7

There you have it—a positive and negative promise for all eternity. Jesus clearly laid out what would happen by choosing either direction—eternal heaven or eternal hell. Every human being will be going one way or the other. The key is which way. It is an essential foundational decision that must not be overlooked by anyone, something that needs to be discussed and built upon in families.

A family from Indianapolis recently lost their daughter, Tessa, a student at the University of Tampa, in a car accident. Lauren and I had a chance to visit with the family and watch how they handled their grief. When we finished talking, I walked away knowing that I was seeing the strength of the Lord in their response.

Tessa's father spoke at the memorial service, and his comments were poignant yet blunt. He noted that while he and his family were grieving, they took solace in knowing they would see Tessa again. And then he said, "But for those who don't believe in Jesus, you've seen Tessa for the last time." He then urged each person there to enter into a relationship with Christ.

We need to stop for a moment and be certain of one essential matter in our lives. We can be the greatest man or woman, the best boss, the best tipper, the nicest customer. We can buy our spouse the most thoughtful presents or take time to affirm our friends whether they seem to need it or not. We can consistently be considered outstanding parents by our children and regularly encourage our children so they always know how loved and precious they are to us.

But if we don't know Jesus Christ, we're simply going through the motions for a few days out of eternity. We may be nice people, but we are still not going to spend our lives with Him forever. The only thing that matters to Him is how we answer the question, Are you a child of the living Lord or not? Have you shared, taught, and ingrained that within your family so that each of them is a child of the living Lord?

Make certain that you are. Make certain that you do.

Recognize you are a sinner and separated from God, thank Christ for what He did for you on the cross so that you can have an eternal relationship with God through Christ, and commit to follow Him as Lord in your life. In other words, put Him first.

If this is something you need to take care of, now's the time for you and those whom you love.

UNCOMMON KEY > *Jesus is the one and only way to an everlasting life with God. Do you need to remind yourself or someone else of that truth?*

September 19

A Father-in-Law's Advice

> You're going to wear yourself out—and the people, too. This job is too heavy a burden for you to handle all by yourself. Now listen to me, and let me give you a word of advice, and may God be with you. You should continue to be the people's representative before God, bringing their disputes to him. EXODUS 18:18-19

Sometimes the better part of valor is learning that we need to ask for assistance. Remember, we are not on this journey alone—family, friends, and others are there to walk with us. I have worked under coaches who were micromanagers, which I found to be both inefficient and dispiriting. Inefficient, of course, because if I was qualified to do the job I was hired to do, it can't be more efficient for both of us to do it. And dispiriting because the message I heard through their actions, whether they meant it or not, was that they didn't trust me to do the job correctly.

I've always tried to take the words that Jethro spoke to his son-in-law Moses to heart. Moses had been leading the Israelites on his own for years. But things were getting out of hand. Moses had to share his frustration with someone, so Jethro got an earful:

> The people come to me to get a ruling from God. When a dispute arises, they come to me, and I am the one who settles the case between the quarreling parties. I inform the people of God's decrees and give them his instructions. (Exodus 18:15-16)

In short, Moses was doing it all. And then Jethro had another, and better, idea—delegate.

Delegation isn't always easy. It requires trust and a willingness to let go of control. It also provides the opportunity for you to build into the lives of your friends, coworkers, and others around you. The hardest part of delegating is freeing up time in the short term to make sure that people are up to speed and can take on more responsibility in the long term. But I realized in my own process of delegating that I was adding value to the lives of my friends—of people I respected and admired and, perhaps more important, people I had a responsibility to help to become all they could be.

Once that's been accomplished, you can let go and watch others grow and perform as you move on to other, more pressing tasks. In the end, your time is used much more efficiently and effectively. And you have built further and new bonds of friendship and respect in the process.

Are you a controller? It might be time for a change.

UNCOMMON KEY > *Whether it is on the job or at home, be willing to relinquish complete control and to delegate to others. You'll help yourself and your delegates—and your friends.*

September 20

Walking the Plank

> We ourselves are like fragile clay jars containing this great treasure. This makes it clear that our great power is from God, not from ourselves. We are pressed on every side by troubles, but we are not crushed. We are perplexed, but not driven to despair. We are hunted down, but never abandoned by God. We get knocked down, but we are not destroyed. Through suffering . . . the life of Jesus may also be seen in our bodies. 2 CORINTHIANS 4:7-10

Pushing us, pinning us, trying to crush and destroy us—the imagery in today's verses is vivid and sobering. Satan is at work to bring us down.

But he's not winning. The reason? Because of the treasure inside us—the fragile clay jars.

My first year as a head coach in Tampa Bay, we began the year with five straight losses.

To make matters worse, I wasn't the fans' first choice to take over as head coach of the Buccaneers—they had hoped for Steve Spurrier, a former Bucs quarterback and successful head coach at Florida and Duke. And I was selling something entirely different than the players had known in Tampa. I had made no secret of the fact that while winning football games was important, it wasn't the most important thing to me. My faith and my family were foremost in my mind, and I was not only talking about improving the football team on the field but also helping to build an organization grounded in character and integrity.

That strategy is easier to sell when you're winning. The franchise had never done well, and the number one priority seemed to be to win football games.

And so, here we were, 0–5. But I was able to take comfort in these verses from 2 Corinthians because I knew God was right there with me.

That was a difficult and very public moment, but frankly, that doesn't rank very high on my personal scorecard of other difficult moments of being pressed, perplexed, hunted down, and knocked down.

We all have them, often when we least expect them. But the treasure within us—Jesus Christ—is the reason why when those moments press in all around us, we will not be crushed, we will not be driven to despair, we will not feel abandoned, and we will not be destroyed. That treasure within those cracked and chipped clay jars of our lives gives us the power and passion we need to get back up and press on.

Whether you are bracing yourself for the inevitable blow or trying to pick yourself up from one that has already landed, Jesus is there to help you get back in the fight.

UNCOMMON KEY > *With Christ in your life, you may get knocked down, but you will never get knocked out. And when you do get knocked down, He will help you get back on your feet.*

September 21

Continually Checking Your Priorities

> Don't let the excitement of youth cause you to forget your Creator. Honor him in your youth before you grow old and say, "Life is not pleasant anymore." . . . Fear God and obey his commands, for this is everyone's duty. God will judge us for everything we do, including every secret thing, whether good or bad. ECCLESIASTES 12:1, 13-14

King Solomon was highly successful by most people's standards—he had fame, fortune, status, comfort, and power—but his life did not end well. That's because those things don't satisfy us. I've seen too many people seeking things that aren't worthy of all the time, expense, and effort to get them. Time eventually shows which of our pursuits were ultimately empty. Excessive time at the office watching game film, or chasing after fame, fortune, or fleeting pleasure. All empty.

We've seen how Christ's priorities are different from the world's value system, and most of us have to reevaluate our priorities from time to time in order to line them up with what's truly valuable. We don't want to end like Solomon did—knowing the key to a meaningful, fulfilling life but never living up to what we know to be true. But how do we shift our priorities? How do we make the changes we want to make?

A life centered on Christ will not only help to free us from the uncertainty of our tomorrows and worries about success and achievements—what Solomon called "chasing after the wind." It will redirect our focus toward what really matters. It will put finances, health, relationships, and our goals for the future in the right perspective. When we "chase after God" rather than chasing after the wind, we find that our relationship with Him rearranges our priorities.

It's never too late to put things in order and enjoy the blessings God has placed all around us—blessings like a beautiful sunset, the face of a newborn baby, the laugh of a child, or any other evidence of His work in our lives. Shifting our priorities will require some changes, and it isn't always easy. Solomon said the key to a meaningful, fulfilling life is God. If we make Him the center of our lives, He changes our perspective and our purpose.

UNCOMMON KEY > *The key to shifting our priorities is focusing on God above all else and letting His priorities become ours.*

September 22

I Didn't Ask to Be a Role Model

| **You should imitate me, just as I imitate Christ.** 1 CORINTHIANS 11:1

John Stallworth was one of my role models. When I joined the Pittsburgh Steelers, I was still just a kid—a good guy who had been raised right but who was trying to learn my way around an unfamiliar situation. John had already been there three years and would go on to be a four-time Super Bowl champion, be named to four Pro Bowls, and become a member of the Pro Football Hall of Fame. And he was (and still is) an outstanding person. Whenever practice was over, he would head home to be with his wife and family. He was friendly, engaging, and faithful to his commitments. As a young player susceptible to peer pressure, I needed someone like him to look up to.

I found myself wanting the kind of life John had—a stable home life with plenty of interests outside of football. John never preached or talked down to people who had other lifestyles; he just lived his life for others to observe. And that's how being a role model works. You don't choose to be one. You just are. People look up to you not because you ask them to but because you live in a way that attracts their attention.

Everyone is a role model to someone, whether for good or bad. We all have influence. We may not want to be or feel that we're worthy of role-model status, but people may be watching and following our examples when we aren't aware they are doing it. We may think our behavior affects only ourselves, but that's not how life works. We don't choose to be role models, we just are. People look up to us not because we ask them to but because we live in a way that attracts their attention.

Everyone is a role model to someone, whether for good or bad. We all have influence. We may not want to be or may not feel that we're worthy of role-model status, but people may be watching and following our examples when we aren't aware they are doing it. We may think our behavior affects only ourselves, but that's not how life works. We have family, friends, and coworkers who see what we do and are influenced by it. Our examples make a difference.

Since you can't help being an example to others, why not strive to be a good one? Understand your influence and use it wisely. Someone may be watching.

UNCOMMON KEY > *What others see in you will make a difference, one way or another. Make it a positive difference today.*

September 23

Protective Padding

> Put on all of God's armor so that you will be able to stand firm against all strategies of the devil. For we are not fighting against flesh-and-blood enemies, but against evil rulers and authorities of the unseen world.... Therefore, put on every piece of God's armor so you will be able to resist the enemy in the time of evil. Then after the battle you will still be standing firm. EPHESIANS 6:11-13

I'm sure you've seen photos of early football players wearing those distinctive leather helmets. We've certainly come a long way since then with football gear, that's for sure. Today, coaches wouldn't send their players out on the football field without protective pads or helmets. Some players are wearing less padding these days, but there are some pieces of equipment no one would go without. The helmet falls into that must-have category, especially with all of the recent concussion incidents that have occurred. The big pieces of equipment seem obvious, but the small ones can make a big difference too. I've learned that mouthpieces can play a huge role in eliminating or mitigating concussions. I believe in the importance of protective gear.

But more important than protective sports equipment is the spiritual armor that Paul describes in detail in Ephesians 6:10-18—armor to prepare us for the spiritual battle we're engaged in each and every day.

I have a friend who says he began to believe that spiritual warfare was real after he read Frank Peretti's books *This Present Darkness* and *Piercing the Darkness*.

These novels, written decades ago, recount human heroes and villains caught up in a spiritual battle between the angels of heaven and the demons of hell. It's sobering to think that what is depicted is actually going on in our world, the heavens, and within us. We are engaged in a monumental battle for our souls between the forces of good, with God in command, and the forces of evil under Satan's power.

No wonder we need the full-body armor of God: the belt of truth and the body armor of God's righteousness (v. 14); shoes of peace (v. 15); the shield of faith (v. 16); the helmet of salvation and the sword of the Spirit, which is the Word of God (v. 17). Once outfitted, Paul says to pray constantly, staying alert and persistent.

The good news is that in the very end, God wins. But we have work to do for Him in the meantime.

UNCOMMON KEY > *Read the entire passage (Ephesians 6:10-18) describing the spiritual armor God has set aside for you. It's true that you're in the midst of a titanic spiritual struggle, but the power of the devil is no match for the power of God.*

September 24

Empowered in Your Weakness

> Three different times I begged the Lord to take it away. Each time he said, "My grace is all you need. My power works best in weakness." So now I am glad to boast about my weaknesses, so that the power of Christ can work through me. That's why I take pleasure in my weaknesses, and in the insults, hardships, persecutions, and troubles that I suffer for Christ. For when I am weak, then I am strong. 2 CORINTHIANS 12:8-10

We live in a world that considers weakness a liability. No one wants to show any weakness, especially on the football field. A physically weak player doesn't last very long in the league. If opponents know where a player's weak spots are, they have a better chance of capitalizing on them.

You might think from today's verses that God wouldn't make a good football coach. After all, He turns the idea of weakness on its head. He applauds weakness rather than criticizes it. That's because to God, it denotes a change of heart.

Scripture never reveals what the apostle Paul's "weakness" or "thorn in the flesh" was specifically. He certainly endured major physical pain throughout his missionary journeys—beatings, shipwrecks, jail sentences, hunger and thirst, homelessness. Certainly to survive such endless calamity attests to Paul's physical fortitude. But Paul was helpless and weak and had no ability to do anything about what was happening, about the circumstances through which God was eventually glorified.

When Paul experienced heartache and despair—when he was physically, mentally, emotionally, and spiritually spent—God was lifted up and magnified. He worked through Paul's weakness to show His greatness.

There were times on the sidelines during crucial moments in critical games when I knew that everyone was going to be looking to me for direction. The head football coach is supposed to have the answer to every situation his team is facing. Fourth down and inches—punt or go for it? Make a sure field goal or take a chance on a touchdown?

I didn't have the answer.

All I could do was seek God's peace and direction in prayer and admit that I couldn't do it myself. And the result was an overwhelming peace that I was not alone—He was there and had never left.

In my weakness, He was lifted up.

And the answer came. Sometimes it worked. But the result wasn't the important thing of that moment. What was important was that I had learned to rely on Him and knew He was always there.

UNCOMMON KEY > *Being vulnerable and showing your weakness is when "the power of Christ" can work through you. In the moments when you can't, He can!*

September 25

Give and Receive Blessings

> "Bring all the tithes into the storehouse so there will be enough food in my Temple. If you do," says the LORD of Heaven's Armies, "I will open the windows of heaven for you. I will pour out a blessing so great you won't have enough room to take it in! Try it! Put me to the test!" MALACHI 3:10

Jesus made it very clear when He was tempted by Satan that we should not put the Lord to the test (see Luke 4:12, in which Jesus cites Deuteronomy 6:16). However, we are actually called to do that when it comes to our tithe.

Many people wait to give to God until they're done taking care of everything else that month . . . of course, we all know how that goes.

Instead, we should give to God first and let Him prove Himself. I have done that for as long as I can remember, and He's been faithful, whether I was making a salary of $20,000 as a rookie player or at the end of my career when I was making much more as a head coach.

The truth is that it's not really "giving to God" but rather using what He has given us. After all, everything we have belongs to Him. Therefore, we have a stewardship responsibility to make sure it's accounted for.

Tithing is not about a percentage but about a principle. God will take what we bring to Him and multiply it for the good of others. And He will continue to provide for our needs as well.

How are you using what God gave you? It may be a tithe of time, talents, or treasure. How can you help those whom God has brought across your path? What about that single-mother waitress struggling to care for and feed her children? Does a coworker going through a divorce need an encouraging word? What about that neighbor who can't pay the electric bill this month and is in jeopardy of having the power turned off?

There are so many ways to tithe from the gifts that God has given us, and when we do, He will pour out blessings upon us. Not blessings in terms of more "stuff," but blessings so that we can continue to bless others.

A godly cycle of paying it forward.

UNCOMMON KEY > *God wants you to be a blessing with the gifts He has given you—whether time, talents, or treasure. It's not the size of the gift, but your willingness to do it that counts.*

September 26

Crowd Support

> Since we are surrounded by such a huge crowd of witnesses to the life of faith, . . . let us run with endurance the race God has set before us. HEBREWS 12:1

What a great image. Running the race—living the life—that God has set before us. And doing so before a great cloud of witnesses, those family and friends who have gone on before us and who are watching with pride as we run.

It's not easy, this race. They know it because they went before us, often being the trail-blazers, the teachers.

The author of Hebrews uses the imagery of a great stadium, with the grandstands filled to capacity with the great spiritual athletes of the past, a great cloud of witnesses encouraging us through the testimonies of their lives as we take our places in the arena as followers of Christ.

They're all there—Noah, Abraham, and Enoch. Isaac, Jacob, Joseph, and Moses. People who not only crossed the finish line but provided encouragement and hope for us in the stories of their faithfulness.

Over my career, I've been in a lot of impressive stadiums as a player, coach, and fan. I've always enjoyed looking toward the corners—when those are full, then you know it's a really big crowd. But there are other sports venues that whether they are full or not, the fans are so passionate, so loud, that when a pass is picked off, the puck is dropped, the ball is dunked, or a home run clears the fence, the roar of the crowd nearly knocks you down. Especially the hometown fans. The ones who are behind you, cheering you on.

But I think that the reaction of even the most rabid fans in the largest stadium can't compare with the loving enthusiasm with which the crowd of faithful witnesses is urging us on. By God's grace and through faith in Him, we have salvation and have promised to make a difference in this world of pain, heartache, sickness, sorrow, pressure, hardship, and even death—all for the glory of His name.

We may be criticized, persecuted, misunderstood, and condemned because of our belief in Christ and for what we do in His name. But we will continue to run the race day by day, drawing strength from Him. Each day our stamina will increase and we will get a little stronger.

UNCOMMON KEY > *This relationship with God through His Son, Jesus Christ, is not something you stand still for. It's a workout! Enjoy the race and listen for the cheers.*

September 27

Pruned for Healthier Growth

> I am the true grapevine, and my Father is the gardener. He cuts off every branch of mine that doesn't produce fruit, and he prunes the branches that do bear fruit so they will produce even more. You have already been pruned and purified by the message I have given you.... You cannot be fruitful unless you remain in me. JOHN 15:1-4

Every fall Nathan heads out into his yard to cut back his crepe myrtle trees, hydrangea bushes, and other plants around the yard. The ones that have gotten too "leggy" he trims back to a joint, where new growth will start. Some bushes don't need pruning at all, while others grow much too fast during the summer months and need to be trimmed back so the plant can actually support the branches.

It's all about maintaining the plant's health. Some plants grow quickly, others more slowly. Some of the fast growers eventually need to be taken back a notch or two. Or more. It's all about helping the plants to grow and produce more and more fruit.

That describes you and me in the hands of the Master Gardener.

We go through times in our lives when we are being "pruned" by God. Maybe an opportunity has been taken away from us. Maybe an unhealthy friendship is withering away. Maybe our church is undergoing transition.

God doesn't want us to wither in His hands. These situations are for our ultimate good, as He cuts off those branches that don't produce fruit. Of course we need to be careful that we don't become unproductive branches, but rather understand that there will be times when we will feel that discomfort of being reshaped by the Lord for our growth.

Pruning is needed and beneficial. It may feel like a setback for you, but ultimately it's not. It will create a stronger, healthier, and godlier life that produces more fruit for Him.

UNCOMMON KEY > *Every time you are out doing yard work, especially pruning foliage, think of what parts of your life need trimming to produce more fruit. Ask the Master Gardener to keep you healthy and growing.*

September 28

No Mistaking Your Identity

> Thank you for making me so wonderfully complex! Your workmanship is marvelous—how well I know it. PSALM 139:14

As an NFL coach, I received performance evaluations every day—from multitudes of people, many of whom were completely unqualified to offer a valid critique. That's how it is for anyone in the public eye, especially those in a performance-oriented field. Everyone thinks they know how the job should be done.

I decided long ago that I wouldn't listen to all of the chatter on talk radio, but I would pay attention to some of the criticism from reputable sources. Of course, I put more stock in what my superiors, assistant coaches, and players said, but I would also analyze some of the comments from sportswriters to see what might be helpful. It's important to listen to criticism if you want to improve at anything.

But I also decided long ago that I wouldn't let any criticism affect my sense of who I am. When you understand the difference between who you are and what you do, you can handle criticism a lot better. I know I'm a child of God. He created me with certain strengths and limitations, and He knows about all of them. When people point out my strengths, it doesn't make me proud, and when they point out my limitations, it doesn't change my identity. I am, and always will be, a child of God.

That attitude had to be a conscious decision, because it's easy to let others define us. It happens naturally if we aren't intentional about remembering who we are. And when our "performance reviews" are negative—whether from our actual employers or from the unofficial commentators around us—it can be devastating. If we can't separate what we do from who we are, we'll be defined by the words of people who really aren't qualified to shape our identities. And if their words are negative, our perception of ourselves takes a huge blow.

Remember that you are not your career or any other responsibility you have to perform. No matter what anyone else thinks, your relationship with God defines your identity. If you are His child, you cannot be shaken.

UNCOMMON KEY > *Only God is qualified to define your identity. Learn from others' opinions, but refuse to let your identity be shaped by them. Learn to see yourself as God sees you.*

September 29

Deep and High

> Those who are rich in this world . . . should be rich in good works and generous to those in need, always being ready to share with others. By doing this they will be storing up their treasure as a good foundation for the future so that they may experience true life.
> 1 TIMOTHY 6:17-19

Almost all of us in the United States have been blessed financially, at least when compared to the rest of the world. This has been true for me personally—I know that I have been blessed monetarily more than my grandparents who were in ministry their whole life and more than many of my fellow citizens.

I was unprepared for the distinction when my family went to South Africa several years ago, however. Corrugated cardboard homes. Old, discarded tires for walls. Streams of dirty water running through the shantytowns.

The question then becomes, what will we do with those blessings God has given us?

In his book *Role of a Lifetime*, my dear friend James Brown shares a number of poignant lessons, but at one point he refers to our lives in terms of the "depth" of our foundation and the "height" we should reach for. His ideas echo my own—that "depth" is comprised of faith, character, integrity, honesty, humility, and stewardship. And the deeper those characteristics go in our lives, the more solid our foundation will be, so much so that these things will come naturally.

That foundation centered on Christ determines the height we attain in and with our lives. As I've said—and JB concurs—it's not about basking in the world's accolades, in whatever form they may come. It's not about how many material possessions we accumulate or how important we may be considered in the world's eyes. Instead, it is how we will maximize what God has given us on behalf of others, "recognizing the opportunities [we] have each day to add value to the lives around [us] and to make a difference in [our] world." And as JB does with everyone he meets, we must treat each person "as someone special—because they are."[8]

We should use our money for good, storing up treasures in heaven, finding ways to share with those in need.

God isn't keeping track of the amount of money you give; He's more concerned about your heart and your willingness to give in the first place. Do you need to rethink your giving plan?

UNCOMMON KEY > *Everything you have—including your bank account—is a gift from God. He expects you to use it in the best way possible to add value to the lives of others for eternity.*

September 30

Starting Over on Monday

> Look here, you who say, "Today or tomorrow we are going to a certain town and will stay there a year. We will do business there and make a profit." How do you know what your life will be like tomorrow? Your life is like the morning fog—it's here a little while, then it's gone. What you ought to say is, "If the Lord wants us to, we will live and do this or that."
> JAMES 4:13-15

Every Monday morning during the season, most teams in the NFL do the same thing—they begin to plan for the next game. Sunday's game may have been a big win or a crushing loss, but that doesn't change the needs of Monday morning. Teams don't have time to continue a celebration or wallow in disappointment. Another game is coming soon.

Our lives are a lot like that. We win big victories, make huge mistakes, experience deep joys, and suffer crippling disappointments. Whatever the case, we have to look forward. It helps to remember what Romans 8:28 tells us: that God works all things together for the good of those who love Him. That doesn't mean everything will work out exactly as we hope, but God has the ability to work everything into His plan. He doesn't miss a thing. One way or another, in His time, all of our past experiences—problems, pain, worries, sins, and "accidents," as well as the victories and celebrations—will serve His purposes for our good.

It takes faith to believe that, because we can't comprehend how all the things that didn't go right in our lives could possibly work out for our good. Like a football team on a losing streak, sometimes nothing looks right. We have worries about our relationships, our kids, our finances, our dreams, and much more. People and circumstances let us down. But God doesn't, and He is sovereign over all of it.

When we begin the "Monday mornings" of our lives with a focus on God's game plan rather than our own, we'll be much more effective. We can look back over situations we have come through and learn from our mistakes, but there's never a need to dwell on them. And we can look toward the future and plan, but we can never control what happens. If we walk with God, following however He leads, we'll always be headed in the right direction.

UNCOMMON KEY > *Keep the faith that God's plan is always best. When we walk with Him, we're walking with someone who knows where He is going.*

October 1

Ignoring the Ratings

A man with leprosy approached [Jesus] and knelt before him. "Lord," the man said, "if you are willing, you can heal me and make me clean." Jesus reached out and touched him. "I am willing," he said. "Be healed!" And instantly the leprosy disappeared. MATTHEW 8:2-3

Don't let anyone rate you, stereotype you, or categorize you or anyone whom you love. A good friend of mine who is a college football coach believes that.

He is the head football coach at a major college and looks beyond all the hype and evaluations, categorizations, and rankings by the media and football talent rating services when recruiting. He doesn't worry about trying to win "best in class" with a bunch of alleged "five-star recruits" who commit as juniors in high school. He'd prefer to wait until they develop and mature a bit more. When they become seniors, he can better evaluate them, not only as players but also as people. By waiting until they have continued to grow into the men they are becoming physically and emotionally, he is able to make better decisions. Then he can sign the guys he really wants, even if they aren't as popular with the fans, media, or national rating services.

The leper who ran up to Jesus in today's verses wouldn't have been given much of a chance by the world's standards in his day, or even ours. Such an outcast in biblical times might not even rate one star. Society considered lepers unclean. Isolated from the rest of the population, they had to keep their distance and shout, "Unclean!" to warn others when they approached.

But Christ saw this leper as a wonderful, valuable child of God. Rejected by the world, embraced by Christ. I even think this leper would have a chance to make it by my friend's standards since he looks beyond the outward appearance to determine the kind of player a person is and can be.

Do you know people who feel valueless, worthless, like societal outcasts? Maybe it's time to seek them out and offer help.

UNCOMMON KEY > *Don't be swayed by how society rates others. Instead, consider that God sees people as His precious creations, made for His purposes. It will not only change your perspective but may inspire you to help empower them.*

October 2

Reflecting His Image

> But whenever someone turns to the Lord, the veil is taken away. For the Lord is the Spirit, and wherever the Spirit of the Lord is, there is freedom. So all of us who have had that veil removed can see and reflect the glory of the Lord. And the Lord—who is the Spirit— makes us more and more like him as we are changed into his glorious image.
>
> 2 CORINTHIANS 3:16-18

There's a song by Phillips, Craig & Dean called "I Want to Be like You" about a father expressing his desire to be who he knew he should be, not only for his Lord but also for his children. You probably remember it because you found yourself singing along the way I did: "Lord, I want to be just like you, because he wants to be just like me."

While we are striving to be good role models for our children and for the others around us who need good examples, we should always look to our heavenly Father, the best role model we could have. As the apostle Paul says, the result of our desire to be more like our heavenly Father is that He will make us more like Him.

When we become more like Him, that image gives our children and others around us an image of who their heavenly Father is and wants to be to them, too. Sadly, too many of us grew up with parents who did not reflect what our heavenly Father is truly like—but their image affects how we view God. If we grew up with absentee parents, we might have struggled—or still struggle—with the heavenly Father's seeming absence from our lives. Or parents who were neglectful, harsh, and critical or made us feel guilty about most everything might make us think our heavenly Father is judging us the same way.

We need to remember that who we are reflects to our children and others not only our image as a parent but also potentially the image they have of their heavenly Father.

UNCOMMON KEY > *You are probably your child's first glimpse of the qualities of God. Make that glimpse a good one.*

October 3

A Worthwhile Building Project

> What good is it, dear brothers and sisters, if you say you have faith but don't show it by your actions? JAMES 2:14

Derrick Brooks always made a difference on the football field. Fortunately for the "Brooks Bunch"—a group of kids Derrick got involved with at the Boys Club in Tampa—he makes a difference off the field too.

Not only was Derrick a great player, he's incredibly bright and generous. He has always been concerned with giving back. So when he arrived in Tampa in 1995, he began hanging out at the local Boys & Girls Clubs. He was amazed by the number of kids who had never been outside of Tampa, and he committed himself to broadening their horizons and helping them see themselves as future leaders who could make a difference. He developed a curriculum in which kids would spend a year learning about a place—the King Center in Atlanta; Washington, DC; even South Africa and Swaziland—and then he would take them on a trip to that destination. It was his way of building into the lives of others.

That's an uncommon sense of commitment. All of us have some kind of impact on those closest to us—hopefully a very positive impact—but not everyone goes out of their way to invest in the lives of those outside their normal circle of relationships. Derrick uses the gifts God has given him to look beyond himself and make a difference. And any of us can do that. We can give a hand to provide unusual opportunities for people who haven't had many. We can volunteer time and invest resources to make a lasting impact in the lives of others. We can see the potential in others and help them achieve it.

That's mentoring. That's what it means to leave a legacy. Recently, the first wave of the Brooks Bunch graduated from college, and I have no doubt that Derrick's involvement played a big part in their success. Anytime we go the extra mile to invest in someone's life, we make a difference—and we help them make one too.

UNCOMMON KEY > *Find ways to build into others' lives. Mentoring leaves a lasting legacy. It increases the impact of your life, and it helps others increase the impact of theirs.*

October 4

Doubtful

> Jesus was standing among them. "Peace be with you," he said. Then he said to Thomas, "Put your finger here, and look at my hands. Put your hand into the wound in my side. Don't be faithless any longer. Believe!" "My Lord and my God!" Thomas exclaimed. Then Jesus told him, "You believe because you have seen me. Blessed are those who believe without seeing me." JOHN 20:26-29

Life batters us at times. We can be banged around and buffeted by the ever-present winds of life—job changes (whether we want them or not), the frailty of our health or the health of our loved ones, rejection by friends, or another failed attempt on our part to do something we have long wanted to do.

This story of Thomas in John's Gospel sheds some light on those moments of despair and offers a solution for how we might move forward through them. Growing up in Sunday school, we may have been introduced to this disciple as "doubting Thomas." Little did we know at the time that we ourselves would exhibit similar doubts as the world came in around us.

Remember Thomas's words to his fellow disciples when Jesus said He was heading back to Bethany to go to Lazarus's grave? He is the one who was initially ready to charge headlong after Jesus: "Let's go, too—and die with Jesus" (John 11:16). Previous trips to Judea had been dangerous for them, and Jesus' notoriety was growing among the religious leaders who wanted Him gone. Thomas was willing to stand at Jesus' side, even to his death. And yet after the death and resurrection of Jesus, Thomas wasn't there when the others saw Jesus, and he wouldn't take their word that Jesus was alive.

And then, in the midst of his swirl of doubt, in walked Jesus. His opening words were, "Peace be with you." Jesus didn't chastise Thomas for his unbelief or insist that he believe without seeing, but He recognized the genuine doubts Thomas was feeling. The struggles Thomas was working through.

"Put your finger here. . . ."

Doubt. Perhaps you've been fortunate and haven't experienced it in a while. I doubt it. It hits us all on a regular basis, and it can be devastating when it hits—causing us to lose not only focus, but hope. The devil uses doubt to get us off track, to sap us of our energy for the day. When it comes, it rocks our world. That certainly has happened to me in my life.

But then Jesus comes to us, as He came to Thomas, to keep those doubts from taking firm root. He calls us to faith, to a belief that in the end, even when it doesn't always seem like it, we will prevail, we will win with Him.

Live as doubt-free as you can. And when doubts start to gather, honestly admit them to God.

UNCOMMON KEY > *What do you have a doubt about today? Give it to the one standing next to you—Jesus Christ.*

October 5

United on the Essentials

> | How wonderful and pleasant it is when brothers live together in harmony! PSALM 133:1

The year the Indianapolis Colts won the Super Bowl, we didn't have our most talented team. Other years we had sustained fewer injuries and probably had more talent, but that 2007 team played so well together. There were plenty of unique personalities, and I'm sure they had their differences at times, but that group was united in thought and purpose like no other team I had had a chance to lead. Even when we were trailing the New England Patriots 21–6 at the end of the first half in the AFC championship game, our guys were unrattled. I saw in their faces that what we had in the locker room—fifty-three players pulling together—was all we needed to make the game better in the second half. We did— and as you probably already know, we won.

The church is Christ's bride, and in that role collectively represents Jesus Christ to the world. For those of us who might be tempted to view church involvement as optional and believe that our faith is private and personal, the church is God's plan. In order for our faith to grow further in a relationship with Christ, we need the fellowship and encouragement of others of like faith to edify and sustain us and our faith. God's plan is that we have a private, personal relationship and time with Him alongside the collective worship, study, and fellowship with others in unity with Christ and His purpose for the church.

And in addition, we need to follow Paul's admonition that we be unified on the essentials of our faith and not worry so much about the nonessentials and our different points of view on them—dress, work hours, color of our hair, the list goes on. But regarding the core elements of our faith in Jesus Christ, we need unity, clarity, and commitment. When that occurs, unity occurs within the body of believers—Christ's church. As a result, Christ is lifted up to draw all people to Himself, and He is glorified.

Are you committed to a body of believers?

UNCOMMON KEY > *If you belong to a church, write down a few reasons why you are committed to that group of people. If you have never found a church home, look for one that is unified in the essentials of faith in Jesus Christ.*

October 6

Standing Strong on Sexual Purity

> The world offers only a craving for physical pleasure, a craving for everything we see, and pride in our achievements and possessions. These are not from the Father, but are from this world. 1 JOHN 2:16

Joe Ehrmann used to be a defensive tackle for the Baltimore Colts. He's a high school coach now, but he came to speak to our team once, and I really appreciated his thoughts on what it takes to be a man. Among his refreshingly candid views is the idea that society's evaluation of men is often based on their sexual conquests. In the eyes of many, manhood is defined by sleeping with a lot of women.

That's nothing new, of course. The world has viewed manhood that way for thousands of years. I've seen it with athletes at every level from high school to professionals. But that's a sad statement on society, and it's a sad example for our young men and women. Besides being an unfulfilling lifestyle, it goes against God's design for marriage and family.

If we really believe sex outside of marriage is wrong, we've got to teach our boys and girls how to go against the grain in the society they are living in. The idea of saving oneself for marriage is subject to a lot of questions and even ridicule. We and our kids need a lot of strength to deal with that kind of pressure. Some parents may be hesitant to talk about it because they made mistakes in their past or perhaps struggle with their thoughts today. But those mistakes and struggles are the kind of experience that can actually give a parent more credibility. Whatever a parent's background, it's important to help children avoid poor choices.

For those who aren't married yet, focus on positive relationships grounded in friendship, and stand firm in the knowledge that you are strong enough to wait. It's difficult, but the benefits are definitely worth it. If you are married, remain pure in your thoughts and actions, but perhaps even more important, encourage young people to pursue sexual purity. Adulthood—whether for men or women—is not defined by sexual activity but by things like integrity, patience, and mature character. That's an uncommon lifestyle, especially in these times, but it's definitely more fulfilling in the long run.

UNCOMMON KEY > *It takes a strong person to live a life of sexual integrity and purity. But strong people end up with far fewer regrets. Commit to being a strong person today.*

October 7

Using Your Feet

> There was a man named Jabez who was more honorable than any of his brothers. His mother named him Jabez because his birth had been so painful. He was the one who prayed to the God of Israel, "Oh, that you would bless me and expand my territory! Please be with me in all that I do, and keep me from all trouble and pain!" And God granted him his request.
>
> 1 CHRONICLES 4:9-10

I prayed a lot during our football games, along with many of the staff and players. Before the game, at halftime, after the game, and many times in between. Sometimes, at least silently, many of us prayed for a play to be successful, a field goal to be made or missed, a game to be won. And sometimes we were willing to help. It was important to pray, but we also had to do our part. I had to coach, and our players had to play—hard!

Of course, the Lord can do anything He sees fit, whether we're helping or not. But that's not how He intended our relationship with Him to be or our time on earth to be lived out, merely our asking Him for favors.

When He created you and me, He had a purpose in mind for us. Our lives were not intended to be inactive. God knew what the world would be like when we were born, and we are designed specifically to carry out His purposes for this particular time in history.

God has done this throughout history—not just with us—by using both willing and unwilling participants for His purposes. His preference is that we be willing, with the hope that we will use the gifts and abilities He gave us. The next time you think you might just sit back and rely on the Lord to find others to pick up the slack from your idleness, remember this African proverb: When you pray, use your feet.

Jabez prayed that God would enlarge his territory. He was ready to do whatever was needed. He was ready to use his feet. He was willing and ready to go where God sent him and to do what God set before him.

Pray often. Ask God for power, peace, direction, clarity, strength, and courage—and that's just for starters. Then get ready to go, because He is going to throw you headfirst into the day.

UNCOMMON KEY > *Be like Jabez. Pray specifically and often. And when you pray, get ready to use your feet. He will get you involved.*

October 8

Trusted with the Small Things

> Do not despise these small beginnings, for the LORD rejoices to see the work begin.
> ZECHARIAH 4:10

When I was a teenager, my parents let me stay out pretty late playing basketball with my friends. But that didn't happen right away. I had to earn the privilege by demonstrating that I could be trusted. They watched me closely at first—I couldn't be out at midnight when I was thirteen, of course. But over time, they gave me more and more freedom, and by the time I was seventeen, they knew I was always where I said I would be and wasn't getting into trouble. They had watched me grow and had given me enough opportunities to test my character that they knew they could trust me.

Over the course of a season, a football player's character is challenged many times and from many different angles. Does he work hard? Take shortcuts and make compromises to get by? Show accountability to teammates? Know how to handle adversity? Know how to handle success?

A man has plenty of opportunities during a season to prove he knows how to do the right thing even when the right thing is hard. But no one just happens to have character. It's built into us by a long process. My parents gradually increased my freedom as I demonstrated responsibility because they understood that character begins with the little things in life.

That doesn't apply only to kids playing basketball or grown men on a football field. It applies to all of us in our relationships with God and with each other. Over time, we have a hand in shaping ourselves and building our character through the little acts we do. Character is developed by facing decisions—at first little ones, then larger and larger ones—and choosing what's right until it becomes second nature. It's tried and tested through many circumstances and the most challenging times. We have to know what is right, and we have to choose to do it. That not only strengthens our own character, but also builds trust with others. If we begin to develop character in the little things today, we will be known for our character even in larger things tomorrow.

UNCOMMON KEY > *So many small things make up your character—your words, your thoughts, your actions—which help form how you instinctively respond to every situation. Don't let the small things slip. Start each day by looking for ways to show character.*

October 9

More Valuable than a Picasso

> Stop deceiving yourselves. If you think you are wise by this world's standards, you need to become a fool to be truly wise. For the wisdom of this world is foolishness to God. As the Scriptures say, "He traps the wise in the snare of their own cleverness." And again, "The LORD knows the thoughts of the wise; he knows they are worthless." 1 CORINTHIANS 3:18-20

Sometimes we simply don't have a choice. There are some things we seem compelled to do no matter how ridiculous, unwise, or insane they may seem to be. That must be how Pablo Picasso felt as he began burning some of his own paintings—simply to keep warm. Even though he had by that time painted thousands of canvases over the span of his career, I think most anyone would agree that for him to get to this point—where his paintings became nothing but his firewood—was quite a loss.

Pablo Picasso decided his own survival was worth more than his paintings. Before you hastily agree that you'd make the same choice, think of what you value in your life. If it wasn't a matter of your survival, would you be willing to sell or walk away from those things? If you listed family as one of them, of course your answer would be no. Many of us simply place value on the wrong things. And oftentimes we do it unwittingly and unintentionally by simply not spending the time with family and other important people and things that we should. The value society places on things becomes a pretty steady drumbeat in our heads and hearts and is very often at odds with the value that God places on those same things.

Society places value on objects, on wealth, on the size of our houses, and on the number of cars in our garage. Society emphasizes things like résumés, trophies, awards, and winning simply for the sake of winning. Society has inverted the things it considers valuable with what God intended for us to place first, the ones He says should guide our lives. To live the life of godly wisdom that seeks a life of significance, impact, and legacy that God created us to live—we need to switch them back!

It won't be easy because people are often assessed in the world by the things they acquire. And so our calendars are often empty of time with our families. But whom will you call to your bedside in your last hours of life—your banker or your stockbroker? Or your loved ones? Will you ask to see your bank statements, trophies, and diplomas one more time—or will you look at photos of loved ones who aren't there at that moment?

What do you value more—things of eternal significance or things that are temporal? Focus on the eternal things, for that is the beginning of godly wisdom.

UNCOMMON KEY > *What do you consider of eternal significance in your life? Consider writing a letter now to your loved ones, telling them what you value the most.*

October 10

Free to Disagree

Barnabas agreed and wanted to take along John Mark. But Paul disagreed strongly, since John Mark had deserted them in Pamphylia and had not continued with them in their work. Their disagreement was so sharp that they separated. ACTS 15:37-39

During football games, we have an unwritten code that if you're on the headsets, whether in the coaches' box or on the sideline, it's a safe place and you are free to say whatever you want to say. We can disagree with one another, float crazy ideas, and change our minds without recrimination. It's not a time for idle chatter, of course, but it's a circumstance where people can speak their minds without fear of insult or of someone holding a grudge against them the next day. We don't always agree—and that's a good thing—but the conversation will be healthy and helpful because different people analyze situations differently. You have your opinion, I have mine, and neither of us will hold it against the other person.

But when we disagree, how will we handle it?

In our case, we could disagree, but usually no one would take their ball and go home. No one would be angry about someone else's opinion on something. The strategy was to allow our game conversations to be free and open interchanges of ideas that would potentially lead to creative new ways and plays to move the ball or stop our opponents, even though some suggestions would sound utterly ridiculous.

In Paul's case, it was an honest disagreement between two godly men, but Paul reached a point where he felt no more fruitful discussion would occur and so he left Barnabas behind to his own choices.

However, there is no evidence in Scripture to suggest that this disagreement between these two men of God alienated them as friends.

When you disagree with a coworker or friend or spouse or pastor, how do you handle it? With grace and understanding or with anger and bitterness? Do you force that person to accept your way? The productivity and harmony of your workplace or home will be directly affected by your response. And your witness may be impacted too; others may see you or Jesus in a different light if you can't handle conflict.

UNCOMMON KEY > *Do you need to look at how you handle conflict in your life? Agree to disagree agreeably with others—for the good of everyone.*

October 11

Pain Management

> And we know that God causes everything to work together for the good of those who love God and are called according to his purpose for them.   ROMANS 8:28

For most people, pain is a powerful teacher. But not for my son Jordan. He's one of the few people in the world with congenital insensitivity to pain. In other words, he doesn't feel pain the way the rest of us do. He has never learned to avoid dangerous objects because cuts and stitches aren't unpleasant to him. Small cuts can turn into long hospital stays because he'll run around on an open wound without feeling the pain. The infection can spread to the bone before we discover the problem. So we have to teach Jordan to notice wounds and deal with them at an intellectual level rather than as a response to the pain they cause.

Aristotle said, "We cannot learn without pain." I wish we could, but I believe God allows it for a reason. When we have the negative feedback of an unpleasant feeling—whether it's physical, emotional, or spiritual—we learn how to avoid the dangers and problems that would otherwise infect us and threaten our health. The pain is an important warning signal to protect us from further harm. Without it, we would miss many of life's most important lessons.

None of us likes to learn life's lessons the hard way, but it's better than not learning them at all. We would rather not experience the pain of mistakes and failures, but the experience makes us stronger and teaches us valuable truths. It's great when others can pass on to us the things they have learned, but many times their advice isn't enough. Most of us have to experience the hard lessons of life on our own for them to really sink in and become a part of our character.

Learn whatever you can from other people's mistakes. Let their pain become your teacher. But there will be times when your own pain is the only way to learn life's deepest lessons, and those are the ones that stick. Those who are wise will take every opportunity to learn from everything they experience.

UNCOMMON KEY > *Don't waste the hard lessons of life, even if they are extremely painful. Experience can be a terrific teacher.*

October 12

In but Not Of

> Do not love this world nor the things it offers you, for when you love the world, you do not have the love of the Father in you. 1 JOHN 2:15

In the world, but not of it.

Today's verse from 1 John is an addendum to Jesus' prayer for His disciples in John 17, when He asks God to protect the followers He is leaving behind in the world. Sometimes I think it would have been so much easier for God to remove His followers from the world rather than leaving us in the world. No, in fact in looking back on my life, I *know* it would have been much easier.

I used to get questions from people all the time about how I could justify working in the football "world" and being a Christian. "It's such a violent game"; "What about all the bad language?"; "How can you justify playing games on Sunday?" I would always answer that I had to be careful to try to bring Christ's light to that "world" without getting swallowed up by it. I believe that's what God calls us to do. Without a doubt, spending time in a locker room or on a football team definitely has its moments of being *in* the world.

But I also have come to realize that God can only use us in the world if we are in fact "in the world." The tension that may arise there requires much godly wisdom and the Holy's Spirit's leading.

So what does it mean to be "in the world but not of it"? Have you ever been in situations where you feel uncomfortable from the first moment? You don't need to merely follow along blindly and do everything the world does. I know a pastor who regularly sees popular movies, not because he wants to support them, but because he feels he needs to understand the culture that the youth from his church are coming from.

Is that being *in* the world? Or *of* it? That's not my call. I can only go by what I see in him. Does he begin to look and act like the "world" depicted in those movies?

Both extremes can be easy to fall into. We can buy into everything the world does, but then we're polluting ourselves with everything that's out there. We can also withdraw from everything in the world. I know a guy who said he was only going to "drink milk from a Christian cow" from now on. I think he was kidding. Sometimes it would be clearer to have an easy solution, but God wants us to work it out, to be salt and light to those around us. Salt and light. Adding His flavor and vision.

UNCOMMON KEY > *How can you live in an R-rated world—in it—while staying clear of it? Have you headed toward either extreme? Determine where you are and make adjustments. Stay close to God, and let His wisdom and leading guide you.*

October 13

No Matter What, Don't Give Up

> I don't mean to say that I have already achieved these things or that I have already reached perfection. But I press on to possess that perfection for which Christ Jesus first possessed me. PHILIPPIANS 3:12

Winston Churchill is someone in history whom I admire. I love how he handled some of his toughest moments as England's prime minister. Not only was he a great statesman, but he was also an outstanding orator.

On October 29, 1941, Churchill visited his alma mater, Harrow School, to hear the traditional songs he had sung there as a youth, as well as to speak to the students.

Reflecting on the previous ten months of "terrible catastrophic events in the world," Churchill stood before the students and shared the lesson he had been learning.

"Never give in. Never give in. Never, never, never, never—in nothing, great or small, large or petty—never give in except to convictions of honour and good sense."

Although Churchill wasn't at the end of his speech when he spoke those emphatic words, that line is what is most remembered. In fact, the speech is called "Never Give In." The essence of his remarks, coupled with his steadfast leadership during World War II, helped England to survive the conflict.

The apostle Paul expressed a "never give in" attitude when he wrote today's verses to the Philippian believers. Using the common metaphor of a race he was competing in, Paul encourages believers to pursue Christ with unwavering determination. His words apply to us as well. We are running a marathon relationship with Christ.

When things become difficult in our lives, we may want to throw our hands in the air and give up. No deal. There will be times when we'll want to simply stop and let someone else do what we know God has asked us to do. No deal. We are called to "press on to reach the end of the race and receive the heavenly prize for which God, through Christ Jesus, is calling us" (verse 14).

The two of them—Paul and Churchill—set the course for things much larger than themselves simply by refusing to give up, and in doing so, they directed the paths of those around them by passion and example.

Never give in. Never give up. Don't quit.

UNCOMMON KEY > *It's very simple—never give in or give up. Encourage someone with those words today. Keep running the race with Christ, keeping your eyes on the prize—the hope of heaven.*

October 14

Faith into Action

> Faith by itself isn't enough. Unless it produces good deeds, it is dead and useless. Now someone may argue, "Some people have faith; others have good deeds." But I say, "How can you show me your faith if you don't have good deeds? I will show you my faith by my good deeds." JAMES 2:17-18

Let me explain the apostle James's thinking in a modern-day context.

Imagine a husband and wife from Boston—die-hard New England Patriots fans—coming to Indianapolis to tour the Colts complex, including our practice fields, coaches' offices, and meeting rooms. I can assure you that the visitors would have a great time because the Colts have great facilities staffed by even greater people. And let's say that when the couple walks out, they declare a newfound appreciation and allegiance to the Colts based on how moved they were by the experience. I am a bit biased, but I can see that as a very understandable reaction.

The couple heads home and lands at Logan International Airport in Boston, and as they are walking past the gift shop, the husband sees a Patriots jacket. "You know," he says, "my Patriots jacket still has a mustard stain from last year that I can't get out. It's time to replace it." And so he buys another jacket, while his wife calls to renew their subscription to *New England Patriots Daily News*.

Did they have a great visit in Indianapolis? Sure, I suppose. Was it life changing? Did they truly bring the Colts into the core of their being? Well, based on their actions when they returned home, it doesn't seem so.

In his letter, James points out that our works shine a light on our faith, leading us to impact the world around us and possibly leading others to a relationship with Christ. But we can't earn our way into heaven with any amount of good works. The apostle Paul makes that clear to us in his letter to the church at Ephesus when he says, "God saved you by his grace when you believed. And you can't take credit for this; it is a gift from God" (Ephesians 2:8).

Grace is free, but our behavior demonstrates the true condition of our hearts—and whether or not we really made a decision within the core of our hearts to accept that free gift.

What about you? Do you think of faith and works as two separate things? Saving faith results in actions that emulate God, the one who gives good gifts.

UNCOMMON KEY > *It is by grace, not works, that you are saved. However, your works may shed significant light on whether you ever had the moment of life-changing salvation that Christ offers.*

October 15

Working for the Boss

> Work willingly at whatever you do, as though you were working for the Lord rather than for people. Remember that the Lord will give you an inheritance as your reward, and that the Master you are serving is Christ. COLOSSIANS 3:23-24

Our duty as Christians is to do our jobs well to please God and not simply to please our bosses or to get a raise.

Have you ever thought about how you might approach your job differently if the Lord were your boss or immediate supervisor? On the one hand, I think that would be great, but in all honesty, it is a bit disconcerting—actually, *very* disconcerting—to think of it as a possibility.

When I was a player with the Pittsburgh Steelers, we were blessed not only to have men who were great players on our team, but also men with a strong faith in Christ, who tried to do everything to honor and glorify God. To them, He was their ultimate Coach.

And things were different within our team as a result. They wanted to please Coach Noll, but they answered to a higher standard. And when I became their position coach a couple of years later, even though I was much younger than them, rather than taking advantage of the situation, they worked harder than ever. They were working for the Lord.

I wonder what would happen if we began to think that way about our work. I suspect our passion for what we were doing would change drastically if we felt God was in charge. I suspect our potential would be enhanced, discovered, and sharpened. Think about all of those gifts, abilities, and talents we have or are just discovering. Imagine how good we would be if God were fine-tuning and coaching us to perform and use them even more!

Our purpose might take on a clearer focus as we see things we can do differently and things we should be doing to help others.

Our platform—our opportunities to influence and add value to the lives of others—would expand as others were drawn to our new and positive outlook.

But wait! Isn't God already our boss? Isn't He the one we ultimately should be answering to each day? Isn't God the one who has given us the gifts, abilities, and talents to use at work, home, and in other settings? Isn't He the voice of encouragement in our lives? And doesn't He offer direction and guidance through His Word and through others?

God is your boss! You've got to love that!

UNCOMMON KEY > *Every day is Boss's Day because God is the one you ultimately work for. Write a thank-you note to your Boss today. And whatever you do and wherever you do it, believe that God is directing, guiding, and encouraging you.*

October 16

Don't Aggravate Your Children

> Children, obey your parents because you belong to the Lord, for this is the right thing to do. . . . If you honor your father and mother, "things will go well for you, and you will have a long life on the earth." Fathers, do not provoke your children to anger by the way you treat them. Rather, bring them up with the discipline and instruction that comes from the Lord. EPHESIANS 6:1, 3-4

Paul takes both parents and children to task in these verses. "Parents" ("father" in verse 4), he says, "don't mistreat your children to make them angry, and children, honor your father and mother by obeying them."

Neither one of these directives seems easy at times. Our eldest daughter, Tiara, once said—borrowing from Mark Twain—that Lauren and I didn't make much sense when she was a teenager, but once she got to college, everything we had told her started making sense. It's funny, but since I've retired and have been spending more time at home, I can see both sides of the relationship more clearly.

When was the last time you talked with your children about God's promise that if they honor their father and mother "things will go well for [them], and [they] will have a long life on the earth"? I wouldn't exactly call it bribery; after all, it is in Scripture. But it may open their eyes to look out for those things that will go well for them in the coming days and years. After all, it's what God promises.

We live in a world today where our children and families are under attack in new ways. The assault comes at them through social media never thought of five, ten, or twenty years ago—and the assault is fast, furious, and potentially devastating to them and to the entire family structure.

Our children need a fresh touch from God in our families. That touch from parents and response from our children must be one of love. Love is the most powerful force available to penetrate the evil and temptation around our children and families. Sometimes it needs to be "tough love," but it always needs to be love.

UNCOMMON KEY > *Never let a day go by without telling your children that you love them. Raise your children any way you wish, but if you want to be successful at it, do it with love.*

October 17

Tips for a Healthy Heart

| Guard your heart above all else, for it determines the course of your life. PROVERBS 4:23

The Bible emphasizes the importance of guarding our hearts. That's because our hearts can determine the course of our lives. Our thoughts, emotions, and intentions will shape everything we do and every decision we make. So it's vitally important for us and those close to us to guard our inner attitudes. Here are some ways to do that.

First, be careful what you take in. Whatever sinks into your mind will often come bubbling back up, whether you want it to or not. Just as your physical health is affected by what you eat, your spiritual and emotional health is affected by the thoughts and images you consume. Avoid spiritual "junk food" and fill your heart with positive messages.

Second, fill yourself with God's Word. Nothing will influence you as powerfully as hearing God's voice and learning His ways. It's not enough to avoid putting negative thoughts and images into your heart; you also need to fill it with truth. The Bible, inspired by God, is the only fully reliable source of truth, and its message is more powerful and life changing than that of any other book you can read. Read His Word and meditate on it often.

Third, stay grounded in prayer. Pray alone and with others—especially your spouse and your children, if you have them, or a friend you're accountable to. If you're a young person and your parents haven't prayed with you recently (or ever), why not ask them to? It may feel awkward at first, but it will help bring you closer to God and closer to each other. Just remember that prayer is simply having a conversation with God. There are no rules or special words. Just talk to Him openly and honestly.

Finally, check your motives for what you do with God and for Him. Motives are a heart issue. You need to do things for the right reasons. If your goals are status and acceptance—impressing people, making a name for yourself, serving yourself—then you need to redirect your motives. Make sure everything you do—especially what you do in your relationship with God—is done out of a sincere desire to know God, discover His will, and do it.

Most people spend more energy guarding their behavior than their hearts. But if you guard your heart, your behavior won't be nearly as difficult to deal with. Pay attention to what goes in, and you'll be pleased with what comes out.

UNCOMMON KEY > *If you want the course of your life to go well, guard your heart well. Is there something you need to stop watching or viewing? Take the steps to eliminate those things from your life.*

October 18

Beyond Planning

> Write this letter to the angel of the church in Philadelphia. This is the message from the one who is holy and true, the one who has the key of David. What he opens, no one can close; and what he closes, no one can open: I know all the things you do, and I have opened a door for you that no one can close. You have little strength, yet you obeyed my word and did not deny me. REVELATION 3:7-8

An old Yiddish proverb says, "Man plans. God laughs." That may make you smile, but planning without God is not a laughing matter. It is not only boastful, it is sinful.

Coaches are always planning. They plan their entire schedule for the year—every practice, every meeting—at the beginning of the year. Then they simply live out the plan. And when things occasionally go contrary to the original plan, they make adjustments.

But without a plan, without a vision, without something to strive for—even if God adjusts it as you go—nothing is going to happen, and you may be missing the very thing that God wants you to do.

Have you had people in your life who have blessed you by spurring you on to greater things? What you might not know is what motivates them. I suspect, more often than not, those people had someone encouraging them to think beyond what was right in front of them, to dream of what might happen if they minimized the moments in their lives when they looked back and said, "I wish I had done that differently." They want you to avoid that.

So what is it that God has laid on your heart and is calling you to do? Sing? Write? Start a ministry? Mentor a child? Be a better husband or wife? Spend more time with your children? Be a friend to someone who has none? There is no doubt that God has a plan for your life and mine—but He expects us not only to plan but to do something about it. If He wants us on a different track, He will lead us there.

UNCOMMON KEY > *Don't wait until it's too late to do the things you wish you had done. Get started on what you think God wants you to do—He'll make the needed adjustments along the way.*

October 19

Free Not to Sin

> Consider yourselves to be dead to the power of sin and alive to God through Christ Jesus. Do not let sin control the way you live; do not give in to sinful desires. . . . Sin is no longer your master. . . . You live under the freedom of God's grace. ROMANS 6:11-12, 14

The goal is for us to die to sin once we ask Jesus Christ into our lives. At that moment, the Holy Spirit comes and resides in us. With the Holy Spirit's help, we seek the way that God wants us to live, a way that is different from the way that the world lives. And it's not just following a new set of rules. The power of conquering sinful desires is the freedom we're given when we follow the leading of the Holy Spirit.

It reminds me a little of Peyton Manning's role in the Indianapolis Colts offense. Some quarterbacks enter a game with a rigid list of dos and don'ts, certain plays they call in certain situations and other things they shouldn't do, depending on the situation.

Peyton, however, understood the offense and what we were trying to do so well that our offensive coordinator would give him merely a "concept" of what to do on a given play with a personnel grouping—two running backs, two receivers, and one tight end, for instance—and a formation to use with them. Then Peyton could call the play he thought had the best chance of success for us, even changing the formation if necessary.

Freedom, not rule following.

From a spiritual perspective, it is being so in tune with the Holy Spirit that you understand the "concept" of what you need to do and not do. You have been given the tools of discernment to make decisions without always running to the rules. With the assistance of the Holy Spirit, you become stronger and more intuitive.

UNCOMMON KEY > *Is there a specific sin you need to die to today? God desires that we die to sin. He paradoxically gives us the freedom to make the decision to die to sin and, with the help of the Holy Spirit, to live in a way that is best for us.*

October 20

Maximum Generosity

| **Give as freely as you have received!** MATTHEW 10:8

The father of a young man called me while I was still coaching the Colts. His son's fiancée had died in an accident, and he was concerned that his son was slipping into depression. I talked with the young man several times over the next few weeks, assuring him that things would get better and that ending his life wasn't the answer. I wanted him to know how the people who loved him would feel if he took his own life. As someone who had lost a son, I understood how real his pain was.

Eventually, I could tell he was beginning to pull out of his depression. Finally, after a number of conversations spanning several weeks, the scheduled date of his wedding passed, and he began to find an occasional ray of sunlight. He assured me he would be all right. Then he asked, "So what do you do?" I told him I was a coach. "Oh, cool," he said. "High school or college?" He had no idea who I was. He only knew I was a man who had lost a son and who cared enough to call him.

My name recognition and what I did for a living didn't matter to this young man. What mattered was that I cared and had some experiences that enabled me to relate to him. And that's the point: we have multiple platforms from which we can impact people. Whatever we have gone through gives us a point of contact with others who are going through similar circumstances. We may think we need expertise in a particular area or a well-known name, but we really only need a little experience and a lot of compassion. We may think we should wait until we have more free time, more money, or a better reputation, but all that's necessary is that we see a need and want to meet it. Influencing the lives of others isn't a job for us to do "someday." It's a possibility right now.

Go ahead and begin investing your life in others now. You have opportunities, and you have the means. Whatever God has poured into your life is something you can pour into others' lives. You have received from Him freely; freely give to whoever needs your encouragement, your advice, and your love.

UNCOMMON KEY > *People don't care who you are. They need you to care who they are. When you do that, you have enough of a platform to influence lives.*

October 21

Saved from the Rubble

> See how very much our Father loves us, for he calls us his children, and that is what we are!
> 1 JOHN 3:1

Much like we would relentlessly pursue our own children through any challenge, God relentlessly pursues us even as we sometimes lead such hectic lives that we end up in our own rubble.

Our friend Mark Merrill told Nathan and me a story about a Turkish father's very public display of love during an earthquake.

After the quake, as the news spread about the devastated areas, the father raced to the school where he knew his six-year-old son, Armand, was at the time of the disaster. When the father arrived at the school, the building was nothing but rubble. Immediately, the father began frantically digging.

He worked as quickly as he could, working his way down through the large pile of wreckage, cutting his hands on the shards of rock and brick as he dug. People tried to stop him, explaining that his efforts to save his son were futile.

"Join me or leave me alone," the father replied. For forty-seven hours, he uttered the same response every time someone would try to get him to stop because they believed all was lost.

"Join me or leave me alone."

Four days, hour after hour, a relentless pursuit of his child.

Finally, the father heard a small voice. "Daddy, is that you?" Beneath the pile of rubble that had been the schoolhouse, he had reached his son who was with his classmates. Armand was safe. When his father pulled the final bricks away to free all the children, Armand's face was beaming. He said to his classmates, "Didn't I tell you? I told you my daddy would come. I told you my daddy would come."

UNCOMMON KEY > *How strong is God's love for you? Read the story of the lost sheep in Luke 15:4-7. God is your persistent Father who is there for you, even when things seem hopeless. Spend as much time as possible with Him.*

October 22

Empty Pockets

> You have planted much but harvest little. You eat but are not satisfied. You drink but are still thirsty. You put on clothes but cannot keep warm. Your wages disappear as though you were putting them in pockets filled with holes! HAGGAI 1:6

What a thing to say: *Your wages disappear as though you were putting them in pockets filled with holes!* Sound familiar? It seems on target and relevant today. How many people do we know who really like their jobs, feel they get paid more than enough, and are totally satisfied with where they are in life? These days it almost goes without saying that our pockets are filled with holes. Nothing of this world satisfies. Contentment seems impossible to find in all the places we look.

The Lord, however, offers us rest. We really can find contentment in the Lord. In Philippians 4:13, the apostle Paul says, "I can do everything through Christ, who gives me strength." Many people consider that verse to be one of the most inspiring in Scripture. But what preceded Paul's proclamation?

Not that I was ever in need, for I have learned how to be content with whatever I have. I know how to live on almost nothing or with everything. I have learned the secret of living in every situation, whether it is with a full stomach or empty, with plenty or little. (verses 11-12)

Paul could do all things—including being content in any situation—through Christ.

This was always a challenge for me when I was coaching. Our players were as susceptible to the pulls and tugs of the world as anyone, but their situations were compounded in most cases by having plenty of money. And so their lifestyles often included multiple cars, large homes, and other expensive items. Unfortunately, I often noticed a lack of contentment from a group of young men whose average salary was over a million dollars a year.

Paul says contentment is found in a relationship with the Lord Jesus Christ. Paul was a prisoner for Christ, and in the trials and difficulties of his ministry for Christ—including prison time—he found contentment and rest for each day and the assurance that he would find contentment in the days ahead.

Are you grumbling and discontent about something in your life? Stop grumbling and start thanking God for everything He has provided for you.

UNCOMMON KEY > *Consider getting a small cross to carry in your pocket. It will remind you that contentment and satisfaction will not be found in the things of the world but in a relationship with the Lord Jesus Christ.*

October 23

Keep on Forgiving

> If another believer sins, rebuke that person; then if there is repentance, forgive. Even if that person wrongs you seven times a day and each time turns again and asks forgiveness, you must forgive. LUKE 17:3-4

I don't know about you, but rebuking isn't really my style. For those who can do that, good for them. It has a way of getting right to the point and bringing whatever the issue is that needs addressing and resolving—through repentance or forgiveness—to the forefront immediately.

I'm a little more indirect in my approach, and yet I try to give constructive, direct feedback where warranted if we get to that place in the conversation. But it's not something I enjoy, and so a lot of times I'll dance around it for a while hoping that the issue resolves itself, that the other person repents of the misdeeds or missteps and figures out what corrective action he or she needs to take.

My preferred modus operandi is to help people hit their target. When I was coaching, there were other members of my staff whose personalities lent themselves better to a more direct approach when the team needed constructive feedback or individuals needed to be singled out and shown the error of their ways.

Sometimes, however, people simply don't hit their targets. They fall short and worse yet, choose to fall short of what God has created for them. This often happens because they allow things that are destructive or distracting to take hold of their lives, or they choose to do less than they know they are able to do with the gifts and abilities God has given them. Forgiveness is always warranted and empowering.

In other instances, they have lost interest in the original target they selected or the goals they were trying to accomplish. The key then is to get them to select or reselect the correct target or goals for their lives. More often than I like I need to help them assess what changed in their mind-set. Instead of rebuking or criticizing them, I try to encourage or persuade them to consider a new direction.

What about you? How do you handle issues that you'd prefer to ignore but you know would escalate if they are not talked through? Have you ever been the person who was confronted? How was the situation resolved? I hope it was with an attitude of repentance and a response of forgiveness.

UNCOMMON KEY > *You can't turn a blind eye to sin because sin separates you from God and others. It festers and can do irreparable harm to your relationship. Is there something you need to confess right now to God or a person you have sinned against and ask forgiveness?*

October 24

An Invigorating Give-and-Take

| Fools think their own way is right, but the wise listen to others. PROVERBS 12:15

On Saturdays in the fall I meet with other members of the broadcast team to rehearse our show, *Monday Night Football*, for the next day and talk about possible story lines and discussion points. Our producer, Sam Flood, has great ideas for us but also seeks input from the guys. It doesn't have to be his idea. He gets his satisfaction from producing a great show.

But what if Sam already made up his mind about what the show should contain? What if he wasn't willing to listen to other ideas because he was resistant to change or felt threatened? Sam would miss a lot of angles and insights that his staff could provide, and he really wouldn't even need a staff in the first place. There would be no point in surrounding himself with bright, creative people like he has. (The jury is still out on me, I'm sure.) He'd be totally on his own, which he has said he doesn't want to be.

We need to surround ourselves with insightful, trustworthy friends and advisers. Then we need to allow them the freedom to offer whatever input is necessary to make us the best we can be. Each of us has a limited perspective shaped by our own personality, background, and biases, so we benefit from those who see things differently and who are comfortable challenging our assumptions and giving us advice. People who like being stuck in their patterns of thought or who feel threatened if someone else comes up with a good idea will have a hard time doing this, but they miss a valuable opportunity to gain insight. We make much wiser and more well-informed decisions when we seek out a variety of opinions.

Be open to receiving counsel. Surround yourself with the best people you can find and give them absolute freedom to disagree with and challenge you. Enjoy the benefit of other people's gifts, skills, and insights. Seek their input, listen to them, decide on the right direction, and then go forward with confidence.

UNCOMMON KEY > *God created you unique for a reason. Use the differences of those around you to your advantage. Tap into the wisdom of many counselors before making a decision.*

October 25

Gaining Perspective

> Everything that has happened to me here has helped to spread the Good News. For everyone here, including the whole palace guard, knows that I am in chains because of Christ. And because of my imprisonment, most of the believers here have gained confidence and boldly speak God's message without fear. PHILIPPIANS 1:12-14

Adversity can have a silver lining. Sometimes good actually flows from unlikely places.

I think the teams I coached grew stronger from the difficult losses we endured. Many times I found myself consoling family and friends after a devastating loss. They may have been surprised by a head coach doing that, thinking, *He's the head coach, and here he is consoling me, a fan?* But I knew how much the members of our team loved their jobs. I loved mine, too. I never thought or responded, "It's only a game." What I would say, however, is that when viewed through the lens of eternity, we'd be just fine. It may hurt now, but someday all things will be made new in heaven.

That's why I can imagine Paul writing these words of encouragement from prison. I think we could safely say that his was a case of bad things happening to a good person. And yet Paul was energized by what had been happening before his eyes. Because he had been faithful in telling others the gospel message, others were boldly speaking out too.

In the last chapter of Acts, we read an example of Paul's boldness. "For the next two years, Paul lived in Rome at his own expense. He welcomed all who visited him, boldly proclaiming the Kingdom of God and teaching about the Lord Jesus Christ. And no one tried to stop him" (Acts 28:30-31).

As long as we stay focused on spreading the Good News of Christ, that He came to earth and died for us that we might have abundant life in heaven, we will continue to gain perspective and peace. Holding up any personal issue—no matter how debilitating—against the backdrop of eternity changes things, doesn't it? And, as in Paul's case, it's hard to keep that change inside. We want to boldly tell other people what Jesus has done for us.

UNCOMMON KEY > *What do you need to hold up against the backdrop of eternity to change the negative into a positive? Keep your focus on the good that can come out of your story.*

October 26

Go and Do It

> The rain and snow come down from the heavens and stay on the ground to water the earth. They cause the grain to grow, producing seed for the farmer and bread for the hungry. It is the same with my word. I send it out, and it always produces fruit. It will accomplish all I want it to, and it will prosper everywhere I send it.   ISAIAH 55:10-11

It was more than twenty years ago that Nike created huge advertising campaigns around three words: *Just do it.* I have to admit, it was pure genius. The phrase doesn't say to *prepare* to do it—just do it. I suggest, with today's verses in mind, you just do it—share the Word of God.

That doesn't mean you can stall because you're "planning to plan." Or that it can't happen today because you have to get it just right before you can go with it. Perfect, actually. Which means it will probably never get done.

We always want to wait until we have just the right thing to say . . . but that's often just an excuse. God wants us to just do it. The truth is, we probably will never feel ready to go and share the Word of God. We probably feel—if we care to admit it—afraid. Afraid we might make a mistake and turn someone off and lose an opportunity for God to work in someone's life. Afraid we'll look or sound silly. Embarrassed that we might not have just the right word, phrase, experience, Scripture verse, or answer to a question that comes up.

We're often waiting for something, but God is waiting for us to act. What we forget is that God is much bigger than all our inadequacies and mistakes. He wants simply our availability and our hearts and for us to share what He has done for us with others He puts in our path.

Even if we get it all wrong, mess it up, or leave folks scratching their heads, God can clean it all up. In fact, He promises that He will, that His Word will produce fruit.

UNCOMMON KEY > *Believe God's promise that the seeds of His Word that you plant for Him will bear fruit. Find someone who needs to hear those words.*

October 27

Incredible Impact, Small Ego

> John told them, "I baptize with water, but right here in the crowd is someone you do not recognize. Though his ministry follows mine, I'm not even worthy to be his slave and untie the straps of his sandal." JOHN 1:26-27

I'm totally not into eating locusts, even dipped in honey, but there was certainly something appealing about John the Baptist. I would have loved to have had him on my teams! Here was a guy who had his own followers, yet he was always clear about his mission—pointing people, including his own followers, to someone else, Jesus Christ.

To John, getting the credit was not what motivated him. Getting the result that God intended was his sole mission. That's the type of coach and player we sought to bring on board, and I believe we were pretty successful in doing that through the years. It's the mark of a good team to have people who don't care who gets the credit, but only that together they fulfill their mission.

When Jesus began His ministry, He first saw John waist-deep in the water of the Jordan River. Matthew tells us in his Gospel that John wore skins of camel's hair tied together with a leather belt around his waist and really did eat locusts and honey. From outward appearances, there was not a lot of basis for him to have a big ego, despite his voice that must have sounded like thunder and had an uncommon authority, as if he had a message from God.

Large crowds gathered, excited with expectation. John's words resonated wherever the people gathered. Words that were clear and compelling and passionately delivered . . .

Repent of your sins and turn to God, for the Kingdom of Heaven is near. . . .

Prepare the way for the LORD's coming!

Clear the road for him! (Matthew 3:2-3)

And for those who came, he baptized them in the Jordan River, saying, "I baptize with water those who repent of their sins and turn to God. But someone is coming soon who is greater than I am—so much greater that I'm not worthy even to be his slave and carry his sandals. He will baptize you with the Holy Spirit and with fire" (Matthew 3:11).

And through all of that, it is remarkable the way John was able to keep himself out of the way without a word of complaint. It was clear to him that it was not about him.

It often seems that the greater impact you have, the smaller your ego.

UNCOMMON KEY > *You will be most effective for Christ when you realize that life is not about you, but all about Him. Is there something you need to change to reflect that?*

October 28

Starting Every Day

> Take delight in the LORD, and he will give you your heart's desires. Commit everything you do to the LORD. Trust him, and he will help you. PSALM 37:4-5

Most of us wouldn't think of just taking a day off work. In twenty-eight years of coaching, I never had a player say, "I didn't come to practice today because I was too busy." We are very committed to our jobs. We should be just as committed to spending time with God.

Do you want to do something that will dramatically change your life and the lives of others around you? Something that anyone can do, and it won't cost you anything except a few minutes of your time each day?

Spend some quiet time every morning with the God who created you.

I know. You've heard that before, and while it sounds good, the benefits can be elusive. But have you ever started to do it and stayed with it on a regular and daily basis?

Think about it with me for a minute—I am suggesting that you spend a quiet period of time with the Lord every morning before you take off for your day. If your schedule is anything like mine, there will be a few days where that commitment will be interrupted. But don't let those exceptions affect your decision to set aside one-on-one time with the Lord and dissuade you from starting this dramatically life-transforming journey.

I highly recommend doing it in the morning. Things tend to come up in the afternoon, and you'll probably be too tired at night. Get up ten, fifteen, or twenty minutes earlier to allow for whatever time you need to start with. Keep a pad and a pen with you. Have a Bible at hand—preferably one that is easy to understand. Maybe start reading a chapter or two each day from the Gospel of John.

Pray for a few minutes—remember, you're just talking to God. Make some notes on what crossed your mind while you were praying. You may think your mind wanders, but maybe God is telling you something He'll come back to later.

I have had folks in my life whom I trust tell me they can tell whether or not I have spent quiet time with the Lord that morning. According to them, I respond better to situations and people when I have spent time with the Lord.

UNCOMMON KEY > *Moments spent with the Lord are always well spent. If you have never done this before, commit to ten minutes each morning to begin with. If you have been doing this on a regular basis, increase your time. I promise those few minutes will change your life.*

October 29

No Rules Required

> Christ has truly set us free. Now make sure that you stay free, and don't get tied up again in slavery to the law. GALATIANS 5:1

Albert Camus once said, "Integrity has no need of rules." Think about that. Rules are designed to keep behavior in order. If someone has strong character and lives with integrity, the rules are unnecessary. That person will act consistently with his or her values.

That's one reason I never had many team rules for our players. (We looked for players who had high integrity, who held *themselves* to a high standard.) They knew where I stood and what I expected of them. As a leader—of both my football team and my family—I realize that people have to grow into their values and learn to be accountable not to me but to their own character. It's important to give people a certain amount of freedom, as well as the responsibilities that go with it, to allow them to grow. If they develop an inner life committed to honor and integrity, they have no need of my rules or anyone else's. They live from the core of who they have become.

That applies not only to people we lead but to ourselves. We need to live with both freedom and responsibility. We need to decide what our true values are—things like inner courage, wisdom, a sense of duty, a commitment to something larger than ourselves—and grow into those values. The character that results is ultimately what assures success for us and for our relationships. That's the glue that holds individuals together in a bond of trust and accountability.

Companies often put a higher priority on character than on competence because they know someone who functions from their integrity will be free to focus on the overall mission without character issues getting in the way. Instead of spending time correcting behavior, they will be able to move forward toward the common goal. Strong character creates trust within any group of people—a team, a business, a family—and develops an uncommon bond.

UNCOMMON KEY > *Don't focus on keeping the rules. Focus on becoming the kind of person who is so strong in character that the rules aren't even necessary.*

October 30

When God Speaks, Listen

Long ago God spoke many times and in many ways to our ancestors through the prophets. And now in these final days, he has spoken to us through his Son. God promised everything to the Son as an inheritance, and through the Son he created the universe. HEBREWS 1:1-2

When preparing my team for a game, I often used a lot of different ways to get my message across. On Wednesday I would start by addressing the team and giving them our plan. Sometimes it would be strictly football, but many times I would relate it to life, using stories from the Bible to illustrate a point about football. I would show a videotape of our upcoming opponent or have the assistant coaches go over scouting reports on that team's strengths and weaknesses. We would pass out our game plan, where the players would see diagrams of plays we intended to run or defenses we would use that week. Sometimes I would have a guest speaker address the team or have veteran players talk about the importance of playing well that week. Many different people and materials, but all delivering the message that I, as the coach, wanted to get across.

The same is true with God. He uses different means to communicate with His family. We are His children, and God has been speaking to us since the beginning of Creation and in our lives since the time He formed us in our mother's womb. He began by using the prophets, but now he speaks to us through Christ and the Holy Spirit. He is always speaking to us, despite that more often than not we are not listening. Sometimes we think we are listening but cannot hear. That's the way family is at times. Sometimes we're waiting to hear that big booming voice of God, but that's not how He speaks. Instead, He speaks to us in the quiet words of our spouse, a parent, or one of our children or a friend.

The key to good communication is for the speaker to enunciate well and use words that can be understood; the listener needs to listen and to focus on what is being said and not what he or she wants to say. God knows what He is saying and how to say it—we need to be still and listen for His voice. It's always a good idea to start in His Word—the Bible.

Have you heard Him speaking to you lately? Have you quieted yourself enough to catch what He is saying? Listen closely. You're in His family.

UNCOMMON KEY > *God speaks to you through many means, including through His Spirit, through others, and through His Word. Start jotting down the messages He is giving you.*

October 31

A Daily Dose of Encouragement

> We love each other because he loved us first. If someone says, "I love God," but hates a Christian brother or sister, that person is a liar; for if we don't love people we can see, how can we love God, whom we cannot see? And he has given us this command: Those who love God must also love their Christian brothers and sisters.   1 JOHN 4:19-21

Joseph of Cyprus was a member of the early church. The name people used more often for him, Barnabas, meant "son of encouragement." He apparently had a reputation for encouraging others. Maybe that's why he was such a good companion for Paul on his missionary trips. Those journeys were long and hard, with a lot of obstacles and opposition every step of the way. A "son of encouragement" is exactly who you need in a situation like that.

Everyone needs a Barnabas—or several of them—in their lives. Life can be tough, and it helps when people encourage and lift us up. Not only do we need that for ourselves, we also need to offer it to others. We need to be a Barnabas when people around us are going through difficult times. That's one way to live out the command to love each other, and Jesus said that love is the essence of all of God's law. When we are encouragers, we are doing for others what we want them to do for us. And the more encouragement we give, the more we will likely receive.

Think about the opportunities you have to encourage someone. When you notice that someone did a good job, do you just make a mental note of it, or do you actually tell them? When your spouse or your kids are going through a hard time, do you only get discouraged about how it affects your home life, or do you take time to pour encouragement into them? When was the last time you sent flowers for no reason or did a favor out of the blue? When have you intentionally tried to create a positive memory for someone else?

We can choose to leave a trail of positive memories in the lives of people around us if we look beyond ourselves and take advantage of opportunities. Everyone needs encouragement, not only in difficult times but even when things are going well. We all need to hear positive words daily. Life is comprised of plenty of memories, but we can create good ones for those around us. Our encouragement can keep those around us going strong.

UNCOMMON KEY > *Be intentional about encouraging others. It lifts others up, and it lifts you up too. Let your life be an encouragement to everyone.*

November 1

Hidden Toxins

> For the word of God is alive and powerful. It is sharper than the sharpest two-edged sword, cutting between soul and spirit, between joint and marrow. It exposes our innermost thoughts and desires. Nothing in all creation is hidden from God. Everything is naked and exposed before his eyes, and he is the one to whom we are accountable.   HEBREWS 4:12-13

I know a few people who were among the thousands who have had houses built using drywall manufactured in China. They didn't know it at the time the home was built and didn't even know that was something they should be concerned about at first. For one family, their first inkling of a problem was when a large bulge appeared in a bathroom wall when the wall got wet. The family considered just patching it but instead had a contractor come out to inspect the situation. They wanted to make sure that the leak, if that's what it was, hadn't spread to other areas of the wall.

When the contractor cut into the wall to assess the problem, he discovered the damage was extensive.

Throughout the entire bathroom.

Throughout the entire house.

It seems this particular drywall manufactured in China absorbed water and would begin to expand, producing toxic fumes. Ultimately those folks had to tear the house down to the foundation, as well as destroy all of their furniture and almost everything else that had been in the house. What was lurking inside the walls had poisoned nearly every aspect of their home and lives.

Sin can do the same thing in our lives. We can cover and paint over issues, or patch them temporarily, but often they will fester under the surface and grow so large and toxic that they begin to affect other areas of our lives and ultimately threaten our very foundation.

Staying rooted in God's Word can help us avoid insidious and deadly issues in our lives. The Bible helps us to see beyond what's on the outside to what is in our hearts, to question our motivations, and to cleanse us from those things we try to keep hidden.

UNCOMMON KEY > *Be sure that the walls of your heart are kept clean and are reinforced by what God is teaching you in His Word. Commit to a regular time of reading God's Word, praying, and getting to know His will for you and your life.*

November 2

Good Is Big to God

> You died to the power of the law when you died with Christ. And now you are united with the one who was raised from the dead. As a result, we can produce a harvest of good deeds for God. ROMANS 7:4

As a young assistant coach, I was eager for the opportunity to rise to the level of coordinator. Once I did, I discovered there were unanticipated downsides to the job, the most fundamental one being that I couldn't remain as close to my players as I had previously. When I only coached the defensive backs, I was responsible for only a handful of guys, and Lauren and I got to be close to them. Once I was responsible for twenty-six guys and how they all fit together, everything changed.

What is our harvest to be? Why has God planted us here? When He says "good deeds," does He mean "good" or "big"?

That's always the rub. Society dictates success for us by telling us that bigger is better. More is preferable. Image over influence. But everything that seems natural and expected to society is contrary to the way of life God calls us to live.

The Bible recounts how God has tried to reach people and get their attention. In the Old Testament, He spoke through the voices of the prophets and revealed His judgment and compassion to leaders like Abraham, Isaac, Moses, Joshua, Esther, and countless others, instructing them on what lives of faith should look like. Their response? Making golden idols, whining about wanting to go back to Egypt, and cowering in fear because of giants seen in the Promised Land. They let themselves be overcome by the situations around them instead of relying on God in faith. They abandoned the laws God established and believed that ungodly practices would fulfill them.

In the New Testament, God's incredible love for us is expressed in His Son, Jesus Christ—sent to die for us, to rise from the grave, and to ascend into heaven. Those who believe in Jesus Christ are assured a place with God forever.

And all He asks in return is that we love Him and love each other. Nothing big, really, by society's standards. No fireworks displays or trophies. Nothing flashy required. Just doing what we can to live like Jesus, finding ways to selflessly imitate Him.

UNCOMMON KEY > *You don't need to think big when you're trying to do what God wants you to do. Think good. Think love. Then put the two together.*

November 3

A Truthful Evaluation

> We will speak the truth in love, growing in every way more and more like Christ, who is the head of his body, the church. He makes the whole body fit together perfectly. As each part does its own special work, it helps the other parts grow, so that the whole body is healthy and growing and full of love. **EPHESIANS 4:15-16**

Speak the truth in love.

We often hear that "the truth hurts." But we have to understand that the truth—spoken in love—helps! With our children, with our friends, with our coworkers.

We can see it happen a lot in Christian settings—churches, ministries, and other outreaches. Many people have an inability to speak truthfully—in a loving way or frankly, any way. We see it particularly with people in supervisory positions; they don't want to write a negative evaluation of someone even if that person's performance is subpar. And so that person who thinks he or she is doing a good job stays in that position, and the ministry's or church's mission suffers. We do a great disservice to people who need to hear an honest critique.

Here's what I believe is the crux of the matter. The supervisor doesn't really believe that the employee is created by God as a unique and special human being! If the boss did believe that, he or she would quickly see that there are two options: help the employee apply his or her gifts to the task at hand by building on strengths and minimizing weaknesses or find the person a different position more suited to his or her gifts.

Who is responsible to ensure that a person's gifts and abilities are drawn out? Both the boss and the employee. That's the starting point of the conversation.

Maybe it will require a change in position. Maybe a change in setting or location. But speaking the truth in love not only helps those around us to maximize their gifts and abilities, it requires that we help them to find the setting where that can be done.

UNCOMMON KEY > *Before you speak the truth in love, consider where a person seems to shine, what gifts he or she can bring to the job. Be ready to present options that will maximize the individual's potential and expand God's Kingdom.*

November 4

Taking Care of His Treasures

> Honor the LORD with your wealth and with the best part of everything you produce. Then he will fill your barns with grain, and your vats will overflow with good wine. PROVERBS 3:9-10

We need to be less quick to possess and more willing to honor God with our wealth in whatever form we find it. Then He will return it to us many times over.

Our lives are all about stewardship—taking care of what has been entrusted to us in terms of our time, our talents, and our treasures. How we end up taking care of them really comes down to our understanding of ownership in those areas of our lives.

In his seminal book *The Treasure Principle*, Randy Alcorn succinctly recaps some of the principles that apply to stewardship:

> Principle one: God owns everything. I'm His money manager.
> Principle two: My heart always goes where I put God's money.
> Principle three: Heaven, not earth, is my home.
> Principle four: I should live not for the dot (my present life on earth), but for the line (heading on into eternity).
> Principle five: Giving is the only antidote to materialism.
> Principle six: God prospers me not to raise my standard of living, but to raise my standard of giving.[9]

Randy has it right, and even though those principles fall somewhat lightly off our tongues, they are not the easiest principles to incorporate into daily living. We want to do it. We believe we can't take it with us—at least we jokingly say we believe it, even though our behavior may not validate that belief.

The real crux of the problem that keeps us from wholeheartedly adopting such an attitude is this: we are not ready to admit it's not ours. We hold our possessions too tightly; we acquire and build more than we need.

Honor the Lord with His wealth—then we are off and running for Him.

UNCOMMON KEY > *It all belongs to Him. Start with that truth first, and stay there until your behavior mirrors your belief in that truth.*

November 5

Keeping Anger in Its Place

> Don't befriend angry people or associate with hot-tempered people, or you will learn to be like them and endanger your soul. PROVERBS 22:24-25

We've all been tempted to do it, even on a small scale. We want to get back at someone for something they've done to us with a snide remark or by criticizing them in front of others. If we haven't done it, at least we've thought about doing it. In either case, it only makes the original issue worse. Once anger, frustration, deceit, or cunning ways get a foothold in any situation in our lives, the devil begins to have a field day. There is no telling when we will be able to turn things around, restore the relationship—if ever—or regain our reputation.

Most coaches frequently talk to players about their behavior both on and off the field. No matter what happens to you, don't compound the problem by trying to get back at whoever did something to you. Did you get that? So often it's not the initial issue or incident that gets you into trouble—it's what happens next. How often have you seen the player who retaliates for a cheap shot get the penalty flag thrown on him instead of on the original offender?

It happens all the time in football, and it happens all the time in life. A friend or a spouse says something, and we retaliate angrily. Now we're off to the races as another sinner right alongside them. God doesn't think in terms of who said what first or how sinful one person's actions may be when compared with another person's. All sin causes a person to be separated from God because God is holy, He cannot look at sin, no matter how small or how heinous it is.

When you find yourself in a volatile situation, don't make things worse by letting anger get the better of you. Be wiser than hot-tempered people with short fuses. If you stay calm, instead of reacting angrily, it will be easier to control yourself in whatever situation you find yourself in. And it may have a lasting effect on someone else.

UNCOMMON KEY > *Do you have angry people in your life? Let them know that anger never helps a situation; it only makes it worse. And as much as you'd like to retaliate with anger at times, always take a deep breath before you lose control.*

November 6

Praying before the Storm Hits

> In times of trouble, may the LORD answer your cry. May the name of the God of Jacob keep you safe from all harm. . . . May we shout for joy when we hear of your victory and raise a victory banner in the name of our God. May the LORD answer all your prayers.   PSALM 20:1, 5

It's hard to remember when we're in the middle of tough situations, but while we are in the midst of them and wondering how in the world they will ever end or how we will get out of them, we are doing nothing proactive to change the current environment.

In the middle of a tough situation, a child instinctively seeks out his or her parents or some other member of the family for help and comfort. But what about us? Well, more often than not, we tend to worry.

Worry is a negative response and does little—other than to focus our attention on the problem causing our worry—to help us overcome the problem. Prayer, on the other hand, is a positive and calming response that draws us back into God's family and allows us to focus on God our Father. It helps calm our inner storm. In the midst of those storms we shouldn't be worrying, but instead we should be praying, a discipline recommended by none other than Jesus Christ. And at the very outset of prayer, it will bring us to a place of peace.

Jesus tells us to pray in those moments of need for ourselves and others:

When you pray . . . (Matthew 6:5)
But when you pray . . . (Matthew 6:6)
One day Jesus told his disciples a story to show that they should always pray and never give up. (Luke 18:1)

Throughout Scripture God makes it abundantly clear to us that we are to pray, to devote ourselves to prayer, to pray without ceasing, to pray continually, and to pray boldly with the God who loves us. Jesus prayed continually to His Father: "Jesus often withdrew to the wilderness for prayer" (Luke 5:16).

Then why don't we pray as consistently and fervently as we should to our Father? Maybe we don't believe anything will happen—our prayers won't result in the answers we seek. Maybe it's not a habit we have developed, and therefore when the opportunity arises for a time of prayer, it is not a default for us—so we turn to worry before we even know all we need to know.

Let me suggest that the next time something occurs and you sense worry taking over, turn to God and let Him draw you back into the center of the family. Turn whatever you're going through to a sense of peace by praying—you'll be pleasantly surprised.

UNCOMMON KEY > *When you see the storm clouds gathering, commence praying!*

November 7

What Forgiveness Will Do for You

> Then Peter came to him and asked, "Lord, how often should I forgive someone who sins
> against me? Seven times?" "No, not seven times," Jesus replied, "but seventy times seven!"
> MATTHEW 18:21-22

Forgiveness is hard. I mean, we can forgive some things. "Sure, Lord, I can forgive him or her. There are a lot of things that have happened that I know he didn't mean to happen. I know he's sorry.

"But what about the big things? The things she did that really cut deep and still hurt? The things she said about me to others, right in front of me? The times I was made to feel small and worthless? You obviously weren't there to hear them, otherwise You would understand that I can't forgive.

"And then there are all those hurtful things, repeated over and over again by the same person. He says he's trying to do better, but it doesn't feel like it. I don't see any change. Do I still need to forgive him, even then?"

I know it's hard sometimes, especially in a marriage. Some of you may have experienced that as well.

Peter thought he was being overly generous when he proposed seven acts of forgiveness per person to Jesus; after all, the rabbis taught that forgiving three times fulfilled the requirements of the law. But Christ said no, not seven—seventy times seven. Instead of being patted on the back, Peter learned that a follower of Christ needs to be willing to forgive without keeping track of the number of times it's done. That describes God's forgiving mercy to us—limitless and free, and beyond anything we deserve.

Whom do you need to forgive today? If you're anything like me, you probably have a list of people. What do you need to do to forgive them? How will you go about doing it? What if the people who wronged you don't say they're sorry?

Maybe the real question you need to ask yourself is who is really set free when you forgive someone else? Maybe the answer is the truth that Christ wants to get across in the first place.

UNCOMMON KEY > *As a follower of Christ, your attitude about forgiveness should mirror the attitude of the one you are trying to be like. Forgive others as He forgives you.*

November 8

Making the Most of His Gifts

| To those who use well what they are given, even more will be given. LUKE 19:26

My mom, who was a teacher, used to look at her students and see beyond the obvious, recognizing their gifts and abilities whether they saw them or not. She wanted to help them become all that they could become—and she got results.

We've all been entrusted with things that might not be obvious to ourselves or others as God's gifts. But He has shaped each and every one of us with abilities, interests, and talents in distinct combinations and differing amounts that no one else has ever had in the past or will ever have in the future. We are unique, and what we bring to the table, thanks to Him, will not only bring us satisfaction and add something to those around us, but it will also glorify God.

There is a reason He has created us unique for this particular time in history. He knows what the world needs, and He has provided us with the gifts and abilities to address those needs for Him. Like the man who entrusted his money to his servants in Matthew 25:14-21, God expects that we will use the gifts He gives us, not hoard them. In the similar story of the ten servants in Luke 19:11-27, one servant hoarded the money the nobleman entrusted to him. He was afraid to use what he was given for fear he would lose it.

How often has that happened? Fear has a way of creeping into our lives and keeps us from becoming all God created us to be—keeping us from using the gifts and abilities we were given. Fear of failure. Fear we will disappoint someone. Fear we won't measure up. Fears ingrained in us by a society that measures all the wrong things.

God is measuring how we use the gifts He's given us. He measures how much we want to glorify Him and touch others—whether we fall short or not.

UNCOMMON KEY > *God has given you incredible gifts and abilities, some more obvious than others. Are you using them? Write down what you think your unique gifts are and then ask your family or friends to write down what they think your gifts are. Compare the lists and prayerfully use those gifts and watch them multiply.*

November 9

Marking the Seasons

> For everything there is a season, a time for every activity under heaven. A time to be born and a time to die. . . . A time to cry and a time to laugh. A time to grieve and a time to dance.
> ECCLESIASTES 3:1-2, 4

In the last decade I have lost both of my parents, my father-in-law, and my oldest son. I've also talked to hundreds of other parents who have lost children, and to children who have lost siblings. It never gets easy, and it often seems unfair. But death is a part of life in this world, and even though it is always hard to swallow, I think God uses those losses to remind us not to take life and love for granted.

When we lose loved ones, we grieve that we won't be able to spend any more time with them. Then we start to wish we had spent more time with them when they were here, and we feel a sense of regret that we didn't. Even if we knew the person for a long time and have many happy memories, we wish there were more to come. But we never know how long God will give us with someone. It may be decades, a few years, or even just a few weeks. It's on God's timetable, not ours.

The uncertainty of life reminds us to keep our priorities in order. When we are aware that our time with anyone may be short, we learn to put our families and friends above work and activities—in other words, relationships above possessions, status, and accomplishments. If we don't, we will eventually regret it.

Shifting priorities may require some changes in your schedule, but it will always be worth it if it leads you to spend more time with the people you love, enjoy them and their gifts more deeply, and make more lasting memories with them. Remember that time is short and people are precious. Then arrange your activities around that.

UNCOMMON KEY > *Relationships matter more than anything else, but you never know how long you will have with the people around you. Don't take them for granted. Make a phone call, send a card, or schedule a lunch date on your calendar today.*

November 10

Honoring the Commitment

> Let all who are spiritually mature . . . hold on to the progress we have already made.
> PHILIPPIANS 3:15-16

My friend Wade Phillips has been integrally involved in One Heart, a campaign and movie concept dedicated to getting people involved with youth, specifically at-risk and incarcerated youth, to help them stay out of trouble and become productive members of society.

The idea for One Heart was inspired by a football game between Faith Christian School and Gainesville State School in Texas chronicled in the book *Remember Why You Play* by David Thomas. Kris Hogan, the head coach of Faith Christian, believed that if his kids were going to truly look beyond themselves, they needed to do something radical. He scheduled a game against Gainesville State, a maximum-security juvenile correctional facility.

The biggest issue for Coach Hogan wasn't that the players there were serving time. Rather, his concern was that the Gainesville State team had no fans. No one encouraged those kids.

Faith Christian divided up their cheerleaders and the parents of Faith Christian players between their team and their opponent. It meant that some parents were fervently rooting for Gainesville players to tackle their sons. But by the end of the game, the hearts of players on both teams had been changed.

Once they heard the story, Coach Phillips and other members of the Dallas Cowboys got involved, hoping to spread the impact of Faith Christian's actions far beyond that night.

But on the day of a fund-raising event for One Heart, word came that Coach Phillips had been fired.

No one at One Heart expected him to show up for the benefit. It was perfectly understandable. And then Wade walked through the door, stunning everyone, said Honor Garrett, one of the event's organizers and the wife of Cowboys assistant coach John Garrett.

Wade Phillips believed in One Heart. He believed in keeping his word. He believed that his life, and what he can do with his days in building a legacy, was bigger than him.

He was able to use his platform for good, just hours after receiving that devastating news about his job. I know firsthand how difficult a day that was for him. It wouldn't have been wrong if he hadn't honored that particular commitment to One Heart. In the end, though, his choice to attend the charity event demonstrated how spiritually mature he was and made an even bigger impact.

UNCOMMON KEY > *Is there a commitment that you need to honor today, on the job or at home? Even if you are having a bad day, complete it if you can. It will speak volumes.*

November 11

The Outside Reflecting the Inside

I know all the things you do. I have seen your love, your faith, your service, and your patient endurance. And I can see your constant improvement in all these things. REVELATION 2:19

When I took over the Indianapolis Colts, I came preaching a manner of football that was slightly different from what they had played before. In the past, they had Peyton Manning, an extremely talented, young, aggressive quarterback and an attacking defense. Both were positive aspects of the team, but I wanted us to play differently.

On offense, I wanted us to focus on taking care of the ball—no turnovers. That meant, at times, that we needed Peyton to be less aggressive, not to take unnecessary chances. There were times we were better off settling for a field goal if it meant we weren't taking the chance of throwing an interception.

Similarly, on defense, our scheme was predicated on taking care of each person's responsibility, sometimes by "staying at home." That is, not every guy was to immediately run to the ball, including some positions that were used to doing only that. The scheme required self-discipline and trust in the plan and each other.

Our guys said the right things during that first year, and we made the playoffs, but in a 41–0 playoff loss, it was clear their words didn't truly indicate their hearts—their actions didn't mirror their words.

It's not that they didn't mean well or weren't being truthful, but rather, in their core, their beliefs didn't quite match up, so in crucial situations they would revert back to old habits. Over the next seasons, we kept working until they believed and their words matched their actions.

Ultimately, our actions really do indicate the state of our hearts as well as the extent of our faith in the living God. If we truly believe that we are seeking God and His will for our lives, that should be reflected in how we conduct ourselves on a daily basis.

UNCOMMON KEY > *The state of our faith in Christ will be reflected in the extent of the Christlike quality of our thoughts, words, and deeds. Be sure the outside matches the inside today.*

November 12

Richer by the Word

> Let the message about Christ, in all its richness, fill your lives. Teach and counsel each other with all the wisdom he gives. Sing psalms and hymns and spiritual songs to God with thankful hearts. And whatever you do or say, do it as a representative of the Lord Jesus, giving thanks through him to God the Father. COLOSSIANS 3:16-17

Let the word of Christ dwell in you. Whatever you say and do, in word or deed, do it all for the glory of God. Daily living. Each day, every day. Regardless of what you are called to do as an occupation.

When I was coaching, I made a point to have regular Bible studies and chapels for our players and our staff. Tuesday was the coaches' Bible study, and Friday was the team Bible study with the players. Many men met in smaller groups throughout the week to pray together. Game weekends always included a chapel service for which we would have a speaker come in and share a message from Scripture. Sometimes I would share. Sometimes another coach on our staff would share. And sometimes we would have a person we knew and trusted from outside our team and organization come in to share with us a word of direction and encouragement.

Our hope in those settings, as should be the case with any Bible study or prayer group, was to continually plant the empowering and affirming message of Christ in the listeners' hearts and then allow that message to work according to God's purposes in each of them.

To let the word of Christ dwell within them.

How might that look in the various settings of your life? Perhaps at home it starts with prayer in the morning with your spouse and then individual prayer with your children. Prayer and thanks at the breakfast table together. An encouraging word as your spouse heads out the door to the office or as you drop your children off at school. Perhaps it involves keeping your home free of temptations and things that are contrary to God's Word—certain movies, magazines, music, or things on the Internet. Perhaps it involves reassessing your desire for the temptations of alcohol, tobacco, and other things that harm your body and could harm your children's lives if they followed your example.

At work you could organize an office Bible study. But it doesn't have to be something formal. Maybe it's getting in the habit of offering an encouraging and kind word to others. Or simply not being a participant in the group gossip session at the watercooler.

Wherever you find yourself, consider ways you can let the word of Christ dwell within you and others.

UNCOMMON KEY > *Incorporate the word of Christ within you and others each day; it will empower and encourage you whatever may come.*

November 13

Make This a Regular Exercise

> Jesus began to tell his disciples plainly that it was necessary for him to go to Jerusalem, and that he would suffer many terrible things. . . . He would be killed, but on the third day he would be raised from the dead. But Peter . . . began to reprimand him for saying such things. "Heaven forbid, Lord," he said. "This will never happen to you!" MATTHEW 16:21-22

Anywhere you look in the Gospels and find Jesus, you will usually find the disciples. Once Christ left His home in Nazareth and set out to fulfill His earthly ministry, He selected a group of twelve men to accompany Him, teaching them with parables and by His example.

Over the next three years, Jesus talked with them, and they talked with Him. With each conversation, each shared experience, He gave them an opportunity to find out more about Him and each other. It was all preparation for what He wanted them to do with Him then and eventually through His power.

The group ate together, traveled together, and spent time learning and teaching others together. Most days were busy, but there were quiet times too. Christ made time for His disciples and for others, and they made time for Him. Not a bad example for each of us to take to heart in our daily lives with the people most important to us.

Are you ready to implement this? When did you last spend time talking with your spouse about whatever he or she wanted to talk about? I don't mean when you're in the car headed to the movies or at a ball game or in the checkout at the grocery store. I mean sitting down with each other, one-on-one, all alone, listening to what your spouse has to say, whether it is what happened that day or the day before. Be prepared: you may be in for a marathon conversation because you have a lot of catching up to do.

Try it. I predict that those moments spent together will be cherished for a long time. And maybe what is said will have far-reaching impact. After all, the impact of the disciples is still being felt throughout the world.

UNCOMMON KEY > *Spend quality time with those you love. It will make a difference in your life and your relationships. And who knows, you may end up being blessed as well.*

November 14

Resolving Differences with Grace

> Don't bother correcting mockers; they will only hate you. But correct the wise, and they will love you. Instruct the wise, and they will be even wiser. Teach the righteous, and they will learn even more. **PROVERBS 9:8-9**

Pick up a newspaper, and you'll find quite a few conflicts to read about. Or turn on a TV or radio talk show, and you'll probably hear some pretty heated arguments. It's human nature to let disagreements get personal, and too often people resort to name-calling, mockery, and personal attacks. We often assume that when someone disagrees with what we think, they are disapproving of who we are. Or maybe we just get frustrated at the opinions of others and lash out. Or we realize we're wrong but aren't secure enough to admit it. Whatever the reason, disagreements can turn into personal conflict very easily.

I don't know many people who really like conflict, other than maybe a few people who like to bully others. But in normal circumstances, I don't think we need to fear it. Conflict is really an opportunity to understand our differences. We have one perspective, someone else has another—and both perspectives, if understood, can be valuable. Sharing different ideas and perspectives—without letting the differences get personal—can benefit everyone involved.

If you find yourself in a conflict with someone else, approach it as a positive opportunity, even if the other person doesn't see it that way yet. Agree to talk about it, and emphasize that you want to focus not on each other but on the issue. Acknowledge that having different perspectives can be healthy. Make it clear that you value the other person's opinion and that you want a constructive resolution. Explore how you can get past the problem in a way that respects everyone involved. If you can focus on the principal interests, not the people, it can turn into a very constructive experience.

When you approach conflict this way, you'll find it can be illuminating—a chance for all parties to grow or to see an issue more fully. If it's handled with respect for others' opinions and perspectives, it can have very positive results.

UNCOMMON KEY > *Approach conflict as an opportunity to learn something. It's often a catalyst for positive change and the best way to grow in understanding.*

November 15

To Be (Married), or Not to Be?

> An unmarried man can spend his time doing the Lord's work and thinking how to please him. But a married man has to think about his earthly responsibilities and how to please his wife. . . . A woman who is no longer married or has never been married can be devoted to the Lord and holy in body and in spirit. But a married woman has to think about her earthly responsibilities and how to please her husband. 1 CORINTHIANS 7:32-34

Some of you are single. Now don't take this the wrong way, but good for you! A lot of the players I worked with in my coaching days were—you guessed it—single.

You may want to be single, or maybe not. You may have thought that your being single was something that was going to change soon, but now you find yourself dealing with the loss of a relationship and the accompanying pain, or perhaps the beginning of a new one and all the hope it seems to bring. Maybe you're simply too young to be thinking about any relationship now at all.

So often in our society we view being single as a burden. We should be married. We want to be married. Why aren't we married? That isn't God's attitude toward the matter, however.

As you can see from today's verses, the apostle Paul viewed marriage as a potential distraction from doing the Lord's work, and Jesus told His disciples that "God helps" those who stay unmarried (Matthew 19:11). Jesus wasn't denigrating marriage; He was simply indicating that the unmarried often have greater potential for ministry, as Paul says.

We spend so much time talking about finding someone to marry. And then we spend a lot more of our time in helping those relationships grow so as to maintain a healthy marriage; and we should do all we can do for our marriages to continue to grow. We need healthy marriages because they are the foundation for healthy families and the health of our society.

There's nothing wrong with being married. But take your time. Don't rush into things if you're not married, because there's nothing wrong with being single. Instead of spending so much time on forays designed to find a spouse, spend it with the Lord. You'll find it easier to stay focused on the Lord and what He has planned for your life—which may include marriage.

If you are married, you need to make sure you are supporting your single friends as well. Is there someone you can reach out to and affirm as a child of God?

UNCOMMON KEY > *If you are single, don't rush into a relationship that isn't part of God's plan. Your time may be coming . . . or maybe God trusts you with singleness! Whatever your situation, prayerfully give it to Him.*

November 16

A Daily Serving of Fruit

> The Holy Spirit produces this kind of fruit in our lives: love, joy, peace, patience, kindness, goodness, faithfulness, gentleness, and self-control. There is no law against these things!
> GALATIANS 5:22-23

Some football players aren't sure who they are when they retire. For years they have been validated and valued for what they do and how well they do it. Their self-esteem has been based on statistics and wins. They are talked about very publicly in terms of performance and treated as a commodity—easily expendable when their worth to the team declines. Sometimes their wives fall in love with their high-profile role and lifestyle.

If they have found their identity in their profession, they face an identity crisis as soon as their accomplishment-oriented profession ends. If they have found their sense of self in their achievements, they don't know their real selves when the achievements are over. Their careers have come to define them, and they don't know who they are deep down inside.

The apostle Paul described the fruits of the Spirit as internal characteristics. They have nothing to do with wins and losses, standards of performance, or accolades. They shape us from within and are expressed outwardly toward others. These inner qualities don't always fit well in a competitive world. They aren't oriented toward winning. But in God's eyes these are the characteristics that shape who we are and make us successful in His Kingdom. When we find our identity in Him, we find fulfillment in whatever His Spirit does within us. That's a sense of self that always grows and can never be taken away.

God created you for more than a competitive advantage against His other children. He didn't design you to "get ahead in the world." He doesn't define you by what you do, how you earn a living, how well you perform or impress others, or what kind of accolades you receive. He defines you by the value He assigns to you as His child, and He shapes you by the Spirit working within you.

Make one of your ongoing goals to cultivate the fruits of the Spirit in your life. Grow in the attitudes and characteristics that come from God. Refuse to be defined by your career or accomplishments. Define yourself the same way He does: by how He made you and what He wants to do in your life.

UNCOMMON KEY > *Review the fruits of the Spirit regularly and continually "ripen" and multiply each of them in your life. They will help define who you are according to God's definition.*

November 17

A Respecter of Persons

In the same way, let your good deeds shine out for all to see, so that everyone will praise your heavenly Father. MATTHEW 5:16

Art Rooney Sr. lived on the north side of Pittsburgh. Though he owned the Steelers and could have lived any lifestyle he wanted, he kept his feet on the ground. He walked to the stadium every day. He never moved out of his house, even as the neighborhood got rougher and his neighbors left for a better environment. He knew everybody in our organization, from the star quarterback to the cleaning staff, and made it clear that they were all important to the success of the team. Everyone in Pittsburgh knew he cared about the community and the people who lived in it.

Pittsburgh's sanitation workers went on strike one year, and trash was piling up everywhere—except in front of Mr. Rooney's house. Some of the workers went out of their way to pick up his trash, not as part of their job, but just because they wanted to. They cared for the man who seemed to care for so many others.

Too many people think they'll get the respect they want if they drive the best car, spend the most money, hang out with the hottest people (whatever they are), or flash the most impressive bling. Somehow we started respecting things that aren't really worthy of our respect. But true respect is earned by having integrity, providing for your family, being involved in the community, and working hard in an honest occupation. In my family, those who were older deserved respect for being good parents, grandparents, aunts, or uncles. It had nothing to do with impressing people and everything to do with human decency.

If you seek respect, seek the right kind—the respect that comes as a result of being honest, caring, and hardworking—and seek it for the right reasons.

UNCOMMON KEY > *True respect starts with the way you treat others, and it is earned over a lifetime of demonstrating kindness, honor, and dignity.*

November 18

Screwtape and Wormwood

> Everything else is worthless when compared with the infinite value of knowing Christ Jesus my Lord. For his sake I have discarded everything else, counting it all as garbage, so that I could gain Christ and become one with him. I no longer count on my own righteousness through obeying the law; rather, I become righteous through faith in Christ. For God's way of making us right with himself depends on faith. **PHILIPPIANS 3:8-9**

Most Americans my age know the significance of November 22, 1963, in our country's history, the day President John F. Kennedy was assassinated. But across the ocean at The Kilns in Oxford, another influential man also died. C. S. Lewis, recently retired as professor of Medieval and Renaissance literature at Cambridge, died from renal failure. During his life and even today, however, he was more than noticed because of the timeless nature of his works, including *Mere Christianity*, *The Great Divorce*, The Chronicles of Narnia, and *The Screwtape Letters*.

I have read *The Screwtape Letters* more than once. This series of fictional letters written by an elder devil, Screwtape, to his nephew, Wormwood, is classic mentoring (of the evil kind), as Screwtape encourages the younger devil to be even "worse" than he is. Through Lewis's skillful hand, Screwtape touches on some of the ways that Wormwood can pull his human charge away from growing in a relationship with Christ by touching on all-too-common aspects of human nature.

For instance, he tells Wormwood to prevent his charge from looking inward to evaluate how he can be a better person. Rather, Wormwood must get his human target to concentrate on the hypocrisy that he can see in the person seated just down the pew from him every Sunday morning, forgetting that he is just as dependent on God's grace as the "hypocrite" is. From there, Wormwood's charge could easily fall into faulty comparisons of "I'm not as bad as he is" or "at least I haven't done *that*," rather than comparing himself to the gold standard of Christ, before whom we *all* fall short.

One point that especially struck me is when Lewis writes about the numbing of passion. He understands that the Christian life is not something to ease into but rather something that God wants us to jump headlong into. That idea causes the elder devil to instruct his nephew to "talk to him [his charge] about 'moderation in all things.' If you can once get him to the point of thinking that 'religion is all very well up to a point,' you can feel quite happy about his soul."[10]

Are you committed to following Christ as passionately as Paul did, discarding the things that might hinder your faith and relationship with Jesus from growing? It might be a good practice to pick up and reread *The Screwtape Letters* once a year as a reminder of how easily it can happen.

UNCOMMON KEY > *God wants all of you, not you in moderation. Think of a way you have been trying to be "moderate" in your faith and what you can do to change.*

November 19

Strive to Be Proud about This

| **Pride goes before destruction, and haughtiness before a fall.** PROVERBS 16:18

Barry Sanders and Deion Sanders came into the NFL at the same time. Behind the scenes, they probably weren't very different. They both worked hard and were considered good teammates by their peers. But each had a public persona that was very different from the other. Deion was known as "Prime Time"—flashy, loud, and proud. Not only was he a great player, he knew how to put on a show. He had figured out that in our society, flash sells.

Barry was just the opposite—the "old school" athlete. Like Deion, he was a great player, but he rarely talked about himself. When he scored a touchdown, he handed the ball to the official and went back to the bench. In postgame interviews, he would praise the linemen who blocked for him and then get out of the spotlight. He was a classic example of the quiet, humble athlete most of us say we prefer.

Both players got a lot of attention for their accomplishments, but Deion got even more for his showmanship. He brought a lot of attention to his own name and as a result got more endorsements and exposure. As much as our society claims to commend quiet humility, we actually reward those who put themselves in the spotlight. Deion still commands the spotlight, but these days it's mostly to talk about the Lord.

Pride comes in many forms, and it isn't always attention seeking. An outgoing person can be very humble, and sometimes a quiet person harbors a lot of pride. So I'm not making any judgments about pride and humility in Deion and Barry. But I do know that society has blurred the lines between confidence and pride, and we tend to reward pride with media attention and financial perks. Yet Scripture says that "pride goes before destruction." It eventually leads to a downfall.

Confidence is a good quality to have. It's a realization that God has given us certain abilities and created us to fulfill a unique role that no one else can fill. It's a humble recognition that life is not about us but about using our gifts and abilities to their fullest to help others and contribute to society. Pride, on the other hand, is all about building ourselves up in the eyes of others. If we want to keep from falling, we need to learn the difference.

UNCOMMON KEY > *Be confident in your God-given gifts and abilities, but always avoid pride. Trying to build yourself up will eventually bring you down. If you catch yourself with a "big head" today, deflate it by confessing your sin of pride to God.*

November 20

Not Wasting Words

> A small rudder makes a huge ship turn wherever the pilot chooses to go, even though the winds are strong. In the same way, the tongue is a small thing that makes grand speeches. But a tiny spark can set a great forest on fire. JAMES 3:4-5

Words are powerful. According to the apostle James, they can turn the course of life like a rudder turns a ship or provoke a conflict like a spark starts a forest fire. In the words of Ralph Waldo Emerson, "No man has a prosperity so high or firm, but that two or three words can dishearten it; and there is no calamity which right words will not begin to address." Whether good or bad, words can have a deep and lasting impact.

That means what we say to each other—especially to our kids—is extremely important. Our families can live in peace or be filled with conflict all because of a few well-timed or poorly timed words. Words can inspire wonder, kindle hope, or provide direction; or they can tear down, dampen spirits, and destroy initiative. That applies to anyone, but especially to kids who are still looking for affirmation and significance from the people they look up to. They need to be affirmed and guided. They need encouragement, counsel, and love. Their lives need to be filled with positive expressions about who they are and what their potential is. Like all of us, they need to hear good things from those who love them.

Resolve to use your words to build people up. If you need to say something negative, phrase it in such a way that it has some element of encouragement and hope. When you commit to encouraging, comforting, and strengthening others with your speech, you are not only making their lives better, you're also making yours better by surrounding yourself with people who are affirmed and encouraged. Words can bring peace, forgiveness, restoration, instruction, and strength to all your relationships. Make sure you communicate openly and lovingly with everyone—especially those closest to you, and especially your children. Your words really can change lives.

UNCOMMON KEY > *Most people are careless with one of their most powerful resources: their words. Use yours as an investment in people's lives.*

November 21

Persistence Pays

> Jesus told his disciples a story to show that they should always pray and never give up. "There was a judge in a certain city, . . . who neither feared God nor cared about people. A widow . . . came to him repeatedly, saying, 'Give me justice. . . .' The judge ignored her for a while, but finally he said . . . , 'I'm going to see that she gets justice, because she is wearing me out with her constant requests!'" LUKE 18:1-5

We don't know the end of this story, how the dispute between the persistent woman and her enemy was settled. We don't know exactly how prayer works either. But the imagery of the story illustrates the point that Jesus wanted to make to His disciples—that persistence gets results.

Jesus applauded the persistent widow who refused to give up and returned day after day with her request.

The same applies to us and our petitions to God. We are told in 1 Thessalonians 5:17 to "never stop praying." For what? For our family, for our friends? For whatever we want? To whom? Our Friend. Will God actually consider granting any and all of our prayer requests? Is the deciding factor for God how persistent we are? Will He consider a prayer to win a game? Will He consider a prayer for healing from an illness contracted while engaging in some activity contrary to His Word? What about a prayer for a better job? Or just a job, period? Or do our prayers have to be about obtaining justice in alignment with God's will or for others who are being abused or oppressed?

Why does the apostle Paul talk about prayer in almost every one of his pastoral letters to the believers? Could it be that this is the one activity the followers of Christ can engage in that connects them directly with the living God? The answer is an emphatic yes.

The writer of Hebrews directs us to prayer by saying, "Let us come boldly to the throne of our gracious God. There we will receive his mercy, and we will find grace to help us when we need it most" (Hebrews 4:16). Notice that he doesn't say, "Let us come boldly to the finance meeting of the church, or to hear the preacher preach," but to come boldly to the throne of our gracious God, because that's where our relationship with God grows. It's where we touch the face of God. It's where we offer our requests and God listens. It's where we find encouragement, courage, and direction for our next step. It's what we should encourage others to do—our friends, our family, those we mentor, teach, coach, and lead, as well as those who come to us for help.

It's where you hook hands with the God who reaches down with His right hand to hold you securely and to guide you, remaining your friend forever (Psalm 73:24-28).

UNCOMMON KEY > *It's where it all happens with God—in prayer on your knees with Him every moment. He is always there and always waiting. How about right now?*

November 22

The Little Things

> Then he said, "Take the arrows," and the king took them. Elisha told him, "Strike the ground." He struck it three times and stopped. The man of God was angry with him and said, "You should have struck the ground five or six times; then you would have defeated Aram and completely destroyed it. But now you will defeat it only three times." 2 KINGS 13:18-19, NIV

God may call us to do some big things in our lives, but being obedient to God in the little things He calls us to do on a day-to-day basis is critical. Too often we don't see the importance of the little things because they seem so insignificant. Or sometimes we are not sure that we can pull them off, so we end up stopping short of where we know God wants us to go.

In almost every football game there are a couple of crucial downs that determine the outcome of the game. You just don't know beforehand which ones they will be. Every play could be game changing. Doing the little things right is critical in those situations.

Third down and eight yards to go. The play call is for the wide receiver to go downfield ten yards and cut out toward the sideline to receive the pass that should already be in the air. The only problem is that the receiver is bumped by the defensive back coming off the line and can't get through, so he cuts outside at eight yards, not ten, and the ball sails over his head for an incompletion or—worse—interception. All because of a two-yard difference between what was practiced and what the receiver actually ran.

The little things we fail to do or fail to see—and the result is less than we planned. The little things we fail to do can make us come up short of where we wanted to be. How many victories in our lives are we missing because we fail to do the little things or we pull up just a couple of yards short? How many victories in our lives are just around the next corner, but we stop walking and never get to that corner?

God has an assignment for your life—it is perfect, and it is filled with purpose. Run the play to the end. Don't pull up short. Press through any obstacle that gets in your way.

UNCOMMON KEY > *God expects you to do the little things—not just the big things—in your life well. Think about what little thing you need to take care of today. Run the play all the way to the end.*

November 23

What Would You Do?

> Then a despised Samaritan came along, and when he saw the man, he felt compassion for him. Going over to him, the Samaritan soothed his wounds with olive oil and wine and bandaged them. Then he put the man on his own donkey and took him to an inn, where he took care of him. LUKE 10:33-34

I've watched with interest a television show called *What Would You Do?* The premise of the show each week is to create a scenario that puts people in an uncomfortable position and film their responses to what unfolds in front of them. For example, one such staged scene took place in a restaurant. A child was begging his "parent" not to drink any more alcohol that day, but when the parent kept drinking, the child begged the adult not to drive him to his soccer game in that condition because people at the game would see them.

Another scenario focused on a man in a park yelling at his "wife." The responses of passersby were all across the board—from ignoring the confrontation completely, to slowing down and watching, to saying something to the man, to actually coming over and intervening in the situation. The scenarios are filmed two ways, alternating between a man and a woman playing the role of the "bad person," to see if it changes the reactions of the passersby. In any event, the scenarios are at best awkward situations, and at worst, incredibly stressful ones. Before anyone is allowed to physically intervene, the television crew stops the action.

The television show reminds me of the story of the Good Samaritan. The Samaritan had to have experienced some degree of stress when he realized the gravity of the situation. Were the thugs who beat up the man still hiding somewhere? It's so much easier to not get involved. And yet there he was—in broad daylight, a hated Samaritan, stopping to help someone else. He could have passed by—people may have understood, if they even knew. But his conscience wouldn't let him.

What would you do?

UNCOMMON KEY > *Whether it's with a stranger or someone you know, if a person needs help and you can provide it, get involved. Don't detour the situation. God calls you to get involved in the lives of others by loving others as He loves you.*

November 24

Taking an Interest

> Remember your leaders who taught you the word of God. Think of all the good that has come from their lives, and follow the example of their faith. Jesus Christ is the same yesterday, today, and forever. HEBREWS 13:7-8

When I was in my early teenage years, I was blessed to have a couple of people, other than my family members, take an interest in me. One was a junior high assistant principal, Mr. Rockquemore, and another was an older high school student, Allen Truman. Mr. Rockquemore would hang out with some of my friends and me in the cafeteria during lunch and take us to area high school basketball games. I was blessed to have Mr. Rockquemore in my life, especially when I had difficult decisions to make in high school.

Even more surprising, in some ways, was Allen's role. I'd like to say that when I was eighteen, I was looking for thirteen-year-olds to befriend, but I was not. Allen, however, was a fairly constant figure in my life as I was beginning to mature. For whatever reason, he decided to be a role model for me. He not only coached me, but also played basketball and other sports with me as well as taking me to pro and college team games in the area. In his mind, he was just being a friend, but for me he was modeling what an older guy should be.

I was fortunate to have great parents who were very involved in my life, but I was just as blessed that people like Mr. Rockquemore and Allen took an interest in me, modeling for me positive aspects of adult life, aspects I wanted to emulate.

Many of us are reluctant to see ourselves as role models because we are very aware of our own mistakes and shortcomings. But those things don't disqualify us. My role models certainly weren't perfect, but they showed me how to live life in spite of imperfections. They made themselves available, even with their mistakes in plain view, and I watched them and learned. We can do the same for others.

Sometimes our society seems to have a vacuum of positive role models, but it doesn't need to be that way. We should be intentional about modeling for others how to live authentic, meaningful lives. Our kids certainly need that—and some of us adults do too.

UNCOMMON KEY > *Role models come in all shapes and sizes—including yours. Don't wait until you think you've got it all together. Step in and be a good one.*

November 25

Getting in Jesus' Way

> Jesus replied, "You hypocrites! Isaiah was right when he prophesied about you, for he wrote, 'These people honor me with their lips, but their hearts are far from me. Their worship is a farce, for they teach man-made ideas as commands from God.' For you ignore God's law and substitute your own tradition." MARK 7:6-8

I heard someone say the other day, "That's not how I use my religion." I don't have any idea what the person meant by that, but I do see that too often our "religion" seems to be getting in the way of really hearing from God—of a real relationship with the living God and a life of words and deeds that demonstrate that we are truly following His Word.

Religion. When Christ proclaimed His message and performed His ministry on earth, He lived in the midst of a complex religious society, not unlike today. The leaders of Jesus' day were split into four primary groups: the Pharisees, the Sadducees, the Essenes, and the Zealots.

> The Pharisees believed that right religion consisted in strict adherence to divine laws, rituals, and traditions.
> The Sadducees focused on the present, relativists who discounted most things supernatural and modified Scripture and tradition to fit their own religious philosophy.
> The Essenes believed that right religion meant separation from the rest of society, piety for the sake of piety, and an austere lifestyle.
> The Zealots were fanatical nationalists who thought that right religion centered in radical political activism.

You will not find any mention of denominations in the New Testament. No mention of Baptists, Methodists (United or Free), Presbyterians (PCA or mainline), Episcopalians, or Catholics. These denominations arose throughout history as believers grouped together around common interests and beliefs, ways of expressing worship, in defense of scriptural truths that had been lost, and other things to which they believed the Lord called them. But to be considered a Christian denomination, their underlying foundational focus must be born out of a relationship with Jesus Christ.

The central focus of Christ's message to every person then and to every person today is that the way of His Kingdom is first, foremost, and above all else a matter of the heart—a right attitude toward God and other people.

Our faith must be shown to be relevant in the world—flowing from the inside out and reflecting a personal relationship with Jesus Christ—to have any lasting and life-changing power in the world around us.

UNCOMMON KEY > *Don't let your "religion" get in the way of your faith. Consider meeting with Christians of different denominations for Bible study and prayer. Unite in your common bond of belief in and love for Jesus Christ.*

November 26

Right over Convenient

> Daniel soon proved himself more capable than all the other administrators and high officers. Because of Daniel's great ability, the king made plans to place him over the entire empire. Then the other administrators and high officers began searching for some fault in the way Daniel was handling government affairs, but they couldn't find anything to criticize or condemn. He was faithful, always responsible, and completely trustworthy. DANIEL 6:3-4

We are constantly faced with choices. Every day brings a series of decisions between doing what's convenient and what's right. And those choices often carry longer-term consequences than we realize. The difference between "convenient" and "right" can last a lifetime.

Integrity is what you do when no one is watching. It's doing the right thing all the time, even when it works to your disadvantage. It's keeping your word "even when it hurts," as Psalm 15:4 describes. It's the internal compass that keeps you pointed in the right direction when there are plenty of other options around and many of them are pulling you away from your purpose. It isn't your reputation—that's the public perception of your integrity, and it isn't always accurate. Other people determine your reputation, but only you can determine your integrity. Integrity will keep you focused.

When you have integrity, people can count on you. A teammate with integrity can be trusted to put in the time to prepare, to learn the game plan, and to know his assignments during the game. A business partner with integrity can be counted on to deal with money honestly and with people respectfully. A marriage partner with integrity can be trusted to be faithful and to be "all in" for better and for worse, not just for better. A friend with integrity can be depended on to keep his word and to stick with you through thick and thin.

Integrity touches every area of life, not just now but in the long run. And it can sometimes seem like a rare commodity. But the choices of a person with integrity become a blessing not only to that person but to everyone he or she relates to.

UNCOMMON KEY > *Integrity is an inward characteristic with outward consequences that make a lasting difference. Approach everything you do each day with integrity.*

November 27

Essential Nourishment

> Jesus replied, "I am the bread of life. Whoever comes to me will never be hungry again. Whoever believes in me will never be thirsty." JOHN 6:35

Since I retired from coaching in 2009, I am home a lot more now. One of the things I've been able to do more often is eat breakfast with the kids. In fact, I'm often the cook while Lauren is getting them dressed. Because I don't have to rush out to work, I usually try to fix them what they ask for, even if it requires some effort. Cereal for Justin, oatmeal for Jade, eggs for Jordan. But Lauren and I don't just want to dress and feed them. We want to share with them those things that will shape the foundations for their future . . . the bread of life through Christ, the importance of character, and so on.

Everything you accumulate in this life will wear out, be destroyed, or fade into insignificance as you go through the seasons of your life. You'll not find the life God intended for you in relationships seeking immediate and personal gratification—even the youngest have learned that the grass is not always greener. You'll not find it by trying to recover what you think you lost or what you believe you were shortchanged on when you were younger.

But you will find the answer in the circle of loved ones and friends in your lives. You will find it and feel it in the warmth of the hand holding yours, the person who cares that you are there. You will find it when you sit with wise and experienced loved ones and ask questions about the important things in life, about what and where you should spend the time you have been given, and about where will you find the true value in life that should be embraced each day.

And you will find it in a relationship with the one who said and continues to say, "I am the bread of life. Whoever comes to me will never be hungry again. Whoever believes in me will never be thirsty."

Jesus Christ is your spiritual sustenance—the essential element needed for your spiritual well-being for the rest of your life.

UNCOMMON KEY > *Take a moment and "break bread" with Jesus right now, thanking Him for providing spiritual nourishment to you.*

November 28

Still in the Miracle Business

> Jesus went throughout Galilee, teaching in their synagogues, proclaiming the good news of the kingdom, and healing every disease and sickness among the people. MATTHEW 4:23, NIV

Coaches and teams often talk about "trap games," games against an inferior opponent, usually with a much better opponent immediately following that game. We tend to fall into the "trap" of looking past the next game to the one that follows. And in the process, we often lose.

The danger, of course, is complacency. We forget about what is right before us or take it for granted, and the next thing we know, we've missed an opportunity. It happens all the time in our daily lives. We go so fast through each day, looking past the blessings and opportunities of today, focusing on what we think will be great moments tomorrow.

In today's verse, we are reminded that Christ went around the countryside performing miracle after miracle. Yet after a while the people began to take Jesus and His miracles for granted, like they were nothing really special. There are so many miracles we could list from the Old and New Testament that you'd think would have astonished the witnesses when they occurred, and should astonish us when we read about them today.

Or have we become a bit complacent? Do we believe in miracles? Do we believe that God is still performing miracles in the world around us? Or do we simply believe that they are a biblical phenomenon and that life today is controlled by the laws of nature, science, and man?

Just like the probability of missing the worthy opponent in a "trap" game, the probability is slim to none that we will ever notice God's miracles in our lives if we don't believe that God is still in the "miracle business."

But He is.

And I suspect that if you're anything like me, you've missed many of them.

Let's not let that happen this week. I have word, from a reliable source, that the week unfolding before us is destined to be another record-setting week for God's miracles that will take place in our lives. Of course, they happen on His time and in His ways, not ours. As Miracle Max said in the movie *The Princess Bride*, "You rush a miracle man, you get rotten miracles."

But this isn't a fairy tale. God is still performing miracles, if only we will notice.

Anticipate them, notice them, embrace them, and cherish them. Try to count them if you dare—but I suspect you'll lose track.

But most important, thank God for them.

UNCOMMON KEY > *Watch for God's miracles in your life, starting today. Don't allow yourself to be complacent by looking past His blessings.*

November 29

Something to Be Full Of

| **Always be full of joy in the Lord. I say it again—rejoice!** PHILIPPIANS 4:4

Protests in Washington, DC. Political uprisings abroad. Kidnappings, drug wars, turf battles, drive-bys, unemployment, the countless social issues of the day.

Wow. It's discouraging just writing that list—and I've only scratched the surface.

And yet we worship a God who tells us that we are to rejoice! Not just occasionally, but *always* living "full of joy."

That's easier said than done. There are days when life makes rejoicing nearly impossible. Jesus cried with those who were mourning and suffered with those who were suffering.

Yet the apostle Paul, who underwent trials and tribulations at every turn, wrote that we should rejoice in the Lord.

There's a great picture Nathan has in his office, a sketch by Frances Hook of Jesus laughing. I imagine that Jesus was often doing this—with His disciples, at wedding receptions, or at dinner with Mary, Martha, and Lazarus. He exuded joy.

It's disappointing to sometimes hear Christians talking with a spirit of fear and worry, of concern and dread. I get it: life is hard. If it feels like the world is stacked against us, it could be true ("God blesses those who are persecuted"; Matthew 5:10). Whether or not we are "happy" on any given day is often dictated by the circumstances around us. But joy is always there on any given day for those who serve a risen Savior.

Sadly, people who don't know their eternal destiny often live with fear and uncertainty. Maybe the joy they see in you—even when times get tough—will compel them to seek God. His joy is in abundant supply.

UNCOMMON KEY > *Approaching each day with joy can be tough at times. God wants us to stay focused on Him, not on the things of this world that can drag us down. He is the source of our joy. Embrace His presence and spread His joy.*

November 30

Learning What's Most Important

> Martha was distracted by the big dinner she was preparing. She came to Jesus and said, "Lord, doesn't it seem unfair to you that my sister just sits here while I do all the work? Tell her to come and help me." But the Lord said to her, "My dear Martha, you are worried and upset over all these details! There is only one thing worth being concerned about. Mary has discovered it." LUKE 10:40-42

Clearly, Mary got it. Martha's intentions were good, very good, but she missed the most important priority right in front of her—Christ Himself.

I would imagine that Martha had heard Jesus say a number of times what is written in Matthew 6:25, 33: "I tell you not to worry about everyday life. . . . Seek the Kingdom of God above all else." Jesus wanted Martha to see the bigger picture, the things of eternal significance, rather than be caught up in worrisome details that tend to stress people out.

Coaches, as a rule, are like Martha. We're so busy and caught up in preparing for our games that we take our eyes off the bigger picture. So caught up in the minutiae of our jobs that we tend to lose focus, often making things harder than they are.

So, too, Martha let her focus on being the best hostess to Jesus take precedence over what He wanted her to focus on—putting everything aside, spending time with and learning from Him. Her sister, Mary, sitting at Jesus' feet, was hanging on every word, learning from the rabbi.

When Jesus said that Mary had discovered the most important thing—something that Martha needed to find herself—He was validating Mary's desire to be His disciple. Those would have been "fightin' words" to any men listening. Women had their place in Jesus' day, and it wasn't as a rabbi's disciple.

Maybe Martha needed to reread what Solomon wrote at the end of the book of Ecclesiastes, after concluding that life rooted solely in the things of the world is vanity. The wise king says, "Remember your Creator. . . . Fear God and obey his commands" (Ecclesiastes 12:6, 13). Solomon's answer to a meaningful, fulfilling life is God, not the perfect dinner party.

Luke's Gospel doesn't include the rest of the conversation Jesus and Martha had that day. But later Martha confesses to Jesus that she has "always believed" that He is "the Messiah, the Son of God, the one who has come into the world from God" (John 11:27).

What about you? Who are you most like, Mary or Martha? When your heart is in the right place—taking root in Him—you will have no doubt about what's most important.

UNCOMMON KEY > *Ask God where He would like you to be busy today. When you enter into and develop a relationship with Jesus Christ, allow Him to determine the areas where He wants you to be involved the most.*

December 1

A Few Life-Changing Moments

> A Samaritan woman came to draw water, and Jesus said to her, "Please give me a drink." . . . She said to Jesus, "You are a Jew, and I am a Samaritan woman. Why are you asking me for a drink?" Jesus replied, "If you only knew the gift God has for you and who you are speaking to, you would ask me, and I would give you living water." JOHN 4:7, 9-10

I saw this story from John 4 embodied in my parents. Growing up in the 1960s, I was confronted with racial stereotypes all around me. My parents, however, raised my siblings and me with the truth that God loves everyone and we were to do the same. It was a gift to learn that at a young age.

In this story from John's Gospel, God's love and compassion is focused on one person whom the world had labeled insignificant. Jesus was in Judea and was taking His ministry to Galilee. The quickest route, approximately a three-day journey, was through Samaria. But because of a centuries-old feud between the Jews and the Samaritans, Jews used an alternate route, east across the Jordan River, then north until they were past Samaria where it was safe to recross the Jordan and enter Galilee. But Jesus, rebel that He was in breaking down cultural barriers, traveled directly through Samaria.

At the town of Sychar, Jesus came to Jacob's well and sat down alone, while His disciples went into the town to buy food. A woman arrived at the well, carrying a large water jar. Her eyes were averted to avoid people's stares. They knew who she was, this woman who had been married five times and was now living with another man. She knew what it meant to love and receive nothing in return.

Jesus respectfully asked her for a drink of water, but she knew that Jews didn't talk with Samaritans, especially Samaritan women. She may have thought, *What is he really after?* Instead, she said, "You are a Jew and I am a Samaritan, how can you ask me for a drink?"

Get the picture: Jesus . . . a man . . . a Jew . . . in broad daylight . . . in a public place . . . talking to a woman . . . a Samaritan . . . with a bad reputation. This was a scenario Jesus should have walked away from, but Jesus wasn't your ordinary Jew. To the woman's surprise, He simply talked to her.

Jesus is all about breaking down barriers between people and helping you—like He eventually did with that Samaritan woman—to become all you are created to be.

UNCOMMON KEY > *What cultural barriers do you need to break down in your life? Read the entire story of the woman at the well in John 4:1-30 to see the impact that Jesus' bold conversation made.*

December 2

At a Moment's Notice

> Those who were ready went in with him to the marriage feast, and the door was locked. Later, when the other five bridesmaids returned, they stood outside, calling, "Lord! Lord! Open the door for us!" But he called back, "Believe me, I don't know you!" So you, too, must keep watch! For you do not know the day or hour of my return. MATTHEW 25:10-13

Whether it's Y2K or 2012, it seems people have been predicting the end of the world on a fairly regular basis these days. Kind of like the old joke about economists predicting ten of the last five recessions.

I don't know when it's coming—and neither do you. Neither did Jesus. As He said in Matthew 24:36, "No one knows the day or hour when these things will happen, not even the angels in heaven or the Son himself. Only the Father knows."

What I do know, however, is that God says we are to stay prepared, spiritually ready for both that moment of Christ's return and that moment when our lives on earth end. In Jesus' parable of the ten bridesmaids in Matthew 25, five of them were foolish and five of them were wise in their preparations. All ten of them knew the bridegroom was coming; they just didn't know exactly when he would arrive. The details of wedding customs in Jesus' day are not known—possibly it was the bridesmaids' duty to accompany the bridegroom to the wedding feast (as told in this parable) or else to escort the wedded couple back to their home. In either case, the young women needed to have enough oil in their lamps to light the path.

When awakened from sleep, five of the bridesmaids jumped out of bed, grabbed their lamps, and hurried out to the waiting bridegroom. The other five had to collect themselves, then scramble to find an open store where they could buy oil. Their delay cost them the celebration.

Do you know Jesus Christ as your Savior and Lord? Have you accepted the free gift He offers through what He did for each one of us on the cross? Are you trying to live according to the ideals He has set forth in His Word?

None of us are promised tomorrow. Don't put off asking Christ into your life until then. Don't be late like the five bridesmaids were.

UNCOMMON KEY > *The gift of eternal life is available to each of us as a free gift. Have you accepted it by asking Christ into your life? Don't be late!*

December 3

The Strength of Humility

| The LORD mocks the mockers but is gracious to the humble. PROVERBS 3:34

Some people wear their statuses on their sleeves. You know immediately that they are a CEO or a media mogul or a person with lots of connections. And if you can't tell by looking, they will let you know by dropping a few hints or names of people they associate with.

Other people have exactly the same status, but you wouldn't know it from the way they look or talk. They may have obvious leadership skills—that's how they got the positions they are in—but they don't have the self-promoting attitude to go with it. When you're with them, they behave as if you're the only one in the room worthy of focus. They know how to make others feel significant.

I appreciate that kind of humility. I admire those who realize that God created each person with unique gifts and abilities. That isn't the same as false modesty—claiming that who you are and what you have accomplished isn't important. False modesty is an attempt to tear yourself down. True humility focuses more on building others up. It's embracing the idea that God created each one for a particular place and time, and it's being completely comfortable viewing others with exactly the same significance. When someone can do that, it becomes much easier to let go of status or an unhealthy need for respect.

It's ironic, but the best way to earn respect is to respect others, holding them in the proper esteem. We need to demonstrate a respect for others simply because they are who they are—just people trying their best to be all they were created to be. Those who have that attitude make the best spouses, family members, teammates, friends, and business partners. Humility earns the respect that pride seeks.

UNCOMMON KEY > *God created you with great worth. He created others with great worth too. When you are humble, you are acknowledging your own worth while focusing on the worth of others. If you know someone who is quietly supporting you in some way, thank that person today.*

December 4

Bottom-Line Love

> I am convinced that nothing can ever separate us from God's love. Neither death nor life, neither angels nor demons, neither our fears for today nor our worries about tomorrow—not even the powers of hell . . . nothing in all creation will ever be able to separate us from the love of God that is revealed in Christ Jesus our Lord. ROMANS 8:38-39

I saw a photograph a missionary took not too long ago of a beautiful little dark-haired, dark-eyed girl near her village in a Central American country. I heard about her brief life story up to that point—that her mother and father were gone, and she was bouncing around from relative to relative. Without a family to support, protect, and nurture her, you couldn't help but wonder what the future held for her. It seems pretty bleak.

As I looked at her picture and reflected upon millions of other children like her around the world who are alone and unloved, one thought kept penetrating my thinking: *God loves her.*

But where is a family that can show her the tangible love she needs, to demonstrate to her in a real way that nothing can separate her from the love of God?

No matter what we are going through, God loves us. No matter where we are or what is happening to us or around us, God's love is always there for us.

That's an amazing, comforting, and absolute truth.

But what about that little girl? Does she know it? What can we do to show her—and others like her—that love, day after day? There are those in ministry trying to demonstrate that love by providing food, clothing, and shelter, along with God's love and His Word to children like that little girl in Central America. Missionaries trying to be family to others such as her.

To show them what we know, that during those times when we feel unworthy or aren't even seeking the Lord, He is there. Loving us. During those times of ultimate tragedy, heartache, disappointment, or despair, He is there, loving us, holding us. During those times when we are lost and have no idea what the next hour, let alone the next day, will bring—He is there, loving us, holding us, carrying us.

I've been there, and so have you. And when you are in your better moments looking back, you can see that He was there. He is not a "here today and gone tomorrow" God.

Thankfully, nothing can separate us from the love of God! Believe it—we are members of His family forever. Help others like that little girl to believe it too.

UNCOMMON KEY > *Everyone has been there—not knowing which way to turn or whom to turn to. Right now, take a moment to thank God that He is there in your certain times as well as the uncertain ones—loving you, holding you, and carrying you.*

December 5

Knowing What You Know

| Spouting off before listening to the facts is both shameful and foolish.   PROVERBS 18:13

I don't know everything. I wish I did, but I can't even get away with pretending to know everything. Too many people have made it painfully clear that I don't. But over the years, I have become more and more comfortable admitting that and listening to others.

Some people pretend to know more than they do. Nathan was told in law school, "If after three weeks of class you don't know who the class jerk is, it's you." Hopefully he wasn't that person—the one who thinks he has all the answers and can't be vulnerable enough to admit needing the counsel of others. That attitude may come from a huge ego, but it's more often a defense mechanism masking insecurity and fear of being exposed as ignorant. When we feel like we have to know everything about everything—or at least make other people think we do—we've got some self-esteem issues.

I've found that "I don't know" is almost always a good answer. It's actually a sign of strength, not of weakness. We have to be secure to say that. When we can, it becomes a great opportunity to learn. When we find people who know more than us about a certain topic—and they are everywhere—it's a great idea to take them to lunch, ask questions, and let them do the talking. My dad always did that, and most people described him as being quiet. But he was quiet because he was always listening. He felt that people had a lot to offer from their own experiences, and he was secure enough to learn from them.

This is the flip side of mentoring. A mentor reaches out to help someone along the path of life. That's important, and everyone should have someone to mentor in his or her life. But when we seek counsel, we're looking for someone who is a little further along on the path of life—or at least on the path of a certain area of knowledge and wisdom. We need to put all pride and ego aside and be open to being mentored.

A need to be "the expert" about something rarely impresses others and can actually hinder your own growth. Always be in the process of learning. Seek the counsel of others. Listen to their experiences. Feel free to say, "I don't know—enlighten me." And let them fuel your growth.

UNCOMMON KEY > *Sometimes the wisest thing to say is "I don't know." And the wisest thing to do is to listen to those who do know. Start practicing.*

December 6

Filled with the Holy Spirit

Be careful how you live. Don't live like fools, but like those who are wise. Make the most of every opportunity in these evil days. Don't act thoughtlessly, but understand what the Lord wants you to do. Don't be drunk with wine, because that will ruin your life. Instead, be filled with the Holy Spirit. EPHESIANS 5:15-18

I wish I could forget some of the moments from the past where I was less than careful and wise with some of the decisions I made. I recall some foolish and rash choices that did not glorify God. I regret them, and at times they haunt me, but I accept that it's God's way of keeping me from doing them again.

We need to live carefully and wisely. Everything we do and say will have an immediate impact—positively or negatively—on at least one other person, possibly affecting them for the rest of their lives. We should make the most of every opportunity, many of which don't look like opportunities at all. What looks like hard work or uphill battles, God may have put in our paths to make us live up to our potential. With that in mind, I didn't want to waste any opportunity because my mind was under the influence of alcohol.

As a coach, I made it clear to my staff, coaches, and players that I didn't have a problem with them drinking alcohol in moderation, but I didn't want them to use it in excess. At times I wondered, though, why anyone would spend money on something that could potentially destroy themselves and others around them. Some players used alcohol as a crutch to get over feelings of insecurity or low self-esteem, feelings that probably went back to childhood. Other players were addicted to alcohol, whether as a result of family genetics, overuse, or abuse. Time and time again, I would see that players who drank picked friends who drank—they couldn't have a good time without it. It gave them "courage" to do some very foolish things.

What about you? Where do you stand on alcohol? Does any of the behavior I mentioned describe you or someone close to you? I don't have a problem with alcohol and its use, but I do have grave concerns about its negative impact in our lives and in the world.

UNCOMMON KEY > *Drinking is a huge part of this culture. If you drink, do it in moderation. Get help if you cannot keep it under control.*

December 7

Serving Others Is Serving Him

Then they will reply, "Lord, when did we ever see you hungry or thirsty or a stranger or naked or sick or in prison, and not help you?" And he will answer, "I tell you the truth, when you refused to help the least of these my brothers and sisters, you were refusing to help me."
MATTHEW 25:44-45

Abe Brown was one of my heroes. I got to know him when I became head coach of the Tampa Bay Buccaneers and he asked me to visit some prisons with him. By that time, he had been visiting prisoners around Florida for two decades, and was known all over Tampa not only for this work, but also for his great success as a football coach at Tampa's Blake High School. After retiring from coaching, he even went on to pastor the First Baptist Church of College Hill. He was a minister, educator, and coach who, before he died at eighty-three, had touched the lives of many the world would consider to be "the least of these."

Reverend Brown's passion was ignited when he was visiting one of his former high school players who was in prison. The young man was excited to see his former coach because he rarely had any visitors, and Reverend Brown learned that his situation was true of most of the inmates. And so Abe Brown began spending time with inmates and enlisting volunteers to do the same. Then he reached out to inmates with programs designed specifically to help them reenter society. He did all he could do to prevent inmates from going back to the environments that got them in trouble and into prison in the first place.

Abe Brown touched the untouchables of our society. He was always picking somebody up and raising them just high enough to see the sunshine at the end of the rainstorm. Reverend Brown believed that when he served another person, he was serving the living Christ.

We're all called to do the same. Maybe it's not specifically through a prison ministry or coaching or teaching, although God does always find ways to push us out of our comfort zones. Maybe it's a place where someone is in need. Maybe it's where we will find the less fortunate and be able to help them, perhaps as a witness to show them what Christ has done in our lives.

UNCOMMON KEY > *When you stand before God face-to-face, He will ask you when you helped the least of those among us. Make sure you can answer—always!*

December 8

Seeing the Possible

Jesus looked at them intently and said, "Humanly speaking, it is impossible. But with God everything is possible." MATTHEW 19:26

Football players and coaches have a platform. Maybe that seems obvious, but I'm talking about more than the platform created by their high-profile media coverage. They are also husbands, fathers, friends, teammates, members of communities and churches, and more. They all have an opportunity to make a difference in the lives of others. And they have all had experiences that prepare them to influence people for good. In other words, aside from their place in the public eye, they are a lot like everyone else.

I think it's important for everyone to be aware of the platforms they have in their lives and to understand them as God-given opportunities. In fact, that's one of the best ways to view the trials and hardships we experience. Losing a son gave me a platform I never would have sought, but that loss has given me opportunities to comfort and encourage others who are going through painful times. It's true that my job has always given me more opportunities to do that than many other people have, but the bottom line is that I'm a coach, a husband, a father, a coworker, a church member, and a guy who has experienced grief and loss. My roles are my platforms, just as your roles are your platforms.

These opportunities are given by God, and with His strength and guidance we can use them for His purposes. He will bring people into our lives who need the wisdom that comes from what we have experienced. He will guide us into situations that allow us to influence people going through difficulties or needing some particular insight into their situation. He will even express His own character and attitudes through us—His love, comfort, encouragement, forgiveness, patience, and more—if we choose to let Him. Our platforms are given by His design.

All of us have a choice whether to be takers or givers. Takers are concerned more with receiving value from others' lives than adding value to them. But giving is more rewarding and actually adds to our lives as well. Use your platforms to give to others and impact lives in a way no one else can.

UNCOMMON KEY > *The platforms we have are not for our benefit but for the benefit of others. If we're watching, we'll see God providing opportunities to use them powerfully and effectively.*

December 9

A Cure for Doubt

> When Jesus woke up, he rebuked the wind and said to the waves, "Silence! Be still!" Suddenly the wind stopped, and there was a great calm. Then he asked them, "Why are you afraid? Do you still have no faith?" The disciples were absolutely terrified. "Who is this man?" they asked each other. "Even the wind and waves obey him!" MARK 4:39-41

Nathan's children loved the movie *The Water Horse: Legend of the Deep.* The movie is set in Scotland during World War II, and the main character, Angus MacMorrow, is trying to cope with that fact that his father, a soldier, is reported missing and presumed dead. He holds on to the hope that his dad will return soon. One day, Angus finds a large egg in the tide pools of Loch Ness and hides it in the storage shed.

An unusual but wonderful animal hatches from the egg, growing so quickly in size that it reminds viewers of the famed Loch Ness monster, but Angus's "monster" becomes a gentle and faithful companion and protector. The boy wasn't sure of what he found when he picked up the egg from the water, but what he got turned out to be beyond his comprehension.

Faith. We all claim to have faith. Faith in something. Faith in God. But if we're really honest with ourselves, the faith we tend to embrace and live by is typically focused—or limited, if you will—to a thing. Some "thing" we have faith in. For example, it could be in a person or a career. Perhaps it is in a particular church setting or a pastor. Perhaps it's in our abilities—for example, the faith athletes have in their ability to perform at the highest levels. We may state a belief that these are all gifts from God and therefore our faith is in Him and His provision. Too often, though, it is only lip service. Because when the "things" are taken away, then the true object or substance of our faith is exposed.

There have been times when I have not felt God at work in my life. Has He ever felt distant to you? There have been times when I began wondering about what shape my faith was in, and then it hit me—true faith in God still believes in God even when I don't feel, hear, or see God. You see, true faith still believes when all the "things" of life are gone.

What do you have faith in? Is it some "thing" or an amazing God?

UNCOMMON KEY > *Be honest. If your faith is in some "thing," confess and release it to God. Place your immovable faith in Him.*

December 10

Don't Cash It In

True godliness with contentment is itself great wealth. . . . But people who long to be rich fall into temptation and are trapped by many foolish and harmful desires that plunge them into ruin and destruction. For the love of money is the root of all kinds of evil. And some people, craving money, have wandered from the true faith and pierced themselves with many sorrows. 1 TIMOTHY 6:6, 9-10

When I was an assistant coach with the Pittsburgh Steelers, I received an offer to take a job with another club. I was making around $25,000 at the time, and they were going to offer me a salary in the neighborhood of $30,000. It doesn't seem like such a big amount to some people, I'm sure, but that $5,000 was a 20 percent increase over what I was making in Pittsburgh and a big difference to me at the time.

I asked Coach Noll if I could talk to him about it. I really wanted to stay in Pittsburgh, but I didn't want to pass up a chance of making more money. I was secretly hoping he would encourage me to stay by matching the offer. He did encourage me to stay, but told me he would support my decision either way.

The one piece of advice he gave me was to not make my decision based solely on money. Coach Noll urged me to consider who I would be working with, what I could learn from them, what type of environment it would be, and how much responsibility I would be given. He felt those were the important things to weigh, and if I became a good enough coach, eventually my salary would reflect that.

Through my years as a coach, and especially as a head coach, I tried to impress that on players. At times guys became eligible for free agency, and I would have to have an "it's not just about the money" talk with them. Certainly they had to weigh the differences of financial offers that they received, but as several of them learned, taking more money and moving to a different team sometimes resulted either in an unhappy, disrupted family or with their careers heading in a different direction than they enjoyed with our team. In a couple of instances, guys ended up out of the league more quickly than they would have if they had stayed with us. For them, the short-term financial gain wasn't worth the long-term results.

Does money have an unhealthy hold on you? Remember, it's not money itself that is the problem. It's the *love* of money that will spin everything out of control.

UNCOMMON KEY > *The decisions you make in your life are based on your priorities. Write down your top five priorities. Where does money rank on that list? If it is high in your priorities, make a concerted effort to lower its importance in your life.*

December 11

Leaving the Party Behind

> Elijah replied, "I have zealously served the LORD God Almighty. But the people of Israel have broken their covenant with you, torn down your altars, and killed every one of your prophets. I am the only one left, and now they are trying to kill me, too." 1 KINGS 19:10

There Elijah sat. The poor prophet felt oppressed. Things were on a definite downturn for him. He was wallowing in self-pity. We've all been there. Maybe several times, maybe recently.

No?

Weren't you walking around recently in a daze with an expression on your face revealing a definite lack of joy in your heart? Someone you love had said something to you that broke your heart. Or perhaps you were the one who felt that because of a bad break or a rotten childhood, the world owed you something. Elijah would have taken one if it had been offered. Well, you'd both be waiting for a long time for that to happen.

Or perhaps a member of your family who followed her heart has found that the grass is not as green as she expected and you are getting an earful. Tough luck or wrong choice, huh? Maybe neither. Have you or those you love considered that God may have you planted exactly where He intended for you to be, but the rain and wind are blowing so hard you can't see His bigger picture at the moment? Yet you haven't turned on the wipers or decided to pick yourself up and throw yourself back into the fray. Instead you've quit and created your own little pity party while the opportunity He has given you passes from the scene and is forever wasted.

My suggestion is that you take the advice others have given me through the years— get over it and be the person God intended for you to be. Step out of the self-centered focus that Elijah was swirling in, to one that perhaps, just perhaps, can help change the world around you.

UNCOMMON KEY > *Pity parties are never attended by many—just one. Take off the party hat and leave. God has too much for you to do.*

December 12

Anchored with Love

> I pray that your love will overflow more and more, and that you will keep on growing in knowledge and understanding . . . so that you may live pure and blameless lives until the day of Christ's return. May you always be filled with the fruit of your salvation—the righteous character produced in your life by Jesus Christ—for this will bring much glory and praise to God. PHILIPPIANS 1:9-11

Paul gets it right in these words of encouragement to the believers in Philippi. It begins with love—love for God. But as we grow as believers, as we share with other followers of Christ desiring to grow in their relationships with Him, we add knowledge, insight, understanding, and implementation through action into the mix. But love is primary.

Growth in knowledge and understanding of God's ways, His will, and His purpose for our lives will come as we grow in fellowship with Him and perhaps through our fellowship with others.

The Bible is full of stories and examples to demonstrate the incredible love of God for you and me. The most familiar verse that epitomizes that, of course, is John 3:16: "For God loved the world so much that he gave his one and only Son, so that everyone who believes in him will not perish but have eternal life."

One of my favorite examples of God's love in the Bible is this scene toward the end of the Prodigal Son story: "But while he was still a long way off, his father saw him and was filled with compassion for him; he ran to his son, threw his arms around him and kissed him" (Luke 15:20, NIV). The story isn't just about a wayward first-century son returning home. It illustrates the love of God for all His children. God runs to us to embrace us when we turn back to Him, no matter where we have gone to get away from Him, what we have done, or how much we have disappointed and hurt Him. God's love and forgiveness looks past our mistakes and shortcomings.

Living in this world isn't easy, with all of its snares, traps, temptations, and pitfalls. God knows that. Living the kind of life Christ calls us to live—pure and blameless and marked by love—is even more difficult. However, with God's love for us and our love for Him and for others guiding our steps, we have an anchor for our lives.

UNCOMMON KEY > *God never gets tired of hearing us say, "I love You, Father." Run to Him often today and say it.*

December 13

Riding above the Storm

| Be still, and know that I am God! PSALM 46:10

"Conditions are beginning to deteriorate."

It's a warning you often hear on the radio or television as a storm begins to roll in or a hurricane gets closer to landfall.

In those moments, when we find ourselves powerless to do anything to stop the storm or fix the condition—when we have absolutely no control—the psalmist suggests that we stop, take a deep breath, and turn our eyes toward the God who is above everything. In the midst of chaos, "Be still." Really.

When we have an eternal perspective—which our relationship with Christ assures us—He is forming the picture we will eventually see. It's the big picture of our lives in the scheme of eternity, written during the storms we face now.

We've all been in the eye of a storm, and I know many of you are there now. But conditions deteriorate, and then we're blindsided. One moment our dad is eating lunch before boarding a plane to come home, the next minute he suffers a massive heart attack. One moment you've received a great review, the next moment you get a dismissal notice. Another moment the phone rings and you hear the words, "There's been an accident." Someone you can't live without isn't going to make it. One moment all is calm and under control, and in a matter of minutes everything breaks loose.

"Conditions are beginning to deteriorate."

Yet through it all, God remains a safe place to hide, ready to help when we need Him. That's the big picture. When conditions begin to deteriorate and everything seems to be spinning out of control, God offers the eternal, everlasting calm that quiets our hearts and buoys up our spirits.

He is always there, calm and in control, when we're not and can't be. And in the big picture of eternity, conditions are fine. Actually, conditions are glorious and heavenly.

UNCOMMON KEY > *In the midst of whatever conditions you find yourself in, take shelter in God. Quiet your heart before Him, and He will show you how mighty He truly is.*

December 14

JB's Eyes

> Let us continue to love one another, for love comes from God. Anyone who loves is a child of God and knows God. But anyone who does not love does not know God, for God is love. . . . If we love each other, God lives in us, and his love is brought to full expression in us.
>
> 1 JOHN 4:7-8, 12

You know who they are, the ones who embody the ideal John wrote about in today's verses. They are the people who leave the house for a five-minute walk in the neighborhood but don't get back for a half hour. They're the ones who say they have to run out for a loaf of bread and a gallon of milk at the grocery store and disappear for an hour. What happened to them between point A and point B? They stopped along their route or in the midst of their errands to talk and listen, advise and encourage, laugh and cry. You'll often find them at the center of a group or with a long line of people waiting to speak with them.

James Brown is one of my friends who is like that. The three-time Emmy winner and current host of *The NFL Today* on CBS Sports and Showtime's *Inside the NFL*, JB believes that every person is a valuable and special child of God. And JB acts like he believes it. He has one of the busiest schedules of anyone I know, yet he goes out of his way to be available to everyone who wants to talk with him or meet him. JB stops whatever he is doing or delays wherever he is going to listen to folks and spend time with them.

One time when Nathan was with JB at a Washington Nationals game, he saw this in action. He watched as JB took just as much time, if not more, to listen to the elevator operator as he did to visit with the chief justice of the United States Supreme Court—who appeared to be a great guy as well as a baseball fan. In God's eyes—and JB's—both of them are very important.

Who needs you to make them feel special today?

UNCOMMON KEY > *Spend time with the people God brings into your life today. The circumstances that have brought you together have been orchestrated by Him. He may want you to pass along the needed reminder of how important they are to God.*

December 15

Thankful

> Not that I was ever in need, for I have learned how to be content with whatever I have. I know how to live on almost nothing or with everything. I have learned the secret of living in every situation, whether it is with a full stomach or empty, with plenty or little.
>
> PHILIPPIANS 4:11-12

Being content is not easy in the world of professional football. It seems like every year everyone expects more and more. If a team has a winning season, they want to win more games the next year. When they feel they are getting better, they want to make the playoffs. If they make the playoffs, they want to reach the Super Bowl the following season. If they reach the Super Bowl, they want to go home with the Lombardi Trophy. If they reach the Super Bowl and win, well, they want back-to-back victories.

The same is true with our personal lives. If our spouses, children, houses, or bank accounts don't fulfill all the dreams we'd hoped for, we feel empty, maybe even cheated, because society says that's the way it works. We think that acquiring more and always replacing what we have with something bigger and better is the only way to find contentment. Don't believe it.

Contentment is possible when you start with a grateful heart. Not a token sense of gratitude, but the realization that the Lord has blessed you with everything you need.

Notice the difference? The first approach says that something is missing in our lives and we need to get it. Maybe we don't have a Super Bowl ring or a fat bank account. It's tough to be content when all we can think of is what we imagine everyone else has and we don't.

But the apostle Paul takes a different approach, expressing gratitude instead of complaining about personal deprivation. It's an acquired attitude. But when we approach everything in our lives with an attitude of gratitude, it comes more naturally.

That's where you and I will find contentment. Crazy, huh? Not at all.

Just as important, contentment is contagious. Think about those people that you surround yourself with and ask yourself, *Are they always seeking more? Are they rubbing off on me?*

Surround yourself with people who understand what it means to be content—and become one of those people for the good of those you influence.

UNCOMMON KEY > *The moment you size up what everyone else owns or has accomplished, often it's only a short leap to feeling that you've been shortchanged. A contented life is achieved when you focus on what God has given you and thank Him for those blessings.*

December 16

More than the World Offers

> And what do you benefit if you gain the whole world but lose your own soul? Is anything worth more than your soul? MATTHEW 16:26

As we got closer to winning the Super Bowl each year that I was the head coach of the Indianapolis Colts, I grew more concerned about this question framed in Matthew's Gospel. What if we reached the pinnacle of success in the world of sports and the result was unfulfilling, as it was guaranteed to be—as I knew it would be?

I kept thinking over and over about the questions we all struggle with. What is really important in life? Do we chase the world's fortunes and accolades at the expense of our own spiritual welfare? Too often the answer to the second question is yes, and that response takes care of the answer to the first question. We can't really deny it, but we can work to change that way of life before it's too late.

I tried to do that in my own life as we continued toward that pinnacle by spending more quiet time with God, reading Scripture and other devotional materials more, and spending more time in prayer and seeking advice, encouragement, and prayer from others I had come to trust through the years.

As a team, we took time to talk a bit more about spiritual things. We made sure to have chapel speakers who would challenge and focus our minds on the important and eternal rather than the urgent and temporal. We talked about doing things for others, spending time with our families, and looking for opportunities to be role models to others in the community—whether to kids or adults.

I felt it important that we realized that the pinnacle for our team was not winning the Super Bowl, if that happened (which it did), but realizing the platform it gave us to do good for others and in the process to glorify God.

UNCOMMON KEY > *Who you are is not defined by worldly "stuff" but by your heart for God.*

December 17

Honorable Choices

> You have proudly defied the Lord of heaven . . . praising gods . . . that neither see nor hear nor know anything at all. But you have not honored the God who gives you the breath of life and controls your destiny! DANIEL 5:23

King Belshazzar summoned Daniel, promising him royal robes and a position of great authority if he could interpret the strange sign. The king had been entertaining guests at an extravagant banquet when a handwritten message appeared on the wall. Daniel could have told the king what he wanted to hear, but he didn't. He had the nerve to stand before this man who defined his worth by his power and wealth—as so many do today—and accuse him of not honoring God. He declared that God would give the kingdom to another power and take the life of the king. And that very night, it happened just as Daniel said.

Our world glamorizes luxury. Many people who live in luxury communities define their worth by the best that money can buy: houses, cars, clothes, exclusive memberships, and more. These things become the definition of success and the basis of self-esteem. And we can spend a lot of time pursuing them. Young girls feel as if they need to live up to the ideals they see on TV, and young boys believe that conquest—of goals or people—is what makes a man. But it's never enough. The result is that we're always running but never arriving.

But that isn't reality, at least not as God defines it. He wants us to base our lives on Him, not on things that don't last. We're supposed to focus on honoring Him rather than on getting more, doing more, or achieving more. When we get to the end of our lives and look at what we have left—and what we have built into our children—we'll find that keeping up with appearances leaves us empty, but serving the Lord is fulfilling. Values that are shaped by a desire to honor Him will always lead us to true success in His eyes.

UNCOMMON KEY > *God deserves to be honored. You can honor Him with your words, how you treat other people, how you spend your time and money. Live for the values that reflect Him.*

December 18

Countless Ways to Honor

> Husbands, this means love your wives, just as Christ loved the church. He gave up his life for her. EPHESIANS 5:25

I was once asked at a press conference what I had done on Friday afternoon to prepare for the upcoming game. It was during the playoffs, but I had learned from Chuck Noll years before that you don't change your schedule just because it's a playoff game. So I had spent Friday afternoon the way our entire staff had done all season. We took the afternoon off as personal time. Lauren had been out of town, and I wanted her to come home to a clean house. So I went home and cleaned the house.

The reporter thought I was joking when I said I cleaned the house. It's not what you expect an NFL coach to do on a Friday during the playoffs. But I was serious. This was something I could do to help her out, and at the time it made more sense than taking her out or buying her some jewelry. I wanted to do something that would actually benefit her well-being.

I still try to find ways to make our home a sanctuary for Lauren. I learned that from my dad, who frequently took us kids out to a park in order to give mom some space and time to herself. And she did the same for him. They took care of each other's needs.

Honoring your spouse is important, and I think it's rarer to find a husband who does it well for his wife than the other way around—although neither seems particularly common. The person God has brought into your life to live with you "till death do you part" is worthy of honor. Honor can be conveyed in large ways but also in the little things—holding a door open, running an errand, or paying a compliment. When you nurture each other like that, you are improving the health of your family, strengthening your marriage, and fulfilling God's purpose for your most important relationship next to your relationship with Him.

UNCOMMON KEY > *Relationships are about love, and love is about sacrificially serving another. Focus on honoring your spouse by taking care of his or her needs.*

December 19

The Fellowship of Believers

> All the believers devoted themselves to the apostles' teaching, and to fellowship, and to sharing in meals (including the Lord's Supper), and to prayer. ACTS 2:42

I wish I could say that since I made the decision to accept Christ as my Savior and follow Him and His teaching for my life, my growth in Him has been a picture of a consistently ascending climb toward Him. It hasn't. The more accurate depiction of my journey is described by my friend, a math major in college, as a sine wave—up and down in its flow, but very irregular in the consistency of time spent between the points.

I know better; we all do. The early Christians devoted themselves to teaching, fellowship, sharing time and meals, and prayer. They were friends who listened, encouraged, and learned from each other. They realized they needed each other to create and maintain a meaningful and consistent pattern of growth in the Christian faith.

In the past few years, I have begun to do much better with that. The most important component for me has been the local church. We lived in five different cities during my NFL career, and my family was always able to find a solid Bible-teaching church in which to worship. Because of my job, however, I was not always able to get to church on Sundays, so finding other ways to study the Bible and grow spiritually became important to me.

I have a group of men—friends, fellow brothers, and believers in Christ—whom I trust and with whom I share on a regular basis. Since we are scattered across the country and can't always get together face-to-face, we have committed to spend time each week via a phone conference, sharing, encouraging, and praying for each other.

I also spend time with my dear friend James Brown when I am in New York for those weekly football broadcasts. JB has brought together a group of employees from the hotel where we stay to study, pray, and share together. It is extremely uplifting and encouraging for me.

And then I try to consistently spend quiet time on my own with the Lord each day—usually in the morning before the day begins to fold in around me.

What about you? Will you commit, along with me, to spend more time with Him each day, to grow more in your relationship with Him? Deal?

UNCOMMON KEY > *It is important to find a gospel-preaching church when you accept Christ as your Lord and Savior. In addition to worshiping with that church body, try to meet with a smaller group of people on a regular basis to study God's Word and pray together. The bonds that you make will strengthen you for Kingdom work.*

December 20

Inner Reflection

> Don't think you are better than you really are. Be honest in your evaluation of yourselves, measuring yourselves by the faith God has given us. ROMANS 12:3

The bathroom mirror.

Reflective glass that's there to help me see that my hair is combed, my tie is straight, my collar is adjusted, and to view the final look making sure that everything is the way it should be.

But as I have grown older and I hope a bit wiser, I have come to realize a mirror's usefulness isn't relegated to showing me whether or not I'm put together on the outside well enough to meet the world. Each morning as I peer into the mirror, I am able to meet myself anew. I am invited to take a long, honest, and introspective look at myself, face-to-face with who I am. To look within and honestly evaluate where I am in the journey toward becoming all that God created me to be.

I learned this as a young man in Pittsburgh, when I played for the Steelers. The veteran players viewed themselves as uniquely gifted. Not in an arrogant manner, but rather recognizing that they were special, but other players were too.

Too often our method of being humble is to drag ourselves down. This can't be the right method—God says that we are uniquely made. Rather, we should be elevating ourselves and others.

From time to time, I need that deep look within to put things back into perspective, especially when the world wants to lift me up for accomplishments on the football field or drag me down for not accomplishing them. To bring myself back to a perspective of all that I am in Christ—not according to the world. I need it to remind myself that the world doesn't define me. I am defined by my relationship with Jesus Christ.

I recommend it for you, too. An honest evaluation in front of a mirror will keep you from thinking too highly of yourself but will also remind you not to be too harsh and think too little of yourself. After all, you and I were created unique and in particular for such a time as this.

UNCOMMON KEY > *Every morning, when you stand in front of a mirror, don't just look at the reflected face. Look within. A regular and honest self-examination has the potential of getting and keeping you on track to become all He created you to be.*

December 21

Going against the Status Quo

To acquire wisdom is to love oneself; people who cherish understanding will prosper.
PROVERBS 19:8

Popular culture sends us a lot of messages about value and worth. In magazines, music, television shows, movies, sports, and any other form of entertainment, we are continually told that the respect we receive depends on the status we have—and that status is defined by wealth, style, or popular opinion. We not only begin to evaluate ourselves that way, we evaluate others that way too. If they don't work a certain kind of job, earn a certain level of income, dress a certain way, or have a lifestyle we envy, they probably aren't successful. And if they aren't successful, they aren't significant or worthy of our attention.

Real significance isn't defined by popular culture. In fact, culture often magnifies less significant things and minimizes truly significant things. If we listen to trends and opinions, we will be driven to seek significance in jobs that provide the status we want, income that provides the possessions we want, and relationships that provide the security and influence we want. And we can spend our entire lives going down that path, trying to find true significance in things that can never give it to us. We will always be running but never arriving.

The Bible tells us what true significance is, and it isn't found in what we have, in the status we attain, or even in what we accomplish. It's found in knowing God, living faithfully for Him, loving Him and others, and doing whatever He has called us to do—even if it doesn't impress anyone else. It's about our identity in Him, not our achievements and possessions. We have worth not because of what we do and have but because we are His children and He chooses to love us. Our worth doesn't depend on us; it's based on how He values us. And He values us simply because He made us and we belong to Him.

Learn to see yourself as being valuable for who you are, and learn to see others that way too. Until you see people the way God sees them—uniquely created with special gifts and abilities that the world may not recognize—you will sell them short. You need to have His eyes, recognize true worth, and stop striving after unworthy goals.

UNCOMMON KEY > *Your mission is shaped by your values, and if your values are misplaced, you'll miss your true mission. Understand that status is fleeting and artificial; pursue what's truly worthwhile.*

December 22

The Gift That Keeps on Giving

| Give freely and become more wealthy; be stingy and lose everything. PROVERBS 11:24

Over the years, I have enjoyed being involved with Basket of Hope, a group that gives baskets full of games, books, and fun diversions to seriously ill children in the hospital. Not only is it a gift to them, but seeing their reaction is a gift to me, and a positive example for my children.

Someone who believed in giving himself to others was Francis of Assisi. Francis was born in 1182 into a wealthy family in Italy. But in early manhood, Francis left his family and a life of luxury and committed himself to full-time ministry. He lived a simple, relatively short life of forty-four years.

Yet what he accomplished continues to have a strong impact to this day—most notably establishing the Franciscan Order, whose members maintain a vow of poverty. A man of prayer, Francis is especially known for one with these poetic lines:

Lord, make me an instrument of your peace,
Where there is hatred, let me sow love. . . .
For it is in giving that we receive;
it is in pardoning that we are pardoned;
and it is in dying that we are born to eternal life.

No matter if we are young or grown, we could all use a refresher course from St. Francis on this lesson: "It is in giving that we receive."

How many times have you said something along those lines at Christmastime to your children? My children don't have any trouble coming up with a Christmas list every year for themselves. Even when we talk about other children who are in dire circumstances and won't have a Christmas, their reaction might be, "You can get something for them, too."

Then something happens. Something happens that finally makes St. Francis's words ring true for people. It may be that first smile from a child who is handed a stuffed animal bought with allowance money. It may be that video showing a close-up of children's faces in a faraway place as they struggle to find enough food for the day.

Something happens, and people understand that giving is all about blessings. That focusing on giving instead of getting adds a gift to their list—the blessing of lifting up someone else's life.

UNCOMMON KEY > *You don't need to give everything away, but it's important for you to be generous to people in need. The blessing you will receive from them lasts forever.*

December 23

A Life Well Spent

> "Everything is meaningless," says the Teacher, "completely meaningless!" . . . I observed
> everything going on under the sun, and really, it is all meaningless—like chasing the wind. . . .
> So what do people get in this life for all their hard work and anxiety?
>
> ECCLESIASTES 1:2, 14; 2:22

Solomon wrote the words of these verses toward the end of his life, when he realized how futile it is to seek worldly things. He called it "chasing the wind." This king who had been given wisdom and wealth beyond compare had spent much of his life chasing pleasure and power, and none of it ever really satisfied him. It all proved to be empty. His priorities were out of order.

Tom Landry said that football was his god before he began to follow Jesus Christ. It was his top priority, and his wife and family were a little further down the list. Becoming a Christian redefined what was important to him. After beginning his personal relationship with Christ, his family became his next highest priority. He remained an excellent football coach, but that wasn't his main focus. Faith and family ranked higher.

That's a much more fulfilling way to live. Relationships are always more meaningful than activities. The most important relationship we can have is with God, and next is with the people we love and spend most of our lives with—our families. Nothing is tougher than looking at the past and realizing the ways it has been misspent, but if we don't invest in our relationships, that's exactly what we will do one day. Like Solomon, we'll realize we spent a lot of time chasing the wind and neglecting what would have mattered more.

We'll always have pressures that pull at us, responsibilities we can't shirk. At the same time, we need to carve out time for our families—without fail.

Examine your priorities often. Order your life according to what really matters. If you've spent much of your life on meaningless things, realize it's never too late to change your direction. Always bring your priorities back to their proper focus.

UNCOMMON KEY > *Never exchange what is eternal for what is temporary. Make sure your priorities reflect what is truly valuable.*

December 24

Uniquely Gifted People

> In his grace, God has given us different gifts for doing certain things well. . . . If your gift is serving others, serve them well. If you are a teacher, teach well. If your gift is to encourage others, be encouraging. If it is giving, give generously. If God has given you leadership ability, take the responsibility seriously. And if you have a gift for showing kindness to others, do it gladly. ROMANS 12:6-8

Stewardship is one of those things that we have an easy time agreeing with but a hard time practicing. An understanding of stewardship involves recognizing that life isn't about us but about God and that everything belongs to Him. When we feel like we're in control of what we spend, save, and give, His ownership of everything sounds great. But when the market drops, prices go up, unemployment rises, or unexpected expenses hit home, our attitude often changes. We get more protective of "our" money. Where that money goes can be a very accurate indication of what we believe.

But stewardship is about much more than just money. A lot of people think that if they don't have money to give, they don't have anything to offer the Lord. But that isn't true at all. We are also called to be stewards of our time and our talents and our abilities. God has given us different gifts because He wants us to use them. He has given us twenty-four hours in a day expecting us to spend them wisely. What do we do with our time, talents, and treasures? When we consider our whole lives an investment, we can find joy and fulfillment in almost anything we do.

Don't assume you have little to offer to God and others. In an attempt to be humble, many people are reluctant to believe they have any special gifts. But Scripture makes it clear that each person has gifts from God to be used for the benefit of His people. It's up to you to make the best use of those gifts that God has given you.

UNCOMMON KEY > *Stewardship includes your time, treasure, and talents. What gift can you offer to God and to others today?*

December 25

The Imitation of Christ

> Those who belong to Christ Jesus have nailed the passions and desires of their sinful nature to his cross and crucified them there. Since we are living by the Spirit, let us follow the Spirit's leading in every part of our lives. Let us not become conceited, or provoke one another, or be jealous of one another. GALATIANS 5:24-26

Whenever something goes wrong, either on the football field or at home, the first words that come out of my mouth are usually, "You've *got* to be kidding me!" So I shouldn't have been surprised when I heard the same words come out of the mouth of one of my sons recently when another son broke his toy. He sounded just like me. He even put the right emphasis on *got*.

Children are imitators. They learn by watching the people around them, especially the authority figures closest to them. What we say as parents may be important, but it's not nearly as important as what we do. When our actions are inconsistent with our words—and kids will notice because they are uncannily perceptive—kids will almost always ignore our words and follow our actions.

True obedience is not just a matter of words but of action and follow-through. That's not only true of obeying God; it's a fact in every area of life, especially our leadership. And it's never more true in our leadership than in our relationships with our kids. Words are powerful, but actions are much more so.

There's no doubt about it: our children are watching. If you tell your son it's important to treat women well but are consistently rude to your wife, guess which message will sink in? But if you teach your kids about the importance of honesty and then show how that plays out in your life—by letting the cashier know she gave you too much change, for example—your words and actions line up to send an even more powerful message. Your values, your motives, and your ethics will be passed on to your kids not through your words, but through your actions. Demonstrate who you want them to be, and that's who they will most likely become.

UNCOMMON KEY > *Actions speak louder than words. The most effective lessons you teach are the ones you live before others, especially your children.*

December 26

True Prosperity

> Hasn't God chosen the poor in this world to be rich in faith? Aren't they the ones who will inherit the Kingdom he promised to those who love him? JAMES 2:5

You or someone you know may have heard it preached—a version of what seems like the prosperity gospel—that God provides material blessings to those He favors. I've even heard an occasional suggestion that maybe the poor are just not praying hard enough or their faith in God is not sure and strong enough.

Growing up, I watched my grandparents, who were tremendous people of faith, minister in small churches for many years. While they weren't poor, they certainly were never wealthy. When I got to the NFL, I sometimes felt guilty about the money I made playing (and later coaching) a *game*. I don't know anyone who did more work for God's Kingdom than my grandfather. Why didn't he make the money I made working in the NFL?

Some people of seemingly solid faith are remarkably wealthy, while others who seem to be the saints of God's Kingdom are destitute.

Is it a function of the quality and depth of their faith?

I would say no. I believe it is a reminder that God doesn't always bless us materially in proportion to our faith or our work for Him. We can't question God's sovereignty; we just have to appreciate that He doesn't measure wealth the same way we do. Faith in God is not about stuff. Christ's earthly life should tip us off. No castle, chariot, silk garments, or golden crowns. Just a robe and some sandals.

Stuff—that's a society thing. It's a measure of most everything in secular society—success, intelligence, image, power, and position.

On the other hand, faith is about a relationship with God. It's about a relationship with Christ and thankfulness for what He did for us on the cross. Faith is about relying on the "Helper," the Holy Spirit, to guide and direct us every day. Faith transcends "stuff" and opens doors to being used by God for His Kingdom purposes.

UNCOMMON KEY > *If you or a person you are close to is expecting God to prosper you because of your faith, think again. Stop dreaming about stuff and start valuing your relationship with God through Jesus Christ.*

December 27

Be Mindful of the Power You Have

> For to me, living means living for Christ, and dying is even better. But if I live, I can do more fruitful work for Christ. So I really don't know which is better. I'm torn between two desires: I long to go and be with Christ, which would be far better for me. But for your sakes, it is better that I continue to live. PHILIPPIANS 1:21-24

William James could have been a football coach because coaches always talk about visualizing success. The great American novelist once wrote, "Be not afraid of life. Believe that life is worth living, and your belief will help create the fact." He understood that human beings can accomplish almost anything if their minds tell them it can be done.

That truth certainly applies to sports teams—the difference between losers and winners is often determined between the ears—but it also applies to any human endeavor. I've even heard of prisoners of war who were able to play golf or invent something new, skills they didn't have before their imprisonment. Isolated in captivity, their minds visualized everything it would take to accomplish new things, and then they were able to do them. Clearly, our minds are powerful parts of us. It was the same with our team. Players who weren't able to practice all week but could watch and visualize themselves doing it, often went out and had a great game on Sunday.

The apostle Paul had two visions of his future. In one, he would live on in his painful body, probably in prison, and teach more people about the Kingdom of God. In the other, he would die and be with Christ. Spiritually, Paul was in a good place: he was able to accept either vision for his life and be content with it. Because God was in charge of his circumstances, Paul could focus his mind on the task at hand—helping people know Christ. And because he knew he would be with Christ for eternity, he could endure his present trials.

What circumstances do you need to endure? What visions has God put in your heart? What's going on in your life that causes you to think, "I just don't know if I can do it"? Whatever it is—whether it's a mission to accomplish, a goal to achieve, or a problem to overcome—if God has called you to do it, you can have complete confidence that it can be done. Let that sink in. Picture how it will work out. Focus your mind on the truth of the vision. Your mind is a powerful part of you—especially when it is filled with faith.

UNCOMMON KEY > *Your mind is an instrument of vision. You can endure and accomplish anything if you envision God's purposes for you and your ultimate destiny with Him in eternity.*

December 28

A Bright Reflection

> You are the light of the world—like a city on a hilltop that cannot be hidden. No one lights a lamp and then puts it under a basket. Instead, a lamp is placed on a stand, where it gives light to everyone in the house. In the same way, let your good deeds shine out for all to see, so that everyone will praise your heavenly Father. MATTHEW 5:14-16

Over the last few nights we've had a waxing moon that culminated in a full moon. A waxing moon is a moon growing from right to left, from a new moon, to a sliver of a moon, to a full and radiant moon. Of course, the moon—bright as it may be—doesn't generate its own light but rather reflects the sun's light.

In John 8:12, Jesus says He is the light of the world. These verses from Matthew are found in what is referred to as the Sermon on the Mount (chapters 5 through 7). Whether Jesus was teaching crowds gathered at one time on a mountainside or the sermon is a compilation of teachings during His entire ministry, Jesus emphasized that "you are the light of the world."

We had many of those conversations in the locker room with our players during the course of the season—not necessarily repeating Jesus' exact words, but urging each other to find places to make a difference. At home, with our wives and family, with friends, and in making our communities and the people we find there better. Players have an opportunity to stand for something positive, and they need to reflect God's light to accomplish that.

I was talking to someone the other day about light and how Christ has called us to be lights—His lights. We might be in a waxing or waning or full stage, but the key is to reflect the Son of God, Jesus Christ. If we reflect Christ's light to the world by our thoughts, words, and actions, we have a good chance to change the world.

UNCOMMON KEY > *Tonight, or whenever the moon is visible, spend a moment looking at it, and pray that nothing clouds Jesus Christ's light in your life. Others need to see the Light, and you may be the only person they know who reflects Him.*

December 29

Spreading the Bounty

> When someone has been given much, much will be required in return; and when someone has been entrusted with much, even more will be required. LUKE 12:48

Some of us have caught a lot of breaks in our lives. A number of people around the world might argue that any person born in the United States is already starting with a leg up on the rest of the world. But even within that group, there are those of us who are so far ahead of the game in terms of opportunities, positions, and other advantages that it's not funny.

Maybe you worked tireless hours to get there. Maybe you saw a vision for what needed to be done when no one else did. Maybe someone gave you an opportunity, and things worked out. Perhaps some people gave you a lift up in life, and you made the most of it.

But here you are. And God wants more of you. He reminds us all that when someone has been given much, they have responsibilities. I think about that a lot when I enjoy the little blessings of life—like heat on a freezing winter day or a cold glass of milk, readily available from the gallon container in the refrigerator. I can't help but think in those situations of people who, right that moment, are sleeping in a freezing house because they couldn't afford to pay the electric bill or who don't have anything in their refrigerator, let alone a bottle of milk. I have to overcome a slight feeling of guilt in that moment—guilt for the times when I have complained about the things I *don't* have.

But I also feel a sense of responsibility to them. Shouldn't I? Shouldn't you? If we are to be the people of impact that we are called to be—much required, remember?—we must keep this before us.

UNCOMMON KEY > *Feeling blessed? Great–thank God. And then share what He has done for you with someone else.*

December 30

A Well-Worn Verse

> For God loved the world so much that he gave his one and only Son, so that everyone who believes in him will not perish but have eternal life. JOHN 3:16

After the University of Florida's quarterback Tim Tebow put the words of John 3:16 on his eyeblack for the 2008 National Championship Game against Oklahoma, I heard that over ninety million people searched for that verse on the Internet.[11] I'm surprised that more people didn't know it beforehand after all the times it has been displayed at sporting events. But I'm glad they looked it up.

In our world of sports with idols and platforms and winning and money, it's refreshing to see something different. In a world of sports centered around *me* instead of *we*, Tim Tebow emphasized what was most important to him. Not the offer of more money, securing more championships, playing in massive stadiums where luxury boxes blot out the sun, or expanding his trophy cases to accommodate his awards, but glorifying the God who sacrificed His Son for Tim and every one of us. Something much different from what the world thinks is most important.

John 3:16 simply states the three profound aspects of salvation: God's love, God's Son, and our belief.

For God loved the world so much—it's the starting place. Do you believe that? Do you really? If you don't, why don't you? Is there something or someone in your past holding you back from believing that the God who created you really loves you?

God loved the world so much *that He gave His one and only Son*—to die as the sacrifice for your sins and my sins. Can you think of any family member or friend who would be willing to do that for you? Don't tell me who you picked. My guess is that you didn't even think about picking one because of how painful that would be. Yet God sent His Son for you and for me.

So that everyone who believes in Him will not perish but have eternal life. Now here's where the leap of faith comes in. The promise of eternal life with a risen Savior. You and I will never understand it all, but we do know that people saw Jesus die on the cross, be laid in the tomb, and over the next forty days, over five hundred people saw Him—alive.

Believe it like Tim Tebow does.

UNCOMMON KEY > *John 3:16 clearly explains the essence of faith in Christ—believe it and ask Him into your heart if you haven't done so already. And then live like someone who is looking forward to a life with Him forever.*

December 31

Beginning to End

> All Scripture is inspired by God and is useful to teach us what is true and to make us realize what is wrong in our lives. It corrects us when we are wrong and teaches us to do what is right. God uses it to prepare and equip his people to do every good work.
>
> 2 TIMOTHY 3:16-17

All Scripture comes from the Lord, not just the selected bits and pieces we like or the ones we agree with. In understanding that all Scripture is God-breathed and inspired, we should be encouraged that it is God's instrument that He uses to talk with us, teach and grow us, and move us closer to becoming the people He created us to be. Many of the most profound lessons and life-changing moments in my life and the life of my family have come from the inspiration and wisdom contained in the pages of the Bible.

Lessons on attitude—helping us expect that things will work out for the best, and when they don't seem to in our view, encouraging and lifting us up. Lessons on faith—that we can have the confidence that what we hope for but can't see will actually happen in God's timing and in God's way. Lessons on integrity, exemplified in the life of Daniel, and of the importance of telling the truth—letting my yes mean yes and my no mean no. Lessons on priorities—of loving God and loving others, of treating my spouse, family, and friends as He wants me to by putting them and their needs ahead of my own.

It's amazing how the Bible, still the bestselling book of all time, has stood the test of time and has remained as relevant today as it ever was. But doesn't that make sense? After all, it was inspired by our God, who is timeless. He is the God of all history—the past, what's happening now, and what's to come—and He knew what the world would be like today and knew what He would need for us to do. God grabbed ordinary people like David, Moses, Matthew, and Amos, and today He uses people like you and me to share His message through us, encouraging and inspiring others.

UNCOMMON KEY > *Have you ever read through the entire Bible? Consider doing it. The Bible is God's love story with His creation from beginning to end. And that includes you!*

Notes

1. See, for example, Brittany Stevens, "Abstinence on the Rise among Teens, Young Adults," *Kansas State Collegian*, April 12, 2011, http://www.kstatecollegian.com/news/abstinence-on-the-rise-among-teens-young-adults-1.2539474.
2. C. S. Lewis, *The Voyage of the* Dawn Treader (New York: Harper Trophy, 1980), 3.
3. Ibid., 82.
4. "Teen Role Models: Who They Are, Why They Matter," *Barna Group*, January 31, 2011, http://www.barna.org/teens-next-gen-articles/467-teen-role-models.
5. Winston Churchill, *Never Give In!: The Best of Winston Churchill's Speeches*, ed., Winston S. Churchill (New York: Hyperion, 2003), 206
6. Ibid., 218.
7. Ibid., 220.
8. James Brown, *Role of a Lifetime: Reflections on Faith, Family, and Significant Living* (New York: FaithWords, 2009), 79.
9. See Randy Alcorn, *The Treasure Principle* (Sisters, OR: Multnomah Publishing, 2001).
10. C. S. Lewis, *The Screwtape Letters* (New York: HarperCollins, 1942), 46.
11. See, for example, "Florida QB Makes 'John 3:16' Hottest Google Search," *WorldNetDaily*, January 9, 2009, http://www.wnd.com/?pageId=85729.

Scripture Index

Matthew 10:8	October 20	John 8:31-32	January 27
Matthew 10:29-31	July 13	John 8:32	July 16
Matthew 12:36-37	January 15	John 9:1-3	May 15
Matthew 13:8	June 9	John 10:10	September 6
Matthew 15:19	March 31	John 11:32-35	September 2
Matthew 15:29-30	May 22	John 13:8-9	August 26
Matthew 16:13-16	June 17	John 14:6-7	September 18
Matthew 16:21-22	November 13	John 14:27	April 7
Matthew 16:26	December 16	John 15:1-4	September 27
Matthew 18:3	July 29	John 15:5	May 3, June 15
Matthew 18:5-6	September 1	John 15:12-13	February 7
Matthew 18:21-22	November 7	John 15:16	August 10
Matthew 19:26	December 8	John 16:13	March 11
Matthew 20:26-28	April 6	John 17:4, 22-23	July 24
Matthew 21:28-31	May 26	John 17:17	August 27
Matthew 22:31-32	September 14	John 20:1-2, 8	April 10
Matthew 23:12	February 26	John 20:21-22	April 14
Matthew 25:10-13	December 2	John 20:26-29	October 4
Matthew 25:23	June 29	John 21:4-6	July 15
Matthew 25:44-45	December 7	Acts 1:8-9	September 7
Mark 1:35-37	January 11	Acts 2:42	December 19
Mark 1:40-41	March 18	Acts 5:27-29	February 19
Mark 2:17	January 24	Acts 9:36	February 9
Mark 3:14	July 17	Acts 12:1-4	June 1
Mark 4:39-41	December 9	Acts 14:19-20	August 19
Mark 7:6-8	November 25	Acts 15:37-39	October 10
Mark 16:19-20	April 21	Acts 16:9-10	May 25
Luke 2:52	February 1	Acts 17:11	June 12
Luke 6:27-28	April 4	Acts 20:22, 24	February 18
Luke 7:33-34	September 15	Romans 2:1	July 21
Luke 9:23-24	August 24	Romans 3:22-24	August 5
Luke 10:27-28	July 4	Romans 5:3-5	May 31
Luke 10:30, 33	February 3	Romans 6:11-12, 14	October 19
Luke 10:33-34	November 23	Romans 7:4	November 2
Luke 10:40-42	November 30	Romans 7:21	July 30
Luke 10:41-42	March 3	Romans 8:3	February 15
Luke 12:15	August 9	Romans 8:5-6	April 2
Luke 12:33-34	September 9	Romans 8:9-10	September 13
Luke 12:48	December 29	Romans 8:28	October 11
Luke 15:27-28	April 28	Romans 8:31	May 27
Luke 17:3-4	October 23	Romans 8:38-39	January 9,
Luke 17:6	January 14		December 4
Luke 18:1-5	November 21	Romans 11:33	June 16
Luke 19:8-10	June 27	Romans 12:1	August 23
Luke 19:26	November 8	Romans 12:2	January 26
Luke 22:42	April 5	Romans 12:3	December 20
John 1:1-3	May 8	Romans 12:4-5	January 31
John 1:26-27	October 27	Romans 12:6-8	December 24
John 3:16	December 30	Romans 12:9	March 28
John 4:7, 9-10	December 1	Romans 13:1-3	January 19
John 5:6-9	August 31	Romans 13:5	August 21
John 6:35	November 27	Romans 13:7	July 28
John 8:12	September 12	Romans 14:13	May 24

TAKE THE CHALLENGE

VISIT WWW.UNCOMMONCHALLENGE.COM TO JOIN TONY DUNGY ON A YEARLONG ADVENTURE

For photos, podcasts, videos, and information on Tony Dungy's bestselling books, visit www.coachdungy.com

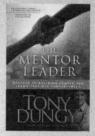
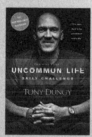

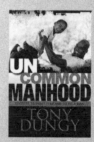

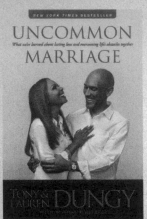

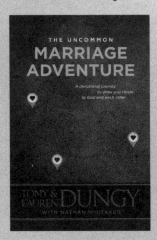

Tony and Lauren Dungy bring together their faith, love of children, and love of sports to tell stories of inspiration and encouragement.

In a family where everyone seems to have found their special talent, all third-grader Linden Dungy knows is that he wants to make people happy. With encouragement from his parents and inspiration from God, Linden learns that if he dreams big and has faith, he can do anything!

ISBN 9781416954613

Jade has been planning to have her birthday party at a water park, but her new friend, Hannah, is in a wheelchair. Is it more important to keep her party where she planned or to make sure all her friends have fun? A beautiful story of friendship without limits.

ISBN 9781416997719

When Mom and Dad bring home a new puppy, everyone is so excited! But who gets to walk Ruby? Who gets to play with Ruby? In this story about the importance of sharing, the Dungy children learn to stop saying, "Ruby is *my* dog," and say instead, "Ruby is *our* dog!"

ISBN 9781442429482

CP0260